Basic Approaches to
Group Psychotherapy
and
Group Counseling

Basic Approaches to Group Psychotherapy and Group Counseling

SECOND EDITION, THIRD PRINTING

Edited by

GEORGE M. GAZDA

Professor of Education
University of Georgia
Athens, Georgia
Consulting Professor of Psychiatry
Department of Psychiatry
Medical College of Georgia
Augusta, Georgia

CHARLES C THOMAS · PUBLISHER
Springfield · Illinois · U.S.A.

Published and Distributed Throughout the World by
CHARLES C THOMAS • PUBLISHER
Bannerstone House
301-327 East Lawrence Avenue, Springfield, Illinois, U.S.A.

© 1968, 1975, by CHARLES C THOMAS • PUBLISHER
ISBN 0-398-03212-2
Library of Congress Catalog Card Number: 74-8890

Second Edition, Second Printing, 1977
Second Edition, Third Printing, 1979

Printed in the United States of America
C-1

Library of Congress Cataloging in Publication Data

Gazda, George Michael, 1931-
    Basic approaches to group psychotherapy and group
counseling.

    Includes bibliographies.
    1. Group psychotherapy. 2. Group counseling.
I. Title. [DNLM: 1. Counseling. 2. Psychotherapy,
Group. WM430 G289b]
RC488.G29 1974   616.8'915   74-8890
ISBN 0-398-03212-2

To my Mother and Father

CONTRIBUTORS

RUDOLF DREIKURS, M.D., Formerly Director, Alfred Adler Institute of Chicago; Professor of Psychiatry, Chicago Medical School, Chicago, Illinois. (Deceased)

DEAN G. ELEFTHERY, M.D., Consultant Psychiatrist; Member of Royal College of Psychiatry, London; Director of Institute for Human Relations, Miami, Florida; President of International Foundation of Human Relations, Amsterdam; President of VI International Congress of Psychodrama–Amsterdam, 1971; Fellow of the American Society of Group Psychotherapy and Psychodrama; Certified Director of Group Psychotherapy, Psychodrama, and Sociometry; Clinical Associate, Dept. of Psychiatry, University of Florida; Adjunct Professor–Union Graduate School–Ohio; Teacher, Lecturer, and Trainer (International) –Group Process and Psychodrama.

ALBERT ELLIS, Ph.D., Private Practice and Executive Director, Institute for Advanced Study in Rational Psychotherapy, New York, New York.

GEORGE M. GAZDA, Ed.D., Professor of Education, University of Georgia, Athens, Georgia, and Consulting Professor of Psychiatry, Department of Psychiatry, Medical College of Georgia, Augusta, Georgia.

HAIM G. GINOTT, Ed.D., Formerly Adjunct Associate Professor of Psychology, Graduate School of Arts and Science, New York University, New York City; Associate Clinical Professor, Postdoctoral Program in Psychotherapy, Adelphi University, Garden City, New York. (Deceased)

WILLIAM GLASSER, M.D., Private Practice and Founder and President of the Institute for Reality Therapy, Los Angeles, California.

ROBERT L. GOULDING, M.D. (Fellow, American Group Psychotherapy Association), Director, Western Institute for Group and Family Therapy, Watsonville, California.

MARTHA HAYS, M. Ed., Huntsville, Alabama.

THOMAS HORA, M.D., Private Practice, New York City.

ROBERT F. KALTENBACH (Ph.D. Candidate), University of Georgia, Athens, Georgia.

ARNOLD A. LAZARUS, Ph.D. (Diplomate in Clinical Psychology), Professor of Psychology and Chairman of the Department of Psychology, Rutgers University, New Brunswick, New Jersey.

BETTY D. MEADOR, Ph.D., Director, Center for Studies of the Person, LaJolla, California.

J. L. MORENO, M.D., Formerly Director, Moreno Institute, Beacon, New York; Physician in Charge, Moreno Sanitarium, Beacon, New York; President, International Council of Group Psychotherapy; World Center for Psychodrama, Sociometry and Group Psychotherapy. (Deceased)

ROGER W. PETERS, Ph.D., Assistant Professor, Team Program, Department of Community Dentistry, University of Tennessee College of Dentistry, Memphis, Tennessee.

BEVERLY POTTER, Ph.D., Formerly School of Education, Stanford University, Stanford, California.

VIRGINIA M. SATIR, ACSW Private Consulting, 10 Sunrise Lane, Mill Valley, California.

JAMES S. SIMKIN, Ph.D. (Diplomate in Clinical Psychology), Private Practice, Big Sur, California.

MANFORD A. SONSTEGARD, Ph.D., Professor of Counseling and Psychological Services, West Virginia College of Graduate Studies, Institute, West Virginia, and Clinical Professor, Department of Behavioral Medicine and Psychiatry, West Virginia University Medical School, Morgantown, West Virginia.

CARL E. THORESEN, Ph.D., Associate Professor, School of Education, Stanford University, Stanford, California.

ALEXANDER WOLF, M.D., Private Practice, New York City; Training Analyst, Division of Postgraduate Studies, New York Medical College; Supervisor, Group Therapy Department, Postgraduate Center for Mental Health; Associate Clinical Professor of Psychiatry, New York Medical College; Associate Attending Psychiatrist, Flower and Fifth Avenue Hospital, New York City.

PREFACE

THE PURPOSE OF THE FIRST EDITION of this book was to provide the practitioners and students of group psychotherapy and group counseling with a convenient reference to the basic theories of group psychotherapy and group counseling. The same basic purpose guided the revision of this book. There were, however, three additional purposes in revising this book in addition to up-dating each original chapter. First, several theoretical positions have achieved the status of being "basic," i.e., having significant impact and predictable enduring influence on group psychotherapy and group counseling since the first edition was produced. Second, there was a need to provide an overview of the effectiveness of group psychotherapy and group counseling as revealed through research; therefore chapter two provides the reader a synopsis of the nature of group research and the effectiveness of the basic small group practices. Third, there is a compelling need to give direction to group practitioners in terms of ethical practices; therefore chapter three was included to summarize current thinking in this domain. The original chapter one, dealing with history and development and definitions of group psychotherapy and group counseling was up-dated and expanded to include the new developments in the movement and the citation of more of the "developers." In addition, a history time-line was added to summarize and highlight key people and events.

The coverage of the "basic" approaches to group psychotherapy and group counseling was almost doubled in this edition. The first edition contained eight chapters dealing with different theoretical positions, whereas the revised edition contains fourteen, with seven being new positions. One position dealing with client-centered group counseling was not included in the revised edition because this position was represented by the addition of Meador's chapter on client-centered group therapy. The editor felt that Meador's chapter served as a client-centered example for both group therapy and group counseling.

Moreno and Elefthery's chapter on group psychodrama represents a revision of the chapter by Moreno and Kipper in the first edition. It reflects the current influence of Elefthery on the group psychodrama movement as well as including the basic elements, a la Moreno.

Wolf was chosen to portray the analytic approach to group psychotherapy because of his long association as a writer, teacher and practitioner of this approach, and also because his approach has remained close to the orthodox position. Criticisms of the first edition came primarily from analytically-oriented group therapists who felt that this position should have been represented by additional chapters from others of this persuasion. However, there are so many variations of the analytic approach to group psychotherapy, ranging from the orthodox-analytic to the experiential-analytic, that it would have required an entire volume to present a representative sampling of analytic positions.

Hora was again asked to present an exposition of the existential approach to group psychotherapy. Even though existentialism as applied to therapy groups represents a relatively recent addition to the group psychotherapy movement, it was included because of its present widespread popularity and because it has become the theoretical foundation on which many popular variations of experiential group psychotherapy have been built. Behavior group psychotherapy, even though it also is one of the more recent approaches to make an impact on the rapidly expanding field of group psychotherapy, was included because it provides a basic rationale for the applications of learning theory to group psychotherapy. Lazarus probably presents the most complete but eclectic position of behavioral group psychotherapy.

The client-centered approach to group psychotherapy was a significant omission from the first edition but is corrected with Betty Meador's chapter. Since she is Director of the Center for Studies of the Person, the center that continues to be influenced by Carl Rogers, the founder of this model, she was in an excellent position to represent this modality.

Although William Glasser, the founder of Reality Therapy was unable to write the chapter on Reality Therapy in Groups, he has edited the chapter and concurs that it represents his position.

Robert Goulding was chosen to present the Transactional Approach to group psychotherapy because he was one of the original small group to study with the late Eric Berne, the founder of this model. Goulding's leadership of TA is evident on the international scene.

James Simkin was an understudy of the late Fritz Perls, the founder of Gestalt psychotherapy, much like Goulding was of Berne with TA. Simkin has been during Perls' lifetime, as well as currently, one of the original small group of individuals who knows firsthand the Gestalt approach to group psychotherapy and therefore is in an excellent position to represent this model.

Rational-Emotive Group Therapy is presented by its originator, Albert Ellis. Since this model is presented by the founder and champion of the position, it would, of course, seem to be represented most appropriately.

The first edition of this book was incomplete without a chapter to represent the rapidly developing interest in and practice of family group therapy. Although it was not possible to have one of the most popular and representative positions produced for this edition directly by the founder, Satir's Conjoint model was written in effect by a "ghost" writer, Martha Hays. Satir, however, edited the chapter and approved it as representative of her model.

Group therapy with children is again represented by the position of the late Haim Ginott. Ginott was originally selected to write this chapter because of his extensive experience in this particular area of group psychotherapy and also because of his ability to present a systematic and theoretically grounded position. Although this chapter has been unchanged, Dr. Ginott was consulted long before his untimely death and he had made the decision not to change the chapter, because he felt that it still represented his basic beliefs and practices.

Part three of this edition contains three chapters that probably best represent the models utilized in group counseling if one considers the fact that Meador's chapter on Client-centered Group Therapy also represents the model for client-centered group counseling. My own eclectic position has changed considerably from the original edition and represents a summary of the model that is more completely described in my book *Group Counseling: A*

Developmental Approach (1971) published by Allyn and Bacon, Inc. My position also reflects the influence of Carkhuff's Human Resources Development model. Insofar as my position reflects the Carkhuff model, the omission of his model from this edition is lessened somewhat. However, he was invited to write a chapter for this edition but unfortunately was not able to do so. The absence of the Carkhuff model from this edition, in my estimation, is the most serious omission.

Since the writing and publication of the first edition of this book, the Behavioral influence on psychotherapy and counseling has been extensive; therefore a separate chapter was added to illustrate its application to group counseling as well as group therapy. Carl Thoresen and a doctoral candidate, at the time of the writing of the chapter, Beverly Potter, represent two of the prominent developers and proponents of this model. Thoresen, perhaps as much as any other single individual, has championed the application of behavioral principles to group counseling.

Finally, the Teleoanalytic model is responsible for the growing influence of the Adlerian principles upon group counseling in the United States. The late Rudolf Dreikurs, perhaps more than any other single individual, was responsible for the development and influence of this model. His coauthor and former student, Manford Sonstegard, has very capably presented this model in its revised form for this edition.

This volume was designed primarily as a textbook for students of group psychotherapy and group counseling to present them with the essential elements of the basic theories in both of these practices. Since only the most essential elements of each theory could be included in a chapter-length exposition, the contents of the chapters were carefully outlined and each contributor was asked to include the following areas in his chapter: The theoretical foundations of the process, including a description of how the process produces attitude and/or behavior change with supporting research; goals of the treatment; unique contributions of the theory or treatment; therapist or counselor roles; patient or client roles; qualifications of the therapist or counselor; composition of the group, including preferred number; limitations of the treatment; modifications of the theory or treatment practiced by others; a short sample protocol; and a list of suggested references to related expositions of the particular theory for the interested student who wishes to make a more comprehensive study of one or more theories.

Although each writer approached his task in his unique style, the topics suggested by the editor were for the most part dealt with in each chapter, thus allowing the reader the opportunity to make comparisons between and among these basic approaches to group psychotherapy and group counseling.

It has been my goal to provide the student, teacher and practitioner with a source of information in group psychotherapy and group counseling which will make their study and teaching more meaningful and their practice more successful. If I have even approached this goal, I shall be most pleased.

Many individuals have assisted me in the preparation of this manuscript. Without the cooperation of each chapter contributor, a volume such as this would of course be impossible. I want each of these contributors to know that I am deeply grateful. To Robert Rigdon, my sincere thanks for his assistance in tracing the history of the development of group counseling in the first edition of this text. For their secretarial assistance, I am most grateful to Mary Brooks and my wife Barbara for her typing of the manuscript. I also wish to acknowledge the encouragement given to me by my students, especially Robert Kaltenbach and Martha Hays for their "ghost" writing of chapters nine and thirteen, respectively. To my son David, and my wife, Barbara, my heartfelt appreciation for the many things they sacrificed to permit me the time to attend to this manuscript.

G. M. GAZDA

CONTENTS

PART III—GROUP COUNSELING

Basic Approaches to
Group Psychotherapy
and
Group Counseling

PART I

INTRODUCTION
AND
OVERVIEW

.

CHAPTER I

GROUP PSYCHOTHERAPY AND GROUP COUNSELING: DEFINITION AND HERITAGE

George M. Gazda

GROUP PSYCHOTHERAPY

I T MAY SEEM PARADOXICAL that the group psychotherapy movement is indigenous to a country where the individual and the rights of the individual are extolled. Nevertheless, it is probably because of the respect for the individual and the favorable political climate that group psychotherapy would come to fruition in the United States. Although there is general agreement (Corsini, 1957; J. L. Moreno, 1962; Z. Moreno, 1966; Rosenbaum and Berger, 1963) that group psychotherapy in its present form is a product of the United States, there is considerably less than a consensus regarding who deserves to be called the father or founder of group psychotherapy.

If one accepts July 1, 1905 (Hadden, 1955), or the introduction of Pratt's "class method" as the beginning of group psychotherapy, rather than some ancient ritual such as Mesmer's treatment through suggestion, then the history of group psychotherapy covers approximately 70 years. There are those among the originators of group psychotherapy who are alive and are still very much involved in influencing the movement; thus we find it is difficult to evaluate its history without emotionalism. Perhaps it must be left to future historians to write a more objective account of the founders of group psychotherapy. It is unlikely that this will be possible until agreement is reached concerning the definition of group psychotherapy.

Corsini (1957) has described group psychotherapy as "a conglomerate of methods and theories having diverse multiple origins in the past, resulting inevitably from social demands, and developed in various forms by many persons" (p. 9). J. L. Moreno (1966) has described scientific group psychotherapy as having its roots in medicine, sociology and religion.

It is not the intent of the writer to present a detailed historical account of group psychotherapy, since several accounts (Corsini, 1957; Hadden, 1955; Meiers, 1945; Z. Moreno, 1966; Mullan and Rosenbaum, 1962) are readily available. However, an outline of significant figures and events will be presented. Before this tracing of the development of group psychotherapy is presented, it is necessary first to define group psychotherapy, or at least present what the writer believes to be the boundaries and ingredients of the current definition.

GROUP PSYCHOTHERAPY DEFINED

Group therapy and group psychotherapy have been defined by several writers (Corsini, 1957; Gibb, Platts and Miller, 1951; Harms, 1944; Z. Moreno, 1966) since the term *group therapy* was introduced by J. L. Moreno in 1931 (Z. Moreno, 1966) and *group psychotherapy* in 1932 (Corsini, 1957). These writers have attempted to interpret Moreno's use of the two terms, but their interpretations lack agreement (Z. Moreno, 1966). J. L. Moreno's (1962) general and brief statement that "group psychotherapy means simply to treat people in groups," . . . offers little assistance in clarifying the issue. Gibb *et al.* contend that Moreno used *group therapy* to represent "personality change which is a by-product of more primary group activities carried on for other purposes than therapy," and *group psychotherapy* to designate "the process by which a professional therapist guides a group in which the immediate and primary objective is the therapeutic welfare of the group" (1951, p. 14).

In general, group therapy and group psychotherapy are used synonymously in current discourse; group therapy has become the shortened or colloquial version of group psychotherapy. Group therapy also is used, on occasion, to represent a more inclusive category of group procedures including physical therapy, recreational therapy, psychotherapy and the like. In this sense, group psychotherapy represents a special type of group therapy, and thus has created a problem in communication.

Much of the disagreement over the historical development of group psychotherapy apparently stems from variations in the definition given to group psychotherapy. Slavson (1959) would not agree that Pratt or anyone else before 1930 was practicing group psychotherapy because the groups of these practitioners did not meet the following criteria: small group size (approximately eight people), permissive group leadership (catalytic rather than authoritative or didactic), grouping of clients on the basis of some diagnostic classification (rather than indiscriminate collections of individuals), and freedom and spontaneity of action of group members (rather than recipients of advice, information, etc.). Many would agree that Slavson makes a strong case. Many others would not agree. For example, Lazarus in his chapter in this text, takes issue point-by-point with Slavson's criteria.

Harms (1944) formulated three categories of group therapy: "(1) group therapy for one or more patients through one or more outside therapeutic agents; (2) therapy in psychopathology of the natural group and the social group; (3) internal therapeutic influence in artificial group settings" (p. 189). Harms (1944) prefers the sociological meaning of *group* which "in its essential sense is that of a not-too-large, organized association of human beings, brought about either by the forces of nature or civilization" (p. 189). A more superficial definition of group, according to Harms, is the numerical concept which simply differentiates large and small numbers of humans.

Harms appears to concur with Slavson regarding the concept of homogeneity of illness as a criterion of a therapy group; however, his preferred use of the term *group* with *therapy* resembles the concept of "social engineering"; e.g., setting up mental institutions to be therapeutic groups, intervening in social pathological groups, environmental group therapy through placing an unhealthy person in a healthy family, and the like. Harms seems to have envisioned group therapy as something quite different from a single therapist working with a small group of patients. His views appear to be best represented in current approaches of milieu therapy, family group therapy, therapeutic social clubs and similar social engineering-like procedures.

The distinction made by Gibb *et al.* (1951) between Moreno's group therapy and group psychotherapy is seldom adhered to in current parlance; however, there are some limited and specific meanings assigned to the two different terms. Our contemporary group therapies frequently represent adaptations of all our individual psychotherapies plus some varieties which may not have their counterparts in the individual psychotherapies. The group psychotherapies practiced today cut across and/or include all three of Harms' categories.

Corsini (1957) has defined group psychotherapy in a parsimonious but satisfactory manner. It is not as detailed as it might be, but it is more specific than J. L. Moreno's definition. I shall therefore use Corsini's definition to illustrate definitions given to group psychotherapy today. The definition is as follows:

> Group psychotherapy consists of processes occurring in formally organized, protected groups and calculated to attain rapid ameliorations in personality and behavior of individual members through specified and controlled group interactions (Corsini, 1957, p. 5).

(See also Z. Moreno, 1966, for a summary of definitions and for additional treatment of this subject.)

SIGNIFICANT CONTRIBUTORS

Although it can be demonstrated that non-professional forms of group therapy have existed since the beginning of recorded history, the basic approaches to group psychotherapy presented in this volume have their roots in the more recent history of the 1900's; therefore only the most significant contributors and their contributions to this period of history will be cited. This brief tracing of the significant contributors to group therapy will be divided into the early period from 1905 to 1932 and the period of expansion from 1932 to the present.

Early Period: 1905 to 1932

The early period is perhaps best represented by the contributions of six men: Pratt, Lazell, Marsh, Burrow, Adler, and Moreno. This period begins with Joseph H. Pratt's application of his "class method" to the treatment of tubercular patients and ends with Moreno's introduction of the terms *group therapy* in 1931 and *group psychotherapy* in 1932.

J. H. PRATT. As early as 1905, Dr. Pratt held group meetings with tuberculosis patients for the purpose of saving time in instructing them in hygienic practices (Hadden, 1955). It is generally accepted that Dr. Pratt did not at first understand the psychological impact on his patients of this group procedure. It is quite likely that Pratt began to understand and appreciate the psychotherapeutic effects of one person on another in his "class" or "thought control" approach to group therapy only *after* he had read Dejerine's work (perhaps as early as 1913). Slavson (1959) characterized Pratt's approach "authoritative-inspirational."

E. W. LAZELL. Dr. Lazell, a psychiatrist, was one of the first to use group procedures, mainly didactic (inspirational) lectures ("lecture method") to hospitalized schizophrenics. The first published accounts of Lazell's work appears to have been in 1921, at least two years following his first application of it.

L. C. MARSH. First an Episcopal minister, Marsh entered the field of psychiatry at middle age. Along with Lazell, Marsh was one of the first to use group psychotherapy in mental hospitals. He used an inspirational, revival-like method of lectures, group discussions, music, art, dance and other media to involve the patients with each other, and he met with all segments of the hospital staff to develop a therapeutic team–the forerunner of the milieu therapy approach. Perhaps Marsh can best be characterized by his famous motto: "By the crowd they have been broken; by the crowd they shall be healed."

T. BURROW. Trigant Burrow, like several other well-known followers of Freud, became dissatisfied with the lack of concern of psychoanalysis with the social forces affecting behavior. Thus he developed group analysis, which was his most significant contribution to group psychotherapy. Burrow's group analysis stressed the importance of studying man in relation to the group of which he is a part. After 1932 Burrow's efforts were devoted to the study of biological principles of group behavior, which he named *phylo-*

analysis. Phyloanalysis did not achieve widespread popularity, and Burrow's contributions to group psychotherapy after 1932 were minimal.

A. ADLER. The form of group therapy that Adler initiated in Vienna about 1921, according to Seidler (1936), would best fit the description of individual counseling/therapy *within* the group setting. Adler counseled children in front of a group including doctors, social workers, teachers, and psychologists. His purpose was to teach the audience how to do individual therapy. However, in the process, he noticed that the group was positively affecting the patient instead of interfering with the patient-doctor relationship. When the group members responded they did so as quasi-therapists and therefore the situation was more akin to "multiple therapy," i.e., the use of more than one therapist with a single patient. Today, Adlerians continue to interview clients/patients in front of others, and usually, but not always, other clients/patients. Current Adlerians consider this practice to be group counseling/therapy. Part of their rationale, like Adler's, is to teach, but they are additionally "treating" as well as teaching.

J. L. MORENO. Moreno was very likely the most colorful, controversial and influential person in the field of group psychotherapy. Moreno emigrated to the United States in 1925, but while still in Vienna he worked with prostitutes in groups. He stated, "Modern group psychotherapy started in the sexual ghetto of Vienna, in a natural setting *in situ* . . ." (J. L. Moreno, 1966, p. 156).

Moreno introduced psychodrama into the United States in 1925; in 1931 he coined the term *group therapy* and in 1932, *group psychotherapy;* in 1931 he began to publish *Impromptu,* a journal concerned with dramatics and therapy; in 1936-37 he founded the journal *Sociometry; Sociatry* was founded in 1947, but was changed to *Group Psychotherapy* in 1949, and *Group Psychotherapy and Psychodrama* in 1970; in 1941-42 he founded the Sociometric and Psychodramatic Institutes and the first society of group psychotherapy (the American Society of Group Psychotherapy and Psychodrama) and became its first president; he organized the First International Committee on Group Psychotherapy in 1951, and was instrumental in organizing the First International Congress of Group Psychotherapy in 1954. He was elected president of the Second International Congress of Group Psychotherapy, 1957, the International Council of Group Psychotherapy, 1962, and the Third International Congress of Group Psychotherapy, 1963. He was Honorary President of the International Congress of Psychodrama and Sociodrama. In addition to the above accomplishments, Moreno has written numerous books and journal articles in the field of group psychodrama, group therapy and sociometry. His more recent works include the editing of the *International Handbook of Group Psychotherapy* (1966), and the authoring of *Psychodrama* (1969), Volume 3, and *Group Psychotherapy: A Symposium* (1972). Moreno provided leadership to the group psychotherapy movement, although he was best known for his championing of psychodrama.

Period of Expansion: 1932 to the Present

The total number of books, articles and dissertations in the group psychotherapy literature for the twenty-five-year period preceding 1931 was only 34, but the increase was steady and rapid. For example, for the five-year period 1931-35, it was 20; from 1936-40, 69; from 1941-45, 203; and from 1946-50, 536 (Corsini, 1957). The annual review of group psychotherapy references published in the *International Journal of Group Psychotherapy* listed 199 references for the year 1965 (MacLennan, Morse, and Goode 1966); 481 references for 1970 (MacLennan and Levy, 1971); and 500 references for 1972 (Lubin and Lubin, 1973). These figures represent a geometric increase for many years in the growth of interest and contributions to the field of group psychotherapy. The number of additional references between 1970 and 1972 was only 19, so perhaps we are approaching a leveling off period. The reviewers (Lubin and Lubin, 1973) remind us that "the boundaries between group therapy and the intensive small group experience that have developed in recent years are not clear" (p. 474). Therefore, the 500 references include related literature from group counseling, T-groups, encounter groups, growth groups, et cetera. The significant year-to-year increase in the group psychotherapy literature has been reflected in the number of different contributors to the field. For the sake of brevity, only some of the most significant contributors will be cited for the Period of Expansion.

Paul Schilder and Louis Wender were two group therapists who were practicing during the latter part of the Early Period but did not publish their results until the middle and late 30's. Both of these psychiatrists pioneered the applications of psychoanalytic procedures to psychotic, hospitalized, adult patients. Schilder also pioneered the use of group therapy with prison inmates, and Wender discovered the value of group meetings for discharged patients, although A. A. Low had earlier recognized the possibility of self-help groups when he organized "Recovery, Inc." in Chicago, Illinois. Wender also recognized the similarity of the group experience to the family and included different generations in the outpatient groups that he conducted.

Samuel R. Slavson, an engineer by training, was one of the leading figures to emerge in the early 1930's. Slavson, an analytically oriented group therapist, is probably best known for his development of *activity group therapy* and other play therapies for children.

In 1934, Slavson introduced a child-guidance clinic that featured a "creative recreational program for small groups of socially maladjusted latency-aged girls–and later boys. These groups became known as "Therapeutics of Creative Activity" and finally "Group Therapy." Betty Gabriel and later Fanny Amster also pioneered group therapy with children (Durkin *et al.*, 1971, p. 410). Slavson also organized the American Group Psychotherapy Association in 1943 and has been a leader of that organization as well as editor of its journal, *The International Journal of Group Psychotherapy.* Slavson has been one of the most prolific writers in the field of group psychotherapy.

Among the leaders in the application of group therapy techniques to play therapy with children have been F. Redl, Lauretta Bender, Gisela Konopka, W. Klopfer, Betty Gabriel, Henriette Glatzer, Helen Durkin, Lawson Lowrey, A. G. Woltman, Virginia Axline, and Haim Ginott. Ginott was instrumental in implementing new techniques in activity and play group therapies. He authored a very useful book on play therapy, *Group Psychotherapy with Children,* and a "best seller" *Between Parent and Child* as well as related books for parents and teachers.

Nathan Ackerman was a New York psychiatrist and a member of the group with Slavson who formed the American Group Psychotherapy Association. He utilized analytic techniques with a wide variety of clientele and was particularly noted for group therapy with adolescents and for his pioneer work with family group therapy. Other current leaders in the family group therapy movement are John Bell, Donald Jackson, Jay Haley, G. Bateson, J. H. Weakland, and Virginia Satir. Satir has recently provided the field of family therapy with two very useful books: *Conjoint Family Therapy* and *Peoplemaking.*

Following in the tradition of Schilder and Wender, Alexander Wolf became one of the leading spokesmen for psychoanalysis in groups. He used psychoanalysis in groups in his private practice and also trained several psychiatrists in this method. He initiated the use of the *alternate session,* i.e., the meeting of patients on alternate sessions without the therapist in attendance. E. K. Schwartz has collaborated with Wolf in producing numerous publications dealing with psychoanalysis in groups. H. Spotnitz and S. Scheidlinger, A. Stein, E. Fried, M. Rosenbaum, A. Kadis, H. Durkin are other significant contributors to the group analytic therapy literature.

Rudolf Dreikurs, who was a Chicago psychiatrist trained by Adler, applied Adlerian principles to group therapy. He is known especially for his work with family groups, child guidance and the development of group-therapy training centers. One of his recent collaborators is Manford Sonstegard, who with Dreikurs, has applied Adlerian principles to group counseling in the school setting with children, parents, teachers and other school personnel. Other group therapists who have been influenced by Adler's writings and/or Dreikurs include B. Rosenberg, D. Dinkmeyer, J. Muro, B. Grunwald, O. Christensen, H. Papanek, to name but a few.

Raymond Corsini has given to the field of group therapy one of the most thorough accounts of its history in his *Methods of Group Psychotherapy.* Corsini has utilized psychodramatic approaches to group psychotherapy and has been the exponent of Immediate Group Therapy. His *Methods of Group Psychotherapy* was a popular text in the field of group psychotherapy, and his *Roleplaying in Psychotherapy* is also a very useful addition to the literature. Other prominent American group psychodramatists include Dean Elefthery, Zerka Moreno, James Enneis, David Kipper, Richard Korn, Lewis Yablonsky, Hannah Weiner, Leon Fine, Doris Twitchell-Allen, Robert Siroka, Ellen Siroka, Ronald Robbins, Gloria Robbins, Martin Haskell, Nah Brind, and Jonathan Moreno. In addition, there are many highly qualified foreign psychodramatists many of whom are operating organizations to train psychodramatists in Canada, South America, Italy, France, Netherlands, England, Austria, Finland, Sweden, Norway, et cetera.

George Bach, a clinical psychologist in private practice, has been a leader in innovations in group psychotherapy. His book *Intensive Group Psychotherapy* represents one of the most complete treatments of the application of concepts of group dynamics to group therapy. Bach, a former student of Lewin's, has recently been one of the pioneers of marathon group therapy. M. Lakin has also utilized Lewinian theory with Bion's in his approach to group therapy. One of the more recent and successful attempts to apply group dynamics concepts and research to group therapy has been that of Irvin Yalom in *The Theory and Practice of Group Psychotherapy*. Jack Gibb is an eminent group dynamicist who is also applying group dynamics research and theory to group psychotherapy; he has developed the TORI process to describe group procedures, including group therapy. Frederick Stoller, along with George Bach, was a pioneer in developing the rationale for marathon group therapy and has also been one of the first to employ video with group psychotherapy; he called this technique "focused feedback." He developed this technique around communication theory and principles.

The followers of Carl Rogers have not been without interest in the application of phenomenological psychology and client-centered principles to groups–witness the work of Thomas Gordon, A. G. Woltman, L. Gorlow, E. Telschow, E. L. Hoch, Nicholas

Hobbs, Walter Lifton, Charles Truax, William Coulson, Betty Meador and Eugene Gendlin. Gendlin, perhaps more than any of the others of the group cited, and perhaps more than Rogers himself, has championed the experiential approach to group psychotherapy. Gendlin's applications of Rogerian principles appears to incorporate some of the principles of certain elder statesmen of experiential group therapy such as Carl Whitaker, Thomas Malone and John Warkentin, who have taught and practiced this method at the Atlanta Psychiatric Clinic and elsewhere. This approach includes a greater involvement of the therapist; his values and feelings are expressed and become a significant part of the treatment. Hugh Mullan and Max Rosenbaum's *Group Psychotherapy* presents a variation of the experiential approach advocated by the Atlanta group. Mullan has become one of the more articulate spokesmen for the existential-experiential approach to group therapy. M. Berger has also become identified as an exponent of existential group therapy. Thomas Hora, like Mullan, a New York psychiatrist, has become an advocate of existential group psychotherapy. Hora has combined his psychoanalytic training with communications theory and has produced a system of group psychotherapy similar to his counterparts in Europe. The trend toward greater therapist involvement with groups of patients growing out of the experiential-existential approaches may produce a new era in group psychotherapy. Its influence is very likely just beginning to be felt.

Behavior theory applied to group therapy is just beginning to make its impact, primarily through the efforts of Arnold Lazarus. His book *Behavior Therapy and Beyond* and his cassettes and films on Broad Spectrum Behavior Therapy plus his chapter in this text, "Multimodal Behavior Therapy in Groups," represent significant additions to the group therapy literature. S. D. Rose's *Treating Children in Groups: A Behavioral Approach* represents a needed addition to this aspect of group therapy. Alan Goldstein's and Joseph Wolpe's chapter in *Comprehensive Group Psychotherapy* adds a behavioral position which will permit a comparison and contrast with the Lazarus model.

Since the first edition of this book, several new methods of group therapy have become recognized. These positions have large followings and are not likely to be passing fads, especially since most of them are also applied in individual therapy. These positions include Transactional Analysis (TA), Gestalt Therapy, Reality Therapy, Rational-Emotive Therapy, and Systematic Human Resources Training.

At the time this text is being written, Transactional Analysis is perhaps enjoying greater popularity than almost any other form of group therapy. Perhaps this is because of its use of unique labels and the structured format. The founder of this movement was the late Eric Berne. Some of the leading proponents of TA are Robert Goulding (see his chapter in this text), Mary Goulding, Thomas Harris, Stephen Karpman, David Kupfer, Ken Everts, Paul McCormick, Leonard Campos, Barbara Rosenfeld, Muriel James, Dorothy Jongward, John Dusay, Claude Steiner, Frank Ernst, and William and Martha Holloway.

Gestalt Therapy, much like TA, is a very popular movement at this time. In some ways it is popular because of the mystique that it brings to therapy—the many different techniques and the gurus who practice this method of group therapy. Fritz Perls, its founder, made no apologies for his guru status; in fact, he seemed to cultivate it as have many of his followers. Some of those who have been or are still prominent Gestalt group therapists are James Simkin (see his chapter in this text), John Enright, the late Richard Wallen, Erving and Miriam Polster, Laura Perls, Joen Fagan, Irma Shepherd, Claudio Naranjo, Walter Kempler, Vincent O'Connell, Elaine Kepner, Wilson Van Dusen, G. M. Yontef, Janet Lederman, and Abraham Levitsky.

Reality Therapy has been the product primarily of one man—William Glasser, a California psychiatrist. Glasser admits to the influence of individuals like Thomas Szasz and Hobart Mowrer. Glasser developed his position while working as a consultant to a juvenile detention facility. He has since expanded its application to the school setting, especially, but also to correctional institutions and hospital settings, as well as group therapy in private practice. Some of the proponents of Reality Therapy are Alex Bassin, Leonard Zunin, Gary Applegate and Edward Ford. Ford is developing a collection of Reality Therapy tapes, including speeches and group application or demonstrations.

Rational-Emotive Therapy (RET) like the other group therapies, is also primarily the product of one man–Albert Ellis (see his chapter in this text). Ellis is the prime mover of RET in the United States, and Donald Michenbaum is his counterpart in Canada.

Robert Carkhuff is the dominant force behind an eclectic position involving the application of relationship and behavioral methodologies to groups. Although this model is also used on a one-to-one basis, Carkhuff (1971) claims that it is more effective with small groups. His model is referred to as Systematic Human Resources Development/Training (HRD). This model, although developed in the middle and late 1960's, is perhaps the most thoroughly researched psychotherapeutic model in existence. The number of Carkhuff's followers are growing geometrically and are too numerous to cite, save for a few who have worked very closely with him. These include David Aspy, Andrew Griffin, Richard Pierce, David Berenson, Bernard Berenson, Thomas Collingwood, George Banks, William Anthony, Ted Friel, R. Vitalo, R. Bierman, Dan Kratochvil, Todd Holder, Rosemary Antonuzzo, and Muriel Santelli.

By now, the reader's head is probably buzzing with names and the list of significant contributors to group psychotherapy seems endless. Yet it would seem unfair to omit some individuals who have made recent significant contributions to the field, especially through their publications, viz., Clifford Sager's and Helen Kaplan's *Progress in Group and Family Therapy;* Harold Kaplan's and Benjamin Sadock's *Comprehensive Group Psychotherapy;* and Morton Lieberman, Irvin Yalom, and Matthew Miles' *Encounter Groups: First Facts.*

There are many others who have made and are making a significant contribution to specialized areas of group psychotherapy. For example, Harris Peck's and Mansell Pattison's contributions to community psychiatry; Irvin Kraft, Beryce MacLennan, and Naomi Felsenfeld's contributions to group therapy with children and adolescents; William F. Hill's development of a group process scale, The Hill Interaction Matrix; Bernard Lubin's literature summaries and reviews; O. H. Mowrer's development of Integrity Therapy for groups are but a sampling of contributors to specialized areas of group therapy.

Several leading English group therapists are included in the tracing of the history of group psychotherapy because of their influence on American group therapists. Joshua Bierer has been one of the most significant proponents of group psychotherapy in England. Bierer is probably best known for his development of the therapeutic social club, a type of self-help therapy group.

S. H. Foulkes, in collaboration with E. J. Anthony, is known for his utilization of Freudian concepts and the application of Lewin's field theory in the development of a group analytic psychotherapy.

W. R. Bion and a colleague, H. Ezriel at the Tavistock Clinic, have promoted the concept of the therapy group as an entity, as has J. D. Sutherland. Bion, in particular, has been the advocate of this concept. He is also well known for his concept of the "leadership by default" group approach to psychotherapy and his use of Kleinian concepts in group therapy. Bion's work has stimulated the interest of Herbert Thelen and his students at the University of Chicago. Dorothy Stock Whitaker and Morton Lieberman have combined the theory of Bion, Ezriel and Foulkes with the focal conflict model of Thomas French and produced an intriguing book, *Psychotherapy Through the Group Process.*

A review of the history of group psychotherapy and contributions on an international scope has been written by Zerka Moreno, herself a leader in the field of group psychodrama and group psychotherapy in the United States. Her account can be found in Part II of *The International Handbook of Group Psychotherapy* (1966). S. B. Hadden is also known for his careful historical account of the group psychotherapy movement.

The list of significant contributors to the field of group psychotherapy is so lengthy that this volume cannot do justice to any of them; and worse yet, some important contributors have not been cited. Aside from the British group psychotherapists–Bierer, Sutherland, Foulkes, Ezriel and Bion–no attempt was made to cite the contributions of the growing number of foreign group psychotherapists.

GROUP COUNSELING

The origin of the term *group counseling* is somewhat obscured. Its historical antecedent was most likely group guidance or case conference. In other words, much like its counterpart, group psychotherapy, group counseling in its inception was very likely a class method similar to what is referred to today as *group guidance*. The earliest use in print in the United States of the term *group counseling* appears to have been in 1931. Dr. Richard D. Allen (1931), in an article entitled "A Group Guidance Curriculum in the Senior High School" published in *Education,* used group counseling in the following context:

> *Group thinking and the case-conference method* usually take the place of the recitation. . . . Problems of educational and vocational guidance require teachers who are specially selected and trained for the work, who understand problems of individual differences and are continually studying them. These teachers require continuous contacts with the same pupils for several years, a knowledge of occupations and occupational problems, and special training in methods of individual and group counseling.
>
> All of these considerations draw attention to the class counselor as the logical teacher of the new unit. There is much similarity between the techniques of individual guidance and group guidance. When the counselor finds by individual interviews that certain problems are common to most of the pupils, such problems become units in the group guidance course. The class discussions of these problems should reduce the length and number of individual interviews with a saving of considerable time and expense. In fact, the separation of group counseling from individual counseling would seem very short-sighted. . . .
>
> If the above principle prevails, the next serious problem concerns its practical application in the time schedule of the school. Ideally, such a course should be *extensive* rather than *intensive* in its nature, in order to accomplish its objectives effectively. Its purpose is to arouse interests in current educational, vocational and social problems, to develop social attitudes, and to build up a back-ground of occupational information. Such objectives require considerable *time extended over several years* (p. 190).

This lengthy quotation is included to show that what Allen described as *group counseling* in 1931 today is generally referred to as *group guidance*. Also, it should be noted that Allen used the terms *case-conference, group guidance,* and *group counseling* interchangeably.

Although Allen's use of *group counseling* appeared in print in 1931, it is very likely that he had used the expression before 1931. For example, John M. Brewer (1937) writing the Introduction to Allen's *Organization and Supervision of Guidance in Public Education,* published in 1937, wrote, "For more than a decade his colleagues in the Harvard Summer School have urged Dr. Allen to put his ideas into permanent form" (xxi).

Jones, as early as 1934, in his second edition of *Principles of Guidance,* states "it [group guidance] is a term that has come into use chiefly through the excellent work of Richard D. Allen in Providence, R. I. It includes all those forms of guidance activities that are undertaken in groups or in classes" (1934, p. 284). Jones (1934, p. 291) also refers to the "Boston Plan for Group Counseling in Intermediate Schools" and cites the source as two circulars[1] developed by the Committee on Guidance of the Boston Public Schools. Although group counseling is used in the title of the Boston publication, the description of the nature of the process described by Jones places it squarely in the realm of group guidance and not group counseling as it is defined today.

In his fifth edition of *Principles of Guidance,* published in 1963, Jones had this to say about Allen's case conference procedures: "A technique that combined the techniques of 'counseling in groups' and 'group counseling' was used by Allen and practiced in the public schools of Providence, Rhode Island more than twenty-five years ago" (1963, pp. 218-219). Jones contends that the purpose of the case conference was to provide the counselor with a means for students to discuss their personal and social relationships. Common problems of group members were used as the basis for discussion. A case was presented to the group to illus-

---

1. Boston Public Schools, Guidance—Educational and Vocational, A Tentative Plan for Group Counseling, Board of Superintendents' Circular No. 2, 1928-1929, and Board of Superintendents' Circular No. 17, 1928-1929, First Supplement to Board of Superintendents' Circular No. 2: Boston: Printing Department, 1929.

trate the problem and each student was expected to compare his own experiences with those revealed through the case. The leader encouraged the group to seek the more permanent values exposed rather than the more immediate temporary ones, and he also encouraged the participants to consider the effect upon others of their proposed action before performing it. Conclusions were summarized to formulate generalizations for other situations. Jones stated that Allen believed his method worked best when "each case represented a common, usual, or typical situation that concerned most of the group. The case should involve persons and personal or social relations" (1963, p. 219).

According to Jones, Allen characterized the case conference leader as one who never expressed approval or disapproval of any opinion or attitude and never stated opinions of his own. In addition, the leader was impartial and open-minded and encouraged the expression of all points of view; he would occasionally restate and summarize the group's thinking, and organize the group so that it was large enough to guarantee a diversity of opinions, but not so large as to prevent each member the opportunity to enter into discussion.

The goals and procedures of Allen's case conference approach described by Jones are similar to those of contemporary group counselors. Most contemporary group counselors, however, do not structure their groups around specific cases.

DEFINITION[2]

Although group counseling is very likely here to stay–witness its inclusion in the *Review of Educational Research, Psychological Abstracts, Education Index* and similar indexes and references– it was not without substantial opposition. A brief tracing of the resistance to its acceptance is outlined below through the use of selected quotations. In his second edition of *Principles of Guidance,* Jones (1934) wrote, "Counseling has such an intimate sound that it would seem advisable to limit it to that intimate, heart-to-heart talk between teacher and pupil. It is frankly admitted that it is

---

2. For additional treatment of this topic, see the author's chapter "Group Counseling: A Developmental Approach" in this text.

difficult to draw the line sharply between the essence of what is done in the personal interview and what is done in small groups. But it is even more difficult to make any distinction between group counseling and the more modern forms of class work . . ." (p. 274).

Almost twenty years later, in his fifth edition of the same text, Jones (1963) wrote, "The values of group guidance are generally accepted, but the term 'group counseling' is still rejected by many guidance authorities. Some believe that group counseling is an 'anomaly' and say that it is as silly to speak of 'group counseling' as 'group courtship' " (pp. 217-218).

In the thirty-seventh yearbook of the National Society for the Study of Education, *Part I Guidance in Educational Institutions,* Gilbert Wrenn (1938) wrote, "First of all, counseling is personal. It cannot be performed with a group. 'Group counseling' is a tautology; counseling is always personal" (p. 119). And in 1942, Brewer, also a highly respected guidance authority, wrote, " 'Group guidance' was invented, apparently, as a term to mean classroom study, recitation, or discussion; is it any longer needed? 'Group counseling' is a similar term, but might it not be best to confine the word counseling to work with individuals?' " (p. 294).

Slavson (1964), too, resists the use of the term group counseling. He stated, "Counseling should be done on a one-to-one relation" (p. 102). He also believes that there are different treatments for different levels of the person's psyche. On the continuum from least to most in terms of depth and intensity of treatment and level of psyche reached, Slavson places group counseling at the level of least depth and intensity and most superficial level of psyche dealt with and group psychotherapy at the level of greatest depth and intensity and deepest level of psyche reached. Group guidance lies in the middle of this continuum. In terms of duration of treatment, the order from shortest to longest is group counseling, group guidance and group psychotherapy. Slavson's conception of group counseling and his placement of it on the above continuum is not in accord with the majority of group counselors.

Gazda, Duncan, and Sisson (1971) surveyed one thousand members of an American Personnel and Guidance Association Interest Group on Group Procedures in order to determine distinctions among various group procedures, among other purposes. (The majority of the 164 respondents held the doctorate degrees and were members of the American Personnel and Guidance Association and/or the American Psychological Association.)

The respondents were asked to indicate distinctions that they would make among group guidance, group counseling, T-groups, sensitivity groups, encounter groups, and psychotherapy groups on each of the following: (1) purposes of each; (2) clientele best served; and (3) "essential" professional preparation requirements. Group guidance was viewed as essentially different (on all three criteria) from the other group procedures. Likewise, group therapy was viewed as distinctly different from group counseling, sensitivity and T-groups on the same dimensions. However, the respondents did not distinguish between group counseling, T-groups, and sensitivity groups on the three criteria. (In other words, they viewed these three group procedures as similar on the criteria.) In the author's chapter of this text, "Group counseling: A Developmental Approach," Figure 1 illustrates the relationships among group procedures. Group guidance and certain human potential-type groups are described as primarily preventive in purpose; group counseling, T-groups, sensitivity groups, encounter groups, and organizational development (OD) groups are described as partially preventive, growth-engendering, and remedial in purpose; group psychotherapy is described as remedial in purpose. The clientele served, degree of disturbance of the clientele, setting of the treatment, goals of treatment, size of group, and length and duration of treatment are, accordingly, reflected in the emphasis or purpose of each of these three distinctly different groupings. Although the lines between group procedures, especially group counseling, encounter groups and therapy groups are becoming more and more blurred because of each borrowing from the other, there is still need, in my opinion, to make certain distinctions based on the criteria described in my *Group Counseling: A Developmental Approach* (1971) and summarized in my chapter by the same title, included in this text.

Lifton (1966) also has dealt with the confusion of "group"

terminology (including group counseling) and concluded "that although some nine years have passed since the earlier edition of this text [his first edition] was written, confusion and disagreement over the meaning of terms still exist" (p. 13). A "group procedures" interest group of some thirty members of the American Personnel and Guidance Association met at the Association's 1966 Convention in Washington, D. C., and appeared to confirm Lifton's conclusion when they had difficulty differentiating between group guidance and group counseling.[3]

To muddy the waters still more, the term *multiple counseling* was introduced by Froehlich (n.d.). Froehlich's use of multiple counseling is consistent with the generally accepted use of *group counseling;* however, Helen Driver (1958) introduced multiple counseling to mean the conjunctive use of individual counseling with group counseling. Still others frequently use multiple counseling when they are referring to the use of more than one counselor.

Granted the confusion over the definition of group counseling, there is evidence that it is abating. A survey of 54 of the more prominent contributors to the field of group counseling for the period 1960 to 1965 revealed that 80 percent preferred the term *group counseling* to *group guidance, multiple counseling, group therapy, psychodrama* and *sociodrama* when they were asked to select the term that they preferred to use to describe "counseling with more than one individual simultaneously" (Gazda, Duncan, and Meadows, 1967). This appears consistent with a conclusion reached by Bennett as early as 1963. She states, "The term group counseling has become very popular, and practices under this name have been introduced rather widely in school systems. One might almost call it an epidemic" (p. 136).

Forty-three of the respondents to the survey by Gazda *et al.* (1967), i.e., those who preferred the term group counseling, were asked to define it. From their definitions, a composite definition was generated.

> Group counseling is a dynamic interpersonal process focusing on conscious thought and behavior and involving the therapy functions

---

3. Personal communication.

of permissiveness, orientation to reality, catharsis, and mutual trust, caring, understanding, acceptance, and support. The therapy functions are created and nurtured in a small group through the sharing of personal concerns with one's peers and the counselor(s). The group counselees are basically normal individuals with various concerns which are not debilitating to the extent requiring extensive personality change. The group counselees may utilize the group interaction to increase understanding and acceptance of values and goals and to learn and/or unlearn certain attitudes and behaviors (Gazda, Duncan, and Meadows, 1967, p. 305).

MOVEMENTS CONTRIBUTING TO GROUP COUNSELING

The previous reference to R. D. Allen's use of the term group counseling suggests that Allen may have coined the expression; however, the author does not contend that he has discovered the missing link. More likely than not, several individuals were using the term in Allen's era. Several movements have contributed to the group counseling movement. The most significant of these contributing movements, in addition to group psychotherapy which was described earlier in this chapter, were child guidance, vocational guidance, social casework, group work, group dynamics, and the human potential movement.

Child Guidance

There exists the possibility that group counseling originated in Europe. Dreikurs and Corsini (1954) contend that between 1900 and 1930 major steps were being made in Europe toward a systematic use of the group method called "collective counceling (sic)." They believe that Alfred Adler, in his child guidance clinics in Vienna, was likely the first psychiatrist to use *collective counseling* formally and systematically.

Ansbacher and Ansbacher (1956) translated many of Adler's works, and in their commentary on his writing they stated, "Although Adler himself never practiced group therapy he suggested its use for the treatment of criminals" (p. 347). It is not because of his suggestion for using group therapy with criminals that Adler is considered by some to be the father of the group counseling movement, but rather because of his application of group techniques in his child guidance clinics. According to the Ansbachers,

Adler was conducting group procedures–perhaps collective counseling–as early as 1922.

The rationale and methods employed by Adler and his followers are described by Ansbacher and Ansbacher (1956). However, the Ansbachers, because they were unable to find "more than a mere mention" of Adler's rationale and methods in his own writings, were forced to turn to secondary sources, i.e., the writings of Seidler and Zilat, and Rayner and Holub. Seidler and Zilat described the "public" character of Adlerian child guidance clinics, i.e., the child was interviewed in the presence of an adult audience. Doris Rayner defends this form of treatment by stating that the child benefits because he comes to view his difficulty as a "community problem" and his audience (parents) receive an education in parent-child behavior. Martha Holub agreed with Rayner's position of the mutual therapeutic benefits to the child and adult through participation in this Adlerian "open-door" treatment procedure.

In 1942 Brewer described the child guidance movement "as yet largely dissociated from the work of the schools . . ." (p. 263). Nevertheless, because of its many similarities, the child guidance movement has influenced, directly or indirectly, the group counseling movement. Currently Adlerian-oriented counselors are making a very significant contribution in elementary school guidance programs and parent and child guidance clinics not too unlike those originated by Adler in Vienna.

Vocational Guidance

Frank Parsons has been recognized as the father of the vocational guidance movement because of his founding of the Vocational Bureau of Boston in 1908 (Brewer, 1942). Just when, where and by whom the word *group* was added to the word *guidance* is not known; however, according to Brewer (1942), Charles L. Jacobs of San Jose was one of the first to suggest a wider use of the term *guidance* when in the October, 1915 issue of *Manual Training and Vocational Education,* he stated that his work included three departments–educational guidance, vocational guidance, and avocational guidance.

CLASSES IN OCCUPATIONAL INFORMATION. As early as 1908 William A. Wheatley was instrumental in introducing a course in occupational information for freshmen boys at Westport, Connecticut High School. Similar courses were offered in Boston and New York City soon after Wheatley's (Brewer, 1942).

HOMEROOM. McKown (1934) authored a text, *Home Room Guidance,* as early as 1934. The content of the text and the fact that McKown proposed the director of guidance as the director of homeroom guidance suggests its close association to group guidance and counseling. In fact, some schools referred to the homeroom as "the 'guidance hour,' or 'guidance room' " (McKown, 1934, p. 53). In a publication of approximately the same vintage of McKown's, Strang (1935) cited the contribution of the homeroom teacher as being fourfold: "to establish friendly relationships, to discover the abilities and needs, and to develop right attitudes toward school, home, and community" (p. 116). Once more the group guidance and counseling "flavor" was expressed in the work of the homeroom teacher.

EXTRACURRICULAR ACTIVITIES. C. R. Foster authored a book, *Extra Curricular Activities,* in 1925, in which he recognized guidance as an extracurricular activity. In the same text, Foster also urged the counselor to "hold many group conferences with the students on the subject of future educational or vocational plans" (p. 182). Pittsburgh was cited by Foster as including instructional guidance taking "the form of tenth-grade group conferences which were held for the purpose of discussing Pittsburgh's industrial life and the opportunities it affords the young people" (1925, p. 183).

The vocational guidance movement was instrumental in the introduction of homeroom guidance, classes in occupational information, and certain extracurricular activities that were forerunners of current group guidance and group counseling.

Social Casework

In reviewing the history of the Marriage Council of Philadelphia, Gaskill and Mudd (1950) stated that group counseling and family life education had been part of the "Marriage Council's service from the agency's inception in 1932" (p. 194). Whether or not the term *group counseling* itself was actually used by the Council as early as 1932 and whether or not the treatment was similar to current group counseling is not indicated. However, Gaskill and Mudd (1950) gave the following definition of group counseling for which they express their indebtedness to Hazel Froscher, Margery Klein and Helen Phillips:

> . . . a dynamic relationship between a counselor and the members of a group, involving presentation and discussion of subjects about which the counselor has special knowledge, which is of general or specific concern to the group, and around which emotions may be brought out and attitudes developed or changed. The relationship between the group members themselves and the counselor's use of this is essentially important in the total process (1950, p. 195).

The definition implies that the counselor gives a presentation and encourages discussion of it. Gaskill and Mudd (1950), in their description of the group counseling sessions, indicate that the group ranged between 35 and 50 persons in size, and they further described the group sessions as a *course* including speakers other than the group counselor. This approach to group counseling seems more closely related to group guidance or a family living class rather than the typical small, eight- to ten-member counseling groups where leader-imposed content is absent or minimal.

Group Work

Sullivan (1952) described a group in the following manner:

> The group must be a small stable one which feels itself as an entity and which the individual can feel close identification. Membership . . . is voluntary. There is a group leader, who is consciously making constructive use of the process of personality interaction among the members. The leader utilizes the desire of a normal person to be accepted by his fellows. He establishes the dignity of the individual and teaches acceptance of differences in race, creed, and nationality. Group work stresses programs evolved by the group itself, in consultation with the leader who guides toward socially desirable ends. Creative activities are encouraged to provide legitimate channels of self-expressions and to relieve emotional stress. Competition for its own sake is minimized and group members learn from situations where cooperation brings rich satisfaction. The trained

leader arranged for leadership practice by group members, individual responsibility and group responsibility grow as the group takes on new functions. The atmosphere is friendly, informal, and democratic (p. 189).

This description of group work contains many of the ingredients that are present in definitions of group counseling, and the possible influence on group counseling of the group work specialists becomes readily apparent.

Group Dynamics

The group dynamics movement, according to Bonner (1959), had its beginning in the late 1800's, notably in Europe. Contribution to the group dynamics discipline came from sociology, psychology, philosophy, and education, but primarily from sociology and psychology.

Bonner is careful not to give major credit to a single individual or discipline; however, he cites Kurt Lewin and J. L. Moreno for making significant, but dissimilar, contributions during the contemporary phase of development—1930's to the present.

The National Training Laboratories (NTL) was established in Bethel, Maine in [1947], "it was not until the middle to late 1950's before the tools and techniques of group dynamics really found their way into education and more specifically, into guidance" (Glanz and Hayes, 1967, p. 4). In 1964, Durkin, after a careful survey of group dynamicists and group therapists wrote:

> In spite of the general impression to the contrary, there was almost no therapy actually being conducted on solely group dynamics principles by group dynamicists. From private correspondence with some of the leading social scientists, I learned that they did not acknowledge group dynamics therapy as an identifiable approach and that they were meticulous in distinguishing between their work and group therapy (p. 4).

One can conclude from the Glanz and Hayes statement above that group dynamics principles and concepts only very recently have begun to affect the field of *group guidance.* Also, Durkin emphasized that, although group dynamics had begun to influence the field of group therapy, as late as 1964 there was still no complete application of group therapy based primarily on group dynamics principles.

The application of group dynamics principles to *group counseling* has a rather recent history. The explication of these applications can be found in the writings of Bonney (1969), Gazda (1971), Fullmer (1969, 1971) and Mahler (1969).

Human Potential Movement

The human potential emphasis began to be felt in the early and middle 1960's. Its origin is multiple and diverse. The disciplines of psychology, education, and management have made significant contributions. Some of the more influential contributors have been Carl Rogers, Abraham Maslow, Herbert Otto, Jack Gibb, and William Schutz. The more practical elements of the movement are being applied to classroom instruction and, in that sense, are *group guidance*-oriented. In the highly experimental and perhaps even ethically questionable forms of group application, it is affecting *group counseling* by introducing more body contact and more structured game playing.

SIGNIFICANT CONTRIBUTORS

For one to attempt to appraise and record some of the most significant contributors to the specialty of *group counseling* while living in the era of the beginning of the movement is to court professional suicide; nevertheless, an attempt will be made to sketch briefly the author's perception of those who have been and, in most instances, are still making significant contributions to the group counseling movement. The author concluded that the leaders of the group counseling movement are citizens of the United States, and this assumption seems supported by Brewer (1942). If this conclusion is erroneous, it might at least stimulate others to investigate and challenge it.

The credit for coining the term group counseling may be attributed to Richard D. Allen, although there is no absolute proof of this. Others who were among the first to publish and teach in the field of group counseling were Margaret Bennett, Ruth Strang and

Jane Warters. Evelyn Gaskill and Emily Mudd should be cited for their early use of group counseling in social casework and Hanna Grunwald for the current application of group counseling in case work agencies.

Clifford Froehlich and Helen Driver have influenced the group counseling movement with their introduction of multiple counseling, and E. Wayne Wright, upon the death of Froehlich, continued the multiple counseling emphasis. However, multiple counseling is now only rarely accepted as the preferred term for group counseling (Gazda, Duncan, and Meadows, 1967).

Merle Ohlsen, Fred Proff and several of their colleagues and students at the University of Illinois, the author among them, are known for their early attempt to research group counseling. Ohlsen has also contributed two significant texts to the field. Ben Cohn (who was influenced by Ohlsen) and his associates of the Board of Cooperative Educational Services of Bedford Hills, New York, researched the effects of group counseling on acting-out adolescents. Stanley Capalan did research with similar groups. Clarence Mahler and Edson Caldwell co-authored one of the first texts on group counseling in the schools and Mahler has since produced his own very useful text.

Among those representing the various schools of group counseling, Walter Lifton has been the most prominent proponent of the client-centered approach to group counseling. Rudolf Dreikurs, Manford Sonstegard, Oscar Christensen, Donald Dinkmeyer, James Muro, and G. Edward Stormer are among the most significant Adlerian-oriented contributors to the field of group counseling. John Krumboltz, Barbara Varenhorst, Carl E. Thoresen, and Beverly Potter are making their contributions with a behavior-oriented application of group counseling.

Dan Fullmer and Harold Bernard have introduced to the field *family group-consultation,* whereas Joseph Knowles has been instrumental in the successful application of the group approach to *pastoral counseling.*

Robert Carkhuff has influenced the direction that group counseling and counseling in general is taking because of his research and writings regarding the "core dimensions" of a helping relationship and his overall model–Systematic Human Resources Development (HRD).

There are many others[4] who have contributed significantly to the development of group counseling through their training procedures, research, and/or writing. Although the list of contributors is lengthy it is by no means inclusive, for example, Lechowicz (1973) identified over 229 "experts" in group counseling. His criteria for defining an expert included:

1. The author must have published in the area of group counseling, group guidance, group psychotherapy, or multiple counseling,

2. At least two different publications of each author had been cited by other authors,

3. The cited publications were dated between 1950 and 1972 (p. 41).

In 1966, Dwight Arnold assumed a leadership role in developing an "interest group" among the American Personnel and Guidance Association members for the purpose of defining the field, sharing information on training programs, and establishing communication among practitioners to provide some form of organization to the loose-knit group counseling movement. The author assumed Dr. Arnold's coordinator role in 1968 and developed this interest group from approximately 100 to over 1,500. On December 8, 1973, the author succeeded in establishing the Association for Specialists in Group Work (ASGW) as the eleventh division of the American Personnel and Guidance Association (the parent organization of over 35,000 members). He will serve as the new division's first president. With the establishment of this new divi-

---

4. Norman Kagan, John Vriend, Wayne Dyer, Joseph Lechowicz, James Lee, Vincent Calia, Jack Duncan, Jonell Kirby, Roger Peters, Charles Truax, Ken Matheney, Sherman Day, Jack Blakeman, Ronald Ruble, William Mermis, Gratton Kemp, Thomas J. Long, Gary Landreth, Sharon Anderson, Marilyn Bates, C. E. Johnson, Richard Caple, Al Dye, Richard Diedrich, David Zimpfer, C. E. Smith, Merville Shaw, Wesley Schmidt, Frank Noble, Cal Daane, Sheldon Glass, William Lewis, W. F. Hill, M. E. Meadows, Al Roark, Betty Bosdell, Earl Koile, Robert Myrick, Robert Berg, S. Dietz, Pete Havens, Oscar Mink, Robert Griffin, Burl Gilliand, Alicia Tilley, Thomas Hennessy, Robert Naun, and Marion Belka.

sion for group work, of which group counseling is the core, the continued growth and impact of group counseling seems likely. Although this chapter focused primarily on the historical development of group psychotherapy and group counseling, many other related group procedures were developing and influencing these two group specialities. In the 1960's, especially, clear differentiations among the many group procedures and disciplines became difficult. Figure 1–Group Procedures Historical Time-Line–is included: (1) to illustrate the concurrent development of several

Figure 1

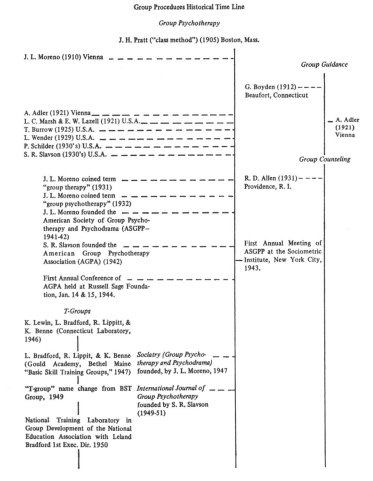

Group Procedures Historical Time Line

Group Psychotherapy

J. H. Pratt ("class method") (1905) Boston, Mass.

J. L. Moreno (1910) Vienna

Group Guidance

G. Boyden (1912)
Beaufort, Connecticut

A. Adler (1921) Vienna
L. C. Marsh & E. W. Lazell (1921) U.S.A.
T. Burrow (1925) U.S.A.
L. Wender (1929) U.S.A.
P. Schilder (1930's) U.S.A.
S. R. Slavson (1930's) U.S.A.

_ A. Adler (1921) Vienna

Group Counseling

J. L. Moreno coined term "group therapy" (1931)
J. L. Moreno coined term "group psychotherapy" (1932)
J. L. Moreno founded the American Society of Group Psychotherapy and Psychodrama (ASGPP–1941-42)
S. R. Slavson founded the American Group Psychotherapy Association (AGPA) (1942)

R. D. Allen (1931)
Providence, R. I.

First Annual Meeting of ASGPP at the Sociometric Institute, New York City, 1943.

First Annual Conference of AGPA held at Russell Sage Foundation, Jan. 14 & 15, 1944.

T-Groups

K. Lewin, L. Bradford, R. Lippitt, & K. Benne (Connecticut Laboratory, 1946)

L. Bradford, R. Lippit, & K. Benne (Gould Academy, Bethel Maine "Basic Skill Training Groups," 1947)

Sociatry (Group Psychotherapy and Psychodrama) founded, by J. L. Moreno, 1947

"T-group" name change from BST Group, 1949

International Journal of Group Psychotherapy founded by S. R. Slavson (1949-51)

National Training Laboratory in Group Development of the National Education Association with Leland Bradford 1st Exec. Dir. 1950

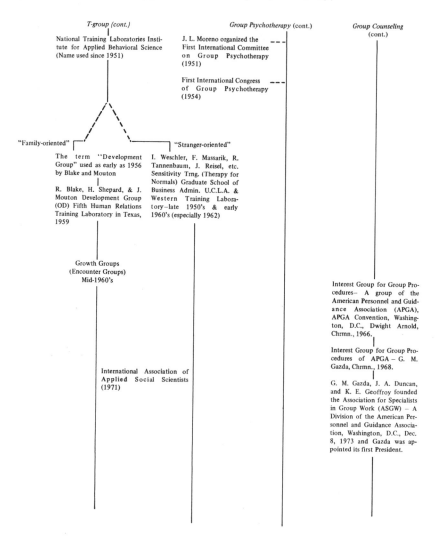

T-group (cont.)

National Training Laboratories Institute for Applied Behavioral Science (Name used since 1951)

Group Psychotherapy (cont.)

J. L. Moreno organized the First International Committee on Group Psychotherapy (1951)

First International Congress of Group Psychotherapy (1954)

Group Counseling (cont.)

"Family-oriented"

The term "Development Group" used as early as 1956 by Blake and Mouton

R. Blake, H. Shepard, & J. Mouton Development Group (OD) Fifth Human Relations Training Laboratory in Texas, 1959

"Stranger-oriented"

I. Weschler, F. Massarik, R. Tannenbaum, J. Reisel, etc. Sensitivity Trng. (Therapy for Normals) Graduate School of Business Admin. U.C.L.A. & Western Training Laboratory–late 1950's & early 1960's (especially 1962)

Growth Groups (Encounter Groups) Mid-1960's

Interest Group for Group Procedures– A group of the American Personnel and Guidance Association (APGA), APGA Convention, Washington, D.C., Dwight Arnold, Chrmn., 1966.

Interest Group for Group Procedures of APGA – G. M. Gazda, Chrmn., 1968.

International Association of Applied Social Scientists (1971)

G. M. Gazda, J. A. Duncan, and K. E. Geoffroy founded the Association for Specialists in Group Work (ASGW) – A Division of the American Personnel and Guidance Association, Washington, D.C., Dec. 8, 1973 and Gazda was appointed its first President.

group disciplines; (2) to illustrate the possible mutual influence of the disciplines/procedures on each other; and (3) to serve as a brief summary of several significant group developments which, for the most part, were cited in this chapter.

SUMMARY

This chapter traces the history and development of group psychotherapy and group counseling and defines each. Significant contributors and a brief summary of their contributions are included. The contributions of related disciplines to the development of group counseling are outlined. An historical time-line is developed to illustrate the inter-relationship in the development of the small group field.

REFERENCES

Allen, R. D.: A group guidance curriculum in the senior high school. *Education, 2:*189, 1931.

Ansbacher, H. L., and Ansbacher, R. R. (Eds.): *The Individual Psychology of Alfred Adler.* New York, Basic Books, 1956.

Bennett, M. E.: *Guidance and Counseling in Groups* (2nd ed.). New York, McGraw, 1963.

Bonner, H.: *Group Dynamics.* New York, Ronald Press, 1959.

Bonney, W. C.: Group counseling and developmental processes. In G. M. Gazda (Ed.): *Theories and Methods of Group Counseling in the Schools.* Springfield, Ill., Charles C Thomas, 1969.

Brewer, J. M.: Introduction. In R. D. Allen (Ed.): *Organization and Supervision of Guildance in Public Education.* New York, Inor Publishing Company, 1937.

Brewer, J. M.: *History of Vocational Guidance.* New York, Harper, 1942.

Carkhuff, R. R.: Training as a preferred mode of treatment (Ch. 6). In G. M. Gazda: *Group Counseling: A Developmental Approach.* Boston, Allyn and Bacon, 1971.

Corsini, R. J.: *Methods of Group Psychotherapy.* Chicago, William James Press, 1957.

Dreikurs, R., and Corsini, R. J.: Twenty years of group psychotherapy. *American Journal of Psychiatry, 110:*567, 1954.

Driver, H. I.: *Counseling and Learning in Small-group Discussion.* Madison, Monona, 1958.

Durkin, H., *et al.* (AGPA Committee on History): A brief history of the American Group Psychotherapy Association. *International Journal of Group Psychotherapy, 21*(4):406, 1971.

Foster, C. R.: *Extra-curricular Activities in the High School.* Richmond, Va., Johnson, 1925.

Froehlich, C. P.: Multiple counseling—A research proposal. Berkeley, University of California Department of Education, n.d.

Fullmer, D. W.: Family group consultation. In G. M. Gazda (Ed.): *Theories and Methods of Group Counseling in the Schools.* Springfield, Illinois, Charles C Thomas, 1969.

Gaskill, E. R., and Mudd, E. H.: A decade of group counseling. *Social Casework, 31:*194, 1950.

Gazda, G. M.: *Group Counseling: A Developmental Approach.* Boston, Allyn and Bacon, 1971.

Gazda, G. M., Duncan, J. A., and Meadows, M. E.: Counseling and group procedures—Report of a survey. *Counselor Education and Supervision, 6:*305, 1967.

Gazda, G. M., Duncan, J. A., and Sisson, P. J.: Professional issues in group work. *Personnel and Guidance Journal, 49*(8):637, 1971.

Gibb, J. R., Platts, G. N., and Miller, L. F.: *Dynamics of Participative Groups.* St. Louis, John Swift, 1951.

Glanz, E. C., and Hayes, R. W.: *Groups in Guidance* (2nd ed.). Boston, Allyn and Bacon, 1968.

Hadden, S. B.: Historic background of group psychotherapy. *International Journal of Group Psychotherapy, 5:*62, 1955.

Harms, E.: Group therapy—Farce, fashion, or sociologically sound? *Nervous Child, 4:*186, 1944.

Jones, A. J.: *Principles of Guildance* (2nd ed.). New York, McGraw, 1934.

Jones, A. J.: *Principles of Guidance* (5th ed.). New York, McGraw, 1963.

Lechowicz, J. S.: Group counseling instruction: A model based on behavioral objectives developed via the Delphi technique. Unpublished doctoral dissertation, University of Georgia, Athens, Georgia, 1973.

Lifton, W. M.: *Working with Groups* (2nd ed.). New York, Wiley, 1966.

Lubin, B., and Lubin, A. W.: The group psychotherapy literature: 1972. *International Journal of Group Psychotherapy, 23*(4):474, 1973.

MacLennan, B., Morse, V., and Goode, P.: The group psychotherapy literature, 1965. *International Journal of Group Psychotherapy, 16:*225, 1966.

MacLennan, B., and Levy, N.: The group psychotherapy literature, 1970. *International Journal of Group Psychotherapy, 21*(3):345, 1971.

Mahler, C. A.: *Group Counseling in the Schools.* Boston, Houghton-Mifflin, 1969.

McKowan, H. C.: *Home Room Guidance.* New York, McGraw, 1934.

Meiers, J. L.: Origins and development of group psychotherapy. *Sociometry, 8:*499, 1945.

Moreno, J. L.: Common ground for all group psychotherapists. What is a group psychotherapist? *Group Psychotherapy, 15:*263, 1962.

Moreno, J. L., et al. (Eds.): *The International Handbook of Group Psychotherapy.* New York, Philosophical Library, 1966.

Moreno, Z. T.: Evolution and dynamics of the groups psychotherapy movement. In J. L. Moreno et al. (Eds.): *The International Handbook of Group Psychotherapy.* New York, Philosophical Library, 1966.

Moreno, J. L.: *Psychodrama* (Vol. 3). Beacon, New York, Beacon House, 1969.

Moreno, J. L.: *Group Psychotherapy: A Symposium.* Boston, Beacon House, 1972.

Mullan, H., and Rosenbaum, M.: *Group Psychotherapy.* New York, Glencoe Free Press, 1962.

Seidler, R.: School guidance clinics in Vienna. *Journal of Individual Psychology, 2:*75, 1936.

Slavson, S. R.: Parallelisms in the development of group psychotherapy. *International Journal of Group Psychotherapy, 9:*451, 1959.

Slavson, S. R.: *A Textbook in Analytic Group Psychotherapy.* New York, International U. P., 1964.

Strang, R.: *The Role of the Teacher in Personnel Work.* New York, Bureau of Publications, Teachers College, Columbia U., 1935.

Sullivan, D. F. (Ed.): *Readings in Group Work.* New York, Association Press, 1952.

Rosenbaum, M., and Berger, M. (Eds.): *Group Psychotherapy and Function.* New York, Basic Books, 1963.

Wrenn, C. G.: Counseling with students. In G. M. Whipple (Ed.): *Guidance in Educational Institutions, Part I. National Society for the Study of Education.* Bloomington, Public School Publishing Co., 1938.

CHAPTER II

AN ANALYSIS OF RESEARCH IN GROUP PSYCHOTHERAPY, GROUP COUNSELING AND HUMAN RELATIONS TRAINING

George M. Gazda and Roger W. Peters

G ROUP PSYCHOTHERAPY and group counseling have several unique features which have permitted distinctions to be made between them in the past. However, in recent years traditional distinctions have been erased while more pragmatic distinctions have been made on the basis of what appears to be convenience. For example, counseling traditionally occurred in a school setting while psychotherapy was reserved for services that took place in a hospital or private clinic. Currently, counseling appears to be tacitly limited to our educational settings, but psychotherapy can take place in any other setting. The choice of psychotherapy or counseling appears to be largely determined by what the investigators want to use rather than according to any established criteria.

For the purposes of this analysis, studies were categorized on the basis of what services the investigators assigned to the treatment groups, viz., group psychotherapy, group counseling or human relations training. In the first part of this analysis, group counseling research since 1938 will be described on the basis of nine criteria: (1) purpose (nature of the study), (2) type of group, (3) group size, (4) control (design), (5) treatment and process, (6) instruments (evaluative devices), (7) test statistics employed, (8) experimental design and (9) outcomes. This description of the literature includes 251 studies. It includes the updating of three earlier reports (Gazda, 1971; Gazda and Larsen, 1968; Gazda and Peters, 1973), and makes the review current through May 1973. Although this review is not exhaustive, it was intended to be exhaustive rather than representative. It includes dissertations as well as studies reported in a variety of professional journals. Only those studies which explicitly referred to group counseling were analyzed. The second portion of this analysis will include a summary of group psychotherapy, group counseling, and human relations training. Recommendations for future research will be made based on the findings in all three areas.

ANALYSIS OF GROUP COUNSELING RESEARCH SINCE 1938

Nature of the Study

About 64 percent of all studies were outcome; 16 percent were comparison; 13 percent were process; 7 percent were classified as miscellaneous, such as a combination of process and outcome. Based on studies reviewed through 1970 (Gazda, 1971), recent studies suggest a decrease in the number of outcome studies by approximately 24 percent. Process and outcome studies decreased by approximately 2 percent and comparison studies increased significantly by 40 percent.

Type of Group

Approximately 72 percent of the studies reviewed used students who were in an educational setting. The breakdown is as follows: kindergarten, 8 percent; elementary school, 8 percent; high school, 19 percent; college, 37 percent. The remaining studies utilized different subject populations such as: adults, 7 percent; inmates, 3 percent; mental patients, 3 percent. Fifteen percent of the studies were classified as miscellaneous. There is growing evidence that investigators are using more diversified subject populations (Lewis and McCants, 1973).

Group Size

Group size refers to the N reported in each study. It does *not* reflect the actual size of the counseling group. The range extended from a process study with an N of 3 to an outcome study with 266 experimental Ss. The average experimental or treatment group for the 1938-73 period was 42. This reflects an increase of 23 over the 1938-70 report (Gazda, 1971).

Controls

Control groups were used in 80 percent of the studies. This means that approximately 20 percent of the studies did not use controls. This includes process studies where controls are not always essential. (See Campbell and Stanley, 1963.)

Treatment

The "typical" treatment, calculated by averaging the number and the duration of the experimental sessions for all the studies that used treatment groups, consisted of approximately 14 hours of treatment spaced over 8.3 weeks. It is important to realize that this figure is affected by the increasing number of studies which used marathon or behavior modification approaches. These approaches generally consolidate a large number of treatment hours over relatively few days. For example, a marathon format may call for 25 hours of treatment over one weekend.

Instruments

Instruments refers to the measures employed to evaluate process and outcome variables. The majority of the studies reviewed used more than instrument. To maximize accuracy the frequency of usage rather than the percentage will be reported.

The relative ranking of the instruments was stable over the period from 1938 through 1973; grade-point average was used 45 times, but it decreased about 10 percent during the 1970-73 period. Ratings by judges, supervisors, teachers, etc., decreased about 8 percent but was still used 41 times. Self-reporting techniques, other than those used on standardized tests, were used approximately 31 times. Researcher-devised questionnaires were used 35 times. Achievement and ability tests were used 20 times which represents a significant increase over the 1938-70 period (Gazda, 1971) where they were infrequently used. Interviews declined in usage especially since 1970. In the total period from 1938-73 they were used only 17 times.

Occasionally used instruments include: Bills IAV (10), Q sorts (9), TAT (9), the Tennessee Self-Concept Test (11), the Semantic Differential (6), the California Psychological Inventory (6), and the Personal Orientation Inventory (6). A sample of the other instruments used at least twice includes: the Hill Interaction Matrix, the FIRO-B, the Rokeach Dogmatism Scale, Rotter's I-E Scale, Cassidy's Loneliness Scale, the Personal Relations Survey, the Adjective Checklist, the Sensitivity Group Rating Scales, evaluation of vocal performance, videotape evaluations, measures of study habits and measures of anxiety.

The majority of process studies reported the use of some forms of interaction analysis (based on researcher-devised instruments and the Hill Interaction Matrix), leadership scales, peer ratings, role-playing, nonverbal classifications and other similar instruments.

Test Statistics

As was the case with instruments, the use of multiple test statistics is more prevalent than the use of a single statistic. Rather than report the results in percentages which would be misleading, frequency of usage will be reported. Overall there were approximately 38 different test statistics used. The t-test was used 82 times. The analysis of variance in one form or another was used 85 times. These figures indicate a significant increase in the popularity of analysis of variance and a decrease in the popularity of the t-test in the 3-year period from 1970-73. Some form of correlation was used 37 times. Some form of descriptive statistics was used 26 times but usage decreased significantly during the 1970-73 period. Chi square (used 24 times) also showed a similar decrease during the same 3-year period. Analysis of covariance was used 23 times and remains in the same relative position for the 1970-73 period. Factor analysis was used 6 times which suggests a slight trend toward the employment of this statistical treatment procedure especially in conjunction with other statistical analyses.

Experimental Designs

The research designs used for categorization of the group counseling research described here are those of Campbell and Stanley

TABLE I

EXPERIMENTAL DESIGNS

True Experimental Designs		
Pretest-Posttest Control Group Design	Solomon Four-Group Design	Posttest Only Control Group Design
N = 138	1	14

Pre-Experimental Designs		
One Shot Case Study	One Group Pretest-Posttest Design	Static Group Comparison
N = 5	12	2

Quasi-Experimental Designs		
Equivalent Materials Design	Non-Equivalent Control Group Design	Separate Sample Pretest-Posttest (No Control) Design
1	7	3

Other Designs			
Descriptive One Group Pretest-Posttest Study	Descriptive Simple Survey	Process	Unclassifiable
6	8	36	18

Total N = 251.

(1963). The various designs are classified under 3 major headings: pre-experimental designs, true experimental designs and quasi-experimental and other designs, including process.

About 74 percent of the outcome studies were classifiable as True Experimental Designs, which means that some form of control group was utilized. About 63 percent of the total studies reported were in the category of True Experimental Designs. The process and unclassifiable studies make up the bulk of the Other Designs Category, representing 14 and 7 percent respectively.

Two notable findings, found by comparing data from 1938-70 (Gazda, 1971) with that from 1970-73, were that outcome studies were classified as to design approximately the same as for the 1938-70 period. At the same time there was a significant increase in the number of process studies from 15 to 36. More important is the rate of increase. There were only 15 process studies from 1938-70 and there were 21 additional studies from 1970-73.

Criteria and Outcomes

The studies analyzed from 1938-70 (Gazda, 1971) revealed that about 50 percent showed significant gains in the predicted direction. This may be somewhat misleading because most of the studies used multiple measures and in many instances only 1 out of several variables showed significant change in the predicted direction. Often these variables were self-reports of self-concept improvement and the like. On the other hand, those studies evaluating GPA increases and/or other achievement increases showed about 50 percent success rates.

An important difference between the 1938-70 period and the 1970-73 period is the greater proportion of studies which showed significant changes in the predicted direction on the majority of evaluated variables. More than 75 percent of the studies in this 3-year period versus 50 percent prior to 1970, showed significant results. This may mean that group leaders are doing a more effective job of counseling, that journal editors are accepting fewer studies which do not show significant results, or a number of other explanations.

The 1970-73 breakdown for the various types of studies shows 40 out of 57 outcome studies, 15 out of 19 process studies, and 11 out of 17 comparison studies reported significant results. The remainder were unclassifiable.

SUMMARY ANALYSIS OF GROUP PSYCHOTHERAPY, GROUP COUNSELING, AND HUMAN RELATIONS TRAINING

The second part of this analysis is a comparative summary of group psychotherapy, group counseling and human relations training.

Summary and Recommendations For Group Psychotherapy*

Nature of the Study/Purpose

Very few of the studies investigated differential treatment effects accompanying variations in group therapy procedures. It appears that the studies included investigations that identified (1) the treatment effects of group therapy, (2) behavior changes that are attributable to group therapy, (3) the types of clients and problems that are amenable to treatment by group therapy, (4) personality variables of those therapists who have a positive influence on group dynamics, (5) antecedent conditions to client improvement and (6) group interaction patterns that appear to benefit participants. There were several studies which explored such concomitant variables as: client attrition and client anxiety.

Type of Group

The data may be summarized as follows: (1) group therapy produces good results when it is used to supplement other treatment methods, (2) group therapy seems to have less effectiveness with psychotic clients; conversely it seems to be more effective with nonpsychotic clients, and (3) individual therapy appears

Summary and Recommendations For Group Counseling

Nature of the Study/Purpose

Of the studies, articles and dissertations reviewed during the 1970-73 period, about 19 percent were concerned with the study of both process and outcome variables; 16 percent of the studies reviewed were directly concerned with investigating process variables. The remaining 65 percent of the studies investigated outcome variables.

The 16 percent of the studies investigating both process and outcome variables represent a trend toward accounting for more of the effects of group dynamics. They may also represent an attempt to get at potential causal relations. A subtle trend that may have remained hidden is that many of the studies which correlate outcome variables used more diversified and, behaviorally, more psychologically positive and diversified variables as part of the outcome. These variables included: musical appreciation, problem-solving competency, self-disclosure, personal and social skills, and weight reduction.

Type of Group

By far the greatest amount of group

Summary and Recommendations For Human Relations Training*

Nature of the Study/Purpose

When considering that a prevalent criticism is the lack of research on human relations training, the quality and quantity of available research is surprisingly good. However, when compared with the standards of research in group counseling and group therapy, and with the desirability of definitive findings about the effects of training, the results are disappointingly inconsistent.

"Too much of the research has a 'bits and pieces' quality, seems opportunistically empirical and lacks an integrating or programmatic directionality" (Gibb, 1971, p. 842). Innovation and change in training methodology is largely clinical and intuitive rather than systematic. New methods do not appear to reflect empirical evaluation and research has little influence upon the evolution of methods and theories.

Type of Group

Creativity-Growth Groups: These activities appear to be most controversial and lack substantial empirical support. Marathon Groups: Although the method is becoming increasingly popular and has generated modifications in many human relations training programs, there

to be more effective with grossly psychotic clients and less effective with nonpsychotic clients.

Characteristics such as severe thought disorders and marked interpersonal withdrawal do not appear to be readily influenced by group therapy. Group therapy, however, appears to contribute to improved self-adjustment.

"Current data in contrast to the data from group dynamic literature, suggest that leaderless groups with psychiatric patients are probably more inherently dangerous than are professionally led groups" (Bednar and Lawlis, 1971, p. 832). Group therapists play an important role in keeping the group focused on relevant therapeutic tasks. Therapists should be reluctant to sponsor leaderless groups with psychiatric patients, although there may be conditions under which periodic absences of the leader can be beneficial.

The most basic factor for inclusion in group therapy seems to be a nonpsychotic disorder. The bulk of the literature

---

*This summary is based in part on a critical review by R. Bednar and G. Lawlis (Ch. 21) in A. Bergin and S. Garfield (Eds.): *Handbook of Psychotherapy and Behavior Change* (1971). John Wiley and Sons, Inc. Reprinted by permission.

counseling studies used college students as participants. The next most frequently used subjects were adult participants. Graduate students were next in terms of reported usage. Elementary and secondary students were used frequently as well as more diverse participants such as: prison inmates, theology students, music students, retarded residents and mental patients. Of all the group counseling studies reviewed, 72 percent originated in an educational setting. This corresponds to one of the trends reported by Gazda and Peters (1973) in which the widespread use of educational settings may limit the type of group and group goals. The use of more diverse settings and participants represents an encouraging trend.

The bulk of the groups were either homogeneously composed or description of the group composition was not given. There is evidence (Gazda, 1971; Peters, 1972; Yalom, 1971) that groups should be heterogeneously composed or balanced in order to provide models of healthier behavior thus increasing the opportunity for the participant to learn an increased repertoire of behaviors. The studies reviewed suggest an apparent neglect of this important variable. It is recommended that group composition or client selection receive greater attention.

is as yet little evaluative research available.

Emergent Groups: There is some evidence that training in groups without leaders produces changes in the behavior of participants.

Authenticity Groups: "There is little available published research on training in these groups" (Gibb, 1971, p. 851).

Sensitivity Training Groups: About 80 percent of the studies reviewed were sensitivity training groups.

Programmed Groups: "There is no clear evidence as yet to indicate differential effects of programmed and nonprogrammed groups" (Gibb, 1971, p. 852).

Microexperience Groups: There is as yet no research evaluating outcomes.

Inquiry Groups: It is difficult to determine from the reports in the literature what was actually done in the training sessions.

Embedded Groups: Empirical evidence on the effectiveness of these programs in changing practices is as yet not available.

---

*This summary is based essentially on the findings of J. R. Gibb (Ch. 22) in A. Bergin and S. Garfield (Eds.): *Handbook of Psychotherapy and Behavior Change* (1971). John Wiley and Sons, Inc. Reprinted by permission.

**Summary and Recommendations
For Group Psychotherapy**

suggests that the brighter, more capable, nonpsychotic clients tend to be more responsive to group therapy than are other types of clients.

There is evidence that indicates about ⅓ of the clients who begin group therapy drop out unimproved within the first 12 sessions.

Research addressing the problems of group composition covers content areas of: group homogeneity and heterogeneity, premorbid history, current adjustment, emotional and intellectual resources and group compatibility.

Goldstein, Heller and Sechrest (1966) present data which "suggest that there are identifiable behavioral and emotional pre-requisites for effective involvement in group therapy ranging on dimensions of severity of disturbance, intellectual and emotional resources and group compati-bility." (Bednar and Lawlis, 1970, p. 830).

The research suggests that clinicians should utilize behavioral assets by placing clients in groups so that sufficient group resources are available to facilitate (1) warm, responsive interactions between group members, (2) sufficient compatibility to increase personal attractions, (3) sufficient courage to discuss

**Summary and Recommendations
For Group Counseling**

Group Size

The average overall treatment sample size for the period 1938-73 was 38. Prior to 1970 the average treatment sample size was 29. From 1970-73 the treatment sample size increased to 47. The increase in the size of the treatment sample reflects the use of methodologies and research designs which simultaneously compare several different treatments and permit greater coverage of the variables under investigation. (See Campbell and Stanley, 1963, for a concise discussion on research designs.) The use of greater sophistication in research designs corresponds to increased use of multiple statistical analyses.

Controls

Approximately 80 percent of the studies used some form of controls. In the 1970-73 period 83 percent of the studies used placebo or Hawthorne control measures. It is strongly recommended that all studies include some form of control as well as control for the Hawthorne effect. This means that some of the controls should be more than in-active recipients of no experimental treatment. Those participants who are in the

**Summary and Recommendations
For Human Relations Training**

Research results suggest that composing the training group of members of the same administrative unit or work team is effective. It is believed by some to be more effective than heterogeneously composed training groups.

"Participants with more self-disclosing trainers more often entered into relationships with other group members. Members of groups that had trainers who were less self-disclosing tended to enter into relationships with the trainer" (Gibb, 1971, p. 854).

Group Size

Data from the studies reviewed were not sufficiently quantified so that a reasonable assessment of the treatment group size could be made. Based on the small number of studies which reported the size of their treatment groups, the average treatment group numbered about 48.

Controls

Less than 10 percent of the studies mentioned any attempts to provide controls for the treatment groups.

Treatment and Process

Total time in the treatment groups

the unpleasant and (4) sufficiently adequate adjustment to provide models for more effective ways of coping.

To provide solutions for the problem of achieving desired group therapy activity, many researchers select candidates for group therapy and submit them to various degrees of pretherapy treatment conditions. Data suggest that the initial therapeutic sessions are of prime importance. Data also indicate "that pretherapy training that clarifies client role expectations and provides models of desirable therapeutic behavior has a positive effect on both the therapeutic process and the eventual therapeutic improvement" (Bednar and Lawlis, 1971, p. 829).

Group Size

Although the data are insufficient for a thorough analysis, a gross approximation based on the available data suggested that an averge treatment group hovered around 30 subjects.

Controls

(No analysis given.)

Treatment and Process

"Mean improvement among treated subjects is masked because of a cancellation effect between the clients who have im-

placebo or Hawthorne group should receive active attention similar, but not necessarily equivalent to, the experimental treatment. An encouraging trend was that several studies included some form of follow-up within the research design. However, the majority of the studies reported no attempt at periodic follow-up after the treatment phase was completed. Since there is apparently no definitive research clearly demonstrating that any change that is likely to occur will do so shortly after the end of the treatment phase, it would appear that the main reasons investigators are reluctant to incorporate relatively long-range follow-up into the research paradigm are inconvenience and the additional efforts that are required. It is strongly recommended that investigators incorporate periodic follow-ups of the participants after the completion of the treatment if at all possible.

Treatment and Process

The average treatment was 13.6 hours extending over a period of 8.3 weeks. This time period is usually too short to expect significant behavioral changes from group counseling. However, this figure may be somewhat deceptive because a number of studies that were reviewed used a group-marathon format

ranged from less than 10 hours to 150 hours. There is a consensus among experienced trainers that continuous time, within indeterminable limits, is more effective than time spent in short sessions spread out over long periods of time. "It is clear that when studies are arrayed simply in terms of amount of time in group, that greater differences are obtained from groups of larger duration than from short-term groups" (Gibb, 1971, p. 855).

Several studies suggest that short-term experiences may not bring changes to a critical point. "When changes become integrated into new behavioral systems that are congruent with new attitudinal substrata in the person, the changes may actually increase over time" (Gibb, 1971, p. 855).

Most human relations training as evidenced in the literature, is too short in duration to be of optimal enduring effect. How long training should be, and what temporal patterns of "booster shots" are optimal for long-range effects, are critical questions that must receive attention from researchers.

Instruments

Measurement is a persistent problem. The more reliable measures often describe trivial outcomes. "Reliable mea-

Summary and Recommendations For Group Psychotherapy

proved and others who have deteriorated. The significant difference in variabilities between treatment and control groups has been used as a basis for inferring the potential value and harm of therapeutic treatments" (Bednar and Lawlis, 1971, p. 819).

Subjects involved in group therapy tended to show more change and variability in interpersonal behavior, while subjects receiving individual therapy tended to manifest more change and variability in perceptual spheres.

As research paradigms and statistical analyses become more sophisticated, it is hoped that group therapy research will emphasize testing group member processes, instead of treating the group as a whole. On the basis of the data, group therapy appears to offer more degrees of freedom for a participant to find the therapeutic personality than does individual therapy.

Instruments

The data on adjustment suggest that group therapy can contribute to improving observable behavior patterns, at least in a hospital setting.

"Studies can be criticized for psychological testing with such instruments as

Summary and Recommendations For Group Counseling

which combined a maximum number of treatment hours over a minimum number of days. Some studies deliberately appeared to give the treatment over a short duration of time perhaps as an attempt to effect some change in a minimum amount of time.

Many studies did not go beyond mentioning the theoretical orientation of the group leader(s). Few studies attempted to assess the leader's level of expertise or competency, and then make efforts to control for this variable so that questions such as whether the results stem mainly from leader variables, or differences in techniques, or both, do not go unanswered. A method for quantifying the level of leader functioning has been developed by Carkhuff, 1969; Carkhuff and Berenson, 1967; Truax and Carkhuff, 1967.

Instruments

The use of instruments for measuring or evaluating change ranged from grade point average (GPA) to information obtained from self-reports and experimental-devised questionnaires. The use of criteria such as GPA suggests a somewhat unrealistic expectation on the part of the experimenter. It reflects the as-

Summary and Recommendations For Human Relations Training

sures are often not validated against acceptable indices of mental health, personal growth or personal effectiveness in a natural setting. Researchers report an increasing resistance to multiple measurements in the training setting" (Gibb, 1971, p. 843).

Statistics

(No analysis given.)

Experimental Design

Design problems appear to be a major obstacle to training research. "Training has almost always been done under field conditions in which the researcher is an unwelcome intruder" (Gibb, 1971, p. 842). In most cases the researcher has apparently settled for the best of poor design alternatives or outcome measures that were permitted by such factors as expense, training conditions, participant resistance and imprecise instruments.

The majority of researchers have not adequately used control or comparison groups. Matching groups that are equally "ready," and then delaying the training of one set of groups so that they function as controls, brings into play effects caused by the delay itself.

One major weakness of training research designs is their lack of "representativeness." Researchers took great care in getting a random sample of only one trainer or one organization, thus limiting the generalizations of their results.

Criteria and Outcomes

Research outcomes indicate that changes occur in: sensitivity, feeling management, directionality of motivations, attitudes toward self, attitudes toward others and interpersonal relationships. Because these effects are closely related to desirable therapeutic outcomes, the data from the literature suggest that intensive group training experiences have therapeutic effects. However, at the present, the data do no more than suggest similarity in outcomes between human relations training and group psychotherapy.

The data from human relations training research suggest that the following conditions for learning occurred with group growth: feedback, behavior visibility, member-member interaction, feeling expression and perceptual diversity.

sumption that a minimum amount of treatment should affect intellectual skills within a relatively short period of time. It would be more realistic to develop criterion variables that are behavioral and observable. The use of behavioral criteria should help attenuate discrepancies between treatment intentions and outcome goals. The increasing use of multiple measures for evaluating outcome leads to 2 possible interpretations. On one hand, it may represent a "shotgun" approach in which the investigator hopes to illuminate some relevant variable among several unknown variables. On the other hand, it may reflect the growing sophistication of the counseling field, because if the majority of the outcome variables differed significantly as a result of the experimental treatment, it would indicate that a relationship exists between the variables being studied. A considerable number of recent studies have used experimenter-devised questionnaires. While this trend raises questions concerning validity, it also represents a creative approach to identify relevant factors within group counseling.

Statistics

The literature shows a definite trend toward using multivariant analyses. Early studies would usually rely on a

the MMPI or Rorschach during actual treatment. As a result of this testing, outcome effects could be attributed to the psychological testing or attention effect instead of to the therapeutic treatment" (Bednar and Lawlis, 1971, p. 821).

"Many studies have used observation techniques such as Bales Interaction Categories or Hill's Interaction Matrix as a quantitative method for describing overt behavior.... Preformed behavioral rating systems run the risk of being invalid because the behavioral categories may be inappropriate" (Bednar and Lawlis, 1971, p. 821).

"Some researchers have used subjective criteria to measure both process variables and therapeutic outcomes. Most of these measures included the individual's own assessment of his personal happiness, his observations of his behavior in the group, and the perceived growth resulting from group psychotherapy.... It is difficult to accept that a participant's feelings of satisfaction with himself or with group therapy can be considered either a major goal of the procedure or evidence of its success" (Bednar and Lawlis, 1971, p. 821).

There were no studies reviewed in which different stages of group therapy were related to physiological measures

Summary and Recommendations For Group Psychotherapy

such as galvanic skin response or pulse and heart rate.

Statistics

In recent years, more application of multivariant statistical analyses have been utilized. "Matrix algebra and nonlinear mathematics may also be adopted to more accurately reflect group processes" (Bednar and Lawlis, 1971, p. 833).

Experimental Design

The majority of the studies reviewed used the pre-postest design in conjunction with no-therapy control groups.

The major criticism of designs using repeated measures is the effect on the instruments and/or reliability deteriorations. "Even with the more reliable instruments test-retest reliabilities are about .90. With as many as 4 administrations these reliabilities would be reduced to .73" (Bednar and Lawlis, 1971, p. 822).

Criteria and Outcomes

Appropriate evaluation procedures should be initiated to provide the therapist with feedback about his general ef-

Summary and Recommendations For Group Counseling

single statistic as a test for significance. Currently, it is more the rule rather than the exception to use at least 2 complementary statistics for the analysis of the data. Bednar and Lawlis (1971) have suggested matrix algebra and nonlinear mathematics as one way to quantify group process variables. The increasing emphasis on quantification and sophisticated statistical analyses are favorable signs in terms of increasing the rigor of group counseling research.

Experimental Design

A salient trend is the increase in the number of process studies which are essentially investigating what happens as well as comparing the efficacy of different approaches toward achievement of common objectives. Overall, almost 65 percent of the studies were classifiable as "True Experimental Designs" according to the criteria of Campbell and Stanley (1963). This means that some type of statistical measure or control group was utilized.

Criteria and Outcomes

Essentially the overall effectiveness of group counseling has not yet been un-

fectiveness, the type of client with whom he is most and least successful.

"Follow-up treatment contracts on an increasing intermittent schedule would probably help arrest the rate of a relapse after treatment is terminated" (Bednar and Lawlis, 1971, p. 821).

equivocally demonstrated. However, in recent years the majority of the studies reported indicate statistically significant results consistent with predictions. Most investigators do not explicitly state the theory or rationale which underlies the predicted outcomes for specific clients. While this may reflect a growing emphasis on eclecticism, by its nature it attenuates, however slightly, the potency of the findings.

Investigators have not yet reported replications of former studies in any discernible amount. This suggests that the state of group counseling literature may be primarily concerned with correlations rather than causations. Studies which are replications and studies which investigate identical treatments for different clients usually herald identifications of causative variables. On the basis of the studies in this review, research in the area of group counseling has not generally progressed to the level of identifying causative factors. However, considerable progress has been made, including the identification of many major variables which contribute to the final results.

RECOMMENDATIONS

The following recommendations are based essentially on the 3 content areas which were summarized. In each case an effort was made to list a recommendation that appears applicable to all 3 content areas.

1. Greater attempts should be made to strive for consistency across studies in terms of operational definitions of terms and attempts should be made to explicitly integrate the findings into a unifying body of knowledge.
2. Efforts should be made to replicate studies which have made significant contributions.
3. Greater use of equipment such as video-tape recorders will aid in the study of the individual within the framework of a group.
4. Emphasis should be placed on stating a rationale which explains why a given treatment should produce the predicted changes.
5. It is recommended that a wider range of clients be considered for participation in group treatment. This will help to assure generalization of results.
6. Greater attempts should be made to investigate the efficacy of precounseling or pretherapy training.
7. Group composition is an important area which is experiencing a dearth of information. It is strongly recommended that investigations explore and take into consideration the effects of group composition.
8. Investigators should make every effort to incorporate a Hawthorne-effect control group.
9. The duration of the experimental treatment should be increased so that more subtle changes have a greater probability of becoming manifest.
10. Greater attention should be directed toward objectively assessing the leader's level of competency and the theoretical model which he employs, in order to use research designs which simultaneously use 2 or more leaders.
11. An integral part of the research paradigm should include opportunity for follow-up measurements of the treatment

groups at regular intervals after the termination of the treatment.

12. When feasible, attempts should be made to use observable behavioral outcomes as indices of change.

13. More sophisticated statistical analyses should be employed such as (a) multivariate analysis (Cohn, 1967), (b) nonlinear mathematics and matrix algebra, which permits analysis of group members (Bednar and Lawlis, 1971) and (c) the Time-Series Design (Campbell and Stanley, 1963) which allows the S to be his own control and avoids matching errors at the risk of lowered instrument reliabilities (Bednar and Lawlis, 1971).

Among the summaries there were a few areas of apparent disagreement. For example, in group therapy as contrasted to human relations training groups, Bednar and Lawlis (1971) suggested that leaderless groups with psychiatric patients are probably more potentially dangerous than professionally led groups. Human relations trainers are reluctant to use multiple measures (Gibb, 1971). Also, human relations trainers prefer to work with relatively homogeneously-composed administrative units of work teams (Gibb, 1971), as contrasted to general preference for heterogeneously composed psychotherapy and counseling groups (Peters, 1972).

REFERENCES

Bednar, R., and Lawlis, G.: Empirical research in group psychotherapy. In A. Bergin and S. Garfield (Eds.): *Handbook of Psychotherapy and Behavior Change: An Empirical Analysis.* New York, Wiley, 1971.

Campbell, D., and Stanley, J.: Experimental and quasi-experimental designs for research. In N. L. Gage (Ed.): *Handbook of Research in Teaching.* Chicago, Rand McNally, 1963.

Carkhuff, R.: *Helping and Human Relations: A Primer for Lay and Professional Helpers,* Vol. 2. *Practice and Research.* New York, Holt, Rinehart and Winston, 1969.

Carkhuff, R., and Berenson, B.: *Beyond Counseling and Therapy.* New York, Holt, Rinehart and Winston, 1967.

Cohn. B. (Ed.): *Guidelines for Future Research on Group Counseling in the Public School Setting.* Washington, D. C., American Personnel and Guidance Association, 1967.

Gazda, G.: *Group Counseling: A Developmental Approach.* Boston, Allyn and Bacon, 1971.

Gazda, G., and Larsen, M. J.: A comprehensive appraisal of group and multiple counseling research. *Journal of Research and Development in Education, 1*(2):57, 1968.

Gazda, G., and Peters, R.: An analysis of research in group procedures. *Educational Technology, 13*(1):68, 1973.

Goldstein, A., Heller, K., and Sechrest, L.: *Psychotherapy and Psychology of Behavior Change.* New York, Wiley, 1966.

Lewis, P., and McCants, J.: Some current issues in group psychotherapy research. *International Journal of Group Psychotherapy, 23*(3):268, 1973.

Peters, R.: The Facilitation of Change in Group Counseling by Group Composition. Unpublished doctoral dissertation, University of Georgia, 1972.

Truax, C., and Carkhuff, R.: *Toward Effective Counseling and Psychotherapy: Training and Practice.* Chicago, Aldine, 1967.

Yalom, I.: *The Theory and Practice of Group Psychotherapy.* New York, Basic Books, 1971.

CHAPTER III

SOME TENTATIVE GUIDELINES FOR ETHICAL PRACTICE BY GROUP WORK PRACTITIONERS

George M. Gazda

INTRODUCTION

T HE TITLE OF THIS CHAPTER was carefully considered, because no single person can hope to do more than present "some tentative guidelines . . ." based on his search and evaluation of the numerous positions taken by a wide range of professionals engaged in group work, especially therapy and quasi-therapy groups. (The reader is reminded at this point that the writer does not intend to deal directly with the training of group leaders since wide variations will be dictated by the potential group leader's discipline.)

A survey (Gazda *et al.*, 1973) of 26 professional associations/ societies and/or individuals representing these associations in which group procedures were a part of the functions employed by the membership, produced 20 responses. The 20 respondents represented all of the basic professional associations wherein the membership would use group work in their practice. The "codes of ethics," "ethical guidelines/standards," and similar documents were obtained from each of these associations. In addition draft documents and published articles on the subject of ethical practices in group work were carefully studied in an attempt to provide this overview of the recommendations that are being espoused by concerned professionals and associations. The Suggested Readings at the end of this chapter indicates the extent of my review.

For this writer, the most interesting outcome of his review was the fact that the literature is beginning to reflect a fair degree of agreement on a number of basic issues or topics that are especially

55

relevant to group work. In other words, a certain consensus is being achieved on what are the basic ethical issues that cut across many and varied group procedures and related disciplines in the "helping professions."

Although the emphasis in this text is group psychotherapy and group counseling, the increasing similarity of other forms of group work to these two forms is blurring the distinctions and therefore suggests a look at the total group work discipline. In Chapter 15 of this text I have illustrated how I differentiate among the various kinds of group work by classifying them along a prevention-remediation continuum, i.e., whether the goals or purposes are primarily preventative or remedial/rehabilitative, including combinations of the two ends of the continuum. For purposes of this discussion I shall attempt to define only "group work" with an emphasis on "small" group work for personal growth rather than task accomplishment, but special types of group work may be the focus with respect to particular guidelines. *Group work refers to the dynamic interaction between collections of individuals for prevention or remediation of difficulties or for the enhancement of personal growth/enrichment through the interaction of those who meet together for a commonly agreed upon purpose and at pre-arranged times.* A number of people meeting in this purposeful way have the potential to become a group if they succeed in clarifying their goals, agreeing on ways to accomplish them, and maintaining the committed participation of all involved.

Lakin (1972, p. 7) has identified what he considers to be the "conditions for membership" in "experiential" groups. His definition of experiential groups includes interpersonal encounter, psychotherapy, and sensitivity groups. His conditions for membership (what I might call "functional" membership) include the following:[1]

1. Contribute to the shaping and coherence of the group;
2. Invest in it emotionally;
3. Help move it toward a goal [metagoal];

---

1. Martin Lakin: *Experimental Groups: The Uses of Interpersonal Encounter, Psychotherapy Groups, and Sensitivity Training,* 1972. General Learning Corporation. Reprinted by permission.

4. Help establish its norms, and obey them;
5. Take on some specific role or function;
6. Help establish a viable level of open communication;
7. Help establish a desired level of intimacy;
8. Make contributions relevant to others;
9. Make a place for each person;
10. Acknowledge the group's significance.

Some exposition of what is meant by ethical guidelines or "ethics" also seems apropos. *Ethics of group work are those agreed upon practices consistent with our broader ethical commitments (political, moral and religious) that we think reasonable and which responsible practitioners and clients will generally support at a given point in time.*

By their very nature ethics are not absolutes. They inevitably change as the culture and scientific evidence dictates. Otherwise they would become prejudicial barriers that restrict rather than guidelines within which professional and client growth can proceed with some measure of order, confidence, and security. Because there are few unchanging, universal absolutes in the field of human relations, codes or guidelines for ethical practices are seldom equally acceptable to all responsible practitioners at the same time. At the present time, commonalities of beliefs are emerging in group work and these commonalities will be the emphasis of most of the remaining portions of this chapter.

GROUP LEADERSHIP

As stated earlier in this chapter, the writer does not intend to focus on group leadership *training* since training standards must reflect the purpose of the professional discipline with which the leader identifies. Currently there are very few disciplines that have clear cut proven guidelines for training group practitioners. More specifically there is a serious lack of well defined standards for training group practitioners to function at various levels of expertise in varying settings and with differing clientele. But, there are some leader-related elements for which guidelines are indicated and, assuming leader competency, can be useful guidelines for all or most group leaders. They are as follows:

1. The group leader should have a generally accepted code of ethics.
2. The group leader should have evidence that he has received training commensurate with his group practice.
3. The group leader should have evidence that his leadership is effective; i.e., post-treatment and follow-up data of group members illustrates that they have benefited from membership in the leader's group.
4. The group leader should have a well conceptualized model for explaining behavioral change.
5. The group leader should possess the necessary certification, licensure or similar evidence of qualifications generally accepted by his discipline.
6. The group leader who does not possess professional credentials must function under the supervision of a professionally qualified person.
7. The group leader should attend refresher courses, workshops, et cetera to upgrade his skills and obtain evaluation of others regarding his skills and/or level of functioning.
8. The group leader should have a clear set of ground rules that guide him in the leadership of his group.

RECRUITMENT OF GROUP PARTICIPANTS

Professional standards as detailed by the group leader's discipline should be adhered to at all times in the recruitment of group members. Often these guidelines are more explicit for those in private practice, but are vague when it comes to policies governing recruitment within an institutional setting such as schools, and business and industrial organizations. Some guidelines that apply to one or both of the above settings are as follows:

1. Announcements should include an explicit statement of the group's:
   a. purpose,
   b. length and duration of group sessions,
   c. number of group participants.
2. Announcements should include an explicit statement regarding the leader's qualifications for leading the proposed group.

3. Announcements should include an explicit statement regarding the leader's fee which specifies:
   a. the amount for professional service,
   b. the amount for any meals, lodging, materials, et cetera,
   c. the amount for follow-up services.
4. Group members should not be coerced to join a group by superiors or the group leader.
5. Claims that cannot be substantiated by *scientific* evidence should not be made.

SCREENING OF GROUP PARTICIPANTS

Since there is evidence that not just anyone can benefit from a group experience, some form of screening procedure should be instituted by the leader to ensure that the prospective group member understands what will be expected of him and to select only those members where there is likelihood that they will benefit themselves and other group participants. Some general guidelines to ensure that these conditions prevail are as follows:

1. The prospective group member should be appraised as to his ability to achieve specific benefits from the experience. High risk members should ordinarily be excluded from group treatment. The American Medical Association's Council on Mental Health cited the following who "run a risk of adverse reaction from sensitivity training": "(a) persons who are frankly psychotic and those with an impaired sense of reality; (b) persons with a significant degree of psychoneurosis; (c) those with a history of marked emotional lability; (d) those who react to stress with psychological decompensation or psychosomatic illness; and (e) persons in a crisis situation" (1971, p. 1854). (Except for "b" these individuals would also be poor risks for therapy groups and quasi-therapy groups.)
2. The prospective group member should be informed that his participation must be voluntary. (Rare exceptions are perhaps defensible; if they are made they must be fully documented.)
3. The prospective group member should be told candidly

what will be expected of him, the risks that he will incur, and what techniques will be employed by the leader.

4. The prospective group member should be told that he has "freedom of exit" from the group.
5. The prospective group member should be told that he has the freedom to resist following suggestions or prescriptions of the group members and/or leader.
6. The prospective group member should be informed whether or not confidentiality is a requirement for group membership. (It is expected that it would be in therapy, counseling, and other experiential groups, although it must be pointed out that complete confidentiality cannot be guaranteed.)
7. The prospective group member should be informed explicitly of areas or instances that the group leader may be required to break confidence, e.g., imminent harm to the group member or others.
8. The prospective group member should be informed of any research that might be carried out on the group and his permission must be secured in writing.
9. Prospective group members must be informed regarding recording of group sessions and their consent must be obtained. Furthermore, they should be told that they can stop the recorder at any point that they choose if they find that it is restricting their participation.
10. Prospective group members should be querried to determine whether or not they are in similar treatment with others. Clearance with the other professional who is treating the potential group member must be obtained.
11. Prospective group members should be informed that the leader may need to remove them from the group if he determines that they are being harmed or are harmful to others.

Ordinarily, superiors should not be placed in groups with subordinates unless they are fully aware of the risks involved and choose such an arrangement. Likewise, students/trainees should not be required to be in therapy/counseling with their teachers or others who may have evaluative control over them.

CONFIDENTIALITY

There is general acceptance among group leaders that confidentiality is necessary as a prerequisite for the development of group trust, cohesion, and productive work in therapy and quasi-therapy groups. The importance of this concept should be discussed fully with a prospective group participant in the screening process (see Screening of Group Participants). It is discussed separately here to specify other dimensions of confidentiality in group work. Some general guidelines regarding confidentiality are as follows:

1. The group leader shall refrain from revealing unnecessary identifying data of group members when seeking professional consultation. He should discuss his group or individuals within it for professional purposes only.

2. All data collected from group participants for research purposes must be obtained only after group members have given their written permission.

3. The group leader must disguise all data that identifies group members if he uses it in his writing and/or instruction.

4. The group leader periodically should remind group members of the importance of strict confidentiality in therapy and quasi-therapy groups.

TERMINATION AND FOLLOW-UP

The major criticism of therapy and quasi-therapy group leaders' handling of termination and follow-up is the abrupt termination of short-term, week-end types of group encounters with no follow-up provided. This condition frequently occurs when an out-of-town group leader provides a training-therapy combination workshop. Since he is just present for the workshop, he is unfamiliar with the local professional resources and is not in a position to make a satisfactory referral when it is needed. And since he often does not plan a return or follow-up session, the participants are left on their own to secure follow-up assistance if needed. The guidelines are thus directed to this type of situation. Suggested guidelines are as follows:

1. The group leader should plan a follow-up for short-term, time-limited groups.

2. The group leader should be acquainted with and have a commitment from a qualified professional to whom he can refer group participants when he cannot continue the professional involvement himself.
3. Group participants should be informed of competent referral sources to whom they will have access provided that such assistance is needed.

"LEADERLESS" GROUPS

Until such time as greater supportive research evidence is available, therapy and quasi-therapy groups without the presence of some kind of professional leader should be discouraged. In particular, groups that are directed by audio-taped instruction should not be permitted unless a professionally trained leader is monitoring the group. (These suggestions may seem to limit the use of self-help groups such as AA and Synanon. This is true only if there is no previously established body of knowledge or evidence to support the use of self-help, and in the case of AA and Synanon such supportive evidence is available.)

GENERAL PROCEDURES FOR HANDLING UNETHICAL PRACTICE/BEHAVIOR

There are generally accepted procedures established by most professional associations for policing their membership. The code of ethics or ethical standards is not only the professional instrument, but often the legal criterion against which an accused person may be held accountable. Therefore it behooves professionals to know their ethical responsibilities and practice accordingly. Most ethical codes also indicate the procedure that one is to follow when he has evidence of unethical practice/behavior.

In general, one should first protect the clients affected by the unethical practice/behavior. Assuming that the client is in no immediate danger, the "accused" should be informed of his unethical practice/behavior and asked to correct the situation. If the "accused" refuses to correct the situation, the professional is bound by his ethics to report (with proper regard to accuracy of details, fairness, and discretion) the incident to the appropriate professional association's "ethical practices committee" and/or the "accused's" superior or institutional representative. A professional person who ignores unethical practice behavior of others is equally guilty in the view of most associations within the "helping professions."

SUMMARY

This chapter contains some tentative guidelines for the ethical practice of group workers, especially for those leading therapy or quasi-therapy groups. The guidelines are based on a careful review of the literature and also upon a questionnaire survey sent to appropriate professional associations/societies within the "helping professions."

A review of the literature revealed that the various professional associations whose membership is engaged in some form of group work are beginning to reach a consensus on a number of guidelines–especially for therapy and quasi-therapy groups.

This chapter begins with the definition of "group work" and "ethics of group work," and includes a listing of Lakin's "conditions for membership" in "experiential" groups. Next, tentative guidelines for ethical practice are outlined under the following specific topics: Group Leadership, Recruitment of Group Participants, Screening of Group Participants, Confidentiality, Termination and Follow-up, "Leaderless" Groups, and General Procedures for Handling Unethical Practice/Behavior.

SUGGESTED READINGS

American College Personnel Association Task Force on Group Procedures: A proposed statement for ACPA regarding the use of group procedures in higher education. *Journal of College Student Personnel, 13:*(1), 90, 1972.

American College Personnel Association Task Force on Group Procedures: Guidelines for Group Facilitators in Higher Education (mimeographed) Author, n.d.

American Group Psychotherapy Association: *Guidelines for the Training of Group Psychotherapists.* New York, Author, n.d.

American Medical Association's Council on Mental Health: Sensitivity training. *Journal of the American Medical Association, 217:*(13), 1853, 1971.

American Personnel and Guidance Association: *Ethical Standards Casebook.* Washington, D. C., Author, 1965.

American Personnel and Guidance Association: *Ethical Standards: Ameri-*

can *Personnel and Guidance Association.* Washington, D. C., Author, 1974.

American Psychiatric Association: *Task Force Report 1: Encounter Groups and Psychiatry.* Washington, D. C., Author, 1970.

American Psychological Association: *Casebook on Ethical Standards of Psychologists.* Washington, D. C., Author, 1967.

American Psychological Association: *Ethical Principles in the Conduct of Research with Human Participants.* Washington, D. C., Author, 1973.

American Psychological Association: Guidelines for psychologists conducting growth groups. *American Psychologist, 28:*(10), 933, 1973.

Berzon, B., and Solomon, L.: The self-directed therapeutic group: Three Studies. *Journal of Counseling Psychology, 13:*491, 1966.

Birnbaum, M.: Sense about sensitivity training. *Saturday Review,* 82, Nov. 15, 1969.

Carkhuff, R., and Truax, C.: Lay mental health counseling: The effects of lay group counseling. *Journal of Consulting Psychology, 29:*426, 1965.

Gazda, G. M.: *Group Counseling: A Developmental Approach* (Ch. 8 Ethics and Professional Issues). Boston, Allyn and Bacon, 1971.

Gazda, G. M.: *Group Procedures in Education.* Washington, D. C., American Personnel and Guidance Association Press, 1971.

Gazda, G. M., Duncan, J. A., and Meadows, M. E.: Group counseling and group procedures—Report of a survey. *Counselor Education and Supervision, 6:*305, 1967.

Gazda, G. M., Duncan, J. A., and Sisson, P. J.: Professional issues in group work. *Personnel and Guidance Journal, 49:*(8), 637, 1971.

Gazda, G. M., *et al.*: Recommended changes and additions to APGA Code of Ethics to accommodate group workers. *Counselor Education and Supervision, 13:*(2), 155, 1973.

Golan, S. E.: Emerging areas of ethical concern. *American Psychologist, 24:*454, 1969.

Jenkins, D.: Ethics and responsibility in human relations training. In I. Weschler and E. Schein (Eds.): *Issues in Training.* Washington, D. C., National Training Laboratories, National Education Association, 1962.

Kelman, H. S.: *A Time to Speak—On Human Values and Social Research.* San Francisco, Josey-Bass, 1968.

Lakin, M.: Some ethical issues in sensitivity training. *American Psychologist, 24:*923, 1969.

Lakin, M.: *Experiential Groups: The Uses of Interpersonal Encounter, Psychotherapy Groups, and Sensitivity Training.* Morristown, New Jersey, General Learning Press, 1972.

Moreno, J. L.: Code of ethics of group psychotherapists. *Group Psychotherapy, 10:*143, 1957.

Moreno, J. L.: Code of ethics for group psychotherapy and psychodrama:

Relationship to the Hippocratic Oath. *Psychodrama and Group Psychotherapy Monograph* No. 31. Beacon, New York, Beacon House, 1962.

National Training Laboratory Institute: *Standards for the Use of Laboratory Method,* Washington, D. C., Author, 1969.

Olsen, L. C.: Ethical standards for group leaders. *Personnel and Guidance Journal, 50:*(4), 288, 1971.

Patterson, C. H.: Ethical standards for groups. *Counseling Psychologist, 3:*93, 1972.

Shostrom, E. L.: Group therapy: Let the buyer beware. *Psychology Today, 2:*(12), 37, 1969.

Zimpfer, D.: Needed: Professional ethics for working with groups. *Personnel and Guidance Journal, 50:*(4), 280, 1971.

Zytowski, D.: Obligatory counseling with college underachievers. *Group Psychotherapy, 16:*8, 1963.

REFERENCES

American Medical Association's Council on Mental Health: Sensitivity training. *Journal of the American Medical Association, 217:*(13), 1853, 1971.

Gazda, G. M., *et al.:* Recommended changes and additions to APGA Code of Ethics to accommodate group workers. *Counselor Education and Supervision, 13:*(2), 155, 1973.

Lakin, M.: *Experiential Groups: The Uses of Interpersonal Encounter, Psychotherapy Groups, and Sensitivity Training.* Morristown, New Jersey, General Learning Press, 1972.

PART II

GROUP
PSYCHOTHERAPY

AN INTRODUCTION TO GROUP PSYCHODRAMA

Jacob L. Moreno[1] and Dean G. Eleftery

J. L. MORENO, a pioneer of group psychotherapy and the originator of psychodrama and sociometry, has devised a method from which other action methods have developed. "The tree with many branches"–Gestalt Therapy, Family Therapy, Transactional Analysis, et cetera. Eleftery calls this "tree" the Moreno "syndrome." Perls, Berne, and Maslow called it the "Moreno problem." All feel one must carefully research the writing of Moreno in the last 50 years before claiming the "discovery" of a "new" action method. Some of their feelings in this regard are presented in the following selected quotations.

Eric Berne wrote: "In his selection of specific techniques, Dr. Perls shares with other 'active' psychotherapists the 'Moreno problem': The fact that nearly all known 'active' techniques were first tried out by Dr. J. L. Moreno in psychodrama, so that it is difficult to come up with an original idea in this regard" (1970, p. 126).

A. H. Maslow wrote the following statement regarding Jane Howard's article on Esalen and other new developments in education and psychotherapy: "I would however like to add one credit-where-credit-is-due footnote. Many of the techniques set forth in the article were originally invented by Dr. Jacob Moreno, who is still functioning vigorously and probably still inventing new techniques and ideas" (1968, p. 15).

William Schutz stated that ". . . Virtually all of the methods

---

1. J. L. Moreno died on May 14, 1974 in Beacon, New York after a long and productive life. He was recognized as the father of psychodrama and sociometry, and he was one of the pioneers in group psychotherapy. He coined the terms "psychodrama," "sociometry," and "group psychotherapy" as well as many others in the field of psychotherapy. Only history will record the greatness of his contribution to the field of human relations.—Dean G. Eleftery.

that I had proudly compiled or invented he [Moreno] had more or less anticipated, in some cases forty years earlier. . . . I invite you to investigate Moreno's work. It is probably not sufficiently acknowledged in this country. Perl's gestalt therapy owes a great deal to it. It is imaginative and worth exploring" (1971, p. 201).

THE THIRD PSYCHIATRIC REVOLUTION

One can speak of three psychiatric revolutions: (1) the liberation of the mentally sick from chains (Pinel) symbolizes the first. (2) The development of psychoanalysis (Freud) and the theory of the conditioned reflex (Pavlov) symbolize the second. (3) The development of group psychotherapy, psychodrama, sociometry, sociatry and psychopharmacology symbolize the third. The third psychiatric revolution began to crystalize in the early twenties and is still in formation. Its ultimate goal is the *therapeutic society*.

At least seven trends of thought prepared the way for group psychotherapy (Moreno, 1956): socioeconomic, biologic, psychoanalytic, psychologic, existentialist, sociologic and sociatric-psychodramatic thought. Karl Marx was the theoretical forerunner of the socioeconomic trend. He states in *Das Kapital* in 1867, "A dozen persons when working together will, in their collective working day of 144 hours, produce far more than 12 isolated men, each working twelve hours, or than one man who works 12 days in succession" (Moreno, 1956, p. 11).

The biologic trend received its incentive from the observation of animal societies made by Espinas in 1878. The psychologic and psychoanalytic trends were stimulated by Bernheim in 1884 and Freud in 1922, that led to a psychoanalytic variety of mass psychology. The existentialist trend received its incentive from Kierkegaard in 1885 and others. Existentialism consists of a rigorous analysis of existence, a new evaluation of the encounter, and an emphasis upon the moment of action. The sociologic trend was initiated by sociologists and anthropologists; indeed, the very term *small group* was first used by Simmel in 1908 and Cooley in 1909. The sociatric and psychodramatic trend prepared the scientific foundations of group psychiatry and marked the transition from authoritarian varieties of psychotherapy to the democratic.

PSYCHODRAMA

Psychodrama in Perspective

Psychodrama is part of a triad: group psychotherapy, sociometry, and psychodrama. Psychodrama can be defined as the science which explores the "truth" by the use of dramatic methods (Moreno, 1946). Psychodrama is an extension of group psychotherapy in which there is not just verbalization but the situation is acted out in as realistic a setting as possible.

Moreno says people are born in groups, live in groups, work in groups, become ill in groups, and so why not treat them in groups. The most important discovery regarding the "group" phenomenon was that every group has a specific structure of its own with a varying degree of cohesiveness and depth, and that no two groups are alike–that the structure of groups can be explored and determined and that groups are phenomena which can be studied scientifically in their own right. This discovery led to the development of sociometry and small group analysis.

Next in importance was the discovery that by means of psychodramatic methods the depth dimensions of the group can be brought to the surface so that the members can recognize the invisible interactions existing between them. Effective therapy is, therefore, that in which the therapist becomes aware of the interactions of the patients towards each other, as well as of their interactions with him. The locus of the therapeutic influence is in the *group* rather than in the *therapist*.

Verbal methods of communication between therapist and patient and between the patients themselves have proven extremely useful in sessions dealing with adult problems, in the treatment of most neuroses, and in counseling of social situations, among others, within the framework of any pathology for which the use of language is an instrument of communication. Whenever it comes to situations where speech restricts the meanings of experience, as in hallucinatory experiences of psychotics, in preverbal experiences of infants, in dreams and fantasies, additional or alternative methods become urgent. It is due to this dilemma in communication that the senior author was compelled about fifty years ago to open up the large area of psychodrama and action therapy and to invent techniques to fill this gap by other forms of communication.

It is instructive to follow the publications in group psychotherapy and to watch the various efforts of many authors to find correctives and replacements which would overcome the deficiencies encountered in the course of treatment.

Theoretical Rationale

The rationale that explains the functioning of the psychodrama can only be sketched briefly in the space allotted herein. Five principles that characterize the therapeutic process in groups and thus psychodrama also will be described. These concepts are *encounter* (therapeutic interaction), *spontaneity, catharsis, reality testing,* and *role.*

Encounter—Therapeutic Interaction

Moreno defined encounter as follows:

> A meeting of two:
> Eye to eye
> Face to face
> And when you are near
> I will tear out your eyes
> And place them instead of mine
> And you will tear out my eyes
> And place them instead of yours
> Then I will look at you
> With your eyes
> And you will look at me
> With mine (Moreno, 1914).

In the center of the group process is the concept of the encounter. The German word *Zwischenmenschlich* or the English word *interpersonal* are collateral terms. Yet they are abstract, academic terms when compared with the living universal concept of the German *Begegnung* or the English *encounter*. The term *encounter* comprises numerous areas of living; it means to be together, to meet one another, the contact of two bodies, seeing, observing, touching, feeling into the other person, withdrawing and uniting, understanding one another, intuitive insight through silence or movement, language or gestures, kiss or embrace, becoming one –*una cum uno*.

The word encounter contains as a root the word *counter;* thus the Latin derivation of *contra* is conveyed–the meeting of opposing forces. It therefore includes not only loving relations but also hostile and threatening ones: confronting one another, acting in spite, and quarreling. Encounter is a concept of being; it is a unique experience that occurs once only and is irreplaceable. A touch and contact between two bodies as in a psychodrama session is a personal outburst of interaction that is unrehearsed. It is not only a challenge to the acting protagonist but also to all the participants. They witness an experience in the making. Encountering is therefore at the core of psychodramatic experience; this comes first. Perception or interpretive analysis comes second. It can not be exchanged through other forms of expression–other individuals, a book, a letter or similar conserves.

Encounter means that two persons do not only meet, but also experience and comprehend one another, each with his whole being. It is not a circumscribed contact like a professional meeting of a therapist with a patient, nor is it an intellectual contact (teacher and pupil) or a scientific contact (a transaction occurring between an observer and an object). The participants are not pushed into the situation by an external force. They are there because they want to be there, propelled by the highest inner calling –the self-chosen path. The encounter is unprepared; it is not constructed or rehearsed in advance. There is in every encounter an element of surprise.

It is thus made clear that encounter is essentially different from that which the psychoanalysts call transference, and that it is also different from what the psychologists call empathy. It does not negate transference and it does not negate empathy. It includes transference and empathy and gives them their natural function in the entire process. It moves from I to Thou and from Thou to I. It is "two-feeling." It is *tele*.

Social interactions may be therapeutic or harmful, depending upon the circumstances. The task is to form groups that are therapeutically effective for all participants. One participant is the therapeutic agent of the other; one group is the therapeutic agent for the other group. This kind of encounter or interaction is the *principle of "therapeutic" interaction;* the autonomy of the participant individuals is not lost, but fully considered. The therapeutic skills of each individual are productively employed.

Spontaneity

Spontaneity may be defined as (1) an adequate response to a new situation or a new response to an old situation, and (2) a response of varying degrees of adequacy to situations of varying degrees of novelty.

Pathological spontaneity may be defined as a new response to either an old situation or to a new situation, but a response that does not adequately solve the problem involved and, therefore, cannot provide any satisfaction to the person involved.

Of equal importance as the principle of therapeutic interaction is the *principle of spontaneity*–the spontaneous production of the group, the free and unhindered participation of group members. The spontaneous character of participation is important for both therapeutic and diagnostic reasons. In the course of therapeutic sessions it may become necessary to restrain a certain member from being overly active. Such restraints should be analytically understood by the participant; they must not be the result of the therapist's own mood or temperament. It should also be clear that the therapist and every member of the group gains new insights about the structure of the group from session to session.

Catharsis

Another important principle is *mental catharsis,* that has two outstanding forms which take place in the group process. These two outstanding forms of catharsis are (a) group catharsis and (b) action catharsis.

The entire group is involved in the process of group catharsis. It is a *catharsis of integration* resulting from the therapeutic interactions between the members of the group. In contrast, there is the individual catharsis through abreaction, which is related to a particular individual who is separated from the rest of the group.

Action catharsis results from the spontaneous actions of one or more members of the group. It results from act hunger and acting-out behavior. Acting out is considered by some as a symptom of pathology; the psychoanalysts hold this opinion. In contrast to them, socioanalysts use acting-out methods for overcoming pathology. Acting out is a general phenomenon observable in all types of therapy groups. In the discussion type of group psychotherapy, acting out has comparatively little structure and often assumes the form of abreactions. The more intensive the form of group psychotherapy, the more acting out is an important source of information. The most elaborate and intensive forms of acting out constitute a regular procedure in psychodrama.

The importance of action catharsis in the process of learning and development is generally recognized. First, in the action groups of children, full and uninhibited spontaneity is allowed. Action groups of children may be left entirely free, without any authoritarian direction. They may develop spontaneous friendships, have fist fights or a free-for-all in which objects are destroyed. The moment comes, however, when special therapeutic intervention becomes indicated. Second, individuals who suffer from a psychicmotoric disturbance, such as tics, stuttering or bedwetting, also benefit from the acting-out process in groups. Third, in the treatment of psychoses, action catharsis is also employed.

Reality Testing

Another important principle is confrontation with reality or *reality testing*. Confrontation is an actual part of therapy that is provided within the group for every member. The group provides each member with the confrontation of reality in the true sense of the word. It is different from the protected and projected character of reality testing in individual therapy. In group psychotherapy the member is confronted with real people and real situations, not only with his own situations but also with those of other individuals. The locus of individual therapy is irrelevant; in group psychotherapy, it must be carefully structured.

It is significant to differentiate the normal group from the therapeutically organized group. In the normal group, the interaction between the members is characterized by common interests and activities. In contrast with this, the therapeutic group may require a greater amount of freedom and spontaneity. In the normal group there is often an inequality of status among the group members and, accordingly, a low degree of internal cohesion. An equality of therapeutic status between all members of the therapy group is definitely required, and the cohesion of the therapy group must be superior to the one which the members face in real life.

Role

Role, originally an old French word which penetrated into medieval French and English, is derived from the Latin *rotula.* *Role* can be defined as the actual and tangible forms that the individual self takes. The role is the functioning form the individual assumes in the specific moment he reacts to a specific situation in which other persons or objects are involved. The symbolic representation of this functioning form is perceived by the individual and others. The form is created by past experiences and the cultural patterns of the society in which the individual lives, and may be satisfied by the specific type of his productivity. Every role is a fusion of private and collective elements. Every role has two sides, a private and a collective side.

Goals of Psychodrama

Fundamentally, the goals or aims of the psychodramatic production are to integrate the individual into life that is meaningful to himself, to the group of which he is a part, and to the world at large. To this end, the various psychodramatic concepts and techniques have been developed and refined.

Procedures

In the course of typical verbal interaction therapy group sessions, one member of the group may experience a problem with such intensity that words alone are insufficient. That member has the urge to make the episode come alive, to act out a problem situation, to structure it and to present it more fully than it had actually occurred in real life. The problem of this individual is then shared by all the members of the group; the single individual becomes their representative in action. In such moments of great emotion, all members of the group step aside to make space for him. It is space that he needs, first of all, in order to move and expand himself. He moves into the middle of the group or in front of it, so that he can be seen and communicate with everyone. In a later phase one or another member of the group may join in as an antagonist.

This is the natural transformation of a simple session of group psychotherapy into a group psychodrama. It is difficult to hinder or interrupt this tendency.

Primary Instruments

The psychodramatic method uses mainly five instruments: (1) protagonist or subject, (2) auxiliary egos, (3) director or facilitator, (4) group, and (5) stage.

1. *The protagonist* is the one who emerges from the group with the most pressing need to explore his life's space. In the psychodrama he portrays his own private world.

2. *The auxiliary ego(s)* are the other members of the group who make themselves available to the protagonist to play the roles he needs in order to explore his private life, e.g., father, mother, brother, sister, et cetera. They are mainly extensions of the protagonist.

3. *The director* (facilitator) has three functions. The director is a producer, therapist and analyst. As producer he has to be on the alert to turn into action every clue that the group member/ protagonist offers, to make the line of production one with the life line of the group member/protagonist, and never to let the production lose rapport with the group. As therapist, confronting the group member/protagonist is at times just as permissible as laughing and joking with him; at times he may become indirect and passive and for all practical purposes the session seems to be run by the group member/protagonist. As analyst he may complement his own interpretation by responses coming from informants in the group, husband, parents, children, friends or neighbors.

4. *The group* supports the protagonist by its silent support during the session as well as through doubling and serving as auxiliary egos. The group's most important function is feedback or sharing in the third or sharing phase of the session.

5. *The stage* is the locus of a psychodrama. If necessary, it may be designated anywhere, wherever the protagonist is–the field of battle, the classroom or the private home. The ultimate resolution of deep mental conflicts requires an objective and secure setting that may or may not include all the dimensions of the "Moreno Stage" with its circular configuration, three levels, balcony, and special lighting. The first step or level is the communication level; the second step is the interview level; and the third or top level is the action level.

Basic Techniques

Psychodramatic techniques are many and varied. The following represent some of the basic techniques.

1. TECHNIQUE OF SELF-PRESENTATION (MONO-DRAMA). The protagonist describes himself or he portrays his mother, father, sisters, his employer, et cetera.

2. TECHNIQUE OF SELF-REALIZATION. The protagonist presents the vision of his life, past, present and future, with the assistance of auxiliary egos.

3. DIRECT SOLILOQUY TECHNIQUE. This is a monologue of the protagonist. The protagonist steps outside the scene and speaks aloud his thoughts freely to himself or to the group.

4. THERAPEUTIC SOLILOQUY TECHNIQUE (ASIDES). This is the rendering and speaking aloud of hidden feelings and thoughts simultaneously with the scenes and thoughts of the main action; side dialogues and actions are often involved. The protagonist remains in the scene. The soliloquy reveals the personal reactions of a protagonist to the role and situation he has just presented, and it occasionally reveals his hidden pathological tendencies.

5. DOUBLE TECHNIQUE. This is applied so as to enter into the inner world of a protagonist through an auxiliary ego. The auxiliary ego provides the protagonist with a second ego who imitates the protagonist in every gesture and movement and acts as if he were the same person. The auxiliary ego doubles as the protagonist and helps him to feel himself more deeply, to see his problems, to hear and evaluate them better. The double has also been referred to at times as the conscience or unconscious of the protagonist.

6. MULTIPLE DOUBLE TECHNIQUE. The protagonist is on the stage and has several doubles. Each double represents another part of his total personality. One double represents the present personality of the protagonist as an adult. Another double represents him as a little child, and a third double represents him as an old man or woman as the protagonist sees himself in the future. The doubles may appear simultaneously; side by side with the protagonist, as an infant in the crib, as a little child, as an old man, and the like. They may act simultaneously on several levels of his life, or they may appear one after another–the first the infant, then the adult, then the old man. With the aid of two or more doubles, ambivalent experiences of the protagonist can be portrayed on the stage.

7. MIRROR TECHNIQUE. (This technique is particularly helpful when the protagonist is unable to present himself in words or in deeds.) An auxiliary ego acts for the protagonist and represents him. The protagonist, himself, sitting in the group, is outside the production. The auxiliary ego acts in lieu of the protagonist. He presents as closely as possible real situations which portray the protagonist's pathology. The protagonist is so presented that he can see himself as if in a mirror or as others see him.

8. ROLE-REVERSAL TECHNIQUE. The protagonist assumes the role of his antagonist(s); for instance, father and son engaged in a violent encounter. The actual protagonist is the son. He may view his father in a distorted way. By allowing the son to play the part of his father, he may disclose to his father the picture he has of him. The father, himself, may have a distorted picture of his son. By reversing roles with his son, he may give his son and himself new insights. In the course of role reversals the protagonist may become aware of the reasons for their interpersonal difficulties. The distortion in the minds of the two partners can be brought to light, investigated and corrected.

In the role reversal between two persons, A and B, the dynamic processes inside each of them as well as the dynamic process of interaction are revealed. We can describe this process in the following way: The son projects the father into himself and in reverse the father projects the son into himself. In this way they see each other through the eyes of the other, as well as with their own eyes. This is an important technique because it facilitates the action of the psychodrama.

9. TECHNIQUE OF FUTURE PROJECTION. This technique helps the protagonist to present the anticipation he has of his future. Every man has in his deepest strivings, hopes and wishes for his future. The future perceptions and visions are strongest in youth. The older a man becomes, the weaker becomes the future projections. The old man has a long past but a short future; the young man has a short past but a long future. In the psychodramatic presentation of the future the protagonist may be required to portray (a) his wishes and desires, which may be entirely unrealistic, but the great contrast between what he is and the important dreams of what he would like to be may be very revealing; and (b) the realistic perception of his future. It is important for the protagonist to portray what he feels will actually take place in his future. The clearer his picture of certain future events, the better will he be able to confront them. In such sessions the protagonist acts as his own prophet. He is not only tested for the future, he is also prepared for it. The protagonist should be encouraged to portray as concretely as possible the place, persons, and events of future projections. This is a good technique to use in projecting upcoming interviews and meetings.

10. TECHNIQUE OF LIFE REHEARSAL. Psychodrama is often called a rehearsal for life. Indeed, it is often supportive to let the protagonist work out in advance situations that he expects to encounter. For instance, a hesitating lover who has failed frequently in the past may rehearse the proposal he is going to make to a woman he loves. Another illustration is when he rehearses an interview with a new employer.

11. THE TECHNIQUE OF PSYCHODRAMATIC HALLUCINATIONS. The protagonist portrays his own hallucinations or the hallucinations of the protagonist are embodied by an auxiliary ego. When the protagonist is in an acute psychotic state he may hallucinate on the stage. He does not have to act the hallucination; he is possessed by it.

When he enters treatment after a long period of hallucinatory psychosis and he has become free of hallucinations, he is not free from a potential relapse. Then the task of the psychodramatist is to prevent relapse. In these cases it is often indicated to instruct the protagonist to reproduce the hallucinatory episodes that may have occurred in the recent past. The protagonist may be reluctant to reenact the gruesome experience from which he has just escaped. The therapist may then explain to the protagonist the reasons for "rehallucinating" the experience. There is no better method of learning than to repeat the hallucination under more favorable and controlled circumstances. He has to train his mind during treatment so that when he returns to the community his mind is conditioned to feel when the hallucination is coming on and stop it at any time during the course of its realization. He has to intervene before it assumes threatening proportions.

12. THE PSYCHODRAMATIC DREAM TECHNIQUE. Instead of telling the dream as in psychoanalysis, the protagonist acts out the dream. In order to make this acting out plausible, the conditions of the dreams have to be recreated on the stage.

There are both daydreams and nocturnal dreams. A daydream is acted out by the protagonist with the aid of a number of auxiliary egos. The daydream is in the here-and-now and *in situ*. The dreamer sees himself climbing a stairway, falling down and breaking his leg, being pursued by robbers, and similar experiences.

In the nocturnal dream, the setting of the sleep situation has to be arranged. The protagonist lies down and goes to bed; he is encouraged to simulate sleep and the states leading up to his sleep. The warmup of going to bed and falling asleep is essential for the sleeper and the group participants. In order to make the sleep and the dream as realistic as possible, the director uses methods of strong suggestion that often take the character of near-hypnosis. As soon as the protagonist is sufficiently involved in the dream, the moment for presentation has come.

Very often the protagonist begins by saying, "I had a dream last night but I don't remember anything." The director should go through the motions of dream presentation just the same. He knows from experience that the denial of remembrance does not prevent presentation; some element will emerge and start the process of dream reenactment. Often the protagonist remembers extremely little, for instance, she may see herself in a strange room, or she may see a man sitting on a beach or her mother crying. By means of acting out, additional material is rapidly added. If the dream content requires it, the protagonist may get out of bed and walk up a stairway. If he sees that the dream space is dark or in a reddish color, the multicolored lights of the psychodrama are used to create the original atmosphere of the dream. If there are other persons appearing in the dream, auxiliary egos help to present them.

The sequence in a dream is often vague and unclear. The director must hold the production closely to the level of the dreamer's perception. The dreamer is a codirector; he directs the auxiliary egos, telling them what to do and what to say, or he may echo or supplement them. Dream objects are just as important as dream persons—floors, ceiling, chairs, trains and every other object should be represented, however fantastic it may seem.

An important part of the technique is teaching the protagonist to correct frightening experiences in forthcoming dreams. This the protagonist learns by repeating the dream in many versions and attempting a correction of the dream pathology. He trains his unconscious states and tries to replace frightening dreams by more harmonious and creative ones.

13. TECHNIQUE OF THE AUXILIARY WORLD. The entire world of the protagonist is built around him *in situ* with the assistance of auxiliary egos. Our theory is that his psychosis is hindering him from living in our world, which is alien to him. We have to establish a world in which he can live with the means at his disposal. Such a technique cannot be used in a therapeutic theater; it requires the entire community as a setting. The community becomes his therapeutic vehicle.

This technique can be a very expensive form of treatment; many therapists will be required to treat a single protagonist (multiple-therapists technique). Yet many modifications may be possible; for instance, friends may be used rather than employees. Also the community may be persuaded to accept the psychotic world of the protagonist without too much fear or reluctance.

14. WARMING-UP TECHNIQUES. They are applied to stimulate

the body to spontaneity states and actions. There are many methods used in preparing the body for athletic events–running, jumping, boxing, and so forth. The warming-up of the body has a special therapeutic value in the treatment of tics, stuttering, and other psychomotoric ailments.

15. TECHNIQUE OF SPONTANEOUS IMPROVISATION. The protagonist or the auxiliary ego plays roles with which he is not identical–a minister, chauffeur, doctor, a policeman, and so on. His task is to suppress his private character and prevent it from influencing the assumed roles.

16. TECHNIQUE OF THERAPEUTIC COMMUNITY. The therapeutic community is a community in which the conflicts are cleared and resolved through the role of therapy and not through the rule of law. For instance, if a member of the therapeutic group steals money from another member of the therapeutic group, he is not put before a criminal court but brought before the group where the illegal acts are reenacted and resolved through the aid of the other group members. This is a variety of a "forensic" psychodrama.

Phases of the Psychodrama

Psychodrama is a sensitive extension to group psychotherapy and no one should be introduced to it in a traumatic manner. Out of the group discussion or traditional interview group psychotherapy will come the possibility of a psychodrama when a group member is prepared to move the problem from verbalization to action and when the director is sufficiently warmed up to move with the protagonist.

WARM-UP PHASE (PRE-ACTION). Phase one is called the warm-up or pre-action phase. There is no specific time alloted to the warm up. It depends on how quickly a protagonist emerges from the group with a need to share a portion of his life with the group. The psychodrama will not proceed until the director is also ready to facilitate the protagonist and to begin the interview phase of the warm up with the protagonist. At this point, the director and protagonist proceed on the interview level of the psychodrama stage or shared space, and then move together in time and space to the second or action phase of the psychodrama.

(Sample Protocol of the Warm-up or Pre-action Phase)

The following brief protocol illustrates the warm-up process. It may occur as a part of the general discussion with the group about the last session or concern recent happenings of group members.

Ann: I feel I can't control my children anymore.

Suzy: Join the majority. My eldest boy is really giving me problems. He keeps putting his sister down. He is always ridiculing her and picking on her. I find I get completely lost.

Director: Could you explain what you mean by being lost?

Suzy: I guess I mean lonely.

Director: Could you tell us a little more about this feeling? (The director stands up and walks over to Suzy. Both are warming up to each other and the group is also being involved.)

Suzy: Well, my husband leaves it all to me.

Director: Could we discuss this further? (The director makes a gesture asking Suzy to stand up and continue the discussion.)

Suzy: Its just that I have to handle the kids—stop the arguments and deal with the general discipline. And you know what happens. I end up being the mean mother and he is "Mr. Clean."

Director: (Realizing the main problem is with Suzy's husband) You feel your husband is not communicating with you, and you feel yourself isolated both from your husband and children.

Suzy: Yes. He just doesn't seem to care. He says he's tired from work, et cetera. But what about me? I'm going to college as well as taking care of the house, et cetera.

(The warm up continues until the director feels that the time is ready to move into action, i.e., he is ready and the protagonist is ready.)

Director: Have you ever discussed this situation with your husband, that is, have you ever confronted him about it?

Suzy: Yes, many times.

Director: When was the last time, or a time that you can remember very vividly?

Suzy: About three days ago; that was the last time.

Director: Could we have a look at this situation—three days ago? Where did it take place, et cetera?

(At this point the director might ask Suzy to select a group member to be her husband in the psychodrama. She would be asked to describe her husband; to warm up the group member (auxiliary ego) to this role. The "stage" is now being set up for the action phase of psychodrama—the director and protagonist working together.)

ACTION PHASE. The action phase includes the involvement in and working through of the problem presented by the protagonist. The action phase may vary considerably in duration, depending upon the director's evaluation of how adequately the protagonist has dealt with the problem. The action phase may be very short (four or five minutes) in a session, but in such unusual instances the problem resolution is continued in the post-action or group sharing phase.

(Sample Protocol of the Action Phase)

(The confrontation that is being reenacted has taken place in the living room following the evening meal about 7:30 P.M.)

Director: Is it happening now.

Suzy: (to husband) I've been having difficulty with John again. I wish you would talk to him about picking on Marie. He will not leave her alone. I find it is all becoming too much to handle by myself.

Husband (auxiliary ego): They will work it out themselves. I'll talk to them tomorrow (yawning).

Director: Is that the way it was?

Suzy: No, not exactly.

Director: (to Suzy and her auxiliary ego) Reverse roles.

Suzy (as husband): You make too much out of it. They are just like all kids. (He continues reading.) You are as capable as me in dealing with these little arguments.

Director: (to Suzy and auxiliary ego) Reverse roles.

Suzy (as herself): You seem more concerned about your paper and the T.V. than about me. I'm left on my own to deal with all the dirty work . . . et cetera.

(Action continues, but the action begins to get more involved. Feelings are called for by the director; doubling gets more intense; the group gets more involved. The protagonist as well as the group gets more insight into the situation. Emotions rise to the surface.)

Suzy: I guess I'm trying to say I feel lonely. Somehow we don't communicate. I feel I'm losing you and I can't handle the children without your support. I feel myself isolated from them as well, et cetera.

(The director allows actions and interaction to take place until he feels like the protagonist has explored the situation from many aspects and insight into the situation has been gained. The director who is always in command, or should be, reaches a moment when he feels that there has been enough of the action phase of the psychodrama for that session. He then stops the action and calls for sharing or feedback.)

Director: Shall we stop here and we can now have the feedback.

POST-ACTION PHASE. The third phase of the psychodrama is the post-action or sharing phase. The group shares their experiences and feelings in a constructive, supportive way with the protagonist. This phase must be under careful supervision of the director to prevent group members from analyzing and confronting the protagonist at a time when the protagonist has just finished sharing personal and intimate life experiences.

The closure of the psychodrama comes during the sharing phase and it is a very important part of the whole psychodrama. The protagonist needs to be reassured and supported and not just rapidly dismissed irresponsibly because the time for the group sessions has elapsed. The protagonist must be psychologically and emotionally integrated once again. It is important that the therapist is sufficiently experienced to assess the length of his session so that there is ample time for the sharing phase within the typical hour to one and one-half hour session.

(Sample Protocol of Post-action or Feedback Phase)

Director: How do you feel?

Suzy: All right—not nearly as tense.

Director: Now for some sharing from the group, but first can we have some feedback from the husband? (the auxiliary ego who portrayed the husband)
Could you share with Suzy as her husband?

Auxiliary ego: You made me feel guilty. I could feel your anger. Then later I suddenly felt very warm towards you.

Suzy: That makes me feel better because I really love you, . . . et cetera.

Director: Can any of the group share with Suzy?

Joe (member of group): I could identify and feel with you. I grew up in a family situation just like this . . . et cetera.

(Several members of the group share with Suzy and then the director closes the session.)

Director: Are you feeling okay, Suzy? Thank you for sharing some of your life space with us.

Selection and Group Composition

Psychodrama, being group psychotherapy, has the same criteria for selection and composition as applied to group psychotherapy in general. That is, age, sex, and type of problems are three basic criteria considered in selection.

Regarding age, psychodrama lends itself to children, adolescents and adults, but the various age groups should not be mixed. For the young child, play therapy represents the extension of psychodrama.

Mixed sex groups (heterogeneous groups) are preferred because they permit a more extensive type of sharing. Nevertheless, it is quite appropriate for male roles to be played by females and vice versa when doubles are needed from the group.

Group psychodrama members should be selected so as to represent a variety of problem-types or pathologies. Extremely homogeneous groups should be avoided, i.e., depressives, destructively aggressive individuals, or acting-out individuals should not be placed in a group with others just like themselves. Heterogeneous groups are preferred; nevertheless, sometimes homogeneous psychodrama groups such as groups of homosexuals can be quite successful. Psychodrama *training* groups may also be successfully grouped homogeneously, e.g., groups of administrators, groups of nurses, et cetera.

Potential group members should be interviewed in a one-to-one situation before placing them in a psychodrama group. When possible, individual psychodrama or some role playing should be employed. This is strongly suggested in order to predict the member's group performance.

Three or four married couples make up a married couple's psychodrama group. Frequently the married partners benefit more when they are in separate groups. Psychodrama is also applied most successfully to family groups. If properly practiced, it may be the most searching and effective type of family therapy.

Group Size

Group size varies with the age of patients. With very young children (preadolescents and younger) and young, acting-out adolescents, three or four is a suggested optimum number. If possible, a co-therapist is recommended for these groups.

Eight to ten adult subjects for therapeutic psychodrama groups is a suggested maximum. A co-therapist is also recommended for the adult subject groups whenever a competent one is available.

With very severely disturbed adults, individual psychodrama would usually be preferred at the outset over group psychodrama; eventually, however, the individuals would usually be placed in group psychodrama. Group psychodrama is therefore quite appropriate and often a very helpful form of treatment for the majority of patients in mental hospitals. In the mental hospital setting, eight to ten persons represent a preferred group size. (There are always a few therapists (psychodramatists) who feel they have the ability to treat and work with much larger numbers in group therapy. However, many psychodramatists feel that this is dangerous and in many situations irresponsible.)

In some institutions the closed T.V. circuit is used and is very effective in getting to the wards. This practice calls for the necessary precautions on the wards. T.V. is also very good for teaching and training purposes. Approximately 15 trainees can be accommodated in a psychodrama *training* group. Once again a co-therapist (trainer) is recommended.

Frequency, Length and Duration of Group Sessions

Once-a-week sessions of one to one and one-half hours is the usual arrangement; however, two sessions a week would be a suggested optimum for therapeutic psychodrama groups. The number of sessions is typically set from about 20 to 25. If necessary the number is extended or curtailed depending on the group members' needs.

Groups are usually open-ended, i.e., new members are added as others terminate. Closed groups, i.e., groups that begin and end with the same individuals, are also quite acceptable.

Qualifications of a Psychodramatist

Psychodrama as well as other psychotherapy can do without "week-end genuises." People with only limited training should not attempt group psychodrama. Psychodrama is a very potent medium that is very harmful when in the hands of untrained persons. This is a very useful medium for people in the helping professions and, therefore, it is a definite advantage to have some psychological background–knowledge of techniques of psychodrama alone is not sufficient. Much more important is why you use certain techniques–to what ends you use them.

It is also fundamentally important in doing any kind of group work that one have a knowledge of group dynamics. Once again, knowing your limitations in handling group psychodrama is very important since it can be very explosive. Training with a reputable psychodramatist is essential. It is also quite important to have been a protagonist on many occasions in a psychodrama. In general, one is as good a psychodramatist as he is a psychotherapist. In the therapeutic field one cannot justify hurting people because of lack of training. One must be aware of his limitations since only then will he grow and develop into a responsible therapist.

Ethical Considerations

Like all forms of group therapy, there is a unique problem of confidentiality because the subjects are not therapists in the professional sense of the word. The director should not assume that all members of the group are aware of the need for confidentiality; therefore he should make a definite point of informing the subjects of the need to maintain confidentiality of everything that transpires in the group. Other ethical considerations have been discussed previously in this chapter under Selection and Group Composition, Therapist's Qualifications and Procedures.

Limitations of Psychodrama

At this time there appears to be no emotional or psychological area in which some form of psychodrama would not be helpful if applied properly–again the importance of good training is emphasized. However, there are some areas that present difficulties in regard to initiating the psychodrama. For example, with potential suicide cases, psychodrama must be used cautiously because of the potential of unwittingly reinforcing a suicidal tendency.

Acting-out individuals with criminal intent and psychopaths and sociopaths must also be dealt with very carefully in psychodrama. With all of the above problem individuals, the psychodramatist must possess the experience and sensitivity to understand and cope with the underlying pathology.

In some situations the very nature of psychodrama fills the egotistical and narcissistic needs of the therapist. Awareness of this possibility should be present at all times and definitely be avoided. The psychodrama director should be always present but as inconspicuously as possible. A good psychodrama can usually move on its own without very much interference. One seeks to have as much freedom in the psychodrama as possible, but with freedom comes responsibility.

Protocol of a Psychodrama—Psychodrama of a Marriage

This is a case of the psychodrama of a married couple, Michele and Paul, held in Paris, France. The couple came to Dr. Moreno, who directed the session, with the intention of exploring their marital relationship. The marriage was in a crisis because of a severe disagreement between the two parties. The case, of which only a few excerpts are reported here, may serve as an illustration of how, by means of psychodrama, matrimonial conflicts can be explored. It will also illustrate the use of some of the psychodramatic techniques previously described.

Michele and Paul have been married for five years. Michele is a Parisian and Paul an American. They live in France and have two children.

> Moreno: Yes, now tell me, you must have a problem, otherwise you wouldn't have come forward to see me.
> Paul: Well, we do.
> Moreno: What is it?
> Paul: We don't get along.
> Moreno: You don't get along? Now what is that? That is so general. Is there any specific problem you have?

Michele: Well, I think that from my point of view, I have a problem.

Moreno: Yes. Be sincere, because only a real problem has a meaning in this session. If it isn't real, if it is fictitious, then you just return to where you come from. It must be true, and it must be felt.

Michele: It's a true problem.

Moreno: What is it?

Michele: I have been studying for several years and after that I have been working. And then after working for only one year I went back to studying to get my license. Then I wanted to go back to work but instead I got married. Since then I haven't been working. My husband is an American and he always wanted to go back to America, but we had fights about that and problems.

Moreno: You had fights because he wanted to be in America and you wanted to be in Paris? (Both nod with a forced smile.) You know, you remind me of a problem which I encountered many years ago. I remember the couple; their problem was that she felt she was the queen of Hollywood and he felt he was the king of New York, and so they decided to have half a year in Hollywood and half a year in New York.

Michele: (Smiling.) Yes, we thought we would have such a solution but in our case that is too complicated. It's across the ocean.

Paul: Well, there's more to it.

Moreno: What is it, Paul?

Paul: Let's talk about this ocean business.

Moreno: The ocean business?

Paul: I know that I have used going to America as a tool of aggression against my wife. (Rubs his hand against his forehead, tries very hard to explain.)

Moreno: Do you beat her up once in a while?

Paul: No. I also know, however, that it is very upsetting to me that she has become very resentful of all things American and is very hostile toward my country.

Michele: No. Not exactly. (Smiles uncomfortably.)

Moreno: No? What is it, Michele? What do you find wrong with him? His nose? His eyes? Is he a good husband to you?

Michele: Well, in a way.

Moreno: Not in a way, either-or. Do you sleep in the same bed with him?

Paul: Not anymore. No.

Moreno: But what is the problem?

Paul: I can bring my mother into it. We have a mother-in-law problem.

Moreno: You have a mother-in-law? Is she in Paris?
Paul: It is my mother but she's not in Paris.
Moreno: Where is she?
Paul: She lives in New York.

The warm-up period moves swiftly. It has the character of an interview and dialogue between the director and two protagonists, Michele and Paul. It is a gradual moving into their world, trying to find a significant clue for the opening episode to be acted out. Two leads for the first episode come forth; one is their present hostility towards one another, which seems to be too loaded for opening the psychodrama. The second lead is the mother-in-law problem.

The director accepts Paul's suggestion to bring his mother into the picture. She would give Paul support against Michele and he needs support very badly–mother's boy. The clue is chosen for the first scene. The warming-up period ends; the action period begins.

Moreno: Let's see the scene.
Paul: Then we would have to describe the whole week.
Moreno: You bring just the essence. Where is your mother now?
Paul: She's in New York.
Moreno: She's back in New York. Let's go to New York and see how she is.
Paul: All right.
Moreno: Let's go back now. Where does she live in New York, on what street? Has she her own house or does she live in an apartment building?

The director again takes the initiative and structures the scene. He does not permit long and vague story-telling, but insists on concretization. By forcing the protagonists to stick to actualities, he warms them up to present the facts directly and to express their actual experiences. Nothing warms up a protagonist better than his real life situation, e.g., where he lives and what he does.

Paul: She's in an apartment.
Moreno: What floor?
Paul: Sixteenth.
Michele: We had a terrible fight.
Moreno: Michele, I am very sorry for you. I want to talk to you alone. Forget him, we are alone for a moment. I understand it is

your mother-in-law who bothers you since you are married, isn't it?

Michele: In a way, yes.

Moreno: In a way? Let us find out. I would like now for you and your mother-in-law to have an encounter and see how you make out with her. You have to realize that the encounters you have had with your mother-in-law in life itself are one thing. But here you can be far more expressive and extensive than in life. You just get going the whole way and expose your feelings and her feelings. All right?

Michele: Yes.

The structuring of a future situation emerges, a future situation that the protagonist fully visualizes but which has never taken place. This offers certain advantages. If it were a situation that actually has taken place in the past, then the protagonist would try to reenact what happened from memory, trying to be as literally accurate as possible. To move from the past into the here-and-now is loaded with difficulty. It is easier to move from the here-and-now into the future. The fantasy is freer from detailed commitments. In the here-and-now both protagonists are present, husband and wife. In the future situation the mother-in-law has to be represented by an auxiliary ego. But this is full of practical learning. We are shown the mother-in-law as the protagonists see her, rather than as she is in reality.

Moreno: Whom do you like to choose as a mother-in-law? Let us see, Zerka (who is in the audience), would you like to portray her? (Zerka steps forward.) All right.

Choosing from the audience the person to enact the role of Michele's mother-in-law is the privilege of the protagonist. She is guided by a special clairvoyance for the right person. But at times the director may have an intuition for choosing the right person, an auxiliary ego trained for playing unpleasant, nasty mother-in-law roles.

Moreno: Now this is what we call in psychodrama an auxiliary ego. She is not your real mother-in-law. But she will try to portray her to the best of her ability and I would appreciate it, Paul, if you would sit down on that couch for a moment and leave the two ladies alone. Now, Michele, you have entered your mother-in-law's home in New York, right? You have flown by Air France to

New York and you are in your mother-in-law's home. Do you remember how the living room is fixed?

Michele: Well, she has . . . (laughs), I don't know.

Moreno: You can imagine it.

Michele: Yes.

Moreno: And what kind of furniture has she?

Michele: Yes, I can imagine it.

Zerka as Mrs. Mark (Paul's mother): Michele?

Moreno: Now you are just coming in; you are taking her by surprise. Here she is. Come in. You just come from Kennedy Airport and it's your projection into the future, you are doing now what you might do tomorrow, because that may be the best solution to your conflict. We'll find out. Now you are coming in and you are opening the door, and here is your mother-in-law.

Michele: Well, I'm ashamed. I shouldn't have said what I did. But at the same time, I thought you were so aggressive with me because you had the feeling that I had taken your son away from you. I couldn't bear your aggressivity for so long and at the same time I had the feeling my husband was resentful to me because of you.

Mrs. Mark: Is he?

Michele: I think he is, yes.

Moreno: Is this how your mother-in-law would act towards you, as this lady does?

Michele: Well, she talks very frankly. At the same time my mother-in-law is more aggressive.

Moreno: More aggressive? Reverse roles and let's see how you perceive her. You take the part of your mother-in-law, because you know her, and she will take your part. But talk a little louder because we have a big audience over the ocean; they all have to hear you.

Role reversal is indicated here for two reasons. First, to obtain more adequate information about her mother-in-law (Mrs. Mark) as Michele perceived her. And second, to bring forward the highlights of the conflict between the two women, as the following illustrates.

Zerka as Michele: You know you got me very upset, and I'm sorry. I shouldn't have said the things I said to you and perhaps you shouldn't have said some of the things you said to me, either. But why do you dislike me so? What have I done? I just married your son. Millions of young women marry sons every day.

Michele as Mrs. Mark: Yes, but Michele, I think you are too nervous. It's your fault.

Zerka as Michele: What's my fault?

Michele as Mrs. Mark: I would be much more with you if you were not like that. And I think my son should be in this country. You must understand that he has to spend some time with me. I am his mother. It's a problem for him to be abroad, and I don't like my son to live in France. (Michele turns to Dr. Moreno.) Well she's never said that, but I think she feels. . . .

Moreno: You are acting your mother-in-law, don't fall out of the role, my dear.

"Falling out of a role" is a special pathology. A protagonist will easily fall out of a role which is displeasing for her to play or when she wants to play her own part again in order to tell her mother-in-law directly what she thinks of her.

To make Michele more apprehensive about the kind of relationship her husband, Paul, has with his mother, she, Michele, is made to be her own mother-in-law (Mrs. Mark), but this time talking with her "son," Paul. This role playing from Michele's side may indicate the degree of conflict she has with her mother-in-law.

Michele as Mrs. Mark: You never tell me things about the children. I'd like so much to know all about you.

Paul: Yeah. But you know that I am very upset about what's going on at home and that I get into situations where I want to ignore the future; I want to ignore all but the present or ignore what happened. I simple don't write to people; I don't take pictures of the children because I really banish the present from my mind; I retreat.

Michele as Mrs. Mark: Yes. Well I think you should reproach yourself and try to keep in touch with me.

Paul: Well, it makes me very sad that I haven't been too patient. It seems to me that. . . .

Moreno: Mother is a little bashful and I know you came to me for advice and for counseling just like your wife, Michele. And it would help me in order to understand your problem better, if I could use a method which we call the double.

Paul: All right, fine.

Moreno: I will invite another lady to be like your conscience, to be also here. Here is a young lady who might do that. You are now the double. There are two Mrs. Marks, now. And to express her-

self better toward you, because we want to know the truth.
Paul: Okay.

"Double" is indicated here because Michele has not succeeded to assume adequately the role of the apparently possessive mother. (If a mother is too possessive of her son she may endanger her daughter-in-law's relation to her husband.) So the "double" should help Michele to assume adequately the role of her mother-in-law –which she could not assume. Furthermore, the double should reveal the real nature of Paul's relation to his own mother.

Moreno: All right, go ahead.

Double as Mrs. Mark: When are you going to come home?

Paul: You know that when I went to Europe five years ago I went on a three-week vacation. I had no intention of staying and I've been here ever since.

Double as Mrs. Mark: I asked you, when are you going to come home?

Paul: You also know that I was very confused about what to do with myself when I got married and so forth.

Double as Mrs. Mark: I mean after all, when are you going to know when to do something on your own?

Paul: Um . . . (laughs).

Double as Mrs. Mark: Well, I really mean it; you need to be around me. I can tell this. Living with her has been. . . .

Moreno as Michele: Don't ler her take over, she's only your double. You are still Number One. Go ahead.

Paul: Anyway, what I was trying to get to is the point that I have now built a life for myself in Paris, so professionally, I just can't come home at this point.

Michele as Mrs. Mark: Well, maybe professionally.

Paul: In about two years I probably will be able to. In fact, I'll have to. Because of the things I've done I'll probably be called to New York.

Michele as Mrs. Mark: You can try to come back professionally.

Paul: At this point I'm too committed. I have to follow a career and the career dictates now. This wasn't true six months ago, but now it dictates that I must stay.

Michele as Mrs. Mark: But you know here I can help you. I have a good friend who can help you to stay in New York if you want to. Can I talk to him?

Paul: Of course. I'd be very interested to have any kind of an offer of a good job, but I have a period of commitment now. In any case, even if I were offered it presently, I wouldn't be able to give up these commitments.

Michele as Mrs. Mark: Yes, but maybe you would have first to . . . to . . . to . . . go to Timbuktu and then you are sure to go back to New York and have a good job.

Paul: Well, yes. That would be fine. But you haven't understood that I'm now committed to Paris.

Michele as Mrs. Mark: Yes, I have understood.

(Michele, thanks to the help of the double, tried to be more demanding of her son.)

Moreno: Now in psychodrama, we place a tremendous emphasis upon the future. And that is why we have a method of projecting the future in advance. I'd like now that you should show us how your life would be five years from now.

Paul: All right.

Moreno: Where will you be, Paul, five years from now?

Paul: Well, I can say that I have several alternatives.

Moreno: What do you think will be five years from now?

Paul: I think in five years, if I work well, I think that I will be offered a job in New York, a more important job than I have now. And I might very well be tempted to take it.

Moreno: Where would you live, so far as you are concerned? Try to predict.

Paul: I would like to be living in New York.

Moreno: Do you think you'll live in New York five years from now?

Paul: I don't know.

Moreno: You don't know. (To Michele): Where do you think you'll be five years from now? Would your marriage still exist?

Michele: I have no idea, really.

Moreno: (To Paul): Now what do you suspect?

Paul: I suspect it will not.

Moreno: It will not?

Paul: Yes.

Michele: I don't know.

Moreno: You don't know. Do you want it to last?

Michele: It depends on the conditions.

Moreno: (To Paul): Do you want it to last?

Paul: I don't know.

Future projection technique was an extremely revealing clue here. The fact that after five years of married life this couple could not produce a clear future-image is the most significant indicator of the grave cleavage between the two. So corporal is the disagreement between them that Michele and Paul were incapable of setting a future scene to act out.

Paul resented the fact that Michele's culture dominates his life. She and the children speak French and prefer French ways of life. Eventually he divorced her and went back to America.

EPILOGUE—DEAN G. ELEFTHERY

Psychodrama, with all of its present offerings to the action therapeutic medium, continues to grow in its use and effectiveness. In the years ahead there is a good possibility that as one looks back, one will recognize that psychodrama's greatest contribution to society was in the area of prevention of mental illness through facilitating people to live in greater harmony with each other. One cannot but feel grateful to this legacy that Moreno has left us.

SUMMARY

Moreno's contribution as the originator of psychodrama is briefly outlined along with the "seven trends of thought" that prepared the way for the development of group psychotherapy. Psychodrama is defined and placed in perspective.

Five concepts are presented to outline the theoretical rationale that undergirds group psychodrama. These concepts include encounter, spontaneity, catharsis, reality testing, and role. Each concept is described as it functions within the psychodramatic process.

The procedures utilized in group psychodrama are subsumed in this chapter under three categories: the "primary instruments," the "basic techniques," and the "phases." The primary instruments of the psychodrama, viz., the protagonist, auxiliary egos, director, group, and stage are defined and their functions are described. Likewise, 16 basic techniques employed in the psychodrama are also defined and their use in the psychodrama is outlined. Finally, the three phases of the psychodrama—warm-up, action, and feedback—are described and illustrated through a sample protocol.

Several topics of importance related to the effective understanding and application of psychodrama are dealt with in this chapter. These topics include selection and group composition; group setting; group size, frequency, length, and duration of group sessions; leader qualifications; ethical considerations, and limitations of this treatment modality. The chapter concludes with a sample protocol of a psychodrama directed by J. L. Moreno. The protocol illustrates the application of several basic techniques, the phases, and the instruments of the psychodrama.

SUGGESTED READINGS

Biddle, B. J., and Thomas, E. J.: *Role Theory: Concept and Research.* New York, Wiley, 1966.

Blatner, H. A.: *Acting-in: Practical Applications of Psychodramatic Methods.* New York, Springer Publishing Co., 1973.

Greenberg, I. A.: *Psychodrama: Theory and Therapy.* New York, Behavioral Publications, 1974.

Lindzey, G., and Borgatta, E. F.: Sociometric measurement. In Lindzey, G. (Ed.): *Handbook of Social Psychology.* Reading, Addison-Wesley, 1954.

Moreno, J. L.: *Psychodrama* Vol I. Beacon, N. Y.: Beacon House, 1946.

Moreno, J. L.: *Sociometry, Experimental Methods and Science of Society.* Beacon, N. Y.: Beacon House, 1951.

Moreno, J. L.: *Who Shall Survive?* (2nd ed.) Beacon, N. Y.: Foundation of Sociometry, Group Psychotherapy and Sociodrama, Beacon House, 1953.

Moreno, J. L. (Ed.): *Sociometry and the Science of Man.* Beacon, N. Y.: Beacon House, 1956.

Moreno, J. L.: *Psychodrama* Vol. II. Beacon, N. Y.: Beacon House, 1958.

Moreno, J. L.: Psychodrama. In Arieti, S. (Ed.) *American Handbook of Psychiatry.* Vol. II. New York, Basic Books, 1959.

Moreno, J. L. *et al.: The Sociometry Reader.* Glencoe, Ill., Free Press, 1959.

Moreno, J. L., Friedmann, A., Battegay, R., and Moreno, Zerka T. (Eds.): *The International Handbook of Group Psychotherapy.* New York, Philosophical Library, 1966.

Moreno, Zerka T.: Psychodramatic rules, techniques and adjunctive methods. *Psychodrama and Group Psychotherapy.* Beacon, N. Y., Beacon House, 1966.

REFERENCES

Berne, E. *Gestalt Therapy Verbatim* (a review), *American Journal of Psychiatry, 10:*1519, 1970.

Maslow, A. H.: Letter to the Editor. *Life Magazine,* August 2, 1968, p. 15.

Moreno, J. L.: *Einladung zu einer Begegnung.* Vienna, Anzengeuber, 1914.

Moreno, J. L.: *Das Stegreiftheater*. Potsdam, Kiepenheuer, 1923. (English edition: *The Theater of Spontaneity*. New York, Beacon, 1946.)

Moreno, J. L.: Philosophy of the Third Psychiatric Revolution, with special emphasis on group psychotherapy and psychodrama. In Fromm-Reichmann, Freida, and Moreno, J. L. (Eds.): *Progress in Psychotherapy*. New York, Grune, 1956.

Schutz, W. C.: *Here Comes Everybody: Bodymind and Encounter Culture*. New York, Harper and Row, 1971.

CHAPTER V

PSYCHOANALYSIS IN GROUPS[1]

Alexander Wolf

CLAIMS ARE OCCASIONALLY made that the beginnings of psychoanalytic group therapy were undertaken by one therapist or another. Perhaps one could demonstrate that group therapy began at meetings of young philosophers around Socrates and Plato or among the Apostles and Jesus. Ernest Jones suggests that psychoanalysis in groups began aboard ship in 1909 when Freud, Jung and Ferenczi analyzed one another's dreams on the way to the United States. If any priority needs to be respected, it should perhaps be rendered to Freud and his shipboard companions.

Group psychotherapy began in the first decade of this century. Psychoanalytically oriented group psychotherapy began in the thirties, years that were especially conducive to the development of all sorts of collective activity for a variety of ends. The leadership of Roosevelt and the concerted social need helped to lay the groundwork for the flowering of group therapy. It was a time of protest against failures in the Establishment, a protest that took various social forms. Today this rebelliousness takes the form of withdrawal, isolation and retreats into fantasy. This is done even in groups, where experiencing one's feelings in acting out inappropriate affect is being promoted as therapeutic when it is, in fact, regressive.

It is of some interest to speculate why there was in the thirties such readiness to seek therapy in a group, when generally there is reticence about exposing subjective disorder. This was the time of the great economic depression. It was a time of restlessness,

1. *Note:* Appreciation is expressed to Roche Laboratories, Division of Hoffmann-La Roche Inc., for permission to reprint Dr. Wolf's monograph, Psychoanalysis in Groups, from a series entitled *Major Contributors to Modern Psychotherapy.*

when people sought one another out in collective endeavor. Most people were short of money and tried to find solutions in common struggle, whether in attempts to deal with their impoverishment or their anxiety. Most patients could not pay the cost of an individual analysis. There were needs that were met by the opportunity to undertake analysis in a group: the availability of reconstructive therapy; treatment at a very reasonable fee; a sustaining and collaborative membership under the leadership of a clinician in a joint effort against an outer threat, an impoverishing social structure, and an inner threat, neurosis.

In the middle thirties I became interested in the possibility of doing psychoanalytic therapy in a group setting. I read the papers of Trigant Burrow, Paul Schilder and Louis Wender, visited J. L. Moreno and participated as an actor in one of his psychodramas.

Moved by the success of these clinicians, I suggested to several of my patients that they forego their individual analytic work and continue their further treatment with me in a group setting. With little obvious resistance they evidenced an eagerness to pursue my proposal. In 1938 my first group had its initial meeting. The patients were stimulated and moved by the experience. Our enthusiasm spread, so that by 1940 five groups of patients were in treatment with me, one of them made up of five married couples.

It is not possible in this space to provide a history of the development of psychoanalysis in groups. What follows then is a brief statement of my present concepts of its underlying theory and clinical practice.

Psychoanalysis in groups is the use of analytic means–free association, the analysis of dreams and fantasies and the working through of resistance and transference–in the treatment of eight to ten patients in a group setting. Psychoanalysis in groups entails an understanding of unconscious processes and motivation. It seeks out the historical basis for current behavior in order to resolve its persistence in the present. It requires the working out and working through of repetitive and compulsive psychopathologic maneuvers. Psychoanalysis in groups pursues the latent as well as the manifest in patient interaction and function. The search for unconscious processes is achieved by the promotion of the freedom to express any thought, fantasy or feeling. The pursuit of unconscious motives moves patients away from attending only to the present and toward an understanding of intrapsychic processes, historical determinants and the working through of transference distortions.

INDIVIDUAL ANALYSIS

The traditional psychoanalyst tends to reject the group as a therapeutic milieu. He is more anonymous and less interactive with the patient than are group members or the group analyst. The individual analysand is thereby rendered more passive, regressed, introspective, isolated and concentrated on the intrapsychic rather than on the interpersonal. He pursues his early history, and the focus of attention is largely upon himself, his associations and reactions. The individual analyst is inclined to reject the idea that his values, his individual characteristics and predilections provoke particular responses in the patient. The group analyst, however, becomes increasingly aware from his observation of group interaction that his commitments, his personal qualities, choices and preferences elicit special reactions in his analysands.

The individual analyst is denied in the dyadic relationship a multifaceted view of his patient. He does not see the analysand in the multiplicity of reactions stimulated by other group members. He is not witness to the patient's responses to his projected nuclear or current family, his boss, his friends, to authorities and peers. He does not actually observe the multiple transferences that a group evokes. He is also less aware of the patient's positive resources in the healthy ways he deals with people. The individual analyst is inclined to regard the patient as more helpless than he is, because the therapist is in the vertical position of helping a dependent person. In the group, however, every member occasionally offers support and insight to a co-patient. This is a new role for an analysand, one that exposes a previously unseen side of his character, the strength and perceptivity to encourage and offer insight to another patient, which is mutually ego-building. The presence of other patients provides new kinds of activity and responsive feelings induced less readily in individual analysis. The group analysand experiences peer interaction that is not available in dyadic therapy.

In individual analysis the patient has more difficulty in asserting himself. Co-patients in a group support each other in dealing with the authority invested group analyst. The individual analyst is more easily able to govern one patient than he is several of them assembled. They encourage one another to express attitudes toward the leader less readily ventilated in isolation with the therapist.

GROUP THERAPY AND PSYCHOANALYSIS IN GROUPS

There are differences between nonanalytic group psychotherapy and psychoanalysis in groups. These differences are relative, not absolute, so that in the following list of distinctions between them there is some overlapping. The group therapist tends to treat the group as a whole and to use group dynamic interpretations. The group analyst is more attentive to individuals in the group and their particular unconscious motivation. The group therapist is more interested in the here-and-now, while the group analyst is more attentive to the there-and-then, its persistence in the present and working through. The group therapist is inclined to organize his membership more homogeneously and to treat the homogenized group as one with a bipersonal psychology. The group analyst tends to organize groups more heterogeneously and to treat the patients with a multipersonal psychology. The group therapist looks for similarities in the membership, so that adjustment and conformity are therapeutic outcomes. The group analyst values differences among his patients, so that insight, individual uniqueness and freedom are therapeutic derivatives. The group therapist focuses on the manifest behavior made evident by interaction and interpersonal processes. The group analyst scrutinizes the latent content, the intrapsychic processes, the unconscious material and promotes self-examination to this end. As a result, there is less anxiety in nonanalytic group therapy and more anxiety in psychoanalysis in groups.

In group therapy which is not analytic, the patient may repeat his submission to the original familial expectation that he yield to parental dictates. This resistance to differentiation repeats the earlier ego-repressive experience. In group analysis the examination of unconscious processes helps the patient to grasp in detail the character of his yielding up his own ego to his parents in the past and to group members in the present. He is emboldened to search for a way out, to repossess his own ego. The analytic group supports his distinguishing attributes, his difference, the emergence of his repressed ego.

Six Primary Parameters

The analyst in groups has in mind the existence of six primary parameters, which in part differentiate group from individual analysis.

The first of these is the presence of *hierarchial and peer vectors* in the group. They become apparent in the interplay of vertical and horizontal reactions that characterize parental and sibling transferences. Co-patients in a group provide a peer vector and peer relatedness. The analyst provides a hierarchial vector, a responsible authority and projected parental figure. The presence of leadership in the person of the analyst and of peers in the patient members makes for a setting in which vertical and horizontal interaction can take place that promotes parental and sibling transferences.

Second, there are *multiple reactivities* in the group in which each patient utilizes other members and the leader in healthy and neurotic ways. Some of the distortions are in terms of multiple transferences, identifications, abuse of another patient seen as oneself, etc. This multiple interaction engages group members with one another and the therapist in their feelings, thoughts and behavior. Multiple interaction tends to impel the more uncommunicative patient to participate. Reserved or silent members find it difficult to maintain their detachment. They are reacted to for their nonverbal attitudes until they are able to speak. In the course of multiple interaction, group members are sometimes inclined to gratify each other's transference expectations, so that the therapist is obliged to analyze the patients' inappropriate fulfillment of one another's archaic demands, until the members themselves are able to undertake this mutual analysis. Some masochistic patients manage to provoke the members into scapegoating them. This, too, requires analytic intervention.

Third is the dimension of *interpersonal and intrapsychic com-*

munication. The intrapsychic process stresses self-knowledge leading to personal integration. The interpersonal process emphasizes knowledge of the self and others leading to personal and social integration. Individual analysis often tends to be more of an intrapsychic experience. Group analysis tends to be more of an interpersonal experience, but properly conducted can be equally intrapsychic. In dyadic analysis the analytic process usually proceeds from the intrapsychic to the interpersonal; in group analysis, from the interpersonal to the intrapsychic.

Fourth is the principle of *forced interaction.* Some patients are reluctant to reveal themselves in the group setting. There is, however, pressure on the less participating to become engaged. It is difficult to hold oneself apart in the face of the general push for collaborative interaction.

Fifth is the principle of *shifting attention* which helps to resolve the expectation of the patient, who was an only child, that he receive all the attention. Group analysis confronts the monopolistic only child with the reality that there are others beside the self who need to be heard and attended. Sometimes it is the originally favored or unfavored child who tries in the group to' exclude his siblings. Such a maneuver is less apparent in dyadic analysis where there is little if any necessity to compete for the therapist's attention.

In a group the focus of attention shifts from one patient to another. No one has exclusive possession of therapeutic scrutiny. The analyst and the patients do not give any one member their exclusive regard. This shifting attention gives each member an opportunity to digest the insight that has been offered him. Others use the relaxation from examination as a breathing spell from what may be experienced as a somewhat threatening exploration. Still others may resistively seek avoidance of such attention in order to maintain their psychopathology.

Sixth is the principle of *alternating roles.* The group structure necessarily gives rise to the phenomenon of alternating roles. Every member is obliged or at least inclined to listen, to try to understand the other. Novel kinds of feelings, of reactions, of activity are evoked. Each patient talks, gives advice, tries to comprehend, responds, feels sympathetic, irritated, bored, and evokes appropriate and inappropriate reactions. He wants help and extends help. He is giver and taker, helper and helped. His roles are enlarged by new kinds of activity. He feels frustrated, angry, flattered, pleased. Now he is trying to understand the others. Later, they are trying to understand him. At one moment he is interacting spontaneously. The next, he is thoughtfully contemplating what has just been said to him about himself.

Group Organization and Goals

The group analyst tries to organize a diversified membership. Although he recognizes similarities among his patients, he tries to be awake to each member's novelty and originality. He is alert to every patient's right to be distinctive. For there is unhealth in the cohesion of a homogeneous group that too often excludes the new member as an alien foreigner. The group analyst sees health in the reciprocity and interdependence of unlikeness, in men and women working creatively together just because of their complementarity, in parents and children acknowledging their reciprocal need of one another. He views homogeneity as separating and isolating.

It is not possible to form a group heterogeneous in every respect. Patients are alike in many ways and their similarities make for some homogeneity. The leader does not assemble children, adolescents and adults in groups. He treats these different patients in groups homogeneously organized with respect to their age. He does not mix the intelligent with the mentally retarded or the sociopath with the responsible citizen. While he is obliged to make some concessions to the need for homogeneity, as analytic treatment progresses, the members become more diversified.

If the leader promotes homogeneity, he limits the intensity of analytic investigation. Patients who make advances in treatment begin to ask for differentiated and complementary others in the group. This kind of request is some indication that the group leader is practicing analytic therapy. The more the analyst and analysands search for the latent beneath the manifest, uncover repressed past history and seek out psychic determinants, the more individual differences, heterogeneity and diversity emerge among the members. The analytic approach to group members sponsors their individuality and makes the group heterogeneous. Each patient emerges as a distinct person with a singular past, evolution and current psychodynamics. The members become more responsive to one another in their differentiation in pathology and in health. A struggle develops to understand and accept the stranger in the other.

Confidentiality

Occasionally patients claim they cannot join a group because there is too much anxiety or danger in exposure to strangers whose commitment to confidentiality cannot be trusted. Such patients can usually be induced to join a group in time as their anxiety and resistance are analyzed. Confidentiality among members needs to be maintained. If a patient reveals to an outsider what goes on in his group, he arouses a good deal of fear and anger among the members. The therapist needs to analyze the resistive gossip. Such a breach of mutual trust is a resistive leak that threatens the secure existence of a group unless the problem can be quickly resolved. If not, the tattler may have to return to individual analysis until this difficulty is overcome.

The Alternate Meeting

The alternate session is a scheduled meeting of patients without the presence of the analyst. It alternates with regular meetings at which the analyst is present. Regular sessions take place once a week for about 1½ hours. Alternate meetings take place once or twice a week and last two or three hours.

There are a number of reasons for organizing alternate sessions. For one thing such a regimen says to the patient in effect: "One of our objectives in treatment is to resolve your need of me. I believe you can function effectively with your peers. I will be available to you at regular sessions or in individual consultations should they prove to be necessary. But I believe it is in your interest to try to use and develop your own resources. You can do this, I am certain, at the alternate meeting." These sessions then are an attempt even at the very beginning of analysis to work through pathologically dependent transferential ties to the parental surrogate in the analyst, to move the patient toward autonomy. It is a movement toward ending at the beginning. It is a trial for the child-self in the patient–a trial without the parental figure. The good analyst, like the good parent, believes in paying judicious attention and judicious inattention.

The alternate session provides the opportunity to compare thought, feeling and behavior in the two climates, the regular and the alternate. Patients, to a certain extent, think, feel and act differently in the presence and absence of the authority figure. And these differences become the basis for defining, elucidating and working through parental transferences to the group leader. Many patients interact more freely in the absence of the analyst when authority transferences are experienced as less oppressive. As a result, often a good deal of material is expressed that is withheld in the analyst's presence. This material frequently is concerned with feelings about the therapist. With the support, encouragement and sometimes the "betrayal" by other members, the attitudes and feelings expressed at alternate meetings are brought into regular sessions.

The parental transferences patients make to one another at the alternate session tend to be somewhat attenuated by an awareness that they are, in fact, among their peers. The absence of the helping analyst at alternate sessions forces the peers to help one another and promote their sharing and their equality at the same time that it reduces their childlike dependency on the analyst.

A by-product of psychoanalysis in groups, more particularly when alternate sessions are provided, is socialization. Socialization is usually looked upon as resistance, and in some instances this may be so. However, this is not necessarily true, if socialization is explored analytically for its resistive elements. Socialization has a reparative and humanizing function. Socializing may, however, limit the pursuit of unconscious processes. As a result, the group leader needs to examine the way patients use or misuse the alternate session, their participation in extra-group cliques or subgroups.

The therapeutic use of the alternate session provides further advantages. One of these is the clinical experience of spontaneous mutual support. There may be concern that patients left to their own inexperienced devices may do wild analysis and psychically, if not physically, damage each other. But patients do not at alternate meetings become decorticate and barbaric. If some of the insight they extend is premature, poorly timed, too penetrating or widely off the mark, the member who is the target for analysis usually discounts or resists it on the ground that the proffered help is coming from an inexpert peer. However, as patients become more experienced, sophisticated and familiar with one another's psychological and pathological maneuvers, they often make very astute clinical observations which tend also to be carefully considered. If these insights fit, they are gradually accepted and worked with. For certain patients who have extreme difficulty in accepting insight when offered by the authority figure of the analyst, these same observations coming from peers appear to be more readily acceptable.

Resistance

Resistance is dealt with quickly in group analysis. Patients question the appropriateness of each other's resistive operations. They will not let a member sleep. They urge the silent patient to speak. They energetically press for an end to resistive maneuvers. They incite one another to change. They ask for new activity, demand interaction, protest against withdrawal or monopoly and object to compulsive intrapsychic self-absorption or to inappropriate ways of relating. They induce participation until there is freely expressed and examined interaction.

Dreams, Fantasies and Free Association

Analysts are often skeptical about whether group members can associate freely in the group, where there are so many interruptions of spontaneous expression. But even in individual analysis free association must to an extent be limited, restrained, and bounded. It needs, in any case, to be used selectively. The leader's concern with interruptions of free association may be looked upon as his wish to do individual analysis in the group. The discontinuity in free association may clarify the fantasy or dream of a given patient but may also be used to analyze the interruptive associations of other members in multilateral interpretations. The leader's view of co-members' communications as discordant prevents the group from engaging in multilateral analysis. It demands individual analysis in the group and supports a competition to interrupt each other, a rivalry to win the attention of the therapist.

Supporting the right of the members to join in with their associations gives all the patients the right to be in treatment rather than just one person at a time. The therapist must, therefore, deal with presentations as reciprocal and interdependent, so that patient mutuality is improved. By this means, all patient free associations are increased rather than limited. In a group a patient in his free associations is obliged to function with some awareness of others. This expectation of consciousness of the other is health-facilitating. Unlimited free association without such awareness may lead to more serious pathology.

Free association may be interrupted or facilitated by co-members. If a patient in a group is searching in his associations for previously unexamined unconscious material, he generally excites and holds the attention of his peers and is, as a result, encouraged to continue. If he reproduces the same pathology, the members become bored with the repetition and usually try to stop him and plead for a more mutually gratifying alternative–like a fresh dream or fantasy. If his free association discloses more realistic or less compulsive imaginings, the other patients become more receptive in the hope that he will continue to make freer choices. If his associations take the course of an isolating autism, the members object to his masochistic and detached free association.

The presentation of a dream is followed by the dreamer's associations. Then the other members associate in relation to the dream. Following this, the patients try to interpret the dream as well as the latent meaning of each member's subjective associations. In this way the dreamer is prevented from monopolizing a group session, for every patient's unconscious contribution to the original dream is made conscious and insightful.

Activity and Acting Out

Acting out is more readily discovered and revealed in the group than in the therapeutic dyad and can, therefore, be more easily examined for resolution. Patients who reveal "secrets" to one another in private dyads outside of group meetings engage in a form of cliquing, a resistive leakage that subverts the analytic process.

It is an acting out, a resistance to treatment. Members are, therefore, encouraged to expose one another in the group setting. They are urged to "betray" one another's secrets to the whole group.

In any therapeutic group there is a good deal more activity than in the therapeutic dyad. The activity may be appropriate or an acting out. Much of the activity is not acting out but a wholesome consequence of vigorous group interaction. There is lively expression of good will, friendliness, and support as well as anger and aggression. When acting out occurs, it is partly a consequence of the strong emotional multilateral excitement. If the analyst pursues an interpretive role with respect to acting out, it can commonly be checked. When analytic confrontation fails to limit acting out, the therapist may, all else failing, be obliged to forbid it. Such imposition of restraint generally provides so much relief from anxiety that patients usually appreciate the superimposed control.

Even when the analyst does not limit acting out, the patients themselves before long put an end to it. If they seem to be unable to do so, they plead with the therapist to help them exercise control. There is finally such frustration among acting-out patients that they turn to the group and the leader for restraint and insight.

Clinical experience has demonstrated that there need be little concern about acting out. If patients can function twenty-three hours a day without the analyst, they can be relied upon as a rule to exercise reasonable restraint. Factors supporting control over acting out are the wholesome realistic goals patients set for themselves and the preservative influences in various healthy ego functions. Other sources of restraint are the projection of reasonable authority, regard for the analyst as an appropriately controlling influence, the wish to be guided by conventionality and tradition, by what is fit and unfit, by rules of conscience. A deterrent to acting out is that it will in time be exposed. All acting out ends in such frustration that self-corrective needs and leadership in the group move the members to set their own curbs on the pathological activity.

Working Through

It becomes apparent in any therapeutic group that the analyst's advocacy of freedom to express associations, fantasies, dreams, thoughts, and feelings lead to a good many highly charged responses. These interactions are both appropriate and inappropriate. Group members become increasingly aware of the typical distortions that characterize each one of them. As time goes on, these transference reactions are traced to specific familial antecedents. The process of working through entails a conscious struggle to choose more reasonable and realistic alternatives to the persistent transference maneuvers.

There is more reality-boundness in group than in individual analysis. In the group, even while the patient reveals what he thinks and feels, he is obliged to be regardful of the thoughts and feelings of his peers. This consideration for others prevents pathological retreats into loss of realistic bounds. It enables each member to become aware of his own provocative behavior. Not only is self-understanding meaningful but consciousness of one's effect on others in equally relevant.

Patients and therapist offer different kinds of help. Patient help is offered more spontaneously, more impulsively and more compulsively. The therapist's helpfulness has more purpose, more usefulness and is suggested with more discrimination.

A concern of some therapists is that a patient may inappropriately offer another an insight with which he is not yet ready to cope. The impression is that a poorly timed proffer of insight may be damaging to a member as yet unable to deal with the anxiety evoked by the penetration of his defenses. Patients, however, seem able to deal with insights from their peers either by rejecting them or by gradually assimilating them. When the analyst poorly times his interpretation, the patient becomes more upset, because the insight comes in the authority vector.

A patient does not have the knowledge and skill in timing interpretations that the therapist has. Patients nevertheless often make useful comments about one another with good intuition and considerable acuteness. They are not by nature experts in psychoanalytic theory and technique. It is rather their common sense, straightforwardness, unpremeditation, plain matter-of-factness, liveliness and naiveté, free of the technical language of psychoanalysis, and the manifest wish to be helpful that enable them to be constructive with one another. The emotional intensity associated with their observations is also an element in their influence on each other.

Understanding and confrontation among co-patients are both more easily resisted and invited because they emanate from peers. The group analyst can more often than not simply permit the patients to interact, for they generate less anxiety than he does. He may then selectively interpose his own impressions when they are most useful. Interaction and interpretation among patients generally invigorates, supports, and intensifies the improvement of the members.

ROLE OF THE GROUP ANALYST

The primary ingredient of psychoanalysis in groups is attention to unconscious material, the study of intrapsychic processes. The therapist sets the tone of group meetings by his lead in the pursuit of unconscious material, free association and the analysis of dreams, resistance and transference. The search for unconscious processes and motivations leads the patients to their suppressed history, awareness of its compulsive repetition in the present, and speculation about the conscious choice of more realistic alternatives.

As multiple interaction develops in the group, the therapist leads the patients into the exploration of unconscious motivations and their genetic determinants. If the leader permits the group simply to interact without analysis, he supports resistive and defensive behavior.

Analytic intervention needs to be made in such a way that the interactive participants are given insight multilaterally. One member should not for long be the exclusive focus of analytic attention. If he is so scrutinized by the whole group, the therapist should examine the contribution of the observing co-patients and confront them with their resistance. In so doing, the analyst does not permit any one member to stand alone under critical analysis. A single patient subjected to group scrutiny often has the support of certain other members. If he does not have such allies and needs one, it is the function of the therapist to afford him whatever support is needed.

TERMINATION

The end of treatment for any given patient stirs the remaining members. Their being witness to one patient's recovery is encouraging to them. The departing member impels the others to try harder to attain a similar state of well-being. He may animate them in a time of relative despondency. He may make them more introspective in order to learn how he attained his goals. He may induce in them a competition to succeed as well. Occasionally, the success of a "graduate" may induce a contentious resistance in which another member may insist on his readiness for discharge when he is hardly, in fact, ready to do so.

OTHER READINGS

A more complete presentation of the writer's position is published in two volumes, *Psychoanalysis in Groups,* by Wolf and Schwartz, Grune and Stratton, New York, 1962 and *Beyond the Couch: Dialogues in Teaching and Learning Psychoanalysis in Groups,* by A. Wolf *et al.,* New York, Science House, 1970. For readers interested in further elaboration, not only are the books recommended, but so too are the papers listed in the bibliography at the end of this chapter.

There are other volumes in this field by clinicians whose experience is at some variance from those presented here, but whose views deserve serious consideration. Among these are S. R. Slavson's *Analytic Group Psychotherapy,* Columbia University Press, New York, 1950; S. H. Foulkes and E. J. Anthony's *Group Psychotherapy: The Psychoanalytic Approach,* Penguin Books, London, 1957; Bohdan Wassell's *Group Psychoanalysis,* Philosophical Library, New York, 1959; Norman Locke's *Group Psychoanalysis,* New York University Press, 1961; S. R. Slavson's *A Textbook in Analytic Group Psychotherapy,* International Universities Press, New York, 1964; and Helen Durkin's *The Group in Depth,* International Universities Press, New York, 1964. These suggested "other readings" do not represent the writer's point of view, but since they are written by experienced clinicians in the same field, the reader should be aware that heterogeneous theory and practice prevail not only in individual psychoanalysis but inevitably in psychoanalysis in groups as well. And since the writer is a spokesman for diversity, he believes these "other voices" should be heard.

SUMMARY AND CONCLUSION

Psychoanalysis in groups can be effective because patients become aware of one another's appropriate needs and develop increasing ability to understand and cope with their transferential distortions. Patients achieve in groups a remarkable ability for mutual exploration and understanding and for multilaterally reparative behavior. In the group, interaction is examined as it occurs, not just between patient and analyst but among co-patients as well.

The psychoanalyst in groups has been up to now the student, the pupil of the individual analyst. Developments in group analysis over the last thirty-five years may now improve and intensify individual analytic treatment. If individual analysts would acquaint themselves with the value of group interaction, of socialization, of engagement with personalities other than the analyst, of resolving hierarchical and horizontal vector difficulties, of working through compulsive preoccupations with rank and status, of multiple interaction in attaining intrapsychic gains, these phenomena would receive the attention they deserve–even in the course of individual analysis.

It is of some interest to set down some of the integral characteristics that determine the content and process of group as compared with individual analysis. The numbers of patients in the group provide for the simultaneous presence of vertical and horizontal dimensions. The analyst is experienced as more distant and co-patients as more accessible. Transference reactions are aimed at both the leader and at fellow-patients. Transferences in the group are less uniform and less entrenched than in the dyad. The number of provocative members in a group makes it more difficult at the outset to detect what is a reasonable response from what is irrational in the course of the manifold interactions. Despite this, the excitation of feeling, whether positive or negative, healthy or sick, provides each patient many opportunities for experiencing assurance and insight. In the group, there are both more securities in reality and hazards in unreality than in the analytic dyad. Still, the leader's distortions are more acutely examined by his assembled patients. And the possibility of the therapist's acting out is generally excluded in a group setting.

The multilateral character of transference becomes more obvious in a group. The affective intensity of transferences among patients is more easily tolerated than is one-to-one transference because its power is lessened when aimed at a fellow-patient. Occasionally, lateral transferences bind patients together and become a force that keeps patients in treatment. Such intense feeling for an individual analyst might induce an analysand to flee therapy or to feel helpless or terrified. In the group, interaction is engaged in by the patients, and the therapist can maintain a somewhat detached but active observing role. It is not easy for a patient to isolate himself in a group, because others push for activity, reactivity, and mutual responses. As a result, relationships become transferentially intensified. The occasion for more provocation of pathology as well as analytic therapy coexist because of the interactive intensity in the group. Following such interpersonal interaction, analytic examination of unconscious processes provides insight.

No one patient monopolizes analytic attention. Examination of intrapsychic material follows the interaction of dyads, triads, etc. No member is expected to play only one kind of role, to subscribe to a group dynamic or to be homogeneous with his group. The patient is so encouraged to engage in noncompulsive and liberating activities that he is finally free to leave the group.

CHRONOLOGIC BIBLIOGRAPHY

Wolf, A.: The psychoanalysis of groups. *American Journal of Psychotherapy, 3:*525, 1949; *4:*16, 1950.

Wolf, A.: On the irrelevance of group psychotherapy in mass conflict. *Group Psychotherapy, 5:*78, 1952.

Wolf, A., et al.: The psychoanalysis of groups: The analyst's objections. *International Journal of Group Psychotherapy, 2:*221, 1952.

Wolf, A., et al.: Sexual acting out in the psychoanalysis of groups. *International Journal of Group Psychotherapy, 4:*369, 1954.

118   *Basic Approaches to Group Psychotherapy*

Wolf, A., and Schwartz, E. K.: The psychoanalysis of groups: Implications for education. *International Journal of Social Psychiatry, 1:*9, 1955.

Wolf, A., and Schwartz, E. K.: El Psicoanalisis de Grupos: Consecuencias para la Educacion. *Criminalia* (Mexico, D.F.), *22:*(2), 70-75, 1956.

Wolf, A.: Code of ethics of group psychotherapists: Comments. *Group Psychotherapy, 10:*221, 1957.

Schwartz, E. K., and Wolf, A.: Psychoanalysis in groups: Combined therapy. Paper read at the Postgraduate Center for Psychotherapy, New York, November, 1957.

Durkin, H., Glatzer, H. T., Kadis, A. L., Wolf, A., and Hulse, W. C.: Acting out in group psychotherapy: A panel discussion. *American Journal of Psychotherapy, 14:*87, 1958.

Wolf, A.: The advanced and terminal phases in group psychotherapy. In Berger, M. M., and Linden, M. E. (Eds.): *Proceedings of the Second Annual Institute of the American Group Psychotherapy Association,* 1958.

Schwartz, E. K., and Wolf, A.: Irrational trends in contemporary psychotherapy: Cultural correlates. *Psychoanalysis & Psychoanalytic Review, 45:*(1-2) 65, 1958.

Wolf, A., and Schwartz, E. K.: Psychoanalysis in groups: clinical and theoretic implications of the alternate meeting. *Acta Psychotherapy, 7* (Suppl.):540, 1959.

Wolf, A., and Schwartz, E. K.: Psychoanalysis in groups: The role of values. *American Journal of Psychoanalysis, 19:*37, 1959.

Schwartz, E. K., and Wolf, A.: Psychoanalysis in groups: The mystique of group dynamics. In Stokvis, B. (Ed.): *Topical Problems of Psychotherapy, II,* Basel, S. Karger, 1960.

Wolf, A.: Discussion of S. H. Foulkes: The application of group concepts to the treatment of the individual in the group. In Stokvis, B. (Ed.): *Topical Problems of Psychotherapy, II.* Basel, S. Karger, 1960.

Wolf, A., and Schwartz, E. K.: Psychoanalysis in groups: The alternate session. *American Imago, 17:*101, 1960.

Schwartz, E. K., and Wolf, A.: Psychoanalysis in groups: Some comparisons with individual analysis. *Journal of General Psychology, 64:*153, 1961.

Schwartz, E. K., and Wolf, A.: Psychoanalysis in groups: Resistance to its use. *American Journal of Psychotherapy, 17:*457, 1963.

Wolf, A., and Schwartz, E. K.: Psychoanalysis in groups: As creative process. *American Journal of Psychoanalysis, 24:*(1) 46, 1964.

Schwartz, E. K., and Wolf, A.: On countertransference in group psychotherapy. *Journal of Psychology, 57:*131, 1964.

Wolf, A.: Psychoanalytic group therapy. In Masserman , J.: *Current Psychiatric Therapies, IV.* New York, Grune & Stratton, 1964.

Wolf, A.: Short-term group psychotherapy. In Wolberg, L. R.: *Short-Term Psychotherapy*. New York, Grune & Stratton, 1965.

Wolf, A., and Schwartz, E. K.: Psicoanalisis en Grupos, *14th Coleccion Ciencias del Hombre*, editorial, Pax-Mexico, Libreria Carlos Cesarman, S. A., Rep. Argentina 9, Mexico 1, D.F., 1967.

Wolf, A.: Group psychotherapy. In Freedman, A. M., and Kaplan, H. I. (Eds.): *Comprehensive Textbook of Psychiatry*. Baltimore, Williams & Wilkins, 1967.

Wolf, A.: Psychoanalysis in groups. In Gazda, G. M. (Ed.): *Basic Approaches to Group Psychotherapy and Group Counseling*. Springfield, Ill., Charles C Thomas, 1968.

Wolf, A.: The discriminating use of feeling in group psychotherapy. In Riess, B. F. (Ed.): *New Directions in Mental Health*. New York, Grune & Stratton, 1968.

Schwartz, E. K., and Wolf, A.: The interpreter in group therapy: Conflict resolution through negotiation. *Archives of General Psychiatry, 18:*186, 1968.

Wolf, A., *et al.:* Training in psychoanalysis in groups without face to face contact. *American Journal of Psychotherapy, 23:*488, 1969.

Wolf, A., *et al.: Beyond the Couch: Dialogues in Teaching and Learning Psychoanalysis in Groups*. New York, Science House, 1970.

CHAPTER VI

EXISTENTIAL PSYCHIATRY AND GROUP PSYCHOTHERAPY[1]

BASIC PRINCIPLES

Thomas Hora

A THERAPY GROUP is a structured life situation designed for the study and treatment of the diseased human being. The group situation illuminates man's mode of being in a dimensional way and provides for a deeper understanding of the individual through the quality of his presence.

The group-psychotherapeutic participation is a living, dynamic process involving all members, including the therapist. In therapy groups the members function not as samples of various psychic mechanisms or disease entities, but as people with specific ways of expressing life and specific ways of dealing and communicating with the environment; that is, as individually characteristic modes of "being there" (Binswanger, 1942; Hora, 1959b). Thus, in fact, the therapy group represents a microcosmos or a segment of the world, and as such it is an existential encounter situation for all participants. It is a crossroads at which eight or more people meet and in this meeting reveal to each other and discover for themselves their particular modes of being-in-this-world (Heidegger, 1953). When they part, the course of their progression through life is often altered to an appreciable degree.

As a personality, man is mostly a product of his family background and his sociocultural environment. As a human being, however, he is an existential phenomenon in terms of his unique characteristics among the living creatures of this world. Survival,

---

1. Parts of this paper were published in the *American Journal of Psychoanalysis*. They are included here with permission of the editor.

growth and fulfillment require man to adapt himself to his fellow-man, his family, to social, cultural and economic conditions. However, beyond all this he is inescapably faced with the necessity of adjusting to the Fundamental Order of Existence as well. Which means that in order to be healthy, man must live in harmony with the ontological realities of his existence.

The objectives of existential psychotherapy point beyond personality integration toward "ontic integration" (Hora, 1958b). A significant aspect of this therapeutic process consists of liberating the patient's cognitive and creative potentialities, which are usually blocked by his defense systems. The awakening of the capacity for *creative perception and response* enables the patient to commune with his fellowman in a meaningful (dialogic) way, and beyond that, opens the door to realization of the transcendental (that is, ontological) aspects of existence. This realization appears to be necessary for man to come to terms with his finiteness and thus find relief from the omnipresent existential anxiety, or dread of nonbeing.

The aim of existential psychiatry is, therefore, to broaden the psychodynamic and sociodynamic viewpoints and arrive at an integrated image of man which includes the contributions of phenomenological anthropology and fundamental ontology. These schools of thought illuminate the human being and his existence in an encompassing and deeply meaningful way. Among the significant contributions of these schools, many have direct bearing on psychiatry in general and psychotherapy in particular, for instance: the problem of estrangement, temporality, intentionality, existential anxiety, human values and various attitudes toward existence. The meaningful realization of these existential coordinates provides the participants of the therapy group with a broader and deeper consciousness of the structure of their existence.

OBSTACLES TO AUTHENTIC GROUP PARTICIPATION

Authentic group participation, i.e., genuine being-in-the-group, is only possible under conditions of *openness, receptivity, and responsiveness*. These human capacities are more often than not thwarted, distorted and blocked to various degrees. The removal of these obstacles to cognition, to authentic interhuman communication and communion is an essential feature of the existential group psychotherapeutic endeavor. Man is to be liberated from the prison of his *idios cosmos* (private world of ideas) and enabled to live in the *koinos cosmos* (shared world of communing). Only here can his essential humaneness come to fruition. The prison of his *idios cosmos* is built on various cognitive and conative disturbances acquired in the course of growing up under the combined influences of the environment and the inherent human inclinations. These result in the so-called "misguided modes of being-in-the-world."

Misguided modes of being-in-the-world reveal themselves as "contact disturbances" and "existential frustration." Man suffers from inadequate relationships with his fellowmen and from inadequate realization of his inherent potentialities. While the various aspects of contact disturbances are well known within the framework of traditional psychoanalytic schools of thought, Existentialism makes its contribution in illuminating the human being from the standpoint of his inherent ontic inclinations, which often cause him to be in disharmony with existence.

The following paragraphs contain a small sampling of certain phenomena of existence which have immediate relevancy to group psychotherapy, inasmuch as they constitute some of the more frequently encountered obstacles to genuine being-in-the-group, that is, to free and authentic group participation.

ESTRANGEMENT

One of the predicaments of man is the peculiarity that his conceptual or abstract thinking tends to be dissociated from his experiential perceptiveness to such an extent that his reasoning power may actually hamper his capacities to experience, perceive and cognize what is. A so-called open mind is difficult to attain because it entails the capacity for temporary suspension of intentional (calculating) thinking in favor of heightened receptivity. Heidegger points up the difference between two modes of thinking which he terms *das vorstellende Denken* and *das andenkende Denken*.

This inclination often results in the phenomenon of estrangement or alienation, where the experiential aspects of cognition are dissociated and the individual may, for instance, seek to arrive at an understanding of his feelings through deductive reasoning. This is illustrated by a patient who, while sitting quietly in a group of rather heavy cigarette smokers, remarked in a casual way, "I must feel hostile towards smokers because I keep losing matches." Instead of experiencing the truth of his condition in the situation, he was deductively being rational about it.

C. G. Jung is known to have said that modern man could be compared to someone who looks out of his apartment window on the twentieth floor and discovers that the house he lives in starts at the tenth floor. Below, there is nothing. The alienated individual is a stranger to himself and to his fellowman. The more he strives to bridge the gap between his thoughts and his experience, the greater it becomes because his efforts are primarily intellectual. (This, by the way, is one of the main pitfalls of introspection and self-analysis.) He is a stranger amidst his fellowmen because he is unable to experience himself as authentically in contact with others. Minkowski speaks of the loss of vital contact *(La perte du contact vital)*, which characterizes modern man, who is dissociated from his existential core. Karen Horney made some important contributions to the elucidation of this problem.

Estrangement makes it difficult for a person to be-in-a-group. Such a person tends to be a nonparticipating pseudo-observer, not an actual member.

PRESENCE

Another obstacle to full and free group participation is the propensity to cling to the past and to be unduly preoccupied with the future. Consequently, the capacity to experience the present and respond to it is hampered. As one patient put it, "Before the group sessions I keep thinking what I will say when I come here, and after the group sessions I keep ruminating over what I have said while I was sitting here. Inside I feel like I am running and cannot stop." Such is the dilemma of a person who finds it difficult to be in full perceptual contact with the lived moment. His mode of being-in-the-world is characterized by a disturbed temporality, that is, he lives in unceasing conflict with time.

Such a person may find it difficult to actually be-in-the-group. He may find himself repeatedly out of step with the context of the moment. He may repeatedly drift off into worrying about the future or may tend to divert the attention of the group from what is to what was. Conflict with time has its interhuman repercussions and is revealed in the group as an agitated mode of absent-mindedness and distractibility. The person whose mode of group participation reveals a disturbed temporality is often overly concerned with becoming. Such striving to become underlies a preoccupation with what was in order to change what will be in accordance with how it should be. The desire to become dislocates existence by interfering with the awareness of what is from moment to moment. Since existence is a process, man cannot really understand himself once and for all, only from moment to moment. Knowing oneself must not be confused with knowing about oneself. Transformation and healing can only occur through man's knowing himself. This entails a continuous awareness of what is from moment to moment. Living in harmony with the stream of time abolishes the problem of temporality. Man and time fuse. In this at-oneness the truth of oneself as process is revealed. Truth liberates and transforms man into that being which he really is.

INTENTIONALITY

Closely related to the problem of being present to the present is the problem of intentionality. This frequently occurring problem could be called "the dilemma of planned or intended experiencing." By living according to the Cartesian principle, *Cogito, ergo sum,* man seeks to experience his thoughts. He plans in his mind the experiences which are to come to him. By putting thought before perception, man of necessity falsifies reality and blocks it from reaching him in its full scope. As a consequence, he finds himself in a state of inner emptiness and hunger for experiences which he tries to satisfy through ever-increasing efforts at feeling what he thinks he would like to feel or should be feeling. Patients sometimes ask, "What should I be feeling, doctor?"

The intention to experience something makes it impossible to experience what really is. The blunting of the capacity to experience can conceivably lead to such affective impoverishment and inward sense of emptiness that it may cause him to resort to violent attempts at providing himself with craved-for experiences. This may be an important aspect of sadism, masochism, manipulativeness and even criminal acting out.

One patient whom the group members called "The Thinker" used to sit in her chair, looking seductively at the therapist and biting her fist in a fierce and disquieting way. Her standard complaint was that she could not "gratify her needs." Her intellectuality and intentionality was like a hard shell which stood in the way of tasting the flavor of life in free and reverent receptivity.

In another instance, a colleague one day confessed that he used to come to the session with the intention of taking home a "few pounds of psychotherapy." The intention to acquire knowledge, to learn, to remember, to accept or not accept, to believe or disbelieve, to agree or disagree, are epistemological barriers to the open mind so essential for understanding to happen.

EXISTENTIAL ANXIETY

Man is the being who can be conscious of his existence. This consciousness presupposes the realization of the potentiality of non-existence. Existential anxiety is an omnipresent aspect of human life and is dealt with either by humble awareness or by attempts at various and manifold escape mechanisms and defensive strivings.

One of the more frequent escape mechanisms is the avoidance of experiencing through flight into intellectuality. This in turn leads to estrangement and the cognitive disturbances mentioned above.

The striving for a sense of security of being drives man to reach out in a grasping and clinging fashion for countless possessions of objects, people, systems, concepts, ideas. He invests these with illusory importance and security values. He tends to objectify people and living creatures for the same end. That is, he wishes to cling to them as illusory protective devices against existential anxiety, as if saying, "I possess, therefore I am safe."

He hangs on to his thoughts and beliefs as onto straps in a subway train, and tends to view the straps to which others cling as inferior and unreal. Anyone who challenges the validity of his thinking or the value of his possessions tends to mobilize existential anxiety and may elicit hostile defensiveness.

The tendency to cling to one's thoughts and beliefs for security is certainly one of the human reasons of conflict between ideologies, schools of thought and frames of references, whether political, religious, scientific, social, economic or psychoanalytic.

Needless to say, such defensive strivings cripple man's existence by robbing him of his freedom and creative spontaneity. Seeking to escape from the dread of losing his life, man lives in dread of losing his defenses. The more he clings to them, the more he becomes immobilized by them. Finally that which he clings to clings to him.

Such a tragically paradoxical dilemma was expressed by one successful businessman suffering from coronary heart disease and high blood pressure in the following way, "I know that my life is a 'rat race' and it is killing me, but I am afraid to stop because I might become a nobody and die." Then he added, "It looks like fear of death is driving me to commit suicide."

ENCROACHMENT

The combination of so-called dependent and domineering, or passive and aggressive tendencies in the same person can create severe interhuman contact disturbances, social anxiety and psychosomatic conditions. What appears as a problem of domination and dependency is here understood as a problem of the tendency to encroach on existence. Domination is the encroachment on the existence of others. Passivity and dependency may be viewed as encroachment on the existence of one's self. In either case, man suffers existential guilt which tends to become manifest in the form of embarrassment and social anxiety.

In group situations, the encroaching person tends to alternate between the supine (feet on the table) position and aggressive intent, leaning forward in his chair. In his manner of speech, he tends to alternate between hard, hammer-blow, staccato expressions and whining, "bellyaching" speech. He is alternately boastful and complaining—or both simultaneously. He is either over-assertive or yielding and timid. His face may have hard, aggressive lines, while in his eyes there may be softness. He may feel guilty if he is aggressive and ashamed of his timidity. He may fear asserting himself and be afraid not to assert himself. He may be afraid to be outspoken and afraid to be reticent. If he speaks, he may be afraid of being considered obtrusive and boastful. If he is silent, he may be afraid of being considered stupid, timid, shy, anxious, ignorant. He may feel himself caught in a double bind. Whichever way he moves, he is liable to bring embarrassment or disaster upon himself. He may finally avoid meeting people–he may withdraw from his friends and limit his existence to a mimimum.

The encroaching person has considerable difficulty in the group. His contact disturbances tend to be maximal; therefore he may require a great deal of preliminary elucidation, preferably in individual treatment.

HUMAN VALUES

As long as man is in throes of existential anxiety, his ethics and morality are of necessity artificial and based on discipline, self-abnegation or hypocrisy. Man's defensive preoccupation with security, status, power and permanence will unavoidably drive him in the direction of egocentricity. Consequently, selfishness, greed, possessiveness, exploitativeness, coerciveness, dependency, domination, parasitism, ambition, vanity, hunger for power and influence, fame and popularity remain problems regardless of moral codes, good intentions or discipline.

The group situation invariably highlights the ethical conflict of the individual in his pathetic struggle to reconcile his sense of moral responsibility with his egocentric defensive needs. The problem of authenticity of being points to the significance of values in human existence in general and in psychopathology in particular. In general, it can be said that distorted human values are to be found in most psychopathological conditions. In a paper entitled "Group Psychotherapy, Human Values and Mental Health" (Hora, 1958a), it was pointed out that sound human values are an inseparable aspect of mental health and that the process of personality integration through the medium of group psychotherapy provides ample evidence that positive principles of ethics and morality are integral to mental health.

The problem of human values is closely associated with the peculiarity of the human condition in general. The human condition as such is characterized by the fact that man is cast into this world and removed from it by forces beyond his control, therefore beyond his responsibility. Yet for the duration of his life he is charged with the task of making the best of his given potentialities. From an ontological standpoint, man has two freedoms: the freedom to fulfill his potentialities and the freedom to fail to fulfill them. If he fails to fulfill his given potentialities he may experience existential guilt.

As for human values, they too are mostly imposed upon man in his formative years by his environment. Man may not be responsible for having acquired wrong values, yet he is responsible and suffers the consequences if he keeps them. It is his responsibility to change his wrong values and adopt healthy ones. In addition to all this, there is a natural propensity for man to submit to group pressures, to deny his inner reality and to conform to social mores. In Riesman's (1950) words, man tends to become "other-oriented," thus losing contact with himself and sinking into unauthenticity.

It is interesting to note that in general there are three types of unauthentic modes of existence. There are the believers, the non-believers and the skeptics, or those who tend to agree, those who tend to disagree and those who like to contend. The believer asserts that he believes and thereby avoids coming in contact with truth. The non-believer asserts his unbelief and withdraws from facing the truth. The skeptic asserts his doubts and ignores the truth. To illustrate, let us suppose that someone would say there is an invisible power active in every body of water. This power is called buoyancy. It can sustain a man and save him from drowning. The believer would believe this assertion, but his belief would not prevent him from drowning. The non-believer would disbelieve, the skeptic would doubt, but both would be at a similar disadvantage. The unauthentic man tends to sink in more ways than one. The authentic individual, however, would neither believe, nor disbelieve, nor remain skeptical. He would neither agree, nor disagree, nor contend. His communications would be dialogic rather than argumentatively contentious. He would be forthright in stating whether or not he has understood the truth concerning the above assertion. In other words, the authentic individual lives in constant relation to truth, rather than personal preferences and opinions.

TRANSFERENCE AND NONTRANSFERENCE

It is sometimes asserted that existential psychiatry neglects transference factors and pays more attention to nontransference factors. However, from the standpoint of existential psychotherapy, the concern with nontransference factors appears to be a mistake similar to the preoccupation with transference factors, for in either case one would fall prey to the self-defeating tendency of studying human beings in parts or in aspects only. A person who is taken apart becomes an object. An object is not a living being. The sum total of parts of a human being does not add up to a whole human being. Scientific objectification is painful to the patient and defeats all endeavors to understand him.

If the issue of transference is considered, it can be said that transference is the misuse, avoidance, misunderstanding, misinterpretation, falsification, denial or unawareness of the reality of a current situation. Furthermore, transference is personal history. To see transference in a person is to see primarily his historical conditioning, rather than the human being as he really is. The analyst or group psychotherapist whose attention is centered on transference factors may tend to objectify his patient in accordance with a particular pseudoscientific bias. Instead of a forest, he may see only certain trees twisted in particular ways by some environmental or other influences in the distant past. Such partial and limited perspectives have their validity and usefulness in specialized areas of scientific research, especially in relation to the object world. But when it comes to the understanding of human beings, a holistic mode of perception, cognition, understanding and response is needed.

The existential encounter is an event where the patient as a whole, that is, as a "being-in-the-world," is revealed to the therapist by way of the phenomenological mode of cognition.

What is the phenomenological mode of cognition? It may be described as the unbiased, open-minded understanding of another as an existent from moment to moment. Why from moment to moment? Because man is an existential process. Therefore he cannot really be known once and for all. Neither can man know himself once and for all. As mentioned before, knowing oneself must not be confused with knowing about oneself. The phenomenological mode of cognition opens up to human consciousness the loving mode of knowledge. It reveals to man the "realm of Love-Intelligence" (Hora, 1961).

If we carefully consider that which in traditional psychoanalysis is called insight, we discover that it is actually hindsight, which means knowing oneself as one was in order to change oneself in accordance with certain mentally projected standards. Now all this at times may lead to a form of psychopathology which could be called the "syndrome of the self-made man." Man who "makes" himself healthy may become sicker than he was, for health cannot be made. It comes into being when the truth of oneself as process is understood.

In the therapy groups, patients reveal themselves to each other and to the therapist in accordance with their particular modes of being-in-the-world. This revelation is a continuous process of elucidation of the ongoing stream of events without causal, genetic, historical, teleological or other considerations. The continuous awareness and elucidation of what is happening contains all the above-mentioned aspects of being human; that is, it contains all transference as well as nontransference aspects of the participating individuals; but it transcends them all. Therefore special interpretations are not required. That which is speaks for itself, provided it is understood phenomenologically rather than interpreted in accordance with certain theoretical presuppositions. That which is understood needs no interpretation. That which is interpreted is seldom understood.

THE DYNAMISM OF ASSUMPTIONS

Mental assumptions are acquired and evolved concepts, habits of thought, patterns of thinking, memories, memory traces, mental constructs, ideas and ideologies, theories, opinions and convictions, etc., which make up man's sense of being a self and having a mind of his own. All assumptions are necessarily of the past. They represent the past facing the present and the future. Assumptions confront the present and the future with a definite reluctance, aversion, even dread, for every confrontation of the past with the present or the future spells the death of the past assumption. "We cannot step into the same river twice." ✓

Since man is inclined to identify himself with his mental content, it usually becomes precious to him and he wishes to keep it alive. Thus arises the battle for the validation and confirmation of the viability and reality of the past in the present and in the future. Man wishes to make the present and the future to conform to his assumptions, and thus, by stopping the flow of time, create a sense of permanence.

Assumptions then reveal a certain dynamism which impels man to engage in a futile but energetic endeavor to confirm the validity and reality of that which is not valid anymore and perchance never was.

Things are never as they should be. In his desperation, the man of assumptions often tries to compromise. He likes to call this adjustment and adaptation, or getting along in the world. However, this tends to create a strenuous life of uneasy balances, subject to frequent upsets, frictions, disappointments, tensions and anxieties. This is a world devoid of love and true understanding. It is a world of calculative thinking and interpersonal manipulation. Here friendships and group life are founded on the tenuous comfort which the sharing of similar assumptions produces. The man of assumptions experiences severe discomfort and anxiety in the presence of clashing opinions. Assumptions are forever in struggle for survival, since there is an underlying awareness of their purely conceptual, i.e., fictitious character. Interpersonal conflicts are here revealed as "frictions of differing fictions."

The inner dynamism of assumptions then manifests an urge to confirm the reality of these assumptions, to defend them against challenging statements and views and to contend against the validity and reality of differing assumptions. But above all, assumptions are forever in conflict with what really is. That means that they produce *impairments of cognition* in man and a sense of *disharmony with the world*. The dilemma of the man of assumptions was expressed by a Zen Master the following way: "The past is gone, the future is unknowable and the present you cannot grasp."

The man of assumptions is very sensitive to people whose assumptions represent a threat to his own. He tends to become a keen observer. He is not perceptive, he is sensitive. However, this faculty is mainly in the service of defending himself against possible challenges which would force him to doubt the validity of his own assumptions. He tends to experience this as danger of annihilation, for he confuses his own existence with the reality of his beliefs.

Anxiety is the dread of discovering the fact that the self as a set of assumptions is dead because it has no reality in the present (Hora, 1962a). Interpersonal anxiety is the dread of discovering that what seems to be so alive in one's mind is really dead. This brings to mind one of the most mysterious utterances of Jesus: "Follow me and let the dead bury their dead."

Much of human suffering stems from the clashing of preconceived notions. Human conflicts are essentially ideological in nature.

Since assumptions are continually in quest of self-confirmation, they impel the individual to seek agreement and the concurrence of other people. Thus it arises that people who harbor assumptions cannot "let-be" (Heidegger, 1953); that is they cannot respect other people's freedom to harbor different beliefs. The inner dynamism of assumptions is such as to press for acceptance. As long as God, religion, faith and knowledge are but assumptions, they tend to make man a proselytizer, a propagandist and the like.

Faith and knowledge which are not conceptual but are *existential realizations* make man free of the need to convince and to convert. Such a man is capable of love for he is free to cognize and understand the truth of what really is (Hora, 1962b). His sense of assurance comes from a cognitive at-one-ment with reality (Krishnamurti, 1956).

The solution of the problem which assumptions pose lies in the recognition of their conceptual and historic nature. The alternative is the *loving mode of being-in-the-world*. This means an absolute and reverent concern with the truth of what is from moment to moment. Love transcends the epistemic barrier which assumptions create in human consciousness.

A full understanding of the dynamism of assumptions is of obvious significance for mental health in general, but is particularly meaningful for the psychotherapist, both in dyadic and group situations, for he must be capable not only of transcending his own epistemic barriers, but also those of his patients. *Cognitive transcendence* is a special capacity which enables one to enter into meaningful communion with people in spite of the dynamic pressures and obstacle which differing mental assumptions tend to exert.

THE TRANSPERSONAL PERSPECTIVE

In attempting to convey something of the nature of existential psychotherapy, one usually encounters some difficulties of a conceptual, semantic, philosophical and epistemological nature. Perhaps the greatest difficulty arises, however, from the fact that the existential psychotherapist is required to meet his patient on a different ground, i.e., he must utilize a different mode of cognition and view his patient from a different perspective than is customary in the natural sciences or in much of everyday life.

Generally speaking, under ordinary circumstances man is inclined to view the world around him either from a subjective or an objective standpoint, or from an intellectual-analytic-interpretative standpoint. The subjectivist is concerned with the question, "How do I feel about what is?" The objectivist asks, "What is it?" The intellectual-analytic interpreter asks "Why is it?" or "What is it for?"

The subjectivist is inevitably egotistical; he is involved with his own feelings and sensations, which he calls personal experiences. The objectivist tends to be reifying and materialistic; he considers himself rational, logical, objective, scientific. The intellectual is inquisitive and knowledgeable; he relies on theories, frames of reference, ideologies; he is an adherent of schools of thought, a member of groups, a partisan. More often than not, however, these three modes of relating to the world are intermixed in the same individuals, with one or the other mode taking precedence.

To illustrate, let us take an example from psychotherapeutic practice. A middle-aged man comes for help for obesity, a lifelong problem which has yielded neither to somatic nor psychoanalytic therapies. The phenomenological analysis of his mode-of-being-in-the-world reveals a disguised concern with being a "big man," towering over others physically, mentally and emotionally so that he would be "immovable." He seeks a situation of unassailable security and advantage in life, and he has succeeded in shaping himself into a Goliath.

The subjectively responding therapist might point out that the patient makes him feel small and helpless; the patient in turn probably would say to himself, "I am glad to hear that; that makes me feel good." The objective therapist might concern himself with the patient's nutrition and eating habits. He may even recommend a diet and drugs. The danger here is that should the patient be induced to lose weight, he may experience this as being robbed of his power, security, or greatness, and it is conceivable that as a consequence he could develop a depressive reaction or a compensatory megalomaniacal psychosis.

It is therefore very important that a patient be helped to lose the meaning of his disease before he loses the symptom. This may very well throw light on the perennial problem of side effects and secondary complications following therapeutic interventions and treatment procedures where patients were treated as objects.

The analytic therapist would be inclined to make psychodynamic interpretations on the basis of historico-causal-genetic explorations. However, causality and meaning are not identical, and causal-genetic interpretations seldom have therapeutic value, because cause-and-effect thinking is too shallow and narrowly circumscribed. It fails to comprehend existence as a meaningful and meaning-oriented process. Furthermore, seeking reasons and causes only results in finding excuses which tend to impede therapeutic progress rather than enhance it. As the French put it, *On ne guérit pas en souvenant, mais on se souvient en guérissant—* One does not heal by remembering, but one remembers as a result of healing.

From an existential standpoint, problems and discordant conditions are consequences of misdirected concerns. Therefore, strictly speaking, problems cannot be solved. The endeavor to solve problems is a misdirected concern in itself and tends to compound the initial problem. For instance, people try to iron out their difficulties by discussing them at length, while paradoxically, they are getting more and more embroiled in conflict. Debates and dialectics tend to compound problems rather than solve them. Nor is it wise, however, to ignore problems, withdraw from them or avoid facing up to them. Problems are resolved when misdirected concerns are corrected. Erroneous or misdirected concerns are corrected by being lost, but to be lost, they first must be found; i.e., phenomenologically perceived and elucidated. Only after they are thus found can they be turned away from. False concerns are lost by a shift of attention toward more wholesome concerns. When false concerns vanish from consciousness, i.e., lose their personal significance, they cease to generate problems, complications and existential crises. Wholesome concerns–a basic element being a transpersonal perspective–lead to wholesome attitudes, and these in turn result in harmonious life experiences and mental health.

In the case cited, for instance, the existential approach would be neither subjective, nor objective, nor analytical–it would be transpersonal. The existential therapist would endeavor to discern the meaning and character of the patient's mode-of-being-in-the-world as it is revealed in the psychotherapeutic encounter. When the meaning of a symptom is phenomenologically elucidated, the patient discovers that his suffering is a consequence of misdirected concerns and erroneous assumptions about existence; he then becomes vitally interested in finding more wholesome concerns.

The general validity and significance of the transpersonal perspective can be illustrated further by considering parental attitudes. For example, should a father's attitude toward his daughter be a predominately subjective one, he will reveal a concern with how his own feelings are stimulated by his daughter. This could take on a variety of meanings, from mildly egocentric to the overtly seductive and incestuous. Should a father's attitude be an objective one, he might reduce his daughter to a "thing" by objectifying her, perhaps causing the daughter a loss of a sense of human worth. Finally, should the father be an intellectually inclined, analytically minded person, he might generate a great deal of anxiety, indecision and confusion by interpreting causal connections and motivations. The psychologizing perspective can engender a variety of tendencies from exaggerated intellectual self-preoccupations to self-conscious inhibitions, from loss of spontaneity conceivably all the way to catatonic rigidity or paranoid delusions.

The subjectivist parent tends to bring up selfish, hypochrondriacal, sexually overstimulated and hedonistic children. The objectivist parent often appears tyrannical, and his children tend to become recalcitrant and rebellious, while the analytical and psychologizing parent may well be a source of schizophrenic reactions in his family. *It is the loving parent who understands, for his concern is with beneficence.*

More often than not, man is quite confused about how to respond to life situations. He may attempt intermittently to be subjective, thus relying on his feelings and sensations; or objective, thus relying on his sensory perceptions; or analytical, thus relying on his preconceptions. Indeed, ordinarily unenlightened man seems to have a choice between these three erroneous modes of responding. This tends to create confusion, uncertainty, and not infrequently, a tendency to unintentional hypocrisy. This is a serious professional hazard often afflicting people in the social science fields, as well as so-called cured patients. It may be described as a predilection toward saying that one feels something, when actually one only thinks it or knows about it from books or lectures. For instance, it is not unusual to hear someone say, "I feel that this man has an Oedipus complex"–or "I feel that this patient relates himself to his wife on an anal sadistic level." Such involuntary hypocrisy indicates a failure to differentiate between what one knows and what one thinks, what one observes and what one feels. Yet personal integrity and clarity of communications are fundamental and must be of primary concern to all who would endeavor to foster mental health.

Another manifestation of unintended hypocrisy is the tendency to pretend interest but to pursue inquisitiveness. At first glance, the difference seems very slight, yet neglecting a clear differentiation, can have far-reaching consequences. To be interested is to love and revere; to be inquisitive, however, is to intrude, trespass, violate. This subtle difference constitutes the essence of the existential attitude, which is called "letting-be" and which allows the therapeutic process to proceed with a minimum of the so-called resistance phenomena.

It seems important, therefore, to realize that all three modes of cognition–subjective, objective, analytical–are in a sense pathogenic and inaccurate. Furthermore, the indiscriminate mixing of the three is incompatible with clear communication and harmonious living.

It is essential to discover a mode of cognition which is neither subjective nor objective nor analytical. This can be attained through the transpersonal perspective. The existential psychotherapist is not a participant observer, a nonparticipant interpreter, an empathizer or a sympathizer; he is an understander. He is a *clairiere de l'Existence,* one who sheds light on Existence. His is a perspective of love. Love is spoken of here as a mode-of-being-in-the-world and a mode of cognition.

Love as a mode of cognition is concerned with truth, with meaning and the unhindered unfolding of human potentialities. A loving man is concerned with participating in existence as a beneficial presence. Such love is neither personal nor interpersonal nor impersonal–it is transpersonal.

Wholesome human existence and mental health are here understood to be contingent on an epistemological principle which makes it possible for man to transcend his tendency toward calculative thinking, *das vorstellende Denken,* and become available to creative, inspired modes of thought, *das andenkende Denken.* The capacity to view the patient from a transpersonal perspective is basic to existential psychotherapy.

THE GROUP PROCESS

In considering patients from an existential standpoint, it is found that notwithstanding their diagnostic categories of psychopathology, they suffer from disturbed modes of being-in-the-world. In the group situation they are revealed as hampered in their capacities to communicate meaningfully with their fellow group members, and consequently they suffer both from a sense of isolation and from frequently recurring conflicts. They are further afflicted by a limited capacity for presence; that is, they are in conflict with time, with their own intentionalities, strivings, ethical codes and defensive attitudes.

Whenever two or more people meet, they affect each other significantly. Most of the impact which people have upon each other, however, remains below the surface of conscious awareness, or as the neurophysiologist J. C. Lilly (1957) put it, "There is evidence that the greatest part of our experience comes into us through paths unbeknownst to consciousness."

When a group of people meets, every participant is exposed to the impact of the sum total of all stimuli present. This total of stimuli is the content of the group atmosphere. This atmosphere is charged with affective currents. The nature of man's ties to his fellowman is largely affective (Hora, 1956). Perceptivity and communicativeness are essential features of human nature. Emotions are communicated through verbal, nonverbal, conscious and nonconscious channels. We even speak of emotional contagion as a group phenomenon.

An undifferentiated state of affective stimulation creates a need to organize this affect into thoughts. This is experienced as group tension. The participants experience an inner urge to do something. This results in a need to talk. Language here is used as a substitute action, serving the need to discharge inner tension. This (vicarious) use of language communicates little that is essential. It clarifies nothing. It is a verbal form of acting out, and as such it serves the purpose of tension reduction. This in turn makes it possible for the participants to avoid becoming aware of what they are really experiencing.

Whenever a group meets, certain basic phenomena are observable from the start. These are (1) the impact of the participants upon each other, (2) unspecified affective cross-currents, (3) a group atmosphere, (4) group tension, and (5) a certain pervasive anxiety.

After the initial tension is discharged and the anxiety relieved, there follows a stage of curiosity about each other. This curiosity does not serve the purpose of really understanding one another, but rather to compare notes and see how one "stacks up" in comparison with the others. Language is used here in a superficial, exploratory or concealing manner.

We see that right from the start the group members are primarily concerned with gratifying their own personal needs for tension reduction, even though they appear to be talking to each other and seemingly are interested in each other. This kind of duplicity or unauthenticity is so universal that few people give it a second thought. It is an accepted mode of social behavior. And yet this phenomenon is the first step in the direction of gradual self-estrangement. It is the first contact with the whirlpool of unauthenticity which threatens man throughout his life.

Patients find it very difficult to refrain from the usual ways of discharging their tensions. One patient remarked, "I feel like an overcharged soda bottle about to pop." This statement is an example of how a patient begins to become aware of what he is experiencing. This is the first step in the direction of broadening of his consciousness into the proprioceptive sphere of awareness. Having given expression to the truth of his inner experience, the patient finds relief from tension. One patient expressed it the following way: "The group is the only place where I feel truly alive because everywhere else I am mostly lying." By this she meant to say that in her social and professional life she is only aware of her thoughts and strivings and there is a disharmony between what she is usually saying and feeling. It appears that language is a hidden door which can lead either to alienation or to integrated authentic existence, depending on how it is used.

Essentially, group members act and talk in pursuit of their needs to escape existential anxiety. This leads unavoidably to conflict between divergent needs. The conflict is accompanied by neurotic anxiety which, phenomenologically, is an awareness of the inner disharmony between thought, feeling, experience and striving. Thus in therapy groups man is revealed as being buffeted between his need to escape from existential anxiety and his need to avoid neurotic anxiety. What balance he strikes or how he goes about coping with his human predicament is quite specific to every individual and constitutes his special mode of being-in-the-world.

This mode of being-in-the-world includes all possible mechanisms of defense, diagnostic categories or nosologic entities of psychopathology as part of a general adaptation to life. The group situation illuminates the significance of Martin Buber's dialogue. For the incapacity for genuine, reciprocal, nonmanipulative communication among the members of the group is indicative of their failure to come to terms with their human condition.

It was described above how inner tension drives the group

members to use language in an unauthentic, essentially noncommunicative way as a form of verbal acting out for the purpose of avoiding awareness of what is experienced. Existential anxiety drives the group members to become preoccupied with one another as objects. This leads to a use of language which again is essentially a form of acting out in a manipulative sense. That is, under the impact of existential anxiety, the members are driven to seek mastery over the object world, and thus they attempt to master each other by a verbal form of manipulation and probing. For instance, one patient said to another in a group, "When you look at me, I feel like an automobile engine which needs to be repaired."

The human situation reveals itself in the therapy groups as a rather complex problem of adaptation, requiring man to fit himself into a world which he is thrown in under rather difficult conditions. As one patient put it, "Life is like being in jail, sentenced to die. Trying to escape makes things worse, you keep hurting yourself in the fruitless effort. There is no way out. I wish I could believe in God and trust Him that all this has some sense and purpose. Then perhaps I could accept my situation." Another patient said, "Here we are sitting in a circle, facing one another, yet we are keenly aware of our separateness. It is almost like being in solitary confinement. My eyes are windows through which I am peering at the world, wishing to get out of myself and fuse with everything that is outside of me to escape aloneness."

Every group session becomes an experience of looking into a multifaceted psychological mirror and discovering more and more details about one's mode of being or failing to be-in-this-world due to a variety of defensive attitudes and strivings evolved in the course of a lifetime.

In the main, the group psychotherapy process could be vaguely considered as consisting of a phase of self-discovery, followed by a gradually increasing amount of self-understanding, which then yields to a phase of experimentation in learning to let go of the defensive strivings. This phase is experienced as rather anxiety-laden. Success in learning to accept one's anxiousness is an important step in the direction of accepting one's ontic condition, and is rewarded by a new phase of discovering oneself as being-

in-the-world in an authentic fashion. This may at times have phenomenological concomitants. For instance, one patient said, "Willingness to be afraid has freed me of my fear and suddenly I noticed that people are three-dimensional." In other words, this patient discovered that her previous existence took place in a two-
dimensional world. Spatiality is a phenomenological coordinate
of human existence, as has been described by Binswanger (1942).

In the therapy group, patients become increasingly aware of the
difference between talking to people and communing with people
(Hora, 1957). Furthermore, they discover the difference between
knowing about oneself and understanding oneself.

Since the group is conceived of as a microcosmos and an arena
for an existential encounter, all conceptualizations, historical references and outside issues are considered as of secondary significance and interactions are viewed in the content of here-and-now.
The focus is on the creative understanding of what is (Krishnamurti, 1956) from moment to moment and from heart to heart;
this means an increasing awareness of the unfolding of the existential process in each participant.

While the group setting is a structured one in terms of time,
place, number of participants, circular arrangement of chairs and
so forth, the group process itself in unstructured except by the impact of the therapist's presence which unavoidably and very meaningfully focuses on certain values reflected by his mode of being-
in-the-world. These values are invariably and unavoidably communicated by the therapist's bearing, facial expressions, attitudes
and responses. The authenticity of the therapist as a being is obviously of utmost importance, since otherwise a great deal of confusion and conflict can arise from the disparity between his utterances and his attitudinal communications. For example, one patient said, "You say that we are free and nothing is demanded of
us, but when you sit there looking at us, we feel that you expect
us to talk."

The road to authenticity of being leads through a rather painful
phase of enduring periods of silence in the group. Since the habitual way of being for most group members is to treat one another as objects, and to attempt to probe, manipulate, influence and

use one another for the purpose of gratification of personal needs of selfish nature, the gradual renunciation of this habitual mode of relating with its acting-out use of verbal and nonverbal language leads eventually to a state which Heidegger (1953) calls "speechless silence."

According to Heidegger (1953), "speechless silence" is the "Soundless voice of Being" which opens up the dread of Nothingness. "Nothingness in contrast to all that is, is the Veil of Being." Which means that Nothingness, if confronted in personal experience, unveils the "All in all" in a meaningful way.

One patient reported a dream to the group which immediately was recognized by the others as a turning point in his life. The patient spoke about it as a "dreadful encounter" with death which he miraculously survived. He dreamed that, while walking with a shadowy companion on a lonely road, he heard from a great distance the hum of an approaching plane. He had a vague premonition of disaster. This premonition grew gradually into panic when he noticed that the plane was actually in a nose dive and heading straight at him. In the last moment, while throwing himself to the ground, all fear left him and the thought passed through his mind that this was the end. He felt the wheel of the plane touch his shoulder as it crashed in flames a few feet away. He got up and his first thought was, "I must try to save the pilot from the wreckage." Suddenly, life became for him a continuous miracle to be deeply appreciated. For this patient, reverence for life became a tangible reality rather than just a philosophical abstraction.

In the periods of speechless silence, the group members experience existential anxiety and develop the capacity to endure it. These painful periods of silence reveal to them the phenomenon of boredom. Boredom is a state of meaninglessness of existence which emerges whenever one attempts to renounce the pursuit of false meanings, or when the pursuit of such meanings is made impossible through psychotherapeutic illumination.

The periods of silent boredom prevail for a while, until, one by one the group participants arrive at the edge of the "wasteland" and begin to communicate in an increasingly authentic way. For example, a patient began his group session with an effusive expression of his gratitude to the group members and personal thanks to the therapist for his having succeeded in getting a job as a school teacher. He spoke with some insistence and tension in his demeanor. He gave the impression of someone who was trying to force a gift on another person. After he had finished, there was a long, uneasy period of silence. Some group members avoided responding; others congratulated him somewhat sheepishly, but there was one member who said the following: "Your expressions of gratitude make me feel as though I were being bribed. It is an uncomfortable and embarrassing experience. You are forcing your thanks on us and trying to corrupt us to accept credit for something we do not deserve."

This authentic response had an immediate tension-relieving effect on all, including the patient. At this point, some of the other members reminded the patient that while his gratitude was now so insistent, he tended at other times to blame people for his failures.

This is an illustration of the difference between the authentic and unauthentic ways of responding and communicating. We see that the unauthentic group members responded either with empty, superficial politeness or with evasive silence, while the authentic group member expressed the truth of his inner experience, thus relieving the group tension caused by the threatened breakdown in communication.

The participants learn to be aware of what they are experiencing, and the interactions between patient and patient or patient and therapist are concerned primarily with the experiential aspects of the communications, while content is given secondary importance. For instance, a patient may break a prolonged silence by telling a dream. Instead of analyzing the content of the dream, the group members may respond with expressing their feelings about the fact that the patient chose to tell a dream at that particular moment; they may respond to the manner in which the dream was told or they may analyze the impact of this event upon the group. For example, one female patient told a dream about sharing the superintendent of the house in which she lived with a roommate for sexual purposes. In response to this, one female group member said, "I feel uneasy about your dream and your way of telling it."

Another patient said he perceived a certain demeaning attitude in the manner of presentation of the dream. Another patient remarked, "It seems that you told the dream in order to cover up your embarrassment over the competitive strivings which you have for the doctor." At this point, the first patient said, "Now I understand why I felt so uneasy about your dream. I think we are competing for the doctor and I am the roommate of your dream." Another patient summed it up by saying, "You are demeaning the doctor because you are ashamed of your cravings for him and find it humiliating to compete for his attention."

The experiential elements of the situation in which an interaction occurs illuminate the content in a particularly meaningful way (Hora, 1959a). The ontological essence and existential meaning of a dream or communication is to be found primarily in its basic climate and only secondarily in its symbolic content.

Significantly enough, the capacity to be aware of the experiential impact of the others upon oneself and vice versa tends to open up a new dimension of consciousness which leads to a growing understanding of one's own structure of being-in-the-world or failing to be-in-the-world due to various defensive attitudes and strivings. As one patient put it, "I am aware of standing in my own way."

The awareness of one's own defensiveness converts the meaning of the defense from comfort to obstacle and impediment. The moment one is aware of one's own defenses as impediments, one becomes eager to let go of them. The moment one is aware of one's own strivings as a source of stress, anxiety and conflict, one becomes eager to give them up. The moment one becomes aware of one's own temporality and spatiality—one's own relationship to time and space—one becomes perceptive of conflicts which arise in contact with others whose temporality and spatiality may be different from one's own. The group situation provides the opportunity for experiencing the self-defeating nature and burden someness of defensive attitudes and strivings.

The change to authenticity of being is characterized above all by truthfulness of expression, mutual regard, respect for the freedom and integrity of all, increased perceptivity and creativity of thinking. The use of language becomes dedicated to communication in its stricter sense, rather than to anything else. This is not easily attained. As one patient put it, "One of the most difficult things is to talk in such a way as to really say something rather than seek to get something." Another patient followed this up by saying, "It is almost as if we had to die before we could really live."

Indeed, the periods of silence are at times so painful that some patients experience dizziness and fleeting reactions of depersonalization on such occasions. The dread of nothingness appears to be related to the phenomena which occur in man when exposed to perceptual isolation (Wexler, Mendelson, Liederman, and Solomon, 1957).

The problem of loneliness and isolation is overcome through selftranscendence in the sense of the existential meeting, which is a mode of relatedness described by Martin Buber (1937) as "mutual spiritual inclusion," or by Gabriel Marcel (1948) as "intersubjectivity." In terms of the therapy groups, it means a mode of "being-there" involving the total experiential sphere and communication potential of all participants. The capacity for this kind of presence is rooted in the attainment of authenticity of being.

Group psychotherapy provides the patients with an opportunity to recognize, understand and liberate themselves from the obstacles and impediments which have hitherto stood in the way of their free, full and conscious participation in the process of existence.

The event of the existential encounter, however, as already mentioned above, is phenomenologically characterized by a *transcendence* of the temporo-spatial coordinates of existence. This means that in the existential encounter itself the experience of the passage of time and the awareness of separation between subject and object are absent.

Phenomena are manifestations of existence. Man's awareness of the phenomena is obscured and limited by his strivings to impose his will upon what is. The pursuit of what "should be" tends to make man unaware of the phenomena as they occur. Therefore a therapeutic process cannot be conducted, intended, managed; it must be *allowed to occur*. The essence of existential communication lies in its nonteleological character.

To understand himself man needs to be understood. By being understood he learns to understand. When two people share in understanding, they experience *communion*. Communion is that union which makes differentiation possible. Man becomes an individual through participation. By losing himself in participation, he finds himself as Presence, for individuals are wholly similar and wholly different at the same time—just as mosaic pictures may contain similar stone fragments but be entirely different in their overall design.

In the moment of being understood, patients experience communion; that is, they experience a release from *epistemic isolation*. The subject-object dichotomy between patient and therapist melts away. This is in marked contradistinction to being given an interpretation which is often experienced as an accusation, an attack or even condemnation.

When striving and intending are recognized as self-defeating therapeutic attitudes, there is a tendency to conclude that passivity might be a desirable one. This, however, is a mistake, since striving to be active and striving to be passive are the same. This points up the futility of the perennial disputations between the so-called active therapists and the adherents to the traditionally passive approaches. The issue is neither activity nor passivity, neither directiveness nor nondirectiveness, but *awareness,* that is, being in a *condition of wakeful receptivity and responsiveness to the phenomena*. This condition of being is vitiated by striving and intending, evaluating, judging, categorizing, pigeonholing into conceptual schemes and psychodynamic patterns.

The existential psychotherapist does not try to "do" psychotherapy; *he lives it*. He meets his patient in the *openness* of an interhuman existential encounter. He does not seek to make interpretations; he does not evaluate and judge; *he allows what is to be, so that it can reveal itself in the essence of its being, and then proceeds to elucidate what he understood*. In contrast to the interpretative approach, this is a "hermeneutic" (that is, clarifying) mode of being with a patient.

Nonjudgmental awareness of what is leads to an understanding of the patient's mode of being-in-the-world with an elucidation of the implications for its existence. Complete understanding of one's mode of being tends to bring about a shift in world view, that is, a changed attitude toward life. Change occurs the moment man can see the totality of his situation. *Change is the result of expanding consciousness.* It is to be emphasized that, contrary to general belief, man cannot change himself. Change happens to man. Darkness cannot be removed from a room. It vanishes when light enters.

It seems therefore useless to claim or to aspire to cure patients. Healing occurs through a meaningful shift in the world view of an individual, brought about through genuine understanding of the structure of his existence. As already mentioned, understanding is an event which happens in the openness of the existential encounter. Understanding is a modality of cognition which constitutes the essence of love. *This love is a condition of being, in the presence of which constructive events have the freedom to occur.*

Thus the existential psychotherapeutic process can be described as a meeting of two or more beings in openness and wakeful receptivity to *what is,* leading to a *broadening of consciousness* through revealment of that which hitherto has been obscured. The broadening of consciousness and capacity to see what is, brings man into harmony with life. Personality integration becomes an expression of ontic integration.

The existential therapeutic action is neither operational nor explorative, nor reconstructive, nor interpretative, nor directive nor nondirective; it is experiential and hermeneutic, that is, clarifying. Since it is *phenomenological-transcendental,* i.e., since the mode of cognition is such that the subject-object dichotomy is transcended, the so-called psychic mechanisms of transference, countertransference, projection, introjection, identification, resistance, empathy, etc., lose much of their significance.

The psychotherapeutic process moves in the temporality which is absolutely real and that is the eternal present. The present contains the past. The proper elucidation of the present reveals the past. This, however, is only a byproduct and is of secondary significance.

The ontologic essence and existential meaning of communication of dreams are to be found primarily in the experiencing of its basic existential climate and only secondarily in its symbolic content. A young man reported the following dream: "I was surrounded by wasps. I tried not to bother them in the hope that they might not bother me. I tried to remain as immobile as possible. When one wasp settled on my eyelid, I was seized with panic and didn't dare to move lest it would sting me through the lid and reach my eye (i.e., "I"). I felt in a real jam. Had I moved, I would have gotten stung. Had I not moved, I would have gotten stung anyway. The anxiety was unbearable. Just at the point where I coundn't stand it any longer, I woke up."

The elucidation of the meaning of this dream led to a realization on the part of this patient that defensiveness is seldom warranted, whether it is active or passive. He concluded that the best solution is to wake up and understand that what we are mostly defending are our preconceptions, i.e., dreams about ourselves. Defending one's dream is just more dreaming.

Cognition and consciousness are fundamental criteria of mental health and along with authenticity of being, they constitute the central issues in existential psychotherapy.

In contradistinction to the traditional psychoanalytic interest in the content of unconscious motivation and its historical context, existential analysis points to the epistemological problem which arises as a result of the mind's tendency to attach itself to mental images and motivations in general. In other words, here the content of the mental preoccupation, or attachment, or striving is secondary. The primary issue is the disturbance of consciousness which results from it.

REFERENCES

Binswanger, L.: *Grundformen und Erkenntniss Menschlichen Daseins.* Zurich, Max Niehans, 1942.

Buber, M.: *I and Thou.* New York, Scribner, 1937.

Heidegger, M.: *Sein and Zeit.* Tuebingen, M. Niemeyer, 1953.

Hora, T.: Beyond countertransference. *American Journal of Psychotherapy, 10:*18, 1956.

Hora, T.: Existential communication and psychotherapy. *Psychoanalysis, 5:* 38, 1957.

Hora, T.: Group psychotherapy, human values and mental health. *International Journal of Group Psychotherapy, 8:*154, 1958a.

Hora, T.: Ontic integration. Paper read at the International Congress of Group Psychotherapy, Barcelona, Spain, September, 1958b.

Hora, T.: Ontic perspectives in psychoanalysis. *American Journal of Psychoanalysis, 19:*134, 1959a.

Hora, T.: Tao, Zen and existential psychotherapy. *Psychologia, 2:*236, 1959b.

Hora. T.: Transcendence and healing. *Journal of Existential Psychiatry, 1:* 501, 1961.

Hora, T.: Beyond self. *Psychologia, 5:*84, 1962a.

Hora, T.: The epistemology of love. *Journal of Existential Psychiatry, 2:* 302, 1962b.

Krishnamurti, J.: *Commentaries on Living.* New York, Harper, 1956.

Lilly, J. C.: Some thought on brain-mind and on restraint and isolation on mentally healthy subjects. *Journal of Philadelphia Psychiatric Hospital,* 1957.

Marcel, G.: *The Philosophy of Existence.* London, Harvill, 1948.

Riesman, D.: *The Lonely Crowd.* New Haven, Yale U.P., 1950.

Wexler, D., Mendelson, J., Liederman, P. H., and Solomon, P.: Perceptual isolation: A technique of studying psychiatric aspects of stress. Paper read at annual meeting of American Psychiatric Association, Chicago, 1957.

CHAPTER VII

MULTIMODAL BEHAVIOR THERAPY IN GROUPS

Arnold A. Lazarus

INTRODUCTION

THE EASIEST GROUPS TO MANAGE are those that are relatively homogeneous and have clear-cut goals. Thus, I have successfully conducted groups for people who wished to lose weight, or to stop smoking. Similarly, separate groups for men and women with sexual inadequacy (so-called impotence and frigidity) have also posed no undue clinical problems. Standard behavior therapy techniques, including systematic desensitization (Lazarus, 1961) and assertive training (Lazarus, 1968), have been shown to be clinically effective in groups. These and other specific behavioral methods in groups (such as the use of operant conditioning procedures) have been applied to several settings and situations, and their overall effectiveness requires no further elaboration here. The present chapter will describe a more extended undertaking than the foregoing–the use of special group behavior therapy principles in developing a constructive *modus vivendi* in a heterogeneous group of clients.

Multimodal behavior therapy is a systematic problem solving process that examines and, if necessary, endeavors to remedy maladaptive responses across six separate but interrelated modalities –behavior, affect, sensation, imagery, cognition, and interpersonal relationships. These modalities were not created *sui generis* but stem from the fact that general psychology has always concerned itself with sensation, perception, cognition, and emotion, as well as the study of innumerable behavior patterns within a variety of interpersonal settings. Recent follow-up questionnaires have indicated that a complete course of therapy requires a thorough search for problems within each modality, followed by precise strategies for overcoming these problems (Lazarus, 1973a).

Thus, multimodal therapy is not concerned with mere "symptom removal." The modification of observed behavior (which includes interpersonal responses) is but one-third of the therapeutic variance. Although the behavior therapy literature has recently recognized the importance of covert processes and private events, the multimodal orientation attends to these variables in much greater depth and detail. Yet the emphasis remains *behavioral* for two reasons: (1) It is explicitly emphasized that all we can know, adduce, or infer from our various transactions and interactions stems from verbal and non-verbal behavioral cues. Even when psychoanalysts dwell on intra-psychic dynamics, it is always something about a person's *behavior* that has led them to speculate about these putative complexes. (2) It would seem that *social learning theory* (Bandura, 1969) offers the most elegant and parsimonious theoretical framework for enabling us to identify the active ingredients behind the acquisition and elimination of simple and complex response patterns. Thus, radical behaviorism gives way to experimentally tested constructs like modeling, cognitive dissonance, and interpersonal attraction, while avoiding all untestable concepts such as energized traits, psychic complexes, and latent dynamisms.

To date, apart from a brief discussion of multimodal group behavior therapy on a cassette recording (Lazarus, 1973b), the present account is the first published report on the subject. My paper on multimodal therapy with individuals (Lazarus, 1973a) emphasized the point that most systems of psychotherapy favor two or three modalities, and either overlook the rest or treat them *en passant*. Thus, Casriel (1972) refers to "Triangular Man," and states that in his groups the "ABC's are man's Affect, Behavior and Cognition" (p. 9). Lowen (1967), using a Reichian-related orientation, deals almost exclusively with body exercises that are designed to generate powerful feelings (or in multimodal terms, he is concerned mainly with sensory and affective modalities). Ellis (1962) has long championed the primacy of the cognitive modality, although his more recent writings on rational-emotive therapy emphasize various behavioral assignments and the use of therapeutic imagery (cf., Ellis, 1971). Progressive relaxation training (Jacobson, 1938, 1964) devotes almost exclusive prominence and attention to the sensory modality, whereas eidetic psychotherapy (Ahsen, 1968) deals almost solely with imagery techniques and processes. Thus, every system of therapy from classical psychoanalysis to the latest innovations in Gestalt theory and technique (Polster and Polster, 1973) can be scrutinized through the viewpiece of each separate modality, and almost every system will be found to overlook, ignore, or merely scratch the surface of at least one or two of the basic modalities. Many behavior therapy programs cover the basic modalities more thoroughly than other therapeutic systems, but as currently practiced, they are a superficial approximation of the multimodal treatment regimen.

SOME BASIC ELEMENTS OF BEHAVIORAL GROUP THERAPY

A distinction must be drawn between *group behavior therapy* and *behavior therapy in a group*. The latter clearly implies a group of people who are the simultaneous recipients of individual behavior therapy. Thus group desensitization using individual hierarchies (where each person pictures his or her own particular scene) is a prime example of behavior therapy in a group. The lines of therapeutic demarcation and communication are primarily between each individual and the therapist. Interaction among and between group members is limited and is of little significance—except perhaps to engender feelings of constructive rivalry.

In group behavior therapy, all the members serve as active change agents for themselves and for one another. Members offer one another advice, constructive criticism, positive reinforcement, and monitor each other's therapeutic progress inside and outside the group. Nevertheless, whether the emphasis is mainly upon behavior therapy in a group (e.g., when administering group relaxation, or when the therapist offers individual assignments to be performed outside of the group) or whether group behavior therapy is the focus of attention (e.g., when group members provide each other with contingent encouragement and reinforcement, or when they deliberately demonstrate and model crucial prosocial response patterns) behavioral processes in groups are characterized by an attempt to use experimentally tested principles and techniques to achieve systematic and measurable results. The hallmark of a behavioral orientation is the manner in which global presenting problems are dissected into specific maladaptive habits and response deficits.

The multimodal orientation reflected by this chapter takes the foregoing even further. A group of people zeroing in on each other's behavioral excesses and deficits, quelling negative emotions (anxiety, hate and depression) while augmenting positive feelings (security, belonging, self-worth and genuine affection) affords a fertile milieu for the development of effective functioning. The addition of sensory exercises (enhancing visual, auditory, tactile and other sensual pleasures while diminishing tension, and what we call "sensual anesthesia") when combined with imagery techniques (e.g., picturing the successful execution of formerly upsetting scenes for desensitization purposes, or flashing back to childhood images that lend perspective to current problems) assists not only in identifying critical problem areas, but also facilitates the invention and discovery of precise solutions for particular difficulties. And finally, multimodal behavioral groups offer a constructive interpersonal terrain for parsing irrational cognitions, for changing self-defeating values and attitudes, and for specifically modifying injurious self-talk.

Thus, in operational terms, multimodal therapy is predicated on the assumption that the more constructive, prosocial, nondeviant reaction patterns one acquires during the course of therapy, the less likely one is to relapse afterwards. A constructive group setting in which the members are schooled to modify their own (and everyone else's) "hangups" across each basic modality offers a unique opportunity for people to enhance their growth, to solve their problems, and in the words of certain existential writers, to self-actualize their basic potentialities.

SOME PRACTICAL AND THEORETICAL ASSUMPTIONS

Social learning theory is a deliberately limited and delimited approach to the understanding of human behavior. Adhering to scientific protocol, it carefully excludes all explanatory principles that are unwieldy, untestable, or that lack parsimony. The attempt, as with all scientific disciplines, is to account for complex phenomena in quantifiable terms, without needlessly compounding the variables under scrutiny. Thus, a concept like "psychic energy" is carefully excluded, while more elegant and testable explanations are sought for phenomena such as so-called "conversion hysteria," psychosomatic ailments, and amnesia which are all so readily "explained" in terms of energy transformations. Concepts involving different levels of awareness, as well as symbolic mediation, are likely to receive increasingly more attention from social learning theorists concerned with therapeutic processes. While social learning theory has few explanatory principles (e.g., positive and negative reinforcement, extinction, vicarious conditioning, and punishment) scores of therapeutic techniques have emanated from (or may be explained by) these fundamental principles.

Although multimodal behavior therapy draws its theoretical underpinnings from social learning theory (Bandura, 1969), it follows the doctrine of *technical eclecticism* (Lazarus, 1971) in selecting promising and effective techniques from other schools and disciplines. Thus, in addition to basic behavior therapy techniques, multimodal groups make extensive use of psychodrama (Moreno, 1958) and Gestalt procedures (Fagan and Shepherd, 1970) without subscribing to the esoteric theories underlying many systems of psychotherapy. A fundamental assumption behind the multimodal orientation is that nearly all significant experiences have cognitive, affective, behavioral, sensory, perceptual and interpersonal consequences, and that therapy must unravel and eliminate the relevant components in each area of malfunction. Thus, for example, a woman embarks on an extramarital relationship and, to her chagrin, finds herself sexually unresponsive. What impact will this have upon her subsequent behaviors, thoughts, feelings, sensations, images and interpersonal relationships?

One of my clients after being involved in an automobile accident tended to tremble and palpitate when exceeding 30 m.p.h. He reported vivid images of his accident, avoided traveling by car, and preferred to be chauffeured by his wife. Whereas a traditional behavior therapist might have proceeded with *in vivo* desensitization (on the assumption that positive response generalization would spontaneously ameliorate undue concerns across all modalities), a more thorough multimodal evaluation revealed that his "driving phobia" was more a device to control his wife, rather than a conditioned avoidance response. In other words, by examining each modality in turn, one readily discovers where primary problems reside, and by extirpating residual complaints across all modalities, therapists can feel more confident that half-baked "cures" are less likely to result.

My students, my clients, and I have found the acronym BASIC ID most convenient for remembering the modalities that need to be covered in each case, namely behavior, affect, sensation, imagery, cognition, interpersonal relationships, and a "medical modality" where the focus is primarily directed at the adjunctive use of drugs, if and when necessary. The multimodal profile enables one to conduct a more thorough functional analysis of significant antecedent and maintaining factors across the fundamental parameters of each client's problem areas. Some clinicians may wish to add additional modalities, but in the interests of parsimony, it can be shown that combinations of two or more of the proposed modalities readily account for added dimensions of human experience (e.g., cognitive-affective interchanges can provide a "spiritual" realm). The multimodal (or BASIC ID) profile is useful not only for thoroughly dissecting presenting complaints into discrete yet interrelated components, it also helps the clinician to direct ongoing therapy into productive channels. Thus, during one of our recent group sessions, a woman remarked that she had been arguing with her husband. Instead of a bland, "Would you care to share the details with the group?" (which would probably have resulted in a narrative that was, at best, incomplete), the woman was asked to recount the actual behaviors that had preceded the argument, as well as those that had occurred during and after the argument. The affective components were then discussed, together with possible sensory reactions. (In the latter regard she reported tight sensations in her chest and an awareness of some constriction in her throat, which led me to spend a few minutes teaching her specific breathing and relaxing exercises.) Her imagery was replete with flashbacks to childhood encounters with her domineering father who often chastised her. A simple group exercise was prescribed to assist in diminishing the helpless-little-girl role that she was inclined to adopt–she was asked to face each group member, look them in the eyes and say, "I am an adult woman now." Most of the group discussion then centered upon ways in which she could improve the interpersonal quality of her marriage, with special reference to irrational ideas (arbitrary shoulds, oughts and musts) that tended to corrode many potentially positive interactions. Thus, her 20 minutes of group time proved especially productive for her, and was also beneficial to several other members who indirectly or vicariously enhanced their own repertories of specific coping responses and personal awareness.

In accounting for the benefits that accrued to this woman, the multimodal emphasis would exclude constructs like "promoting insight into unconscious processes," or "lifting repression," and in their place one would stress the effects of modeling, cognitive restructing (or modified self-talk), behavior rehearsal, and so forth. In essence, the group procedures are seen as a didactic process that enables people to emerge with *coping devices*. The groups enable people to see themselves in relation to others, to learn to give to others and to receive emotional support from others, and thereby to overcome feelings of alienation and personal isolation.

BASIC ORIENTATION MEETINGS

The First Meeting

In order to set the stage for a particularly constructive climate of multimodal group interaction, the first two meetings are conducted in a relatively well-structured manner. Initially, the group members are introduced to each other and are asked to provide a summary statement of their individual backgrounds, main problems, and what they hope to derive from the group. The members are encouraged to ask questions of one another so that *self-disclosure* becomes an obvious expectation from the very outset. However, participants are informed that if any question strikes them as too personal, unduly penetrating, or premature, they are to voice their feelings in this regard instead of lying or feeling obliged to answer the question in point.

At the end of the introductory phase, each person is asked to make at least one positive observation about every other group member. It is then clearly shown how some people have inordinate difficulty in making and/or accepting positive remarks. Apart from well-documented virtues of positive reinforcement, the main reason for carrying out this constructive feedback exercise is to set multimodal groups apart from the many group settings in which people verbally attack each other, and in which they are encouraged to let their anger out at one another. As in all behavioral systems of therapy, the multimodal approach constantly encourages *assertive* responses, but actively discourages *aggressive* behavior.

The foregoing preliminaries usually take between one to two hours. Our multimodal groups have generally met once a week for no less than three hours (including a coffee break). We have found it best to have groups of 10 to 12 members, conducted by a male and female co-therapist.

The next phase of the initial group meeting consists of a brief lecture by the group leaders regarding the specific advantages of interpersonal *cooperation*. Emphasis is placed upon the fact that a competitive milieu usually fosters the development of social distance, distrust, antagonism and deception. Particular attention is paid to the absurd Annie-get-your-gun philosophy of "I can do anything better than you." It is pointed out that many aspects of our culture seem to follow the ridiculous notion that one must hide one's shortcomings in order to appear perfect, and also in order to pretend that one can indeed do all things better than other people. The complete absurdity of any doctrine of perfectionism or plerophory is strongly emphasized in the following statement that is made to the group. "Everyone in this room has different genes, chromosomes, and social learning experiences. We have all seen and done things that nobody else in here has seen and done. Being different people with different backgrounds we all have different abilities and disabilities. Everyone in this room has certain bits of knowledge or information, certain skills or capacities that other people in here do not possess. By pooling our resources, that means by openly showing what we can and cannot do, what we know and do not know, we can each trade off various strengths and weaknesses, and grow as a result." The therapist then elaborates on the virtues of avoiding falseness and showmanship in the group.

The first meeting concludes with a specific exercise in "cooperation trading." Each member is asked to state a personal ability and disability, whereupon the group is enjoined to see if anyone can offer a trade-off. A typical excerpt follows:

> Bob: Well, I guess that one of my shortcomings is the fact that I have never learned how to fix a car. Maybe this sounds unimportant in here, but no kidding, I hardly know how to change a flat. It's one of those little things I've always meant to do something about but never got round to. Anyhow, on the positive side, I guess I can tutor math and teach the clarinet.
>
> Mike: Bob, I can gladly show you the basics about car engines, and flat tires and things like that, but I don't want to learn math or how to play the clarinet.
>
> Therapist: That's fine. You don't need a perfect trade off. If Mike shows Bob how to fix simple things that go wrong with cars, maybe someone else in the group may want some musical or mathematical tutoring from Bob. If not, that's also okay. As the group goes on, other things will undoubtedly come up with which Bob can be of service.
>
> Mike: Bob, why don't we get together on Sunday and I can give you your first lesson in mechanics?
>
> Bob: Okay. Fine.
>
> Marilyn: There must be something that Bob can do for Mike.
>
> Mike: Well, perhaps Bob can introduce me to some of the women he's always fighting off.
>
> Bob: (Laughing) Only with pleasure.
>
> Nora: Bob, would you really be willing for instance to help my kids with their math?
>
> Bob: For a free supper, anytime.
>
> Nora: You've got yourself a deal.

Some group therapists expressly discourage the group members from forming friendships outside of the group. As the foregoing clearly indicates, multimodal group therapy deliberately encourages the development of independent friendships between group members. My only justification for adopting this position is the fact that numerous firm and lasting friendships have emanated from these group meetings with very positive overall effects.

The Second Meeting

If no group member has a particularly pressing problem that he or she strongly wishes to share with the group, the second meeting begins with a brief talk by one of the therapists who re-emphasizes the basic points about personal integrity, openness, trust and group solidarity, and the meeting then continues with the "cooperation trading" process outlined above. However, if members bring particular problems to the fore, group counseling procedures are first employed in an endeavor to find solutions to the specific problems that have been raised (cf. Lazarus, 1971).

During the second meeting, group members are given five basic group principles that they are encouraged to write down.

1. What transpires in the group is strictly confidential.
2. Outside of the group, members are required not to share feelings or information with other group members that they are unwilling to disclose to the group as a whole.
3. If any group member has negative reactions pertaining to the group, it is important to air these complaints inside and not outside the group.
4. Withholding feelings and observations–whether positive or negative–diminishes one's own role in the group and retards group progress in general.
5. Constructive criticisms are those that are directed at negative or offensive behaviors, not at people *per se.*

Thus, when one group member called me to complain that in his opinion the meetings had become too unstructured, I pointed out that he had violated principle #3 and urged him to be sure to express his feelings at the beginning of the next group session. Similarly, when one of the women reported that her husband–also a group member–often ridiculed her on the way home from group meetings about things she had said in the group, the husband was told that principle #3 had been infringed. The factors underlying their marital disputes were then dealt with in the group.

Regarding the importance of principle #4, it is emphasized that in most social settings, people are dishonest, although they prefer to think of themselves as "tactful." When group members place tact, diplomacy, and social graces before frank and forthright feedback, they transform the group into a club, a game, or a tea-party.

Presentation of the five basic principles usually provokes considerable discussion. Some people call for the amplification of specific points and seek clarification of their exact boundaries and implications. The general tenor of the discussion readily facilitates the promotion of a helping ethos in which the significance of intrinsic values are spelled out such as in the following statements. "In here we will not play games of status and prestige. We will try to come across as concerned people who value each other for our human qualities. Ridicule, scorn, sarcasm and derision will be outlawed, but we will try to learn to enjoy and to welcome helpful and constructive criticism. We will recognize that everyone on earth is a fallible human being, and that nobody can hope to become infallible. All we can do is to help each other become less fallible. We will try to be unafraid of making mistakes, for unless our mistakes are identified, we cannot profit from them. We want to provide a pervasive feeling of safety and trust in this group so that you will be willing to take risks and extend yourself. Remember that the more psychological risks you take, the more you reveal yourself as you really are instead of letting the members of the group see you as you appear to be, the more rapidly you will grow emotionally and also facilitate the emotional growth of others."

OBTAINING THE INITIAL MULTIMODAL (BASIC ID) PROFILE

By the last hour of the second group meeting, or at the beginning of the third session, the members are presented with the acronym "BASIC ID" and are told that the letters stand for behavior, affect, sensation, imagery, cognition, interpersonal relationships and drugs. They are given the following brief explanation to begin with: "Just about everything that happens to you is reflected in your behavior. The term 'behavior' refers to the way you walk, talk, stand, move, et cetera, in other words, anything that can be observed about you. The word 'affect' means 'emotion' or strong feelings like love, hate, anxiety, depression, anger, et cetera. 'Sensation' refers to your five senses–sight, taste, smell, touch, hearing. We will be interested in discovering what sensations are especially pleasant and unpleasant for you. One goal of therapy is to train you to decrease or eliminate the unpleasant sensations while enhancing those that are pleasant for you. 'Imagery' refers to the mental pictures we all have in our heads. We often recall past events not in words but in mental pictures; also future planning is often carried out in images. Your self-image is particularly important. The term 'cognition' refers to one's thought processes, such as beliefs, values, attitudes, opinions, and so forth. All of us have undoubtedly picked up some irrational beliefs along the way, and in the group we will try to replace them with rational and constructive attitudes. 'Interpersonal relationships' refer specifically to the manner in which you relate to other people and the way in which they react to you. We will want to know how well you get along with other people, what you do for them, what you expect from them, and the subtle ways in which you are influenced by others. Finally, we use the word 'drugs' to cover medication that you take with and without a doctor's prescription–this will alert us to possible physical ailments, addictions, et cetera. These different modalities are interactive and interrelated. If you alter your behavior this also will immediately change significant thoughts, feelings, relationships, et cetera. Similarly, a change in cognition will alter your affective processes–do you all know what these terms mean now? Anyhow, in this group, we will leave nothing to chance but we will scan everybody's 'BASIC ID' from time to time."

The outline just described usually precipitates a host of questions that permits the therapists to underscore the salient features of the multimodal orientation. Often, simple sensory exercises (such as taking turns to massage each other's shoulders and neck, or closely scrutinizing everyday objects in the room) serve as additional ice breakers and tend to consolidate the group while promoting further discussion and a sense of togetherness. The next step is to obtain preliminary *modality profiles* from each group member. The following edited protocol illustrates the process:

Therapist: I think it's a good idea to help Ellen work out her modality profile at this point. How about it Ellen?

Ellen: Nancy is a very hard act to follow, you know.

Peter: What's all this competition crap that's going on?

Bob: It's called "Count the hangups."

Therapist: That's a strange attitude Bob. Anyhow, may I suggest that it really is Ellen's turn. Okay? So let's start with *behavior*. Ellen, will you give us some specific behaviors that you want to stop doing, and others that you want to start doing?

Ellen: Um. Yes, sure. Well, for one thing I want to quit smoking, uh and uh I also want to stop yelling at my kids, uh. . . . That's all I can think of.

Therapist: Who's acting as scribe? Sally are you taking all this down? Okay, good. Ellen, what specific constructive behaviors do you want to start doing?

Ellen: Well, let's see. (Pause) I guess I'd like to learn to be more independent.

Therapist: Being *more independent* is too vague. Can you break it down into specific behaviors?

Ellen: (Pause) Yes, uh, I'd like to start going places on my own.

Co-therapist: Where would you like to go and what would you like to do on your own?

Ellen: Well, I get anxious if I have to drive more than 10 minutes from the house, and Pat, that's my husband, usually does the shopping for me, or else we go together.

Co-therapist: Sally, write down "anxiety" in the Affective Column, and write "dependent on husband" in the Interpersonal Column.

Ellen: Okay, well I can think of some behaviors I'd like to start doing. For instance, I'd like to take up tennis again, and I'd like to start watching my weight, you know, sticking to a diet and maybe losing 10 pounds.

Therapist: Fine, we've got enough for starters. Now apart from getting anxious when you drive some distance away from your home, can you tell us about any other emotions you would like to change?

Co-therapist: What makes you so sure she'd like to change her feelings about driving?

Ellen: Oh, I would! I really would! I mean it's so ridiculous to be so frightened.

Co-therapist: I understand. I just don't want us to take anything for granted. After all, you must get some rewards from being so dependent on Pat, but we can look into that later. Meanwhile, let's hear what other things you want Sally to write down under the Affect Column.

Ellen: It all boils down to fear, really. I mean I don't really get all that depressed or anything.

Therapist: What about anger or irritation? You mentioned yelling at the children.

Ellen: Oh, yes. I do blow up at them a lot. But like I said, the main thing is anxiety. I mean, I'm afraid sometimes of my own shadow. I'm the same as Nancy insofar as I must learn to stand up for my rights.

Sally: Does that also go in the Interpersonal Column?

Several People: Yes.

Co-therapist: Ellen, will you keep a close watch on all the things that make you feel anxious this coming week, and will you write them down for us?

Ellen: Everything that gets me up-tight?

Co-therapist: Yes.

Ellen: God! That may be quite a list.

Co-therapist: That's fine. Will you do it?

Ellen: I'll try.

Therapist: That will really assist us in rounding out your Modality Profile. Now where were we? I think we're up to the Sensory Modality. What can you tell us about any negative sensations?

Ellen: Well, right off, there are two things that come to mind. Whenever I get upset I have a horrible sensation at the back of my head, like a hand tightening inside my brain. Do you know what I mean?

Therapist: A tight sensation at the back of your head that radiates right into your head?

Ellen: Right! It's awful!

Therapist: It sounds very much like muscle tension which we can teach you to overcome. What was the other thing?

Ellen: It's a knot in my stomach. When I'm very anxious, both the headache and the stomach thing can hit me together.

Co-therapist: Do you ever have these sensations when you aren't anxious?

Ellen: I think so. Like, I mean to a greater or lesser extent the knot in my stomach is nearly always there, even when I don't feel particularly anxious or up-tight.

Co-therapist: Perhaps some abdominal breathing exercises will be helpful for that. Shall we move onto imagery now?

Ellen: I don't exactly know what you mean by "imagery." I couldn't follow it when Nancy was doing it either.

Therapist: It might be helpful if we did a group imagery exercise. Sally, do you want to put down the note pad and join in the exercise? This will just take a few minutes but I think it will help Ellen and everyone else experience what we mean by imagery. Okay, what I want you to do is picture your childhood home. You may have moved around as a child, but nearly everyone has one place that they regard as their childhood home. Picture it clearly in your mind. (Pause) Now picture yourself walking through your childhood home room by room, and pay particular attention to your feelings as you go from room to room. You can blend the sensory modality with the imagery by not only seeing the rooms, but by also getting in touch with sounds, odors, et cetera. (Pause) Ellen, what's making you cry?

Ellen: (Blowing her nose and still weeping) I'm sorry. It's just that I pictured mom dying and dad selling the house, and the funeral, and all that, and it was all so vivid.

Therapist: There's no need to apologize. That's a lot of important imagery in there. Tell me, how long ago did all this take place?

Ellen: Oh, let's see, mom's been dead 10 years now. . . .

Therapist: And there's still a lot of anguish tied up in that imagery, in all those recollections.

Ellen: I sometimes dream about it. I have nightmares about that funeral. And there's another image that's stuck in my mind. When I was about 12 years old, I pushed one of my friends and she fell and broke her arm. God! I can just hear the way her bone snapped, and I can see her and hear her screaming.

Therapist: Well, we have some negative imagery to work through with you. Sally, what have you managed to write down under the Imagery Column?

Sally: I've got "mother's death," "mother's funeral," and "friend's broken arm."

Ellen: (Still weeping) Put down "selling the house." I can still picture all those people coming to look at the house and my hating the people that bought it from us. (Several group members spontaneously embrace Ellen.)

Therapist: Ellen has given us many important clues about separation, loss, and attachment. I am sure that much of her anxiety hinges around this theme. And when we get to the cognitive modality, I would guess that there will be a lot of self-devaluation stuff.

Co-therapist: Sooner or later I feel that we will have to add *guilt feelings* to the Affective Modality.

Ellen: I guess I don't think well of myself. I should have done so many things differently.

Therapist: I guess we all wish that we had done many things differently. But regrets and self-hate don't help at all. Anyhow, that gives us some cognitive clues. Is there something about your inter-personal relationships that seems to stand out?

Ellen: Oh, I guess the fact that I would like more friends.

Sally: I'm not sure I've written everything down properly.

Therapist: I'll give you a hand in a moment; we're almost done. Ellen, anything about drugs that you can tell us?

Ellen: Well, I take Valium® when I get anxious.

Therapist: How much?

Ellen: I think it's 5 mg. strength. I take about one or two pills a day.

Therapist: Anything else?

Ellen: Oh, maybe aspirins when my headaches get bad.

Co-therapist: Do these things help?

Ellen: Somewhat, I would say.

Therapist: That was very honest and useful, Ellen. Shall we break for coffee? Sally, would you like us to go over Ellen's profile with you?

The multimodal behavior therapy approach stresses the fact that patients are usually troubled by a multitude of specific problems that should be dealt with by a similar multitude of specific treatments. A general emphasis upon problem specification is beginning to come into its own in psychiatry (Hayes-Roth, Longabaugh, and Ryback, 1972), although in general medicine a problem-oriented approach is slightly older (e.g., Weed, 1968). The multimodal orientation not only underscores the value of this new approach, but also provides a conceptual framework for its psychiatric implementation. As the foregoing protocol illustrates, the construction of a Modality Profile is primarily diagnostic, but the process also has immediate therapeutic value. Ellen's Modality Profile is outlined below.

MODALITY PROFILE

Modality	Problem	Proposed Treatment
Behavior	Smoking	Contingency contracting
	Yells at kids	Learn positive reinforcement principles
	Limited range of free movement	Risk-taking assignments
	Over-eating	Contingency contracting
	Physically inactive	Prescribed assignments
Affect	Anxiety	Look for secondary gain; also use graded assignments
	Irritability	Differential relaxation training
	Self-hate	Rational disputation

Sensation	Tension at back of head	Massage and relaxation
	Knot in stomach	Abdominal breathing with relaxation
Imagery	Mother's death and Mother's funeral	Possibly use Gestalt techniques such as "completing unfinished business"
	Sale of childhood home	Use abreactive techniques
	Breaking friend's arm	Use abreactive techniques
Cognition	Should's, ought's, must's (needless regrets)	Challenge irrational self-talk
Interpersonal	Dependent on husband	Self-sufficiency exercises
	Does not assert her rights	Assertive training
	Lacks friends	Social behavior rehearsal
Drugs	Requires 5 to 10 mg. Valium® daily and uses aspirins for tension headaches	Teach relaxation skills in place of drugs

The majority of the techniques alluded to under "Proposed Treatment" are described in my book *Behavior Therapy and Beyond* (Lazarus, 1971). The reader will find other suggested readings listed towards the end of this chapter. It should also be stressed that when evaluating each client's Modality Profile, the therapists decide on the most likely treatment strategy based on whether or not a particular technique seems feasible in a group and also what can be inferred about the client's personal preferences. Thus, Ellen had once voiced her strong dislike for any aversive techniques–hence our decision to use contingency contracting rather than aversive imagery for combating her smoking and eating problems.

When the initial Modality Profiles have been completed for each member, they are typed and photocopied so that everyone receives a "blueprint" of his/her main problem areas together with the blueprints of all the other group members. The group then becomes a highly focused, cooperative, problem-solving enterprise that capitalizes upon everything from tacit support and interpersonal guidance to collaborative exercises and peer pressure. Additional items are often included on the Modality Profiles as new understandings and more data emerge through individuals revealing hitherto unsuspected nuances of their own and one another's significant difficulties.

The group format is then largely dependent upon the group leaders' preferences. In addition to problem-solving procedures, some of my students believe in using several general group exercises and encounter techniques to enhance a feeling of solidarity within the group. We have tried breaking the group into small units comprised of people who are endeavoring to solve similar problems, and/or who are using the same procedures at a given time. The women in the group sometimes spend an hour on their own using "consciousness raising techniques" (e.g., Brodsky, 1973), while the men exchange confidences that sometimes prove difficult in the larger group setting. Regardless of the specific format, the Modality Profile serves as a constant reminder of unresolved problems and alerts everyone to remember that the most relevant index of improvement is a significant change in the problem areas outside of the group that led the people to become group members in the first place.

The group, qua group, really comes into its own when group members provide one another with new and helpful techniques based upon their own serendipitous findings. A case in point is outlined below.

One of the group members suffered from what we termed "pleasuris interruptus." Quite often, while enjoying himself, he would find that an exceedingly unpleasant thought or image had intruded and, as a result, his fun or pleasure was truncated. For example, during sexual intercourse, he might suddenly think, "I'm probably going to lose my erection," and then become sufficiently tense about this negative expectation to make it a self-fulfilling prophecy. Similarly, while enjoying a concert he would frequently find that horrible images–disease ridden corpses, or mangled animals caught in bear traps–would effectively undermine his pleasure. A BASIC ID analysis of this particular problem area suggested that a strict religious upbringing had probably led him to believe that any protracted pleasure was intrinsically sinful. However, years of insight therapy with a traditional psychiatrist had failed to mitigate any of his problems, and the group decided to waste no further time in searching for an effective antidote. He was taught to use "thought stopping" and the "blow-up technique" (Lazarus, 1971), but to no avail. One of the other group members then made the suggestion that a quiet "No!" directed at the intrusive thoughts or images, very much as one would address a disobedient puppy, might prove more effective. At the next meeting, to everyone's delight, the group was informed that the latter suggestion had proved extraordinarily effective.

RESEARCH FINDINGS AND TREATMENT GOALS

Research results involving immaculate double-blind controls clearly demonstrating that multimodal group procedures produce significantly superior therapeutic outcomes to other therapy groups and/or attention-placebo processes would be most desirable. It is less than two years since the first multimodal group procedures were put into effect. Again, it must be emphasized that the multimodal orientation was developed when follow-ups of individual cases treated by behavior therapy revealed a 36 percent relapse rate after a median of 2.6 years (Lazarus, 1971). Approximately 50 people have been involved in multimodal group therapy procedures. There are only two participants who can be said to have derived no significant benefits and who made no noteworthy life changes.

In developing a philosophy of life, multimodal groups overlap to a great extent with Mowrer's (1973) integrity groups, but without any theological underpinnings. As the various elements across modalities are monitored and scanned, the principles of integrity, authenticity and openness, emphasized during the initial meetings, are constantly reinforced. Dishonest responses are brought to the fore in a non-pejorative manner. For research purposes, frequency distributions can readily be kept. The emotive consequences are extremely powerful. For example, it was pointed out to a female client (after she had described some imagery involving her father) that she had been explicitly taught to tell lies in order to avoid negative sanctions. For her, this was a basic insight. But behavior therapists know all too well that insight alone is usually of limited value. Hence, following this revelation, a role-playing procedure was employed with the therapist acting the part of her father while the client was required to confront him with the truth about past misdemeanors, as well as with the truth regarding her feelings towards him–past and present. She was then asked to take the risk of being completely honest for the next seven days, and to keep a record of her failures and successes in this regard. The same assignment was then given for the next two weeks, after which time she sent me the following letter:

"At last I am an honest woman, and I feel very wise. It is as though I am seeing everyone for the first time through my new straight eyes. I want to describe what happened to me on Wednesday (after the 'insight' plus role-playing sequence). As I thought about what had happened, I put my head down on the desk and sobbed—long, drawn-out child sobs and moans that shook my body. I felt weak, moved slowly. I tried to walk, but couldn't. I got down on the floor and crawled toward the door of the room, crawled short distances in circles, a wounded animal in a cage. I could only whimper and moan. I remembered what it was like to be four years old. I had returned to myself at that age. I felt I was surrounded by nothing, empty space inside me. I didn't know who I was, kept repeating, 'I'm so bent.' All the tension left my body. I felt it go. My lips felt like they were new; licked them to make certain they were mine. I got up and walked down the hall. I had to deal with my children. Make their lunches and plunge a plugged toilet. I cried while I did these things, stopped long enough to face the children, then cried again. I sat on the floor in the bedroom and played with the children's blocks and little cars. When the children left to play with their friends, I felt as though my playmates had abandoned me. I sat on the floor and played with the blocks and cried because my playmates had left me alone. My body felt bent and out of shape. . . . Slowly I began to come together; I began to trust myself. . . . My integrity and being true to myself is all important. I don't know where I'm going, but I know *how* I am going. I'm not afraid. . . . I am so excited about myself and my life. I feel I have enormous creative gifts. A few days ago I felt like a snake shedding its skins, a magician pulling scarves out of a hat, a kaleidoscope constantly turning and sliding into new shapes. Now I wait expectantly for the next event to happen, the next bolt out of the blue, the next vista to open up."

Verbal and written reports like this are all well and good, but multimodal therapists look for more specific indices of change. Covering each modality, one inquires about exact changes in behavior, affect, sensation, imagery, cognition, interpersonal relationships, and the need for drugs. In assessing the results of therapy, the primary question is whether or not there is clear-cut evidence that the client appears to be coping (without the aid of drugs or other crutches) in all situations in which he or she was disturbed and unable to cope before treatment. The Modality Profiles provide convenient tally sheets for determining the exact parameters of change that occur (and fail to occur) in every case.

It is too soon to report on any long-term follow-ups of people who participated in multimodal behavior therapy groups. However, all reports to date have been singularly gratifying–suggesting not only an absence of relapse or new maladaptive problems but a general tendency to progress beyond the gains derived during the course of therapy.

SELECTION OF GROUP MEMBERS

Multimodal groups violate everyone of Slavson's (1959) criteria: group size is always more than 8 people (we find less than 10 rather limiting, but more than 15 very cumbersome); group leadership is didactic, not permissive; clients are not selected or grouped on the basis of some diagnostic classification; and group members are very much the recipients of advice, instruction, information, and the like.

The general effectiveness of multimodal groups has led me to invite nearly all of my clients to join a group rather than to see me individually. I do not invite people into my groups who are likely to have a disruptive effect (e.g., extremely depressed, or overtly hostile, paranoid, or deluded individuals). Highly obsessional people locked into their own thoughts and rituals also seem incapable of benefiting from multimodal group therapy. Finally, if a client is strongly opposed to participating in a group, I will treat him or her individually (or in an interpersonal context that seems relevant and clinically congenial, such as conjoint or family therapy).

ETHICAL CONSIDERATIONS

A logical point of termination for group members is when they reach the point where all items on their Modality Profiles have been adequately dealt with. Often, over the course of three or four months, about four or five group members will leave the group, generally because they are satisfied with their gains. In order to maintain a minimum of nine or ten group members, new people are invited into the group when the number of persons falls below this optimum number. (They are individually primed before joining the group–Modality Profiles are drawn up, and they are taught the essentials of multimodal group procedures.) However, many people find the group process so rewarding that they elect to remain in the group even when their problem areas seem to be completely resolved. As one member put it: "For me the group is a haven of sanity in an insane world. . . . There are not many places where people are really 'up front' with each other and where trust is not misguided." Should people who are no longer in obvious "psychic distress" be asked to make room for people who are clearly in need of therapy? When group members overcome most of their own difficulties and become, in effect, co-facilitators in the group, should they be charged (or should they receive) professional fees? A tentative solution is to have these ex-members "graduating" to the position of voluntary co-facilitators.

THERAPIST/COUNSELOR QUALIFICATIONS

The foregoing considerations lead directly into a discussion of who is best qualified to conduct multimodal group behavior therapy procedures. To date, all of my students and trainees have been Ph.D. students in clinical psychology, or post-doctoral fellows (including residents in psychiatry). I can see no reason why para-professionals could not conduct multimodal group therapy equally well. It is well-known that therapeutic skill depends on individual and personal attributes more than it does upon professional background and training. Warm, emphatic, witty, wise, honest and flexible people with an articulate and expressive ability, and a talent for sympathetically directing and instructing others seem to make the best group leaders. Proficiency at multimodal therapy is best obtained through an apprenticeship served under competent therapists. There should be no barriers to the practice of multimodal group behavior therapy by any trained and responsible person, and certainly, no profession should exercise a hegemony over these methods.

SUMMARY

Multimodal behavior therapy groups endeavor to remedy mal-adaptive responses across six separate but related modalities–behavior, affect, sensation, imagery, cognition, and interpersonal relationships. A basic assumption is that the more constructive reaction patterns one acquires during the course of therapy, the less likely one is to relapse afterwards. The multimodal approach enables the therapist to obtain a *specific and comprehensive* list of problems and to prescribe an equally specific and comprehensive list of solutions to these problems. The group setting can foster a non-threatening and truly cooperative milieu to enhance the acquisition of new prosocial interactions and the elimination of maladaptive or deviant response patterns. Some verbatim protocols are included to show exactly how problem identification and therapeutic implementation fit together in multimodal groups.

SUGGESTED READINGS

The burgeoning world of behavior therapy with its accompanying deluge of writings makes it easy to find dozens of suggested readings. Much of the literature, however, is repetitive, and some of it is scientifically questionable and clinically limited. The few selected readings below have been carefully chosen with the busy scientist-practitioner in mind who has neither the time nor perhaps the inclination to search for journal articles or to peruse a library in search of some active theoretical ingredients and some effective therapeutic techniques.

The reader who wishes to read a sophisticated and critical view of social learning theory as related to the entire field of abnormal behavior is referred to the introductory text by Gerald Davison and John Neale on *Abnormal Psychology: An Experimental Clinical Approach* (New York: Wiley, 1974).

The Annual Review of Behavior Therapy (New York: Brunner/Mazel, 1973) edited by Cyril Franks and Terry Wilson presents a kind of "Consumers Report" of behavior therapy. The Review contains 47 of the best papers published during 1971 to mid-1972 with critical commentaries by the editors that underscore various strengths and weaknesses throughout the entire field.

My own book, *Behavior Therapy and Beyond* (New York: McGraw-Hill, 1971), will amplify many of the techniques alluded to in this chapter. My cassette recording on *Aspects of Broad*

Spectrum Behavior Therapy in Groups (obtainable from Sigma Information, Inc., 485 Main Street, Fort Lee, N. J. 07024), will also highlight many of the basic points emphasized in this chapter.

The book by David Watson and Roland Tharp, *Self-Directed Behavior: Self-Modification for Personal Adjustment* (Monterey, California: Brooks/Cole, 1972), lucidly describes contingency contracting and numerous self-monitoring procedures. This clearly-written volume can serve several functions–from a prescribed textbook to a self-help and self-instruction compendium.

I also highly recommend *Behavioral Self-Control* by Carl Thoresen and Michael Mahoney (Holt, Rienhart & Winston, 1974) and the book *Self-Control: Power to the Person* by Michael Mahoney and Carl Thorensen (Brooks/Cole Publishing Company, 1974).

Donald Keat's *Fundamentals of Child Counseling* (Houghton Mifflin, 1974) contains two exceptionally informative chapters on children's groups–with lucid descriptions on how to conduct them.

Finally, the reader who wishes to become *au courant* with numerous therapeutic systems that lie outside the psychodynamic tradition is referred to *Direct Psychotherapy* edited by R. M. Jurjevich (Coral Gables, Florida: University of Miami Press, 1973). The first two volumes cover 28 systems that employ direct strategies of therapeutic intervention.

REFERENCES

Ahsen, A.: *Basic Concepts in Eidetic Psychotherapy.* New York, Eidetic Publishing House, 1968.

Bandura, A.: *Principles of Behavior Modification.* New York, Holt, 1969.

Brodsky, A. M.: The consciousness-raising group as a model for therapy with women. *Psychotherapy: Theory, Research and Practice, 10:*24, 1973.

Casriel, D.: *A Scream Away From Happiness.* New York, Grosset and Dunlap, 1972.

Ellis, A.: *Reason and Emotion in Psychotherapy.* New York, Lyle Stuart, 1962.

Ellis, A.: *Growth Through Reason.* Palo Alto, Calif., Science and Behavior Books, 1971.

Fagan, J., and Shepherd, I. L. (Eds.): *Gestalt Therapy Now.* Palo Alto, Calif., Science and Behavior Books, 1970.

Hayes-Roth, F., Longabaugh, R., and Ryback, R.: The problem-oriented medical record and psychiatry. *British Journal of Psychiatry, 121:*27, 1972.

Jacobson, E.: *Progressive Relaxation.* Chicago, University of Chicago Press, 1938.

Jacobson, E.: *Anxiety and Tension Control: A Psychobiologic Approach.* Philadelphia, Lippincott, 1964.

Lazarus, A. A.: Group therapy of public disorders by systematic desensitization. *Journal of Abnormal and Social Psychology, 63:*505, 1961.

Lazarus, A. A.: Behavior therapy in groups. In G. M. Gazda (Ed.): *Basic Approaches to Group Psychotherapy and Group Counseling.* Springfield, Ill., Charles C Thomas, 1968.

Lazarus, A. A.: *Behavior Therapy and Beyond.* New York, McGraw-Hill, 1971.

Lazarus, A. A.: Multimodal behavior therapy: Treating the "BASIC ID." *Journal of Nervous and Mental Disease, 156:*404, 1973a.

Lazarus, A. A.: *Multimodal Behavior Therapy.* Fort Lee, New Jersey, Sigma Information, Inc., 1973b.

Lowen, A.: *The Betrayal of the Body.* New York, Macmillan, 1967.

Moreno, J. L.: *Psychodrama.* New York, Beacon House, 1958.

Mowrer, O. H.: Integrity groups today. In R. M. Jurjevich (Ed.): *Direct Psychotherapy.* Coral Gables, Fla., University of Miami Press, 1973.

Polster, E., and Polster, M.: *Gestalt Therapy Integrated.* New York, Brunner/Mazel, 1973.

Slavson, S. R.: Parallelisms in the development of group psychotherapy. *International Journal of Group Psychotherapy, 2:*451, 1959.

Weed, L. L.: Medical records that guide and teach. *New England Journal of Medicine, 278:*593, 1968.

CHAPTER VIII

CLIENT-CENTERED GROUP THERAPY

Betty D. Meador

INTRODUCTION

IN 1942, CARL ROGERS published a book, his second, called *Counseling and Psychotherapy* (Rogers, 1942). Contained in these pages are the seeds which were to be nurtured into a theory of therapy and human growth which came to be called client-centered therapy. Three decades and countless books, articles, papers, research projects, students and clients later, Rogers remains the productive center of the proliferation of the client-centered approach.

For the past ten years, Rogers' primary professional interest has been in intensive small groups. He and a number of colleagues have developed during this period a type of group leadership which can be called client-centered. Because these ten years coincide with the wave of popularity of group experiences, Rogers and his co-workers have had to question, compare, and defend their way of leadershjp against a smorgasbord of other styles. The consequence has been a firmly grounded theoretical and experiential base to the client-centered group. What follows in this chapter is a look at the client-centered group as it has emerged during this period.

DEFINITION OF GROUP PSYCHOTHERAPY

The basic principles of client-centered therapy have been applied in a number of fields where human relations are primary, and including human interaction in group psychotherapy. Here is a recent statement of those principles (Meador and Rogers, 1973):

Client-centered therapy is a continually developing approach to human growth and change developed originally by Carl Rogers in the

175

1940's. Its central hypothesis is that the growthful potential of any individual will tend to be released in a relationship in which the helping person is experiencing and communicating realness, caring, and a deeply sensitive nonjudgmental understanding. It is further unique in being process-oriented, in drawing its hypotheses from the raw data of therapeutic experience and from recorded and filmed interviews. It has been determined to test all its hypotheses through appropriate research. It has application in every field of human endeavor where the healthy psychological growth of the individual is a goal.

A client-centered group is characterized, then, by three attitudes of the therapist. He tries to experience and communicate his own reality, the process of his inner self as that moves and changes in the group; a caring for the persons in the group marked by a respect for their uniqueness; and a "deeply sensitive nonjudgmental understanding." If he can live most of the time in the group within the framework of these three attitudes, he will help to establish a climate in which the growthful potential of the other persons will be released. This is the basic definition of client-centered group therapy.

THEORETICAL FOUNDATIONS OF THE PROCESS

Nature of Man

The theoretical base of client-centered therapy is a particular view of the nature of man. It sees man as an organism with an inherent tendency to develop in a positive or actualizing direction. The view holds that man's growth, like that of plants and animals, is guided by forces within toward the development of "all his capacities in ways which serve to maintain or enhance" him (Rogers, 1959, p. 196).

Rogers quotes biologist Lancelot Whyte:

Crystals, plants, and animals grow without any conscious fuss, and the strangeness of our own history disappears once we assume that the same kind of natural ordering process that guides their growth, also guided the development of man and of his mind, and does so still! (Whyte, 1960).

The task of therapy, indeed of life, is for the individual to become aware of and to work consciously with the natural ordering processes within him as they guide his development. Jung calls this the process of individuation, a process which bogs down without man's conscious participation.

> . . . instinct insists that the higher level of consciousness be attained. This urge to a higher and more comprehensive consciousness fosters civilization and culture, but must fall short of the goal unless man voluntarily places himself in its service (1954, p. 262).

This powerful urge for development lies within the individual, masked by the oughts and shoulds of the culture, frail from lack of nourishment, weak against the ambitions of the ego, but a forceful, unique potential ready to be released. An individual can participate in, can facilitate his own growth by becoming aware of and working with his inner life forces. In coming to trust and value the inner wisdom of his developing self, man sides with his "natural ordering process" and thus with the forces of his own actualization.

Rogers (1972, p. 8) tells a story of one of the first times he was aware of a client knowing better than he what she needed for her own growth. He had been a practicing psychologist for several years and was the director in the mid 1930's of the Rochester Guidance Center which dealt with children and their parents. His method of working was to gather thorough data about an individual, his history, intelligence, personality, etc., then form a diagnosis. This he would convey with tact and clarity to the child's parents, to appropriate agencies, and perhaps to the child himself. Though experience was beginning to erode his confidence in this method, his goal was to communicate his interpretation of the case and his advice for solving the problem with objectivity, professionalism, and personal aloofness from the persons involved.

> An intelligent mother brought her very seriously misbehaving boy to the clinic. I took the history from her myself. Another psychologist tested the boy. We decided in conference that the central problem was the mother's rejection of her son. I would work with her on this problem. The other psychologist would take the boy on for play therapy. In interview after interview I tried—much more softly and gently now, as a result of experience—to help the mother see the pattern of her rejection, and its results in the boy. To no avail. After about a dozen interviews I told her I thought we both had tried but

were getting nowhere, and we should probably call it quits. She agreed. Then as she was leaving the room, she turned and asked, "Do you ever take adults for counseling here?" Puzzled, I replied that sometimes we did. Whereupon she returned to the chair she had just left, and began to pour out a story of the deep difficulties between herself and her husband, and her great desire for some kind of help. I was bowled over. What she was telling me bore no resemblance to the neat history I had drawn from her. I scarcely knew what to do, but mostly I listened. Eventually, after many more interviews, not only did her marital relationship improve, but her son's problem behavior dropped away as she became a more real and free person. . . . This was a vital learning for me. I had followed *her* lead rather than mine. I had just *listened* instead of trying to nudge her toward a diagnostic understanding I had already reached. It was a far more personal relationship, and not nearly so "professional." Yet the results spoke for themselves.

This incident marked a beginning as Rogers came to trust his clients' own unfolding more than his theoretical knowledge.

Therapist as Facilitator

Along with his growing trust in the developmental or actualizing forces within the individual, Rogers was discovering new ways of working with his clients which seemed to allow more room for their growthful change. "Psychotherapy," he said in 1959, "is releasing an already existing capacity in a potentially competent individual (1959, p. 221)." The thrust of client-centered therapy in the forties and fifties was to discover what sort of relationship between a therapist and his client best allowed for the release of these positive growthful forces.

What Rogers and his colleagues discovered through groping experience and painstaking research was a simple formula: If a therapist in the relationship with his client can be transparently real, can be understanding, and can be caring, his client will begin to change and unfold in a positive direction.

This "discovery" seems to be contained in the ancient wisdom of Lao-Tse (Buber, 1957):

The perfected man . . . does not interfere in the life of beings, he does not impose himself on them, but he helps all beings to their freedom. Through his unity, he leads them, too, to unity, he liberates their nature and destiny, he releases Tao in them.

Or again:

It is as though he listened and such listening as his enfolds us in a silence in which at last we begin to hear what we are meant to be.

It is through the *person* of Lao-Tse's perfected man that the other in relationship with him discovers his own nature and destiny. The perfected man has attained a unity within himself, a trust in his inner wisdom which enables him to listen to the other with assurance that the other's nature and destiny lies within, waiting to be discovered.

Applied to a therapist, this means that he is well on his way in his own development, that he is consciously working in consort with the inner forces of his own actualization. It means that he listens in a special way, with full confidence in the growth forces of his client and in his client's ability to become aware of them. He listens in such a way that his client is able to hear his inner self and discover "what he is meant to be."

A group provides the occasion and the safe climate where the members can begin to explore the incongruencies between their beliefs and behaviors and the urgings of their inner feelings and experiencing. As the group member becomes more aware of these incongruencies and begins to resolve them, his concept of himself changes and expands. He learns to trust his inner self, to listen to its ebb and flow, and to rely on it as a basis for his behavior.

PROTOCOL ILLUSTRATING THE PROCESS

The excerpts which follow are taken from a weekend encounter group, portions of which are available in the film, "Because That's My Way" (McGaw, 1971). The group was composed of eight individuals, strangers to each other, and two therapists. They met for about 16 hours. The excerpts are representative of the process of client-centered group therapy, showing how the therapists can be understanding, caring, and real in establishing a climate in which the participants are free to be deeply personal.

In the first example, the group helps Amy discover what her feelings of the moment are about. The therapist is Carl.

Carl: I feel you're close to saying something, but I don't know what.

Amy: I think I feel like crying, but I don't know why.

Diane: I've had a feeling about you for the past ten or fifteen minutes, that you were going to cry at any moment. Please do.

Russ: I don't see anything wrong with crying.

Carl: If you let it come, you may know what it is you're crying about.

Russ: When you cry or when you laugh, you let yourself open up more to everyone else around you now. That means that that person sees that you really are somebody; that you have feelings.

Amy: I think that's what I was feeling all of a sudden when you started talking about who I am really as a person, and really, like I have feelings of pain and fear and all that; and that's really me, that's what it is (cries).

Carl: You're not just a middle-class college girl; you're someone that has pain and fear and all kinds of things.

Amy, before, and Paul, in the next example, are both letting themselves be known at another level other than the roles they carry. Paul is a policeman.

Paul: My dad passed away in 1955, and that's 15 years; and there's still things that I do, that I know displease him. When I go to do it, it gets me. Yet, I was, in my young years, a non-conformist, a real one.

Paul goes on to explain how hard he is trying to let his boys do and be what they want, not imposing himself on them.

Carl: It sounds like you're trying to make sure that they don't have to carry you around inside of them, the way you carry your father around inside of you.

Paul: That's right. You can't imagine some of the things I do now, fifteen years later. Would Dad approve of this?

Carl: One thing that you've done. You've done me an awful lot of good by letting me know you're a real non-conformist.

George: After all these hours, it all comes out.

Diane: I feel a lot more comfortable right now.

Russ: And now the cop is gone and the human is there.

The therapist in the group does not remain a bland sounding board. He is actively present in his listening as well as in his reactions to the group members.

George: I still have to get back to the fact that sure, right now this is real. Okay, that's all well and good, but yet we all do know that if we're going to take what this here and now gives us and go out into tomorrow's here and now, then for us to really apply this to our life and the future, we're going to have to be revolutionaries . . . we're going to have to tear down society, aren't we?

Carl: Okay, I feel there are quiet revolutionaries and violent ones. I think most of my life I've been a quiet revolutionary.

George: We don't all have the channels open to us that you have open to yourself to be a quiet revolutionary. For the masses of kids, we tried to be, the hippie movement tried to be quiet revolutionaries. . . . Now, these very same kids, and it just makes me all the more bitter and cynical. We got our heads beat in after trying to get McCarthy elected. (cries) I'm really bitter about that, you know.

Carl: Just full of rage about that, really.

George: The only way I can deal with rage is to be violent! I can't be a quiet revolutionary. They won't let me. You can sit over there, sanctimonious, and say, "I'm a quiet revolutionary." They won't let me!

Carl: You're mad at me and call me a sanctimonious revolutionary. Okay. But by God, I am a revolutionary; but I will not be a revolutionary in your way, and that's what you don't like!

George: Well, you see, I tend to feel . . . that your way has been proven time and time again to be totally superficial, totally ineffectual, totally . . . counterproductive. You're channelling off a lot of students' energies.

Carl: Both of us could say that same thing to each other, because I can say to you, look what violence has done, and it is ineffectual and counterproductive and these other things.

In many ways the group is a learning situation in which the participants are discovering their own reactions and feelings. The therapist tries to keep the interaction personal, as in this example. Tony is the therapist.

Amy: When we have real deep feelings and we expose them, we want people to listen and to care all the time, but God, it doesn't happen that way, you know.

George: But, Amy, it's just as human for people to hate each other. People won't always love you. That's just unreal, too.

Amy: I know, I know that too.

George: But it seems to me the way society is, the only thing we can freely express is hate. We're not allowed to express our love in society as it is today.

Russ: What do you mean?

Amy: That's not true!

George: I mean like I can't walk up to the bus stop, and there's three or four people standing at the bus stop. It's socially acceptable for me to walk up and sneer at them all. Stand over in the corner and read my paper. But I'm not free to go up there, and not even to put my arms around somebody, but I'm not even free to go up and talk to them. They'll look at you like some kind of a nut. And it's in those interpersonal relations that you have with strangers where the real kind of repression has its real effect on you.

Tony: Right now, just at this moment, I heard you not talk to Amy. She was saying something about herself, and you started talking about the people out at the bus stop who you can't talk to. That to me, is stepping on somebody. Somebody you ought to listen to, or respond to, as a person when she's saying something.

George: Yeah, that's true, and I'm not saying this by way of excusing myself, but maybe just giving a reason why I did that, because it just seems to me easier to verbalize a hypothetical situation that we would all relate to, rather than trying to fight for words and relate directly to you. You know what I mean. I'm not trying to excuse myself.

Amy: Yeah, okay, but I've got the time for you to fight for words to relate to me because that's what matters to me.

George: That's right. I'm sorry. I feel I should.

Carl: At least there was some communication there.

Tony: What do you feel now?

George: I feel good that I apologized.

A deep personal response from one member of the group tends to strike a deep chord in others. Tony has just held Amy in response to her plea for someone to reach out to her. A discussion follows of whether or not such caring can be translated to the "real" world outside of the group.

Diane: Children at the age of five reach out to a mommy or a daddy or brother or sister; and sure enough there's mommy shoving the hand away. And suddenly that little child grows up and nobody's going to reach out. Are we building false hopes in these little children?

Carl: Somebody is going to reach out. I've got to stop this for a minute because a lot has been going on in Russ, and he's just been sitting quietly here weeping; and I really would like to know what the score is. I'm sure the others would, too.

Russ: (crying) My mother reached out for me, but my dad didn't. He never showed one lousy, stinking bit of compassion for me. He never held me, never cried with me. That made it worse for me to face life than if somebody would hold me. At least you've got one person. You only had that one split minute of compassion and held each other, that's a hell of a lot; but it sticks in your mind for a hell of a long time. . . .

Carl: For me it was very, very true when you said just to be held for one minute by your father would have made a hell of a lot of difference.

Russ: The way he shook my hand the other day, it meant more in the world than any time he screamed and hollered at me. He shook my hand. He made me feel like he had some kind of pride in me.

These examples have tried to show some of the many facets of a client-centered group as the interactions bring the participants a broader awareness of who they are.

RESEARCH OF THE PROCESS

One characteristic of client-centered therapy is, as the definition given earlier states, that "it has been determined to test all its hypotheses through appropriate research." Studies during the first 20 years of its development were concerned primarily with individual therapy. During this time the factors in the therapeutic relationship and the process of change in the individual were thoroughly examined, and the client-centered hypotheses were repeatedly confirmed (Barrett-Lennard, 1959, 1962; Halkides, 1958; Rogers, 1967; Rogers and Dymond, 1954). An excellent overview of this research and its influence on client-centered theory and therapy has been published recently by John Shlien and Fred Zimring (1970).

Although there were some studies of groups in this earlier period, most have come in the last ten years. One of these involved a self-report reaction from a large number of people to their experience in intensive groups. Rogers (1970) developed a questionnaire which he sent to 500 participants in small groups which he and his colleagues led. The questionnaires were sent three to six months following participation in a group. With 82 percent replying, two felt the experience was mostly damaging and had changed their behavior in ways they did not like. A moderate number reported no change, and a moderate number reported initial change which had disappeared. "The overwhelming majority," Rogers states, "felt it had been constructive in its results, or had been a deeply meaningful, positive experience which made a continuing positive difference in their behavior (p. 126)."

A persistent question in the mind of client-centered group therapists is how to assess the effects of group participation. Rogers says of his questionnaire survey:

> To my way of thinking, this personal, phenomenological type of study—especially when one reads all of the responses—is far more valuable than the traditional "hard-headed" empirical approach. This kind of study, often scorned by psychologists as being "merely self-reports," actually gives the deepest insight into what the experience has meant. . . . For me this kind of organized, naturalistic study may well be the most fruitful way of advancing our knowledge in these subtle and unknown fields (p. 133).

Nevertheless, traditional, "hard-headed" studies continue to be the acceptable mode of psychological investigation, as the remainder of the research reported in this section testifies.

Basic to the client-centered approach is the contention that growth takes place in a climate which the therapist establishes by being transparently real, caring, and understanding. The therapist's realness was examined in an interesting and complex study by Culbert (1968). He compared two groups, one with a "more self-disclosing" (mSD) leader, and one with a "less self-disclosing" (lSD) leader. He found that participants with the mSD leader formed more "mutually perceived therapeutic relationships" with each other than in the lSD group, while those in the lSD group formed such relationships with the therapist. One could surmise that the mSD leader seemed more on a par with the participants, and therefore they were freed to interact therapeutically *either* with him or with each other. It seems likely that this kind of group learning is more transferrable to outside situations.

Culbert also found that the participants in the mSD group showed much higher self-awareness in the initial sessions of the group, which met weekly for two hours over 14 weeks. Participants in the lSD group eventually caught up with the self-awareness level of the other group, but not until the final sessions.

A study of the process of change in individuals in a group (Meador, 1971) examined change along the seven process strands which Rogers found to be the discernable growth variables (1961). The seven are feelings and personal meanings, manner of experiencing, degree of incongruence, communication of self, manner in which experience is construed, relationship to problems, and manner of relating. Blind ratings of film segments found that each of the eight individuals in the 16-hour weekend group made significant ($p < .01$) positive process movement. This means that each person in the group moved closer to his inner experiencing, became more able to express congruently what he was feeling, and became more real in his relationships. Movement along the process strands is what therapeutic movement is about in client-centered therapy, and this study showed that participation in a group, particularly an intensive weekend group as this one was, can bring about significant change in the group members.

A much earlier study of a weekly group (Peres, 1947) showed comparable results to Meador's study, although the methodology was quite different. Members of this group, which met for one hour over eight weeks, were divided into a "benefited" group and a "non-benefited" group according to members' self-reports after all the sessions had been completed. Peres found that in the "benefited" group the individuals' talk of their personal problems, of the insights they had gained, and of positive action they would take greatly increased over the sessions, while in the "non-benefited" group, the amount of personal talk was minimal throughout.

Another finding of this study which other process studies confirm (Rogers, 1967; Tomlinson and Hart, 1962; Walker, Rablen, and Rogers, 1960) is the correlation between process level and benefit or success in therapy. All these studies show that persons operating at higher process levels, that is persons who are in touch to some extent with their inner selves and can express this to some degree, make more therapeutic movement in groups and individual therapy and are judged to have benefited or changed in a positive way from the experience, more than persons who have great difficulty being aware of their inner selves.

Client-centered therapy is probably the most thoroughly researched therapy there is. Indeed, the interaction between theorizing and research results has been the cornerstone of the client-centered approach. It did not come into existence as a full-blown theory, but carved itself step by step along the way out of notions and hunches which were painstakingly evaluated. By the time Rogers and his colleagues turned their attention to groups, 20 years of research lay as a foundation to their method. Their confidence in the client-centered way of working is based on this foundation as well as on the group research which confirms it.

GOALS OF GROUP THERAPY

Believing as it does in a directional, ordering force within each individual, called the actualizing tendency, the goal of client-centered group therapy is that the individual become aware of and live in harmony with the wisdom and intentions of this force. Client-centered theory trusts the potency of a relationship with a certain character to release the actualizing tendency in an individual. The character of the relationship involves one person being real, caring, and understanding of another. In a group, the real, caring, and understanding person is as likely to be a group member as the therapist, but in order to get more understanding of the two sides of the relationship, we'll talk in terms of therapist and client.

Of the therapist, the theory asks that he maintain three attitudes. First, he will be genuinely, transparently real. This means that the other group members will know to some extent who the therapist is and what he is feeling; they will come to trust that what the therapist says comes genuinely from himself as a person and not from learned techniques. They will know that the therapist will express his persistent feelings even if they are risky, unpopular, or "untherapeutic." This means that the character of the group will be influenced by the *person* of the therapist as much as by the individuality of the group members. He is known in the group to the extent that he feels comfortable, just as the others. His relationship with individual members is person to person, not expert to patient.

Second, he will hear and understand what the participants are saying. Not only that, he will try to hear the feelings behind what the person is saying, the feelings on the edge of the person's awareness. In the process of understanding, he will try on the feelings the member is reporting, and out of this stepping into another person's shoes, he will communicate what this situation or these feelings would be like for him. Through his listening, his hearing, the individuals "begin to hear" themselves.

Third, the therapist will have an attitude of nonjudgmental caring for the group members. This attitude grows out of his trust in the actualizing potential in each individual and in the individual's ability to know himself and find his own pace and direction for change.

If the therapist can create a climate of caring, understanding and genuineness, then members of the group will begin to change along certain dimensions and in a particular direction. An individual will move from being remote from or unaware of his feelings toward acknowledging and expressing his feelings as they change and flow inside; from remoteness from his inner experiencing toward trusting and using his inner experiencing as a referent for his behavior; from dogmatism to flexibility of constructs; from hiding his inner self to openly communicating and prizing his inner self; from playing roles and wearing masks to being transparent; from finding the cause of problems "out there" to owning his own part in creating problems; and, finally, from fearful, hesitant closed relationships with others to more open, expressive personal relationships. Individuals move toward their own freedom, toward knowing, trusting, and allowing their inner selves to be the primary guide for their behavior.

An appropriate summary comes from a talk Rogers gave recently (1972, p. 17):

> On the basis of my experience I have found that if I can help bring about a climate marked by genuineness, prizing, and understanding, then exciting things happen. Persons and groups in such a climate move away from rigidity and toward flexibility, away from status

living toward process living, away from dependence toward autonomy, away from being predictable and toward an unpredictable creativity, away from defensiveness toward self acceptance. They exhibit living proof of an actualising tendency. Because of this evidence, I have developed a deep *trust*—in myself, in individuals, and in groups, when we are exposed to such a growth-promoting climate.

SELECTION AND GROUP COMPOSITION

There are no rules for selection of group members for a client-centered group. One therapist might try to keep a balance of ages and men and women, while another would have a group just for women or just for men.

Weekend encounter groups were generally open to the public. The La Jolla Program, a training institute for group leaders, provides a practicum experience for the participants. They may lead two encounter groups during the program, and the public is invited to participate. Several thousand persons have gone through these weekend groups over the seven years of the Program's existence with no incidents occurring which have made the leaders want to be selective in composing the groups.

A therapist may find a particular person so obstructive to the group process and his way of working that he would ask the person not to return, but this would be an entirely individual matter. (We have never heard of it happening.) More likely, the therapist would tell this person exactly how he feels and hope that his honesty and the group's reactions would bring about some change in the person's behavior.

GROUP SETTING

Groups are generally held in a comfortable, quiet setting where there will be no interruption. This may be an office or a home, while weekend groups are often held in a retreat setting. Again, the setting is up to the discretion of the therapist.

GROUP SIZE

The usual size for a client-centered group is between 8 and 12 persons. This would be true for the usual intensive small group. There are notable exceptions. A number of therapists have experimented with larger groups. The La Jolla Program holds daily community meetings of over 100 participants. These sessions may last several hours, and are in every sense an intense group experience.

FREQUENCY, LENGTH AND DURATION OF GROUP SESSIONS

The time factor of client-centered groups varies principally with whether or not the group is time-limited or on-going. The on-going groups usually meet weekly for an unspecified duration. Participants are added and terminate the groups at will. These groups usually meet for a minimum of four hours each week.

Time-limited groups have a specified duration, with all participants beginning together and remaining throughout the group. For a weekend group, the meetings are usually held from Friday evening until Sunday afternoon, with time out for meals and sleep. These groups usually meet a minimum of 16 hours. Other time-limited groups may agree to meet weekly for three or four hours for perhaps eight weeks.

In both cases it is thought that each session must last three or four hours for there to be adequate time for the process of the group to develop. This ripening time seems to be necessary even for groups in which the participants have a lot of experience together.

MEDIA EMPLOYED

Generally speaking, client-centered therapists use no media in their groups. In this as in all that happens in the group, it is up to the individual therapist, and some have used video, art, dance, creative writing, non-verbal experiences, among others at their own discretion.

THERAPIST QUALIFICATIONS

Recently, a therapist from Holland came to visit Carl Rogers. She was grateful, she said, for the vacation from a group she was leading of therapists-in-training. She had found herself session after session of the group sitting on feelings of anger and frustration. "What do you want the trainees to learn?" he asked. "Why, to be open, to express their feelings of hurt, anger, caring." "But you are unwilling to do that yourself. Is the model afraid to be human?" (personal communication, Nov. 1972).

This incident expresses what is asked of a client-centered group therapist, that he be able to open himself to the others in the group, that he be able to be himself there and to be met. Bill Coulson says (1972, p. 79):

> What is needed is an occasion for meeting. It will happen if the leader will allow himself to be met. In so doing, he does all that is necessary, all that is justifiable, to make the occasion for others also to be met. And that is enough, for when people meet, they are made to grow.

A related factor is that the therapist be involved in his own growth. If he is open to others, more than likely he is also open to himself. He sees the process of individual growth as a never ending one, and one which requires his conscious participation. A good therapist has reached a point in his growth where his own needs and problems are not always getting in the way of his being with the other group members.

A host of descriptive qualities are subsumed under these two basic qualifications, but if a person is able to be open and available to others and if he spends time working on himself, he can be in relationships which help others to grow.

ETHICAL CONSIDERATIONS

What is the implied ethical position of the client-centered group therapist? He probably adheres to the ethical guidelines of his profession, but does his way of conducting groups have ethical implications?

Because the client-centered therapist is in the group as another human person with his own feelings and foibles, his specialness has to do with his being the convener, he who provides the occasion, rather than the expert with a body of knowledge which he gives to the others. This stance avoids many of the ethical problems which arise when group members see the therapist as an authority who stands outside the human interaction making decisions and judgments for them. With the expert leader, ethical problems grow out of the power the group members assign him to tell them how to live their lives and even how the group will go tonight. "The group is in a better position for multi-directional, life-implicated learning," says Bill Coulson, "if the facilitator is in it with them than if he is exempted, standing back, arranging for them to go into areas that he hasn't charted himself or will not bear the consequences of exploring" (1972, p. 78).

The emphasis in client-centered groups is on each member being responsible for himself, determining what he will talk about and setting his own pace. Other members come to respect this responsibility in each other and to understand their individual differences. The temptation to direct others is taken for what it is, the wish or need of one for another to change in a certain way. The recipient of these suggestions learns to follow his own values and feelings, as self-determination and self-responsibility are repeatedly encouraged.

> Can you see that the situation is different when the doctor becomes a participant? Then the answer to "Is this right, Doctor?" can be neither opinion nor dodge but has to be something like, "How should I know? I'm a human being, too." Then, at that moment, if the patient believes the doctor, there is no more patient, no more doctor, just persons *(just persons!)*—humble, damaged, potent as hell to invent healthy lives when help reciprocates between them. Anything else is counterfeit (Coulson, 1972, p. 19).

The task of the therapist who believes this is to keep reminding the others and himself that each is responsible for what he will do and say in the group, that each has responsibility for his own life, for the changes he may or may not make, that they can depend on each other for help in learning more about themselves, but whatever insights are gained or risks are taken, each must finally do alone.

LIMITATIONS OF GROUP THERAPY

The principal limitations of group therapy are those of time and the attentive energies of the participants. These limitations are manifested in different ways. The first and most obvious way is that each person has a limited amount of time he can spend on himself. Participants are constantly caught in the bind of wanting time for themselves yet hesitating to claim it. This is different from individual therapy where the focus on the client is a given in the situation; therefore the deep personal searching, characteristic of individual therapy, probably doesn't occur as often in a group.

Limitations of time and energy may exclude certain types of

people from group therapy. An individual who consistently dominates a group or whose problems are so urgent and severe that he needs most of the members' time and energy may be excluded simply in fairness to the others.

Another limitation of group therapy is inherent in its nature. Because a number of people come together, it is more likely that interpersonal happenings will be discussed, again taking time away from deep, intrapersonal searching. Of course, this is an asset to the person who wants to work on his interpersonal relationships, but it does change the character of the therapy in contrast to a one-to-one situation.

A final limitation has to do with the ability of the participants to transfer their learnings from the group to the world outside. It is not uncommon for a participant to become dependent on the warmth and caring acceptance he finds in the group, and be unable to develop similar relationships in other parts of his life.

Each of these limitations can be overcome in one way or another. Participants should simply be aware of them, and if an individual finds himself caught in one of these limitations, he can find a solution.

SUMMARY

There are many reasons persons come into groups, but common to most is a wish to change. The process of individual change is a slow emergence, a coming into consciousness of factors the individual hadn't known before. The addition of these new awarenesses and their interplay with his present self slowly changes his way of being in the world.

Practitioners of the client-centered point of view try to answer the question, "How can this process of change begin or expand, and what can I do to help it happen?" It begins when a person decides to involve himself in his own growth, when he decides consciously to participate in the process. The therapist helps as he listens to the deep concerns of his client, as he tries to hear and understand what his client is saying, what new awareness is trying to make itself known. He helps as he states what he hears, thus giving a substance to the new. He helps as he responds honestly to the other, with a total presence of himself in the interactions.

The group setting has proved a viable structure in which an individual can participate in his own change. Here it is safe. Here there are persons who will listen and help him to hear what is wanting to be known. Here he can risk honesty, about himself and about the others.

And underlying the motives of the therapist is a kind of seriousness about what is going on in a group. There is often hilarity, boredom, chit-chat, but the unfolding process of human change has an awesomeness he cannot take lightly. This seriousness is basic to the client-centered way. When a therapist calls himself into seriousness, realness, caring, and understanding naturally follow.

SUGGESTED READINGS

Coulson, W. R.: *Groups, Gimmicks and Instant Gurus*. New York, Harper & Row, 1972.

Hart, J. T., and Tomlinson, T. M. (Eds.): *New Directions in Client-Centered Therapy*. Boston, Houghton-Mifflin, 1970.

Meador, B. D.: Individual process in a basic encounter group. *Journal of Counseling Psychology, 18:*70, 1971.

Meador, B. D., and Rogers, C. R.: Client-centered Therapy. In R. Corsini (Ed.): *Current Psychotherapies*. Itasca, Illinois, F. E. Peacock, 1973.

Rogers, C. R.: *On Becoming a Person*. Boston, Houghton-Mifflin, 1961.

Rogers, C. R.: The process equation of psychotherapy. *American Journal of Psychotherapy, 15*(1):27, 1961.

Rogers, C. R.: The actualizing tendency in relation to "motives" and to consciousness. In M. Jones (Ed.): *Nebraska Symposium on Motivation, 1963*, Lincoln, Nebraska, University of Nebraska Press, 1963.

Rogers, C. R.: *Carl Rogers on Encounter Groups*. New York, Harper & Row, 1970.

FILMS AND TAPES

McGaw, B. (Producer): "Journey Into Self." Western Behavioral Science Institute, 1150 Silverado, La Jolla, California 92037.

McGaw, B. (Producer): "Because That's My Way." G. P. N. Films, Box 80669, Lincoln, Nebraska 68501.

Rogers, C. R.: "How To Use Encounter Groups" (26 cassettes). The Human Development Institute, Dept. 3000, 166 E. Superior Street, Chicago, Illinois 60611.

REFERENCES

Barrett-Lennard, G.: Dimensions of perceived therapist response related to therapeutic change. Unpublished doctoral dissertation, University of Chicago, 1959.

Barrett-Lennard, G.: Dimensions of therapist response as causal factors in therapeutic change. *Psychological Monographs,* 1962, Whole No. 562.

Buber, M.: *Pointing the Way.* New York, Harper & Row, 1957.

Coulson, W. R.: *Groups, Gimmicks and Instant Gurus.* New York, Harper & Row, 1972.

Culbert, S. A.: Trainer self-disclosure and member growth in two T-groups. *Journal of Applied Behavioral Science, 4:*47, 1968.

Halkides, G.: An experimental study of four conditions necessary for therapeutic personality change. Unpublished doctoral dissertation, University of Chicago, 1958.

Jung, C. G.: *The Collected Works Vol. 16.* New York, Pantheon Books, 1954.

McGaw, B. (Producer): "Because That's My Way," National Educational Television: WOED, Pittsburgh, 1971.

Meador, B. D.: Individual process in a basic encounter group. *Journal of Counseling Psychology, 18:*70, 1971.

Meador, B. D., and Rogers, C. R.: Client-centered therapy. In R. Corsini (Ed.): *Current Psychotherapies,* Itasca, Illinois, F. E. Peacock, 1973.

Peres, H.: An investigation of non-directive group therapy. *Journal of Consulting Psychology, 11:*159, 1947.

Rogers, C. R.: *Counseling and Psychotherapy.* Boston, Houghton-Mifflin, 1942.

Rogers, C. R.: A theory of therapy, personality, and interpersonal relationships, as developed in the client-centered framework. In S. Kock (Ed.): *Psychology: A Study of a Science,* Vol. III. *Formulations of the Person and the Social Context.* New York, McGraw-Hill, 1959.

Rogers, C. R.: The process equation of psychotherapy. *American Journal of Psychotherapy, 15*(1):27, 1961.

Rogers, C. R.: *Carl Rogers on Encounter Groups.* New York, Harper & Row, 1970.

Rogers, C. R.: My philosophy of interpersonal relationships and how it grew. Address at Association for Humanistic Psychology, Honolulu, Hawaii, September, 1972.

Rogers, C. R., and Dymond, R. F. (Eds.): *Psychotherapy and Personality Change.* Chicago, University of Chicago Press, 1954.

Rogers, C. R., Gendlin, E. T., Kiesler, D. J., and Truax, C. (Eds.): *The Therapeutic Relationship and Its Impacts: A Study of Psychotherapy With Schizophrenics.* Madison, Wisconsin, University of Wisconsin Press, 1967.

Shlien, J. M., and Zimring, F. M.: Research directives and methods in client-centered therapy. In J. T. Hart and T. M. Tomlinson (Eds.): *New Directions in Client-centered Therapy.* Boston, Houghton-Mifflin, 1970.

Tomlinson, T. M., and Hart, J. T., Jr.: A validation study of the process scale. *Journal of Consulting Psychology, 26:*74, 1962.

Walker, A. M., Rablen, R. A., and Rogers, C. R.: Development of a scale to measure process changes in psychotherapy. *Journal of Clinical Psychology, 16:*179, 1960.

Whyte, L.: *The Unconscious Before Freud.* London, Tavistock Publications, 1960.

CHAPTER IX

REALITY THERAPY IN GROUPS

Robert F. Kaltenbach and George M. Gazda
(Reviewed by William Glasser[1])

INTRODUCTION

R EALITY THERAPY is a set of theoretical principles and methodologies developed by Dr. William Glasser. The principles attempt to explain the condition of those patients that he worked with and the means by which they were helped to lead productive responsible lives. Emerging in the 1950's, Reality Therapy has rushed to the forefront in popularity of the modern psychotherapy theories. Straight-forward, logical, jargon-free, warm and human, it offers an explanation of healthy and unhealthy behavior as well as basic principles for dealing with others, especially those with so-called psychological problems.

Reality Therapy is considered unconventional in several respects. First, it rejects the concept of mental illness. Instead, it places the responsibility for behavior on the individual and professes that his behavior is under his control and is chosen by him. Second, since it rejected the concept of mental illness, it dispenses with the traditional psychiatric classification of persons such as schizophrenic, paranoid, manic-depressive. Third, it is antithetical to psychoanalysis in several respects. Little importance is placed on probing into the patient's past life; instead the concentration is on current behavior. Transference is rejected. The therapist is a real person and is the person to whom the patient is relating. The gaining of insight and understanding, which was the end goal of psychoanalysis, is considered insufficient to resolve the patient's problems. He must be taught new behavior. Finally, morality and

---

1. I have reviewed the material in this chapter and I believe it to be essentially accurate in its representation.

196

responsibility are very much a part of Reality Therapy. Behavior cannot be excused because of a patient's unconscious conflicts or reasons for it. In addition to these differences, Reality Therapy further rocks the boat of the conventional approach by the contention that the helping person need not be trained in the psychiatric community. They need only be concerned individuals trained in the principles of Reality Therapy.

Applied in a variety of fashions, Reality Therapy appears to be most promising when used in a group setting. Dr. Glasser discovered that the group approach was most effective and economical while consulting at the Ventura School for Delinquent Girls in California. There, therapy was primarily conducted in groups. It was found that group therapy is extremely effective in such institutions where there are many patients who have similar problems but are at different stages of resolution.

Glasser further developed the group approach when he utilized it as a preventative intervention approach in the school system (Glasser, 1969a). Conducting group sessions (class meetings) in educational settings was found to improve the educational environment and stimulate learning. In this setting, three types of meetings were defined: the social-problem-solving meeting, the open-ended meeting, and the educational-diagnostic meeting. Although designed for an educational setting and addressing the problems of that setting, it appears that they have more general applicability.

Social-problem-solving meetings attempt to solve individual and group problems of living. In the school setting, of course, the problems would pertain to the educational and school world. This group prototype can be used just as easily and is just as valuable in other types of institutional settings. Similar groups intended to prepare patients for life outside the hospital were conducted in Dr. Harrington's project (Glasser, 1965). Such groups are basic task-oriented problem solving groups used to anticipate or identify problems and move toward their resolution.

Open-ended meetings allow discussion of any area related to the lives of individual group members. This type of meeting stimulates thinking about social and behavioral concerns. Members are encouraged to express their feelings, opinions, or anything that will stimulate a thoughtful conversation regarding the lives of the members.

Educational-diagnostic meetings are directed at the topics the class is studying. They are probably the least generalizable to general group counseling situations. Since they provide an evaluation of teaching methods and the impact they have on students, it appears they can be used in similar situations where such information is valuable. Possibly they will also prove useful in organizational problem solving groups.

Dr. Glasser has used extensively these three types of group meetings in the school setting with much success. Underlying each of these is the theoretical rationale and principles of Reality Therapy that have been used so successfully in individual therapy. The process is the same. The group leader needs only to be skilled at applying the principles in a group setting to be successful.

THEORETICAL RATIONALE

Reality Therapy presents the proposition that regardless of how one expresses his problem, everyone who needs psychiatric treatment suffers from one basic inadequacy: he is unable to fulfill his basic needs. These needs, which appear to be built into our nervous system, cause pain and suffering if not satisfied. The person needing counseling help has chosen unsatisfactory behavior that attempts but does not alleviate the pain of unfulfilled needs. The severity of the symptoms displayed reflects the degree to which the individual is unable to fulfill his needs. When the needs are satisfied, the unsatisfactory behavior or symptoms disappear.

Even though the behavior displayed by a patient may appear to be quite irrational and aberrant, it has meaning and validity to him. The unsatisfactory behavior has been chosen and is directed toward meeting the person's unfulfilled needs. The disturbed behavior manifestations are actually an indication of the person's inability to fulfill his needs within the limits of his environment. The common characteristic displayed by disturbed persons is their denial of the reality of the world around them. The denial may be slight and partial, as in denying that a rule of society is relevant to oneself, or extreme and complete, as is often found in back ward mental patients; but it is present never-the-less.

Patients will be able to be successful when they are able to give up denying the world and recognize that reality not only exists but that they must fulfill their needs within its framework. A therapy that leads all patients toward reality, toward grappling successfully with the tangible and intangible aspects of the real world might be called a therapy toward reality, or simply Reality Therapy.

It is not enough to have the patient accept the reality of his existence; therapy must also concentrate on helping him to learn behavior that will allow him to fulfill his needs in the real world, thereby reducing his pain. Unless this is done, the patient has no way except old, ineffective behavior to cope with the stress he will experience in his lifetime. To do Reality Therapy then, the therapist must not only be able to help the patient accept the real world but he must then further help him fulfill his needs in the real world so that he will have no inclination in the future to deny its existence.

The Basic Needs

It is widely acknowledged that man has both physiological and psychological needs that cause discomfort if they are not satisfied. Among the physiological needs, there is little disagreement as to which are the more basic. There is somewhat more discussion, differential labeling and variability or disagreement as to what are the basic psychological needs. Most people agree that the same psychological needs appear universally across cultural patterns, age, sex, and races, even though individuals vary in the intensity of needs and in their ability to satisfy them. For Reality Therapy, the two psychological needs with which we must be concerned are the need to love and be loved and the need to feel we are worthwhile to ourselves and others.

There is an impressive collection of evidence from both animal and human research as well as from clinical practice that indicates we need to be loved from birth to old age. The indications from studies in early experimental isolation, enriched environments (Fiske and Maddi, 1961), motherless monkeys (Harlow, 1958), and the Hospitalism syndrome of human infants described by Spitz (1945) are that unless love and attention are present, the growing infant will display abnormal, maladaptive behaviors. To love and be loved seems to be based upon the need to survive and is a necessary ingredient for successful growth and development. It must be fulfilled early and continually throughout our lives; our health and happiness depend upon it. We must be able to give love and to have someone love us in return.

In many respects, love is synonymous with involvement. It implies that there is another person who cares about us and whom we care for in return. In the context of school, love can best be thought of as social responsibility. Children must learn to be responsible for each other, to care for each other, and to help each other, not only for the sake of others but for their own sake. One does not fulfill this need by either giving love or receiving love separately; we must do both. The only way one loves and is loved is by being involved with at least one other person, preferably a group, throughout their lives. The extent to which we become involved with others is directly related to the degree to which this need for love is fulfilled. Those who are involved with others are generally successful; those who are uninvolved are lonely and suffer.

The need to feel worthwhile to ourselves and others is equally important as the need to feel loved. This need, closely related to self-esteem, stems from the feelings, "I am worthwhile; my life does make a difference; I am doing something worthwhile with my life." It appears to validate the very existence of an individual. Like love, it is a condition that must be reciprocated. There must be others whom one feels are worthwhile and whom he respects and who, in return, feels he is worthwhile and respect him.

To be worthwhile, one must maintain a satisfactory standard of behavior. We must behave in ways that will gain the love and respect of others. Only when we behave in such ways and perform tasks that are worthwhile to others as well as to ourselves do we gain the feelings of self-worth. Morals, standards, values of right and wrong behavior as well as work behavior are all intimately related to the fulfillment of our need for self-worth.

It should be realized that although the conditions for love and for worth are separate, generally a person who loves and is loved will feel that he is worthwhile, and one who is worthwhile is usually someone who is loved and who can give love in return. However, even though it *is* possible to satisfy one need and not the other, i.e., to be loved but not to be worthwhile or to be worthwhile but unloved, this is not enough. The unfulfilled need will cause pain and discomfort. Both needs must be fulfilled independently of each other, but both must be fulfilled.

The degree and manner in which the conditions of love and worth are met determine how the person feels about himself. Actually, love and self-worth are so intertwined that they may more properly be conveyed through the use of the term, *Identity*. Thus, we may say that the single basic need that people have is the requirement for an Identity: the belief that we are someone in distinction to others, and that the someone is important and worthwhile. This need is universal and is found across race, cultural, age, and sex groupings. The person who can love and is loved and feels worthwhile fulfills his needs and develops a *success identity*. It is this end that we struggle to develop in childhood and strive to maintain the rest of our lives.

Two Basic Life Styles

There are two types of life styles that develop as a result of the identity one chooses for himself; one that is based on a *success identity* and one that is based on a *failure identity*. If one chooses to behave in a socially responsible manner and becomes involved with others, it is most probable that he will satisfy his need for love and worth. From such behavior and need satisfaction, the person will develop a success identity. On the other hand, if a person chooses to act irresponsibly and does not become involved with others, he will not feel loved or worthy and will invariably develop an identity of himself as a failure.

Success Identity

Characteristic of a success identity is a positive appraisal of oneself. This person has needs, encounters problems, and has conflicts; however, he has confidence in his decisions and chooses behavior that he knows can resolve his difficulties. Acting responsibly, he satisfies his needs with regard to others and the social environment in which he lives.

People with a "success identity" are involved with other people in their family and in the community. Thus they feel loved and are capable of loving others in return. They are able to look at the reality of a situation and be aware of and evaluate their behavior to determine whether or not it is responsibly appropriate. They know that they must take the consequences of their behavior, so irresponsible behavior is out. They involve themselves in tasks that are worthwhile to themselves and others, thereby receiving recognition and gaining respect from others as well as feelings of self-worth. Each day is not necessarily a good one, and there are periods of bad times and stress; but over the long run, successful persons have the belief that happiness is always a possibility and that they will experience good times in their lives. Generally, they would appraise themselves as succeeding, going in a successful direction, and being able to influence what happens in their lives.

Failure Identity

In contrast, people with failure identities are lonely and appraise themselves and life in general as being characterized by suffering and pain. They develop a response set that "I can't" and generally feel that "Everything is wrong and I can't do anything about it." They are not sure that anyone worthwhile cares for them and even less sure that they can establish such a relationship; therefore they do not care much for anybody else. The normal give-and-take of a healthy relationship appears to be nearly impossible to them. They mostly "take" in whatever meager relationships they develop. To give would expose them to rejection, which causes too much pain for them to even risk. They seldom initiate anything that is worthwhile to themselves or others. As a result, they are withdrawn and uninvolved, typically fail to express any need for others, stifle relationships with others, and are afraid to risk rejection.

It must be remembered that these people hurt very much. Unfortunately, they have chosen behavior that denies the reality of their loneliness and is therefore ineffective in eliminating all the pain emanating from loneliness. To the professional or helping person, the ineffective ways a patient uses to reduce pain are typically viewed as symptomatology. There are four primary unrealistic modes used to reduce the pain of uninvolvement: disturbances of emotions, behavior problems, disturbances of thought, and sickness.

DISTURBANCE OF EMOTIONS. This type of disturbance takes a variety of forms but is best exemplified by depression. Unable to reduce the pain of loneliness through more realistic ways, the person mistakenly withdraws into the self-involvement of depression. Depression does aid the person by partially reducing the pain he feels and by providing a rationalization for continuing uninvolved behavior. After all, how can anyone expect a depressed person to become involved with others when he feels so bad? Instead of dealing with the real problems that face him, the person generally becomes involved with the depression. He then deceives himself by denying the realities of the world around him.

When a successful person feels depressed, he realizes that he must do something about it. The failure fights to maintain the depression since it provided some relief to him. In giving up the symptoms of depression, he is exposed to greater pain from feelings of being unloved and worthless. To experience increased pain is more than the person can do, so he withdraws again into the depression. Thus, we see the well known pattern. Without some kind of help, depressives have much difficulty dealing with their feelings. Developing depression symptomatology may have some value—now at least the person can ask for help.

BEHAVIOR PROBLEMS. This type of disturbance is manifest in numberous anti-social, acting out behaviors. Alcoholism, drug abuse, sexual excesses, delinquency and crime are all behavioral manifestations of failure. Unable to develop meaningful relationships with others, those with a "failure identity" often exhibit behavior that is irresponsible, shows little regard for and often hurts others. "Kicks" are gained at the expense of the community. They are indifferent to social rules and show little concern at breaking them. Anti-social and delinquent, they reinforce their lack of regard for others by casting the blame on others for their own irresponsible behavior. They are not afraid of punishment; that is what they expect. They do not fear failure; it is all they have known and they have nothing to lose anyway. Responding only to the "take" of a relationship, they wish to gain things easily without working, so frequently they are in trouble with the law. Because of their behavior, one of society's major institutions is maintained for them–the prison.

DISTURBANCES OF THOUGHT. This type of disturbance ranges from the occurrence of unwelcomed thoughts to obsessive concerns, delusions, and finally hallucinations. On this continuum, there is a progressive use of denial of reality in an effort to reduce pain. In the world of the psychotic there is a profound denial of the world around them and a retreat into a world of their own creation–a world of their own choosing. The deception is obvious. Obsessional, delusional and hallucinatory disturbances direct attention to these phenomena and away from the loneliness the person feels. Once self-involved, the person no longer has to deal with the pain of failing. Most people who choose this form of self-deception are found in another institution of society–a mental hospital.

SICKNESS. Without doubt, sickness is the most frequently used mode for relief of the pain of failure. A large number of persons who consult an M.D. do not have treatable organic illnesses. There are myriad vague, non-descript aches and pains that are more likely linked to psychological rather than physiological causes. One cannot underestimate the power of the mind to influence the body. Presently, investigations are being conducted in predicting the occurrence of physical illness as a result of the amount of psychological stress an individual has recently experienced. Hans Selye (1950) has shown an undeniable interrelation between stress (both physical and psychological) and illness. Instances of this deception range from the infrequent desire to stay in bed rather than face a hectic day at work to the chronic complainer who centers his life around physicians and medications and tales of his problems. Unless the treating physician is perceptive, it is quite likely that the person will receive only medical attention which, unfortunately, will not be sufficient to help him.

Identity in Reality Therapy*

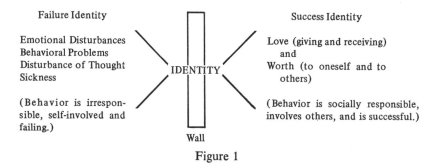

Failure Identity

Emotional Disturbances
Behavioral Problems
Disturbance of Thought
Sickness

(Behavior is irrespon-
sible, self-involved and
failing.)

IDENTITY

Wall

Success Identity

Love (giving and receiving)
and
Worth (to oneself and to
others)

(Behavior is socially responsible,
involves others, and is successful.)

Figure 1

*Presented at the East Coast Training Seminar on Reality Therapy, Augusta, Georgia, Dec. 1973.

The relationships among the various aspects of success and failure identity is shown in Figure 1. If one envisions a hypothetical wall separating success and failure life styles, Identity would be a break in the wall shared by both successful and failing persons.

A TRANSITION SOCIETY

Since World War II, our society has been involved in a rather sudden transition from a goal-oriented survival society to a role-oriented identity society. The survival society, based on power, suppressed man's need for involvement in favor of goal attainment and self-enhancing gain. The survival society fostered constant hostile, destructive, competitive behavior directed toward getting an individual higher in the social structure. In such a society, the essence of each individual is lost, most men are forced into a dependent role, and institutions rule supreme. The only identity possible for most people in this type of society is usually limited to supporting the goal; their role is dependent upon their work or class, the only means to secure a place in the power structure. Only after years of striving for security by working hard in the dependent role could a person begin to look for the human satisfactions in his life under this regimen.

Less anxious about fulfilling goals to obtain security within the power hierarchy, people today concern themselves more and more with an independent role–their identity. Of course, people still strive for goals, but they may or may not lead to economic security. They, however, do give verification of the person as a human being. In the survival society, too often one had to reject the messages received from his nervous system and fulfill the "should" of a goal orientation. When such a condition arises, pain will be experienced. Our nervous system often tells us to protect ourselves, yet our conscious mind tells us to override the nervous system in order to meet the goal. Young people today are rejecting such incongruity. They strive for greater harmony between the nervous system and the conscious mind. We must learn to satisfy the urges of our nervous system as well as to choose the best options available in a new society so that we can feel good. In this identity society, the role the individual takes becomes his most important concern–he is concerned with his identity more than anything else.

Concern with power, which caused competition and alienation, is greatly reduced. It has been replaced with the long denied needs for involvement and intelligent cooperation. These latter needs of man have been suppressed by the culture of the survival society for so long that they appear rather strange and unnatural when compared to the hostile, aggressive behavior to which we are more accustomed. However, hostile, destructive, competitive behavior is not natural; it is not built-in. Our present evolving identity society recognizes this and has chosen to reject these behaviors and respond to the natural felt needs for involvement and cooperation with other human beings. Then, to live successfully in our present society, we must recognize that the need for stimulating social and intellectual involvement is a part of us, that it evolved from a need that kept us alive, and that it warns us to seek each other's company through the same urgent nervous pathway that its ancient predecessor used.

Identity in such a society is of paramount importance to the individual. Those who are involved with others and cooperate through responsible, worthwhile behavior, develop success identities. Those who are uninvolved, irresponsible and lonely, develop failure identities and cannot survive in the society. It is to these failures that Reality Therapy addresses itself.

PRINCIPLES OF REALITY THERAPY

The principles of Reality Therapy, when applied in a systematic manner, provide a good probability of success both for the person with a failure identity and for the therapist. These principles are applied in a progressive or phase-like manner, each building on the previous phase and each contributing to the total process that is Reality Therapy.

Principle I: Involvement

Since the person who acts irresponsibly and has a failure identity is alienated and lonely, it follows that a major therapeutic tool is involvement. Involvement is a necessary prerequisite for anyone to develop and maintain a success identity or to change from failure to success. It appears to be a universal condition that a relationship with a successful person, preferably a group with whom we are emotionally involved, is essential to fulfilling our needs.

Lacking a warm emotional involvement with a responsible person, failures withdraw and become self-involved, ruminate over their symptoms, and behave in an irresponsible manner that causes increased suffering to themselves and those around them. Feeling unloved, they are unable to love. Feeling unworthy, they are afraid to try anything worthwhile. They avoid the very things they need rather than face rejection. Using irresponsible behavior, they are prone to hit first, thus stifling the development of any meaningful involvements.

Involvement is the foundation of therapy. All other principles build on and add to it. The therapist strives to establish a warm, intimate, emotional involvement to break the loneliness and the self-involvement in which the patient indulges. This is the most important, yet the most difficult phase of therapy. Without involvement, there can be no therapy. When Reality Therapy fails, it is usually because the therapist is unable to get involved in a meaningful way with the person who is unsuccessful. The patient needs, usually desperately, someone with whom he can become emotionally involved, someone who cares about him and whom he can care about in return, and someone who can convince him that he will help to fulfill his needs. The therapist's purpose, then, is to provide enough involvement himself to help the patient develop confidence to make new, deep, lasting involvements of his own.

The ability of the therapist to get involved is a major skill required for practicing Reality Therapy, but it is quite difficult to describe. It is not enough simply to establish rapport with the patient and then remain aloof, impersonal, and objective. No one can break through the patient's intense self-involvement with such emotionally detached behavior. This, by the way, is a major failing of traditional psychotherapy. Many are trained to avoid the personal involvement, to remain objective and somewhat detached. Usually, personal feelings expressed towards the therapist, whether hostile or caring, are explained as transference. Simply calling the personal feelings expressed toward the therapist transference avoids the basic needs of the patient and begs the question. The guiding principles of Reality Therapy are directed toward achieving the proper involvement–a completely honest, human relationship in which the patient, perhaps for the first time in his life, realizes that someone cares enough about him not only to accept him but to help him fulfill his needs in the real world.

Involvement is extended by the therapist in a warm, friendly manner, showing that he is open and willing to become emotionally involved with the patient. He is willing to talk about almost anything the patient wishes to discuss, with little emphasis, however, on symptoms. The patient must be introduced to this ideal and understand that there is more to life than being self-involved with his misery, symptoms, and irresponsible behavior. He must recognize that another human being cares for him and is willing to discuss his life and talk about anything that both of them consider worthwhile and interesting. Current books, movies, hobbies, recreational activities, aspirations, personal relations, and family are all appropriate areas of discussions. The patient should be challenged with values and opinions to stimulate him. It is unwise to focus on problems or his misery. Doing so reinforces his behavior by giving value to his self-involvement and failures. The less we talk of his problems and his behavior and the more we discuss the possibilities that are open to him, the better he feels.

Patients are frequently genuinely surprised to discover that they feel better and function better even though they did not focus on their problems. They find they talked about and enjoyed a wide range of subjects. They need to be reassured that these discussions have been worthwhile. The therapist knows that the warm, involved conversations have directed the patient's energies away from self-involvement and towards involvement with others, thereby helping him expand his life space. It is, however, better not to explain this dynamic fully and technically since it would detract from the involvement. Reassurance that the discussions have had an effect and encouragement to continue are more appropriate.

A substantial problem in the formal patient-therapist relationship is to establish warmth and friendship yet limit the involvement to what is possible in the therapeutic situation. To the uninvolved person, the warm, accepting therapist becomes a real source of need gratification that is desperately desired. The therapist's problem becomes how to become involved enough to help the person risk making other long-lasting involvements yet not become overburdened as the sole source of gratification for the patient. It is not possible to become extensively involved with every patient in time-consuming relationships and still lead a life of your own. In addition, such an emotional dependency on the therapist is not desirable for the long-term goals of therapy. Practice has shown that the therapist must not promise too much. He must be honest and never promise more time than he can give. Patients will usually accept honest statements from the therapist once involvement has been established. With respect to time and involvement, whatever the amount of time the patient has with the involved therapist is usually more productive time than he had with any other person. The therapist must convince the patient that such relationships are available with other people and that he must risk seeking them out.

It is at this point in treatment that the advantages of group therapy become apparent. The other people in the group each offer the opportunity for involvement. Collectively, the group can provide greater support, need gratification, and assurance than a single individual. In group therapy, there is more opportunity for and safety in risking new behavior. The therapist does not have to hope the patient will spread his involvement to others outside of therapy; the individual can do it right there in a less threatening and haphazard way. Listening to and becoming involved with the concerns of others reduces self-involvement and allows a wide range of emotions to be expressed. Involvement is stimulated by the warm, non-punishing environment of the group setting. Instead of one person who cares and who feels the patient is worthwhile, now there is the whole group. To stay in the group means the person has to get personal, has to be warm, has to develop concern for others and, most of all, has to develop more responsible behavior. Acting in this manner, the patient has a taste of success and feels better about himself.

Principle II: Focus on Current Behavior

Traditional therapy focuses at length on the past history of the patient. Reality Therapy considers this practice to be of little use to bring about change and may even be detrimental by reinforcing the apparent importance of past events and their association with the person's present predicament. Instead of getting involved in the fruitless pursuit of past explanations for present behavior, Reality Therapy focuses attention on the present behavior of the patient. Self-involved, most patients are unaware of the impact their behavior has on themselves and others. The only way a person can work toward a success identity is to become aware of the ramifications of his present behavior. This is the focus of therapy.

Reality Therapy emphasizes behavior, not feelings. To focus on feelings rather than behavior offers the patient an easy way to avoid facing and taking responsibility for his present behavior. Feelings are important in any relationship; however, the crucial factor in a relationship is how we behave toward other people. Behavior is readily observed and responded to; feelings are not. If changes in the way one relates to others are to occur, they must start with changes in behavior.

Patients typically will, however, want to talk about their feelings rather than their behavior. The therapist neither denies feelings nor says they are wrong or unimportant. He accepts them but points out that the way one feels is not as important as the way one behaves. He therefore often surprises patients when he responds, "I believe you; you have convinced me of your complaints (or depression, or whatever); I appreciate that you are upset, but what are you doing?" In this way he redirects attention to their responsibility for their behavior. By continually doing so, the therapist is able to get through the defense and point out the unreality of the present ineffective behavior.

Questions like, "What are you doing?," "What did you do then?," "What are you doing now?," "What did you do yesterday?," provide the impetus to becoming aware of behavior and provide the opportunity to choose or consider new behavior that will lead to involvement with others. The patient must learn to distinguish responsible from irresponsible behavior and to accept responsibility for his behavior. The skill of therapy is to put responsibility with the patient. The only help that will do any good is that which guides him toward the responsibility he is so steadfastly avoiding.

It is a basic premise, whether one realizes it or not, that the behavior we exhibit is chosen behavior. Concentrating on the "What are you doing?" rather than the "Why?" of behavior is directed toward helping the patient gain conscious control of his behavior and toward learning that he can control the choices he makes. Further, he must realize that he has the responsibility for his behavior choices. If he chooses to continue acting irresponsibly, he will continue to hurt. Hurting will stop when he decides to act responsibly and become involved with others.

Principle III: Evaluating Behavior

At the point of becoming aware of one's behavior and before change can occur, the patient must examine and evaluate his behavior to see if it is beneficial in helping to meet his needs. He must determine if it is good for him and good for those that he cares for or would like to care for and if it is socially acceptable in his community. Since how a person behaves is his choice, he must make the judgment whether or not he wishes to continue the behavior. It is the patient's responsibility to evaluate and decide what he wants to do about his behavior. The Reality Therapist does not do this by imposing value judgments or giving cheap advice nor does he present the "should" expectations of society. He must, however, help work towards having the patient make a decision and point out the reality consequence of that decision.

Often there is no clear choice as to which behavior is more responsible. Choice is not always as it is when the alcoholic who is aware that drinking is not beneficial still says, "Fill her up, Joe." He knows he is acting irresponsibly. In some instances, such as divorce or establishing independence from parents, it is difficult to make a choice. Making the choice to separate will probably, at least temporarily, hurt others. Nevertheless, the person must come to the decision not to prolong a bad situation. Frequently, such a separation must occur before responsible behavior can occur. The Reality Therapist must operate on the premise that coming to a decision offers a better chance of success than prolonging the situation. He provides the patient the opportunity to examine the situation and to urge him to make a decision.

There are two points that need to be emphasized here. First, a person must be involved with at least one other person before he can make an honest self-evaluation. Lonely people, involved with failure, find it almost impossible to do this. On the other hand, a characteristic of a person with a success identity is his ability to judge honestly what he is doing in a wide context; he faces reality and decides how he might act differently whenever a situation arises. The failing person must feel that the therapist, or better the group, cares about him. It is only when this occurs that he will be willing to examine his behavior and try new behavior. Second, once involved, any person can evaluate his own behavior. A person can judge his behavior without a therapist; he can determine if he is acting responsibly or irresponsibly. Whoever the helping person, he should be careful not to make judgments but to lead towards patient self-judgment. Even though the ability to make reasonable value judgments is fostered in the therapy hour, the judgment, "I ought to change," belongs to the patient. In a group of peers, however, it is perfectly all right if members judge each other's behavior. We want this to occur, but the therapist should not do it; it is not his job.

The therapist must help patients reevaluate their behavior by asking questions like, "Is this the best thing you can choose now?," "Does your behavior seem to help the situation?," "If you behave in other ways, would the outcome be different?" For instance, in working with the alcoholic, the therapist helps him understand that when he drinks, he makes a value judgment–the drink is worth more than anything else–and that he must examine his choice if he wants to change. To quit drinking, he must decide that alcohol is a bad choice; it is not the best thing he can do. As long as he continues drinking, alcohol is his choice and he will have to accept the consequences. Since behavior is a choice, there is no justification for excusing moral or legal transgressions. Furthermore, if a patient is unwilling to make such value judgments about his behavior and stick to them, there is nothing that can be done in therapy.

Principle IV: Planning Responsible Behavior

Once someone makes a value judgment, acknowledges that his behavior is irresponsible, and indicates that he wants to change, it is the responsibility of the person or the group to assist in developing realistic plans for change. Too many people, especially those with failure identities, have no experience or background for planning a more successful life. They have such a limited repertoire of behavioral responses that they are simply not able to suggest a variety of preferred alternatives to their present behavior. The therapist, because he has more experience in this area, and the group, because of the variety of experiential backgrounds, are usually able to generate enough ideas to allow the person to develop much of the plan for himself. It is possible that resource persons aside from the group may be used. These people can frequently provide much needed information that provides a good basis for implementing the plan.

At this phase, relearning begins. Through involvement with

others, the patient learns new behavior. Both therapist and group members encourage and support experimenting with new behavior via the plan of action the patient develops. In some respects, planning proceeds in a trial and error fashion in which a plan is made, tried, and possibly modified until one that adequately fits the situation is derived. Usually several plans can end at the same goal; the person has the right to determine the plan he prefers.

A plan that attempts too much should be avoided because it will usually fail and reinforce the already present failure. A failing person needs success, and he needs small individually successful steps to gain it. A reasonable plan should be made to begin with; it can be changed and expanded if necessary. The importance of the plan is that it provides a success experience for the person. Success, no matter how small the dose, is what is needed. The failure identity must be given up. The only way this is accomplished is by experiencing success through responsible involvement. Little but successful steps can be extended; big steps that fail are devastating. The therapist encourages the development of subgoals that lead through several intermediate successful steps to the attaining of the major goal. Each successive subgoal should involve little risk and maximize the probability of success. Success experience reinforces the person's decision to try new behavior and encourages continuing effort.

In certain situations, it is not possible to develop a plan of action. Examples of these situations are long-term prison sentences, terminal illnesses, severe senility, and other severely disabling impediments. How does one develop a plan for a prisoner to be implemented twenty-five years from the time it was developed? In the case of the terminally ill, it becomes even harder to develop a plan, especially if they know they are dying and have accepted their fate. All one can do in both situations is to create an involvement that will make them comfortable. In terms of planning, there is little that can be done. Situations such as these, although frustrating, occur very infrequently for the therapist. For 99.9 percent of the people with whom a therapist works, plans are possible. In this stage, the therapists and group members must help the patient develop skill in evaluating his behavior and his plan for success.

They are supportive and encourage exploration with new behavior that will lead to success. If the plan is feasible, they must be firm in seeing that it is implemented; if it is not feasible, they and the patient must be flexible enough to revise it.

Principle V: Commitment

After a reasonable plan is made and appears to be feasible, a commitment must be obtained that the plan will be carried out. A commitment to any plan is maturity–a part of responsible behavior. It may be verbal or written; it may be given to an individual or a group; nevertheless, commitment is necessary, for without it, without saying, "I'll do it for you as well as for me," plans are less likely to be implemented.

Commitment is at the same time motivating and binding. Adding commitment to others to the individual's own desire to implement his plan becomes a powerful extrinsic motivator. Nothing is wrong with trying new behavior to please someone else; we cannot be successful by remaining uninvolved. The support and encouragement of the group is especially critical at this time. If the norm of the group is to carry out the plan once a commitment is given, the pressures stemming from group cohesiveness and uniformity will bind the person to the plan. It is much more difficult to give up on a commitment when it is made to a group than to oneself or a therapist. There is much more at stake. At the same time, it becomes somewhat easier to carry out the plan when one has the support of a group. For these reasons, the use of groups in Reality Therapy is strongly recommended.

Getting a commitment is not an easy task. For people with failure identities, commitments are difficult. If one has failed frequently, he fears that to commit himself and fail will expose him to painful rejection. Even though he is already lonely and believes no one cares, he does not want to risk the potential rejection that would verify his feelings of worthlessness. In order to protect himself from possible rejection, he frequently will resist making a commitment. Commitment is involvement. Until the person is willing to make a commitment to others, it is likely that he will remain self-involved and unable to gain a success identity. The therapist and the group must be able to assist the patient with a failure identity to overcome his fears and risk new behavior.

Verbal commitments are acceptable, but written commitments are stronger, more binding, and clearer. There is little doubt as to the terms of the commitment when they are written out and signed by the person. Written contracts appear to work especially well with children. Two copies are made so that the therapist and patient can easily refer to it. This quasi-legal process may seem a bit strong. However, the fact remains that it is harder to escape from a written commitment than from a verbal one. For many persons attempting to change their behavior, a firm commitment such as this is necessary.

Principle VI: Accept No Excuses

Plans may fail, but it is the obligation of the therapist and the group to make it clear that no excuses are acceptable. Excuses break the involvement; they allow the person to avoid responsibility. They, at best, provide only temporary relief; they reduce the patient's tension but impede change. If the therapist accepts an excuse, the patient frequently interprets this as lack of concern and confidence. To the patient, the therapist is saying, "O.K., this time. After all, what could I expect from a miserable failure."

The therapist must be tough; he must accept no excuses, none at all. The therapist cannot hold the patient to the commitment in a legal or punitive sense nor can he withdraw. The most powerful course of action open to the therapist is never to excuse the person from the responsibility of the commitment. No matter how valid the excuse, it does not matter; it still represents failure. To be successful and change his identity, the patient must fulfill the plan. To search for "Why?" opens the door to a myriad of conscious and, when they run out, unconscious explanations, all of them rationalizations, intellectualizing or other defenses that excuse accepting responsibility. A commitment made is a commitment important enough to be worth keeping. Those concerned must hold the person to it.

When a commitment fails, the value judgment that leads to the plan must be reevaluated. If the value judgment is still valid, then the plan must be reconsidered. If the plan is reasonable, the person must decide whether or not to recommit himself. If he does not, he is no longer responsible; if he does, he is expected to honor the commitment. The therapist does not emphasize the failure. He simply asks, "When are you going to do it?" Time is rarely important. The patient will eventually begin to fulfill his commitments if the therapist holds him to them and continues his involvement with him. This kind of therapist toughness is difficult but essential, because the only commitments that many patients have made are to their irresponsibilities, their emotions, and their self-involvements.

Principle VII: No Punishment

Equally as important as not accepting excuses is not punishing. Punishment is one of the surest ways to break the involvement, to reduce the trust and confidence, and to eliminate the feeling of caring that exists between the patient and the punishing individual.

It is known from many sources that punishment is absolutely of no benefit to bringing about enduring change. Yet, to many, punishment is a preferred response to irresponsible behavior or failure. Most people who are successful feel that part of their success stems from their fear that punishment will follow failure. It is difficult for them to realize that punishment is not an effective means of changing behavior. Many incompetent and irresponsible people have been punished many times in their lives without any beneficial changes. Instead, for these people, the usual recipients of punishment, it reinforces loneliness by confirming that no one cares about them.

Punishment, here, refers to any treatment of a person that is intended to cause him pain—mental and/or physical. Punishment must be distinguished from the natural consequences for irresponsible behavior. Consider the following analogy. If a policeman stops you on the highway for doing 80 mph and courteously tells you, "Look, I know it's a clear day and these are good roads, but you can't go eighty on this particular highway. I am going to write you a ticket." There is nothing punitive about that situation. The reality of it was that the driver was going too fast and it was the policeman's job to maintain safety on the highway by making sure people do not travel that fast. In this situation, the driver knew the rules, chose to act irresponsibly, and had to face the natural consequences of breaking the rules. Punishment would result, however, if after giving the ticket the policeman took out his revolver, shot the driver through the right foot and said, "This will teach you. For the next six months, everytime you press the gas pedal you are going to feel pain." This behavior of the policeman would be entirely unreasonable; nevertheless, when we examine how we respond to situations requiring discipline or enforcement of rules, all too often we discover it is punishment (Glasser, 1969b).

Praise given when the person succeeds is much more effective motivation than punishment for failure. Praise helps solidify the involvement. When praise is used, there is no question that the therapist and the group are concerned and care about the individual. The warm, accepting support displayed by these essential persons goes a long way in encouraging continuation with the commitment and experimentation with new behavior.

Failures do not fear punishment; they identify with it. For many delinquents, punishment serves as a source of involvement. They receive attention through their delinquent behavior, which is often directed at that goal. The punishment is painful, but it is better than being ignored and lonely. One young man involved in stealing hubcaps from cars actually brought them home and stored them behind the living room couch. The pile got so high that they became visible. It was, however, a maid that first noticed it. She reported it to the boy's father, who, being the District Attorney, was aware of the recent rash of thefts. In counseling, the boy commented, "The only time my old man knows I am alive is when he picks me up in juvenile hall." Actually, this was the boy's first encounter with the police, but it was a logical extention of similar behavior—poor grades, fighting at school, expulsion from several schools for discipline problems—all bids for attention. The punishment, though somewhat uncomfortable, had a payoff. He became involved with several new people and also received the attention of his father. He found a way to reduce loneliness, irresponsible behavior, and punishment became the means by which he could reduce that loneliness.

In addition to these principles that present the process for Reality Therapy, Alexander Bassin, a Regional Associate of the Institute for Reality Therapy, has added an eighth principle. Principle VIII states: "Don't give up." In Reality Therapy, persistence pays off. In the most frustrating times in therapy, when it seems that the patient will never change, when he refuses to give a commitment or even evaluate his behavior, the therapist's refusal to give up will maintain the therapeutic involvement. The support and concern inherent in such an involvement will eventually allow the patient to take the risks involved in change.

ROLE OF THE LEADER

The therapist above all must be a successful, responsible person. He must have warmth, strength, confidence in his ability, and be able to satisfy his needs in his environment. Phrasing it rather concisely, he must be able to serve as a model of a responsible person. The effect of modeling along with encouragement and support is an important tool in helping a patient to develop a successful life style. The therapist should reflect an internalization of the principles of Reality Therapy to his patients.

In the early stages of the group, it is the therapist's responsibility to begin involvement among the members and gradually move them to even deeper involvement. This is done in an active, direct manner in which he becomes highly involved with each group member. He may ask questions, request information, encourage others to make comments or tell about themselves, or do anything that will encourage interaction among the members. He takes a task-orientation that focuses on current behavior. Deep investigation into the personality problems of the patients are not considered fruitful. During this process, he is displaying warmth, concern, and a willingness to become involved. He models openness, trust, and other qualities of a successful person. This initial activity tapers off as the group becomes more involved and interacts more freely among themselves.

Once the involvement is established, the leader focuses attention on "here and now" behavior and relationships. Events discussed in the group are kept timely; rarely is the remote past allowed to take the group's time. Encouragement is given to analyze and evaluate via questions like "What are you doing now?," "Is it good for you?" In this manner, the therapist keeps bringing the members back to the reality of the situation and does not allow indulgence in the fantasy they often create. The leader must not evaluate the behavior; he can only help the person become aware of the behavior and come to a decision. The other members of the group may, however, evaluate behavior. They may also make suggestions as to how they would handle a certain situation or what they think the person should do.

Planning with the group members is an important leader function. Because of his greater experiential background in such matters, it is expected that he will lend his expertise to developing alternative plans. He will also encourage other members to become actively involved in developing plans in conjunction with a given patient. The leader must ensure that the plan is a reasonable one that maximizes the probability of success. When an acceptable plan is decided upon, the leader must obtain the patient's commitment to the plan. After commitment is obtained, should the plan not be carried out, the therapist firmly but nevertheless refuses to accept any excuses. *He* cannot "let the person off the hook" from *their* commitment. He supports and encourages the patient further by asking, "When are you going to do it?" but he does not punish nor does he allow other members to punish the person.

Through the therapy process the leader is teaching, through modeling or directly, the principles of Reality Therapy. To the patient, these principles are the way to learn new behavior and become more responsible.

There are various levels of therapy which can utilize Reality Therapy. The training of the leader should be consummate with the level and purpose of the group and the intensity of therapy. It should be emphasized that the leader need not have an M.D., Ph.D., nor have received extensive training in psychiatric or psychological theory. The basic requirement is that he is a successful person who is interested in Reality Therapy and has received training in the basic principles. In schools using classroom meetings, training begins with discussions of the educational philosophy of Reality Therapy. Someone, preferably from the school, who has experience conducting these meetings will demonstrate the "classroom meeting" to the teacher. After several demonstrations, an experienced person will work with individual teachers in conducting meetings in their classrooms. The teacher is encouraged to develop further skill by conducting the groups themselves and by consulting with the trained person.

More extensive training is obtainable through workshops conducted regionally in various parts of the country. Each summer, the Institution for Reality Therapy, under Dr. Glasser's direction, conducts several training programs in elementary and advanced theory and technique. A person having completed these programs would be well prepared to function in the capacity of a therapist.

SELECTION AND COMPOSITION OF GROUP

It is an important concern to Reality Therapy that the composition of the group be relatively heterogeneous. If one is to use the group involvement to help persons with failure identities, it is extremely important that they come into frequent contact with as many persons as possible who have success identities. Generally, failures can learn very little from other failures since they have so little to offer. A drinking alcoholic, for instance, has little to offer another drinking alcoholic that can help him resolve the drinking problem. It is most likely that all they can do together is foster and support the drinking by exchanging "war" stories, similar feelings about themselves and others, and providing companionship for each other while drinking. A dry alcoholic can help a drinking alcoholic because he has already made the decision to live his life more responsibly. His strength, resolve, encouragement and support can serve as a model to the yet unsuccessful person. Successful persons can offer a successful model for dealing with problems. They may be able to conceive of several alternatives to the problem situation and help with the development of a plan to relieve it. Therefore, it is important that they be included in the group.

School counselors, because of the demands of their situation, sometimes unknowingly compose groups that are probably destined to fail. They gather into one group the delinquent behavior problems, the potential dropout, or the academically poor student.

The intention is to help, but all have chosen the same way to handle their problems. This approach does appear to work well with persons who have similar problems but all members must not be at the same stage of resolution. They need to see other ways to handle the problem. They need to be exposed to and motivated by the more successful students. If they are not so exposed, their behavior is not likely to change.

Selection of the group members is somewhat of a luxury, especially in the institutional (such as Ventura School for Delinquent Girls) or school setting. The group need not be so painstakingly matched and counterbalanced as some group proponents suggest. The critical factor is that members be at different stages of accepting responsibility. In institutional settings it would be nearly impossible to provide the needed help with complex selection procedures. Everyone can benefit from involvement with others in a group. Everyone should be allowed (sometimes required) to attend since by being there, they will gain something. The only exclusions from the group would be those persons whose behavior is so disruptive that it does not allow the meeting to proceed. Even here, once the behavior meets minimally acceptable standards, the person should be allowed to participate in group activity.

In mental institutions, using the milieu of Reality Therapy, placement in groups that have different ward status should be based on the individual's ability to accept responsibility. Dr. Harrington's (Glasser, 1965) early program divided a 150-man building into a 50-man closed ward, a 50-man semi-open ward and a 50-man open ward. Movement among the wards, which differed substantially in privileges, was determined by the amount of responsibility a person was willing to take. This is a somewhat different situation than the counseling groups being discussed here even though the same basic principles apply.

An ideally composed group for Reality Therapy would be heterogeneous in the amount of responsible behavior displayed by the members, but approximately one-third should be responsible, successful persons. The variety of symptoms included or excluded does not matter because as soon as involvement occurs and the persons satisfy their need for love and worth, they will disappear anyway.

GROUP SIZE

The size of the group is dependent on the purpose of the group and the setting in which it functions. The primarily preventative groups conducted in the school classroom average between 30 to 40 students. Here, the size will be determined by the number of students in the room. It is desirable that all children be given the opportunity to express their thoughts and opinions.

In institutions using Reality Therapy to establish the milieu, the size of the group can be quite large. At Ventura, even though small groups were used, the basic and most effective group size was the cottage group which consisted of 50 members (Glasser and Iverson, 1966). Glasser (1965) reports that Dr. Harrington implemented this therapeutic approach in a 150-man hospital unit. This group, however, was broken down into three 50-man wards. Twenty-three patients were placed in a treatment program for living outside the hospital, which utilized three small group settings averaging eight men to the group. Glasser (1965) also cites Dr. Mainord's use of a reality-type therapy that was used in treating 125 patients in about a one-year period; however, the average group membership was 10 to 12.

Dr. Glasser leans toward a somewhat larger group than is typically used for group therapy. This is the result of successful experience with large groups in the institutional setting. In private practice the groups are somewhat smaller averaging between 10 to 15 members.

LENGTH AND DURATION OF TREATMENT

There are requirements for both the length and duration of group treatment. These are determined by the purpose of the group and the setting in which the group is to function. Of more importance from a therapeutic viewpoint than either the length or the duration of the group is the regularity with which the group meets. It is recommended that no matter what time has been set or how long the meeting period, the group should meet regularly at that time. Group meetings are important to the life of the individual and should not be pushed aside as incidental, or shortened in time. Each group member should be allowed the opportunity to plan a regular pattern of attendance. This planning ideally includes both the starting time as well as (within reasonable limits) an ending time.

In *Schools Without Failure*, Dr. Glasser (1969a) recommends that duration is dependent on age and meeting experience of the class. Beginning primary grade children should start by meeting only 10 to 15 minutes per day, building to 30 minutes per day. Fourth, fifth and sixth graders can easily meet for 30 minutes, and high schoolers for 45 minutes, two or three times each week. The absolute minimum frequency for meeting is once a week.

In institutional settings, because of the conditions of institutionalization, there is often a definite time limit for therapy. Knowing how long they will have in therapy appears to be motivating to patients and makes them more responsive in the group sessions. As a result, time-limited groups of 90 days are frequently used. Typically, some form of advancement ranging from change in ward status (both forward and backward) to discharge, results at the end of the group. The length of meetings and the frequency of meeting may vary. At Ventura, large group meetings were held five days a week for 1½ hours each (Glasser and Iverson, 1966). A discharge group conducted by Dr. Mainord met five days a week for 1½ hours at a time. Some treatment time limits are now being set with private patients but not with the frequency found in institutional settings. The results have been quite good.

Counseling groups outside the institutional setting should not meet less frequently than once each week. Generally such groups initially agree to meet for about 6 months and then can extend that time if they desire. Glasser and Zunin (1973) report success meeting once a week with a group of relatively normal, healthy military widows. Those patients needing more involvement with others would probably do better if the group met more frequently. For the average outpatient group, meeting once or twice each week for approximately 1½ to a 2-hour maximum is probably adequate.

MEDIA AND SETTING

The primary media used is verbal interaction utilizing the principles of Reality Therapy. Involvement with other group members, focus on current behavior of individuals via inquiries as to "What are you doing?," the development of a plan, and the commitment to the plan are all powerful tools to help the individual develop responsible behavior. The support the group can give when success, no matter how small, is achieved has much greater impact than can be received from one individual; thus, it tends to maximize the success. Holding the person to commitment for responsible behavior and support for achieved successes, in addition to offering more opportunity for involvement, are the more important reasons why groups are more efficient than individual therapy.

Assuming responsibility to develop feelings of worth is an important aspect of this approach. Thus, especially in the institutional setting, work responsibilities are an important media for developing feelings of worth. The person should perform some task no matter how simple or brief. The difficulty or importance of the task should increase as the person's willingness to accept responsibility increases. Gradually the person will work himself into a full-time position.

The setting for the group meeting can be varied just as long as it is large enough to accommodate the group so that no one is uncomfortable. A large office, a classroom, part of a gymnasium are all adequate meeting places if they provide some privacy and keep interruptions to a minimum. The ideal arrangement for seating is a circle. In large groups a double circle with the members of the inner circle sitting on the floor is the best arrangement. This pattern places members in a face-to-face relationship and as much as possible equidistant from each other, thus maximizing the opportunity for involvement.

ILLUSTRATIVE GROUP MEETING

The following protocol[2] of a demonstration group is presented to illustrate both the beginning interchanges as well as the applica-

---

2. Protocol: Courtesy of Ed Ford, Regional Associate of the Institute for Reality Therapy.

tion of several principles of Reality Therapy. Group members are professional persons who are role playing "someone they know." The group is meeting for the first time. They have been referred from several sources to a small mental health clinic.

There are five members in this group. Anna, a 74-year-old female, is depressed and stays in bed most of the day. Pat, a mother in her early forties, has a seriously disturbed child with learning disabilities. John portrays a retired man in his fifties. He is seeking help with a problem of incest between himself and his two older daughters. Jean is a married woman about 25 years old. She is frightened and nervous most of the time, especially when she must leave the house. Sue is single, about 35 or 40. She was referred by the police for a window breaking incident. Others hold the view that she is "crazy."

Protocol

> Glasser: I'd just like to introduce myself to you. I'm Dr. Glasser, and I'll be meeting with you here and we'll be meeting once a week for about an hour and a half on Tuesday mornings. Can everybody attend at that time?
>
> Sue: I don't care.
>
> Glasser: Can you explain to the rest of the group what you mean when you say you don't care?
>
> Sue: I'd rather not talk much.
>
> Glasser: O.K. You want to listen then. All right. We'll continue to meet and if you find it beneficial, come; and if you don't, there's nothing compulsory here. Could someone tell me, so that the rest of us understand, what brought them here to the group. Is there some particular reason that you've come? I think everyone would be interested.
>
> Pat: Well, I came here because I have a problem with one of my children who is different from all the other children on the block, and I feel a little embarrassed about telling my family that he's in a special class. I've talked to the counselor many times, and it took a lot out of me to come here today, and I'm very, very nervous about it because it's very hard for me to talk about Tommy. He's very dear to me. He's a skinny little boy and he doesn't eat and he has trouble in the class, even though it's a small class. There are two teachers there, and there's just nothing that he wants to do except play and work on his hobbies.
>
> Glasser: O.K.

Pat: I'm very, very nervous about it and I just don't know what to do. Even my mother and father don't know that he's in a special class.

Glasser: O.K. The counselor suggested you come to the group here?

Pat: Right.

Glasser: All right. How about somebody else?

Jean: Well, I'm very scared when I go into a grocery store, and going out at all makes me very nervous. I want to talk it over with you and see how I . . .

Glasser: I see. How about coming in here? Are you frightened to come in here, too?

Jean: No. Uh, yeah, it took me a lot of courage to get in here.

Glasser: O.K. How about you?

John: I'm on medical retirement. I'm the father of several girls. My wife teaches school. We have a problem of incest in the family—my two older daughters and myself. We're engaged in this kind of thing and I need help in the relationship to my younger daughter. I'm home all the time and not too sure that I can handle the situation. I would like some help in working it through.

Glasser: Is this something that you've been advised to come for legally or are you coming voluntarily?

John: No, it's voluntary.

Glasser: I see.

John: It's really not voluntary. My oldest daughter married an alcoholic and he's spreading the news around the neighborhood that we used to sleep together. That's causing some concern among the people in my church and the rest of my family.

Glasser: O.K. Some people would kind of be upset when they hear a story like this. Does this affect any of you?

Jean: It worries me a little bit.

Glasser: You're nervous anyway, aren't you?

Jean: Yeah.

Glasser: What worries you about hearing something like this?

Jean: If I go out to the store or something like that, it's one of the things I worry about—somebody looking at me.

Glasser: I see. Then one of the things you worry about is men when you go out, is that right?

Jean: Yeah.

Glasser: O.K.

Jean: That's when nearly everybody stares at me.

Glasser: Do you go out very much?

Jean: No, it's a real effort. Sometimes I wake up nearly four o'clock in the morning. Even if I'm supposed to pick up some clothes from the cleaners, I just stay awake for hours just thinking I have to go pick up the stuff from the cleaners.

Glasser: Just the idea, you mean, of having to go out. Do you sometimes not go out?

Jean: Well, it's such an effort to get out. I get panicky just thinking about it.

Glasser: But do you make it out or do you stay home lots when you're supposed to go?

Jean: I stay home lots.

Glasser: You don't go then?

Jean: I get sick or something like that. I gripe to my husband when he gets back.

Glasser: Your husband does a lot of things for you then?

Jean: If I can get him to do it, he will. He doesn't like it though.

Glasser: O.K. How about you?

Anna: What?

Glasser: You're a little bit older than the other people here, but you've come here for a problem and we'd be very interested to hear about your problem.

Anna: Well, my husband thought I ought to come.

Glasser: Uh-huh.

Anna: I'm just so tired all the time. I get up in the morning and get his breakfast and then go back to bed after he leaves to go out and do his farming.

Glasser: You live on the farm?

Anna: Uh-huh.

Glasser: Do you stay in bed most of the day?

Anna: Yes.

Glasser: Do you get up for dinner?

Anna: Yes.

Glasser: And then what happens?

Anna: After I do the dishes, I go back to bed.

Glasser: I see. She's a little bit like you, isn't she?

Jean: Well, I don't stay in bed; I just don't like to get out of the house. I feel put upon if somebody comes over for coffee or anything like that.

Glasser: How about in your case? What if someone drops in?

Anna: I visit with them.

Glasser: Will you get out of bed then?

Anna: Oh yes.

Glasser: How about leaving the house?

Anna: I've got so much to do around the house that I don't get done, and I don't go out unless I have to.

Glasser: O.K. We haven't heard from you either. You said you were just going to listen for a little bit; but I wonder, do you stay around the house a lot, too, just listening?

Sue: I stay around the house with the door shut.

Glasser: I see. You stay home most of the time then? How did you get here today?

Sue: I didn't want to go to the police station. They said I could come here.

Glasser: I see. Who said that to you?

Sue: The police. I broke all the windows in the house near where I live because they had somebody shut up in there and I wanted to let him out.

Glasser: I see. How did you do that?

Sue: I just took a stick and broke them out.

Glasser: I see, just the ground floor windows.

Sue: Yes. That's all I could reach.

Glasser: But most of the time you stay in your house? It's interesting. We've got three people who stay in the house most of the time. Do you stay in the house, too, or do you get out quite a bit?

(After several interchanges with the other group members, Dr. Glasser focuses on Sue, who has been sitting quietly in the group.)

Glasser: Do you have children?

Sue: No.

Glasser: Are you married?

Sue: No.

Glasser: Do you live just by yourself?

Sue: No, I don't have any money, so I live with my mother, father, and part of the time with a friend.

Glasser: Is this the first time you have ever had real trouble with the police?

Sue: Yes.

Glasser: Poking out windows . . . is this the first time you have done it?

Sue: It was that conspiracy, though, people who are trying to hurt other people.

Glasser: Were they trying to hurt you?

Sue: Yes!

Glasser: How did you know that?

Sue: I could feel it.

Glasser: I see—just something that you felt. Did you see the people?

Sue: No.

Glasser: Did you get concerned when you broke the windows?

Sue: No. Just because the man hollered.

Glasser: Did you expect the police to come?

Sue: No.

Glasser: What did you say when the police came?

Sue: I ran home.

Glasser: I see . . . but they saw who it was.

Sue: Yes.

Glasser: You don't deny breaking the windows, though?

Sue: No!

Glasser: Do you think maybe you ought to go to jail for that?

Sue: No!

Glasser: Why not?

Sue: Because I had to let the people out.

Glasser: What do you think of that? Breaking all the windows in those people's house?

Anna: It doesn't seem like the right thing to do. . . .

Glasser: I see. What about you? What do you think about that?

John: It's crazy.

Glasser: Think it's crazy.

Glasser: He kinda' says that what you are doing is crazy. What do you think of that?

Sue: Maybe it is but . . . you can't keep people shut up in a house.

Glasser: Uh-huh. Did they get out when you broke the windows?

Sue: I ran away. I don't know.

Glasser: I see. Why did you run away?

Sue: The man hollered.

Glasser: The man who lived in the house. What did he holler?

Sue: He just screamed.

Glasser: Got you scared then. How about you? Does that sound crazy to you?

Pat: It sure does. My mother told me that some kids came to her house and broke three panes out. They are retired and can't really afford the $18.00 that it will cost . . . if we can get the men to come. I think it's terrible.

Glasser: Who's going to pay for the windows you broke?

Sue: My brother is going to put the panes back in.

Glasser: I see, it's going to cost some money, won't it? Do you have any money?

Sue: No!

Glasser: Your brother's going to do this because he's just a nice guy?

Sue: Maybe he doesn't want me to go to jail.

Glasser: I see! Are you worried about that? Don't you think maybe it would be a good idea if you went to jail and then you wouldn't have to break any more windows?

Sue: Maybe.

Glasser: Ever been to jail? Ever broke any windows before?

Sue: No.

Glasser: How would you feel if someone came and broke the windows in your home?

Anna: Well, I wouldn't like it.

Glasser: What would you do?

Anna: Probably call the police.

Glasser: Would you get out of bed?

Anna: Yes.

Glasser: It would mean something to you. Do you keep your house pretty nice?

Anna: Yes. I clean before I go back to bed, do the dishes and everything.

Glasser: Uh-huh. You'd call the police though?

Anna: Yes.

Glasser: How about you? I guess you would be pretty scared?

Jean: Well, I sure do wonder why. I sure would be surprised. I would wonder why you would do that.

Glasser: She told you that she wanted to let people out that were locked up. What do you think of that story?

Jean: Well, if I was really locked up I would appreciate it, but I can go out when I want to.

Glasser: This gentleman said it sounded crazy to him. How does it sound to you?

Jean: Well it really sounds a bit different.

Glasser: What do you think that these two people think it's odd that you broke windows?

Sue: They don't understand about the conspiracy.

Glasser: Something that just you understand.

Sue: Well, I try to tell people.

Glasser: Do your mother and father listen?

Sue: They don't believe me.

Glasser: Do you work at all?

Sue: Not very much.

Glasser: I see . . . you just stay in the house mostly.

Sue: I did work for awhile, but I lost the job.

Glasser: How about you? Do you plan on going back to work?

(At this point Dr. Glasser begins to work more intensively with Pat. Since time for the group is running out he then works to get a commitment from each person, to return for the next meeting. After doing so he simply states that time is up and he will see everyone next week, thus ending the session.)

SUMMARY

The theoretical rationale and the principles of Reality Therapy are based on such a common sense philosophy that it appears that they can be used by minimally trained persons in a broad range of situations. It appears to be equally effective in the back ward of mental institutions as in the average school classroom.

What are the secrets of such a therapeutic approach? There are no secrets, just a straightforward approach that treats the persons with dignity, appeals to them to evaluate their behavior in a rational way, encouraging them to take responsibility for the behavior they have chosen, and finally to plan alternate, more effective ways of responding to others. During this process, it is necessary that the person becomes involved with another person or preferably a group of persons. It is only in this way that one can reduce the loneliness and feelings of being unworthy that cause so much pain. Only then can the person feel successful.

Developing successful identities is the goal of Reality Therapy. It makes a great deal of sense, then, not only to use these principles in a remedial fashion but to use them to prevent failure. In this respect, Reality Therapy can have long-term and far-reaching impact. The movement to introduce Reality Therapy into the schools is gaining momentum. Correctional systems and mental institutions are also using the principles more and more. Regional Associates of the Institute of Reality Therapy are introducing it to those yet unexposed as well as providing training to those desiring it. In institutional settings, a one-to-one counseling relationship simply cannot reach enough persons. With this in mind, it is no wonder that groups have been found to be the most effective means to implement Reality Therapy.

SUGGESTED READINGS

Glasser, W.: *Mental Health or Mental Illness?* New York, Harper & Row, 1961.

Glasser, W.: *Reality Therapy.* New York, Harper & Row, 1965.

Glasser, W.: Reality therapy. In J. H. Masserman (Ed.): *Handbook of Psychiatric Therapies.* New York, Grune and Stratton, 1966.

Glasser, W.: *Schools Without Failure.* New York, Harper & Row, 1969.

Glasser, W.: Reality therapy and group counseling. In G. M. Gazda (Ed.): *Proceedings of a Symposium on Group Procedures for the Disadvantaged.* Athens, Ga., Center for Continuing Education, University of Georgia, 1969.

Glasser, W.: *The Identity Society.* New York, Harper & Row, 1972.

Glasser, W., and Iverson, N.: *Reality Therapy in Large Group Counseling.* Los Angeles, The Reality Press, 1966.

Glasser, W., and Zunin, L. M.: Reality Therapy. In R. Corsini (Ed.): *Current Psychotherapies.* Itasca, Illinois, F. E. Peacock, 1973.

Reality Therapy: An anti-failure approach. *Impact, 2:*(1), 6, n.d.

REFERENCES

Fiske, D. W., and Maddi, S. R. (Eds.): *Functions of Varied Experience.* Homewood, Illinois, Dorsey Press, 1961.

Glasser, W.: *Reality Therapy.* New York, Harper & Row, 1965.

Glasser, W.: *Schools Without Failure.* New York, Harper & Row, 1969 (a).

Glasser, W.: Reality therapy and group counseling. In G. M. Gazda (Ed.): *Proceedings of a Symposium on Group Procedures for the Disadvantaged.* Athens, Ga., Center for Continuing Education, University of Georgia, 1969 (b).

Glasser, W.: *The Identity Society.* New York, Harper & Row, 1972.

Glasser, W., and Iverson, N.: *Reality Therapy in Large Group Counseling.* Los Angeles, The Reality Press, 1966.

Glasser, W., and Zunin, L. M.: Reality therapy. In R. Corsini (Ed.): *Current Psychotherapies.* Itasca, Illinois, F. E. Peacock, 1973.

Harlow, H.: The nature of love. *Scientific American, 13:*673, 1958.

Selye, H.: *Stress.* Montreal, Acta Inc., 1950.

Spitz, R. A.: Hospitalism: An inquiry into the genesis of psychiatric conditions of early childhood. *Psychoanalytic Studies of the Child.* Vol. 1, New York, International University Press, 1945.

CHAPTER X

THE FORMATION AND BEGINNING PROCESS OF TRANSACTIONAL ANALYSIS GROUPS

Robert L. Goulding

ORIGIN

THE EARLY BEGINNINGS of Transactional Analysis (T.A.) came from the late Eric Berne, genius, shy, extremely near-sighted–he used to put his head right into a small notebook in order to write his ideas while flying, sitting in his office, or riding in a car. In the mid-fifties, Eric began to notice the extreme variability in a given person's behavior. For example, at one moment a girl might be curled up on the chair behaving and sounding like a 5-year-old, and at the next moment she would be sitting bolt-upright and shaking her finger and scolding, and at still the next moment she would be giving information in a calm, grown-up manner. As he studied further, Eric noticed that this behavior repeated itself, and that when the girl behaved like a child, she would look similar to the way that she looked when she had previously behaved as a child. When she behaved like a scolding parent, she was also consistent in the way that she looked and sounded, but this was entirely different behavior, different voice, different vocabulary, from the child-like behavior.

From this awareness grew the concept of Ego States–that people, as they develop, begin to have three different personalities–one that they maintain from an earlier time, one that they copy or introject from their real parents and parent surrogates, and one that fits their chronological age. These three ego states Eric called the Parent, the Adult, and the Child.

In the early days, most of the talk and the meetings around these interesting observations were held in Eric's office in San Francisco and Eric's home, in Carmel, California. He shared them at poker games with me and other friends, and he shared them

234

with Barbara Rosenfeld and David Kupfer and other professionals in Carmel. Later, in his San Francisco office, he started the Social Psychiatry Seminars (SPS). During these early days, in the very late fifties and early sixties, the seminars were attended largely by Mel Boyce, Joe Concannon, Frank Ernst, Ken Everts (now President), Vi Litt, Frances Matson, Ray Poindexter, and Myra Schapps. Barbara Rosenfeld went off to Philadelphia to get her M.D.; Claude Steiner, who had been in the early movement was in Ann Arbor getting his Ph.D.; Gordon Haiberg and Tom Harris from Sacramento joined the group; Paul McCormick and Bill Collins from the Department of Corrections were also in the early seminars, which I joined in January, 1962.

I mention those early days because it was there, in San Francisco, that the theory of Transactional Analysis began to develop from the ideas of all of us. The early *Transactional Analysis Bulletin* (now the *Journal of Transactional Analysis*) that was first published in January 1962, contained many clinical notes from which the theory developed. Eric's first book on T.A., *Transactional Analysis in Psychotherapy* (1961), described the development of the theory in detail, and *Games People Play,* published in 1964, conveyed the theory of Games more completely. We had a difficult time getting *Games People Play* published. Grove Press was having some financial difficulties, and they were not willing to take the financial risk. Finally, Eric offered to pay them $3,000 for the first edition and a private printing of 1,000 copies. He persuaded all of us (about 30) to agree to sell 30 copies each—at regular cost to us! We agreed, of course, and the first printing was done. As everybody knows, the book, to our complete surprise, became a tremendously popular best-seller.

SELECTION AND GROUP COMPOSITION

The concept of group therapy as practiced by most Transactional Analysts is quite different from the classical process group that I learned from psychoanalysts in Baltimore. In the first place, the very selection of patients for a group is different. I learned all kinds of principles about selection in the Veteran's Administration Clinic and Hospital, that we totally disregard now; there is no criterion except that the patient is alive, we have space in the group

for him, and he comes to a group. I put all patients in groups, regardless of symptoms, classification of diagnosis, age, sex, marital
status, or race, or even if his mistress is in the same group with
him and his wife. All our groups are of two kinds: (1) open-
ended, ongoing groups, or (2) limited weekend, or week-long or
month-long groups. The on-going groups operated by my associates are completely open-ended, although a few Transactional
Analysts have tried limited groups of ten sessions, three months,
and the like.

My own groups, at this time, are primarily for professionals,
and are all of the marathon-type. Patients who come to my marathons are all referred from other therapists, and they are mixed
with the professionals. These professionals might include, for example, chairman of departments of psychiatry and leading psychoanalysts, or a counselor from the California Youth Authority with
a B.A. degree. We see no objection at all to such a wide range of
"patients." In ten years, we have had no difficulty with this arrangement.

The type of group determines, to some degree, the selection
process and the composition of the group. There is a wide difference between the once-a-week, open-ended group and a marathon
group. The open-end type is just that. Patients have been coming
and going for ten years, so there is no longer any "opening remarks," or the like. Patients are generally seen privately at least
once and often more than once. Frequently they call when there
is no time for a private interview, and then they are put uncere-
moniously for that week into whatever group has an opening.

GROUP SIZE

The average size of our ongoing groups is eight, although we
do take up to ten, but no more than ten. Our marathons are held
to 14, although I prefer 12. Fourteen is the number that is necessary to allow us to operate the groups economically. Our one-week
workshops are held to 20, and our four-week workshops enroll a
maximum of 32.

PATIENT CONTRACT

The first therapeutic move with any new patient is the contract.
If the patient had been seen individually, he may already have

worked out his contract. Even so he will do it again, since all of our groups are run by co-therapists. (This is not generally true of all T.A. groups, because Eric was against the use of co-therapists. But all of our groups operate with the leader co-leading with another staff member, who is truly a co-therapist and not an assistant.) The contract is reached by carefully working with the patient toward his particular desire to change. We need to be very careful to work for a contract that comes from the patient's Child or Adult Ego State, and not from his Parent Ego State. For instance, I did a three-day workshop for professionals last year. One of the professionals stated that he wanted to gain better control of his anger. I was very surprised at this, because I had known him for six years and I had never seen any evidence of his anger. Further questioning of this contract provided me information about his recent marriage. He was becoming angry at his step-children, who were somewhat disruptive. It was important first for him to get in better touch with an anger that he had never before allowed himself, because of the old parental injunction: "Don't get angry!" This man spent so much energy "controlling his anger" that he had very little energy left for other feelings, and he was thought to be a rather cold individual. When he did some work on anger, he was then able to begin to drop it, rather than to involve us in collusion with his early parents to "control" it.

The contract is extremely important, and it is honored by all T.A. therapists whom I know, because through it we do two essential things: (1) We have a concrete place from which to work, rather than sitting around for ten years allowing the patients to "process." (2) We have a point from which to measure success of treatment. If a patient states that he wants to "understand himself better," there is no way of measuring this, whereas if he states that he wants to stop feeling depressed, or get rid of his headaches, this can be measured.

In summary thus far, I have discussed the origins of T.A., the selection and composition of a group, and getting contracts.

BEGINNING A GROUP

If a new group is begun, or if we are doing a marathon, we get contracts from everyone before any definitive work is done. Thus, the first "group time" in a new group may be spent in just getting contracts. The first half-day of a marathon may be spent the same way. Here, however, there are some differences. We do not lecture to a new group, or to a new patient in a group, but we begin all our marathons with about three hours of theory before we start the contract time. This serves a number of purposes. As mentioned earlier, all marathons are comprised of patients and therapists, and the theory is presented for the benefit of the therapists so that they are able to follow the theoretical structure of the practical work. We have learned, however, that everyone does better work during the marathon if they have a theory on which to formulate their understandings. Lieberman and Yalom's most recent research on encounter groups, presented to the American Group Psychotherapy Association in February, 1972, and in Lieberman, Yalom and Miles' (1973) *Encounter Groups: First Facts,* demonstrated that those patients who had the most "head-work" confrontation were among those who improved the most. We are thus, in a way, giving them permission to use their head, whereas Fritz Perls and other Gestaltists have told their patients to lose their heads to come to their senses. We need to rethink the possibility of giving some theoretical rationale to all patients, whether they are in on-going groups or marathons. We do give most of them McCormick's and Campos' *Introduce Yourself to T.A.* (1969), which is super.

Next is a discussion of the early work done in groups operating within a T.A. framework. When describing the initial procedures in a T.A. group, I must consider two quite different frameworks: (1) the classical, Bernian position, and (2) the Goulding tradition. Many therapists around the country who have been trained by me use my method, whereas most of the old San Francisco group use Eric's method.

Eric was very careful, after the contract was selected, to do therapy in four steps. First, he analyzed ego states of the individuals in the group; second, he analyzed transactions; third, he analyzed games; and fourth, he analyzed scripts. The script work was done very carefully, with close attention given to the patient's early memory of favorite stories or fables that fit his life style and to the people in the patient's life that fit the people in the story. This procedure is an analysis of displacement, and we (Goulding Method) usually do not do it.

Following the contract, we are more likely to start working with individual patients in the group concerning their "racket." We define *racket* as the chronic bad feelings of people that usually lead to no action. *Rackets* are remnants of childhood, such as anger, depression, confusion, anxiety, and boredom. We never ask, "What makes you angry," but rather, "What do you do to maintain your anger?"; "What did you do last year?"; "What did you get angry about in college, in high school, in grade school, before you went to school?" By this chronological regression, we usually can reach an early memory of anger very easily. We do not just accept a "telling about" an experience, but rather we get the patient to be in the scene, to tell it as if it were happening right then.

When we get to an early scene, we ask the patient to "act out" not only his response, but also the response of mother, or father, or sibling. We do this by setting up a two-chair dialogue in which we ask the patient to move back and forth between the two chairs. This, of course, is a Gestalt technique; it is an excellent way to help the patient get some clear definitions of his ego state boundaries.

At this point, when we have professionals in the group, they begin to get restless and ask questions like, "We might as well not be here, don't you ever use the other people in the group?" Or they might become involved by asking, "How does that make you feel?" To this line of questioning, we cry "tilt." We are not inclined to sit back and listen to a group talk, but we are more inclined to work with one patient for a period of about 30 minutes.

The other transactions from the group members may be from their Adults, "straight" and good confrontations; or they may be ostensibly Adult, but actually the first move in a *Game*. If we see them as the former, we would probably stroke for good work; if we see them as the first move in a *Game*, we would more likely wait to see what develops. For instance, someone in the group may ask a patient who is working on his anger, "Have you ever tried Librium®?" This sounds like the first move in a "Why don't you, Yes but" *Game* and we would probably wait to see who else gets in, how the patient responds, and what feelings develop. If the patient's answer after every question is "Yes, but I . . . ," we would probably stop the process after two or three interactions. Then we would ask the patient what he feels, and we would also ask the other group members who have been involved, what it is that they feel. If the patient feels discouraged, or angry, and the others feel frustrated, we are sure they have been in a *Game*. We would then define the *Game*, draw it on the blackboard, and point out to the patient how he uses the *Game* to maintain his anger. We would also tell the other group members how they use the *Game* to maintain their frustration.

I referred to "tilt" earlier to call attention to the fact that many, if not most, individuals, honestly believe that people can make other people angry, depressed, bored, confused, and anxious. One of the major propositions of T.A., or at least our brand of T.A., is that each person is responsible for his own feelings, and that he chooses to respond in a fairly stereotyped way, depending upon his own *rackets*.

Thus, when we hear a professional in a group ask another, "How does that (or he, or she) make you feel?," we immediately question the question by our code word "tilt"–meaning that you have just made an illegal movement and the pin ball game is over! For too long, parents have blackmailed their children by saying to them, "You make me so depressed when you get C's and D's on your report card," or "You give me a headache when you make all that noise." Therapists who do the same thing in groups just accentuate this blackmail–that an individual is not responsible for his own feelings. We see the *Games* people play as the means by which they maintain their own feelings or *rackets*.

Thus, in the first group session, we get contracts and we begin to teach people that they are autonomous and responsible not only for their own actions, but also for their own feelings. This self-responsibility is extremely important from the very beginning. We call to the attention of our patients each word and gesture they use which denies that he is responsible for himself. We respond to words like "can't," "try," "want," "wish," "hope," "perhaps," "would if," "if it weren't for," and many others. For patients who say, "I can't quit smoking," or "I want to quit smoking," while puffing on a cigarette, we ask him to say, "I won't quit," and then get in touch with what he feels as he says that. Children are taught that they are not allowed to say "won't" but that it is all right for them to say, "I can't, I'll try," or whatever response they can use that gets both parents and child off the hook. Most of these words, that we call cop-out words, are a result of internal Parent-Child conflicts that have not been resolved, and we see no possibility of resolving them until the patient claims his own power.

If we are doing a marathon, there is an entirely different tempo to the whole problem of autonomy than there is with an ongoing group, which is the reason why many T.A. therapists are now doing marathons, either as a regular function of an ongoing group or as a way of working certain patients through the impasse they are in. A patient having an hour and a half of group per week and then 166½ hours away from the group will probably not make as many changes as he will working for 20 hours over a weekend, where he can practice some of his newly discovered potency with others in the same position.

The first time we see a *Game* being played, and someone picking up a pay-off of bad feelings, we will ask him first to become aware of those feelings, and then we ask him if he knows how he got there. For instance, recently in a practice group, the therapist was getting contracts from the five members of the group, with the other participants observing and making notes of *rackets, Games,* body movements, etc. Three people in the group, in a counterclockwise order, made contracts. Then the fifth started to work. The fourth waited until he was through, then turned to him angrily and said, "How come you didn't let me speak?" (Note the "let me speak.") "Are you angry?" asked the therapist. "Of course," she replied. He then very carefully drew on the blackboard how she had maneuvered herself into the position of feeling angry because he "didn't let her speak" when she had a very clear option of speaking immediately and stating that it was her turn. "But that wouldn't be polite," she said. And then the whole archeology of the *Game* became obvious. In the service of her childhood anger, she allows her Parent ego state to say to her, "Don't interrupt; it's not polite," which is obviously a rehash of an old family scene, repeated many times. She is still angry about all those times, and still plays out the scene in many little ways.

There are several other points to make concerning this practice group session, which lasted about 20 minutes, that illustrate very well the progress of a T.A. group. In ten minutes, the leader had heard four contracts, had picked up a *racket,* that gave him clues to pick up a *Game,* had confronted the patient with the *Game,* and in five minutes more had a contract from her to stop setting herself up for anger. This doesn't mean, of course, that she will never "play" again. The next time she played (which happened about 15 minutes later), she started to become angry, and then suddenly she howled with laughter and said, "I did it again, didn't I?" and dropped her anger. Such a recognition, in the "guts," that she had played a *Game* permitted her to replace the anger with genuine enjoyment of something that she had learned for herself.

Very early in our T.A. groups, we pick up the principal *rackets,* the principal *Games,* and how these *rackets* and *Games* fit a life-long style, or "script." It is the theory in T.A. that most, if not all of us, live out our lives in some kind of a self-defeating *script,* which may be "heroic" or may be "banal." In the heroic *script,* the protagonist may go down fighting the Holy Crusades, such as being disbarred, being carried off the field on the shields of his friends, becoming bankrupt, penniless, or killing himself. In the banal *script,* he lives out a life without a great deal of excitement and without a great deal of joy.

To illustrate a *script* being played, let me refer to another 20-minute group practice session. One of the professionals stated that his contract was to "stop not asking his own patients for contracts." He stated also that he did several groups, and somehow he failed to make clear contracts with most of the patients in the groups. As a result, he then felt inadequate, incompetent, and sometimes felt depressed, and thought about quitting psychiatry—maybe running away, perhaps killing himself. The leader very quickly moved into the frequency with which the patient had had these feelings in the past, moved back into a childhood scene in which the patient remembered that he could never please his mother–might as well run away. He then recognized how his group work fitted the same kind of early scene. The leader, in the classical T.A. way, said, "You never had permission to make it for yourself when you were a kid, and you have never given it to yourself. You have my permission." This procedure follows the Three-P concept of Pat Crossman, described in the *Transactional Analysis Bulletin* in 1966, page 152. Crossman stated that the therapist gives the patient *permission* that he does not have to change, *protects* the patient from any harm while he is trying out his newly found strengths, and is *potent* about the permission and the protection. The patient theoretically develops a new Parent in his head who is different than the old, and he can then make changes.

We, at the Western Institute believe, however, that it is more important for the patient to do it for himself, and thus we would handle the scene a little differently. We would ask the patient, while he was in the middle of an early diaglogue with a fantasied parent, what he felt when Mother just said, "You never do anything right." We would then ask him to respond to Mother. He may stay in his old position with his response, in which case we would ask him to be Mother and to reply. Next, we would ask him to be himself and to reply. Eventually, he will usually become disgusted with the scene, and say angrily, "I'm not going to listen to you anymore," or something similar, that declares his own autonomy. We then may ask him to respond one or more times, and during his response(s) we watch his body movements until we feel that he is congruous. This may all take place in the first 20 minutes of a group.

The most important work in the first few group sessions is to look for evidence of the patient's early decisions, and to allow him to reach an understanding of those early decisions. We are not at all interested in the "process" of a group; we do nothing to formulate the intimacy that develops, except by indirection. We are not interested in the "family" as a group, i.e., we do not care who the patients pick out as mother, father, siblings, and uncle John. We *are* interested in the bad feelings patients have, the *Games* they play to develop those bad feelings, or to support them, the early *decisions* patients made about their lives and how the *Games* support those early *decisions*. We *are* interested in the life style, or script, and how the script is based on the early *decisions* and is supported by the *Games* and *rackets*. We *are* interested in picking up evidence of the original *injunction* of the parent from which the patients' early decision was made, and the kinds of strokes that the patient got to support the *injunction*.

INJUNCTION-DECISION-GAMES-RACKETS COMPLEX

I have given a full description of the Injunction-Decision-Games-Rackets in another chapter, "New Directions in Transactional Analysis: Creating an Environment for Redecision and Change," in Sager and Kaplan's (1972) *Progress in Group and Family Therapy*. However, a brief summary of the connections seems relevant at this point. The T.A. position is that everyone has three parts to their personality: a Parent Ego State introjected from their real parents, an Adult Ego State that stores and processes data and acts upon that data without feelings, and a Child Ego State, comprised of all the previous experiences.

Injunction

An irrational message that is called the *injunction* is often given from mother's or father's Child Ego State. This *injunction* stems from the parent's own discomforts, hurts, and disappointments that may be rational for the parent, but are somewhat irrational for the child. For instance, a mother who didn't want this child may get an abortion, or she may not, and wish she had; then, when the child is born, she may blame the child for her own feelings, and tell him, non-verbally and verbally, that he is not loved, not wanted. She may say things like, "If it weren't for you, I would not have had to marry your father," which means: "Don't exist and I will be happier." Thus, she gives the child a "Don't exist" *injunction*. Another example of an *injunction* may occur when a mother is disappointed that she got a little boy; therefore she dresses him in girl's clothes, with the *injunction* "Don't be you," or "Don't be a boy." A mother may also want her son to act like a man at five years old by admonishing "take care of little sister," "don't cry," "don't play," and "there is too much work to do." The *injunction* is "Don't be a child." (Most psychotherapists have this one.) A father may not like physical closeness, either with the child, his wife, or both, and the *injunction* is "Don't be close."

A mother may have wanted the pregnancy to end in abortion, becomes guilty, and then over-protective by not allowing the child to swim, run, roller skate, or climb trees. She says to father, "Go see what Susan is doing and tell her not to." The *injunction* is "Don't." A father may not want his daughter to be sexually provocative, because of his own fear of an erection when he sees his pre-teen girl; therefore he tells her not to wear sexy clothes, lipstick, and so forth. The *injunction* is "Don't grow (up)." A father may be jealous of his son's ability to beat him at chess, or ping-pong, or wrestling; therefore he stops the activity and says, "I won't play if you beat me." The *injunction* is "Don't make it."

Parents may not allow the child to tell how good he is, or to tell how really important he feels. The *injunction* is "Don't be important." Parents who only show concern for the child by holding him and petting him when he is ill, communicate the *injunction* "Don't be well." (This *injunction* describes the common phenomenon of a group member who stays forever.) There are other *injunctions,* but those just described are most important. Most important of course, is the "Don't be" *injunction* from which the child starts to develop depression and suicidal feelings.

Decision

The second element of the Injunction-Decision-Racket-Games complex is the *decision.* When a child frequently hears and feels the *injunction:* "Don't be," and when he is getting negative recognition (strokes), he may decide that life is pretty tough and say (in his head or aloud), "If things get too tough, I can always kill myself" or "I'll get you to kill me." These kinds of *decisions* may lead to a life style involving potential suicide, death by violence, death by coronary occlusion (while showing them), or death by accident. If a child doesn't make a *decision,* in our opinion, he is not "stuck." (This position differs from the classical Bernian position in which most of us are victims if we get the *injunction.*) The child decides to go along with an *injunction* in order to survive, physiologically and psychologically, at that time and in that place. Some children get support from the opposite parent, e.g., "Don't listen to her. She is nuts. It has to do with her, not you." Sometimes the child may get his support from a grandparent or even an older sibling, and then they do not buy the *injunction:* they don't make a decision.

It is obvious that, if some day a child made a decision to kill himself, or not to trust, or not to be close, or not to grow up, or not to be a child, then he can remake it or change it, at a later date, and begin to get out of his "bag." This is the area we quickly look for early in the group: "What did you decide to do to screw up your life, and what are you going to decide now to unscrew it?" We listen for all the evidence we can get to demonstrate the early decision. Some of it can be heard in the non-autonomous words people use; some of it can be picked up by listening to the change of pronouns in a sentence, such as *"I'm* so tired; *you* work like hell and *you* never have any fun." In the first pronoun, *I'm,* we hear a report of how he feels; in the second and third *(you)* we hear the *injunction* being repeated: "You work like hell; you don't have fun." (Don't be a child.) We might ask the patient at this point, "Who told you not to have fun, and how did they tell you?"

Racket

The third element of the I-D-R-G complex is the *racket*–the chronic bad feelings of people that support the flow of *decisions* and the flow of the script. If a child decides at age four that someday, if things get too bad, he'll kill himself, and if the familiar feeling around his house is depression; that is, if he gets his strokes for being depressed, or sad, then the familiar feeling he has as he grows up is sadness. Thus, when he is grown, he says, "I wouldn't know how to feel if I didn't feel sad." Other circumstances might start off a *racket* of anger, or frustration, or confusion.

For an example of *rackets* around one, listen to one's colleagues in staff meetings. One says, "That patient *makes* me so angry."

Another returns, "You haven't seen anything. *Y* makes me so *anxious* when she calls at 3 A.M. threatening suicide." Another, a famous chest surgeon, says, "My terminal patients *make* me so *frustrated* when I can't cure them"; yet he accepts only difficult patients.

The individual, then, picks a feeling that fits with his original *decision*–the atmosphere of the family and the kind of strokes he receives–and then looks for ways of supporting his feelings. The chest surgeon, for instance, not only was frustrated by his dying patients, but also chose to be psychotherapist and clergy to the families of those patients. Then he complained about their *frustrating* him when he could not solace them. "For 15 years," he said, "I have been asking how to deal with families, and no one ever told me anything worthwhile." (Of course; he was in the frustration *racket!* When he decided to drop his frustrations, he began to feel good about his tremendous skill, rather than frustrated by the dying patient. He also left the counseling of the families to others who would allow them to mourn.)

People can maintain their *rackets,* then, by choosing situations, or actions, or behaviors that will support the *rackets.* At any given moment, a person can fantasize to "stay in the bad feelings." For example, while lying in bed after a happy, exciting and satisfactory sexual encounter, a man can think of income tax due April 15, and be depressed; or he can think of the opportunities he missed last week in his business contacts, and feel saddened; or he can think of the hostility among nations and be depressed, thus taking himself out of the now-time and here-place into another time or another place in order to maintain his depressed feelings.

Early in a group, then, it is necessary for the therapist to create an environment in which the patient is *rapidly* aware of how he maintains old, chronic, bad feelings by his behavior, fantasy, or selection. The therapist must then be prepared to confront him with alternate choices.

Game

The fourth element of the I-D-R-G complex is the *Game,* first defined by Berne as a series of transactions with a con, a gimmick and a payoff. Earlier in this paper I defined the *Game* as an ostensibly straight (usually [A]) stimulus–an unterior transaction as a response to the ulterior transaction, ending in a bad feeling, and out of awareness of the [A]. Let me clarify this definition by providing an example of the start of a *Game*. When I was in Miami recently, I was sitting on one of the benches at the airport waiting for a plane to New York. A little child, probably 9 or 10 months old, was in a stroller parked across the aisle from me. His mother was reading the paper and ignoring him; he had a bottle in his hand. He looked at his mother, looked at the bottle, and dropped it on the floor. He then pulled at mother's pant-suit until she looked at him; she got up, and with a scowl, walked to where the bottle was, picked it up, shoved it at him, and sat down to read her paper. He looked at the bottle, looked at her, pitched the bottle again, and once again pulled on her pant-suit. She looked up, swore, got up, picked up the bottle, thrust it at him, and said to him, "Hold onto the goddamn thing!" Then she sat down again and began reading her paper. He looked at her, looked at the bottle, threw it again, waited a few seconds, and once more pulled at her pant-suit. She looked at him, hollered at him, got up, got the bottle, shoved it in his mouth, and scolded him harshly. He cried and looked pained. She went back to her paper.

I interpreted the child's behavior as, "How do I get attention around here? Oh yeah, if I bug Mom, she will scold me, which is better than being ignored in this big strange place!" At this point, the child made a decision about getting strokes, even if the result was painful. This was just a little *decision,* but it may be the prologue to a major *decision* later on; that is, if mother scolds and ignores long enough, so that it seems to him that she is saying "Drop dead"; or "Don't be"; or "Get out of here"; he then at some point makes another, and more permanent *decision:* "If things get too bad around here, I can always knock myself off." He then has a connection of references or negative strokes that can be obtained by playing "Kick Me," a small *decision* to play the *Game,* and a larger *decision* to die someday if things get too tough. And, if he continues to play the *Game,* things, indeed, get too tough, and he collects more and more evidence that he should kill himself. He may, indeed, find stories or fairy tales to support his position (from his *decision*) and may even begin to live out his real life according to that fairy tale. However, we don't use fairy tales to establish a *script,* but rather use them only to give us support for our hunches, based upon the information we receive. Neither do we use the fairy tale to set up treatment, which we consider to be an analysis of a displacement. For instance, if a man of 45 is depressed, we assume that he has made a *decision* at some point to kill himself, and we look for the evidence. We employ specific kinds of questions, leading to early memories, such as the following:

1. What is the myth of your birth? (I was unwanted, and besides, I tore-up my mother and caused her hemorrhoids.)

2. When you were born, what did they say about you when they looked at you?

3. If you keep on with the present behavior and feelings, where will I find you in 5 years? 10 years? 20 years? (A hermit. You won't, I'll be dead.)

Joen Fagan (1971) asks the patient for his first memory. This is probably a good idea, but we are more inclined to ask: "And when did you feel depressed last year?"; "When did you feel depressed in college?"; "When did you feel depressed in high school?"; "When did you feel depressed in grade school?"; "When did you feel depressed before you attended school?"; "When did you feel depressed the first time?" In other words, we do not ask: "Were you depressed?" But we ask: "When were you depressed?" Our belief is that if we ask the questions chronologically, but begin with the most recent events and then go to the earliest events, we are far more apt to get associations and connections than if we start with the earliest events and work forward.

Once we have established or have a relatively strong indication (hunch) that there was a *decision,* we may ask for a two-chair dialogue, and proceed with our hunches. Our method includes: obtaining the "early memory" by asking the patient to sit in the other chair and assume the position of his mother or father. In the role(s), he is to tell the patient (himself) what they feel or think about him—in the present tense. We then get the patient to respond and, often in a few transactions, pick up the early *decision,* e.g., "I'll get you even if it kills me." This type of patient then may be one who drives his sports car at 90 m.p.h. down the mountainside while he is drunk and without seat belts, plays third degree rapo, and cops and robbers–from either the cop or the robber side.

We think that the early *decision* is made in response to both the stress and the way to get strokes in order to survive in this place at this time. We believe that the movement of the *script* is more likely the result of following the pattern of *Games* and strokes, and not so much the result of pre-selected stories and identification with the hero or heroine and others. Accepting a *racket* (summation of bad feelings) in the direction of the *decision* is the result of the experiences, the modeling, and the strokes. If a child is sad, sees that mother is sad, gets strokes (negative or positive) for being sad, then his sadness fits into playing "Kick Me." And compounded by being depressed after the fourth divorce and the fifth firing, he finally can say, "After all that has happened to me, and all the bad feelings I have had, I am now entitled to kill myself."

In order to draw out a *Game* for the purpose of confronting the patient, we must first allow the *Game* to move to completion, or, at the very least in the case of a lethal or third degree *Game,* we may ask the patient to fantasize or project the end. We then *must* have a report from the patient of his bad feelings. (Without evidence of bad feeling, the patient may deny the *Game,* and go underground.)

Earlier in this chapter, I mentioned the *Game:* "Why don't you, yes but." This is the most common *Game* played in new groups. The *Game* has been thoroughly discussed by Berne in *Games People Play* and *Transactional Analysis in Psychotherapy.* Essentially, in this *Game,* the player ends up feeling disappointed that no one (parent) ever does anything to help, and the playee, who usually plays from a rescue position (I'm only trying to help), also ends up frustrated that nothing he ever offers is really accepted. I saw this version of this *Game* played out classically while fishing on the river in Kashmir, India, recently. I shall describe the conditions surrounding the *Game* and the *Game* itself.

I am an expert fly fisherman and I almost always catch my limit anywhere. In this instance, I had to rent a fly-rod and reel that included just enough back-up line, no fly-casting line, and all wet flies. Even with these odds and with three eager Kashmir fishermen surrounding me with nets, umbrellas and advice, I caught a nice 17 inch Rainbow Trout on my first cast. This catch was extremely difficult because I carefully had to avoid my grandstand on my back cast and to cast a line that was made for following bait, not for carrying a fly. However, despite these obstacles, I hooked the fish. Immediately upon my bringing the fish close to the shore, one of my "helpers" rushed to the "rescue" with a landing net, and dislodged the fly. I quickly had to gill the fish with my finger in order to avoid losing him. "I was only trying to help, sahib," said my "helper," looking crestfallen. I smiled (I had my fish) and said nothing. A few minutes later, I landed my second, slightly smaller Rainbow. And within another ten minutes, I landed a ten-inch fat Brown Trout. At this point, as my "helper" took the fly out, he said, "Why don't you use a peacock fly?" (Hell, I had just caught three fish on the Kashmir version of a wooly worm with white wings, but it was now a little worn, so instead of saying, "Yes, but I caught three," I decided to try the peacock.) I started to tie it on–I only trust my own knots–but my helper took it away from me and tied it. "That knot won't hold a big fish," I said. "But sahib, that's a good knot, why don't you use it?" I shrugged, made a few casts, had a huge strike. I played the fish for a few minutes, and then he made a rush up the river, and swam away with my fly in his mouth as the knot pulled loose. I glared at my helper, who said again, "I was only trying to help." Once again he looked crestfallen.

But wait! Don't go away; there is more to follow. It was obvious that in the first instance, I had not played. In the second instance, I had not initiated the *Game,* but I allowed him to play when I didn't retie the knot, and my mild anger at the end, the remnant of my *racket,* proved that I had played; his crestfallenness proved that he had played. The transactions are translated below.

The *Game* went on. He tied a weight to my line–no self-respecting American fly fisherman would use a weight, because the American Rainbows would see it. So do Kashmiri Rainbows! Af-

Helper   1.

o   o   o   A   o   1. A. OST(A) stimulus — Let me tie the
                                        knot.

o —A— o   o   o   B. OK.

o —B— o   o   B   o   2. Secret message (a) Let me do it so that I
                                        can feel crestfallen (already had a proven
                                        pay-off).

                                     (b) I know it won't hold, but I'll let you
                                     do it so I can be angry at your interfer-
                                     ence.

                                     3. Response to S.M. (see 2b above for
           RLG   mine).

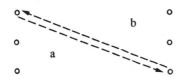

                                     4. He felt crestfallen; I felt angry.

                                     5. Both sides really not aware in Adult that
                                     each set up himself to feel angry/crest-
                                     fallen.

ter 30 minutes of fruitless fishing, I waded across the ice cold
stream in my $40.00 Bostonians, eluded my "helpers," removed
the weight and the second fly they had tied, tied on a wooly worm,
and caught 19 trout in 30 minutes, all of which I returned to the
water before rejoining my Moslem friends for a rice and vegetable
lunch, saying nothing. They were sure I had caught no more, and
all of us were happy.

The incident just described illustrates some of the options of a
therapist:

1. Play the *Game* and don't accept the secondary payoff (I
caught the first fish).

2. Play the *Game* and accept the payoff (I lost the fish and became angry).

3. Ignore the *Game* (cross the river).

In (2), the therapist can confront the player and ask him if he has any other options than the payoff, e.g., "Wow, I played; I understand it; I don't have to feel crestfallen, but I feel good that I understand."

Of course, in a non-contractual situation, I would be out of line to confront my Kashmiri friends; therefore I did not confront them. This would be playing hostalysis (analysis with hostility as the motive) a favorite couples *Game* when they first start a T.A. group.

I have now discussed briefly some of the essential theory of T.A. ego states: *decisions, injunctions, rackets, Games, scripts.* I have briefly discussed therapeutic considerations–the non-selective group, on-going vs. marathon groups, getting the contract, picking up *rackets* and *Games,* looking for the *primary decision,* and creating an environment in which the patient can make a *redecision.* I have also briefly discussed some of the work done to teach the patient how to be aware of his incongruities and non-autonomy, and how to become more congruent, and autonomous.

Redecisions

The essential difference between the kind of work done and taught at the Western Institute and other therapy training centers is in the area of *redecisions.* The difference stems from the different philosophical position that we take compared to Berne's position and, I think in all fairness, compared to the position that most therapists have. I know few therapists who really believe that most patients can get well. We at the Western Institute do so believe and we have a lot of evidence to support our belief. The Berne position is that people are primarily victims of their *injunctions,* that they are "scripted" by their parents, and to quote Eric in the book *What Do You Say After You Say Hello?*

> The script matrix is a diagram designed to illustrate and analyze the directives handed down from the parents and grandparents to the current generation. These will, in the long run, *determine* the person's life plan and his final payoff (1972, p. 294).

This sentence gives no responsibility to the child to accept or reject the script. On pages 113-114, Eric describes the injunction as follows:

> For an injunction *to be locked in* solidly in the mind of a child, it must be repeated frequently and transgressions must be punished, although there are exceptional cases such as in battered children, where a single shattering experience may ingrave an injunction for life (1972).
>
> The injunction is the *most* important part of the script apparatus and varies in intensity (1972).

Eric describes the "electrode" (which is the Child of the parent) which Eric describes as being "inserted into the Parent of the Child, where they act like a negative electrode. This keeps Jeder from doing certain things such as talking or thinking clearly . . ." (1972, p. 115). Over and over again, Berne sees that the parent is everything and the child is nothing–with no choices, having electrodes "inserted," injunctions "inserted," et cetera.

Our position is that every child always has a choice. He makes his decisions based upon the information available and how he interprets this information. He makes a decision in order to survive psychologically and sometimes physically in an environment that is not of his choosing and in which he usually cannot leave at an early age. He does not always make the decision based upon the *injunction.* Often he does, because he can see no other way of getting along at this time.

If you take the position that the child does make a decision, then it is the Child in the patient who obviously can make a new decision. Thus, the focus of our work from the very beginning is to establish an environment in which the patient can in some way make a *redecision* for himself. Preferably, and for a real cure, this must come from his Child ego state, but we are willing to go along with one made from the Adult ego state, at first.

For example, let us examine a patient who has been suicidal for years. He is a psychiatrist who has made several suicide attempts, and was seen by us in a workshop in 1971. The first day of the one-month workshop, we asked him if he were willing to state that he would not kill himself while in the workshop. He looked me straight in the eye and said, "I promise you I will not kill myself this month." I said, "I am not interested in promises; this is not for me; it's for you." He said, "I understand. I will not kill myself this month." For this period, I was satisfied with this decision and asked him if he were willing to do more work around that decision during the month. He stated that he was willing.

During some of the small group work that the trainees conduct with each other under our supervision, he did some more work in this area with one of our participant therapists, but he was still in his Adult. At the end of the work, I asked both him and the therapist if he was willing to do some more work with me. He agreed. I asked him to fantasize that his mother was sitting in the chair across from him, and say to her, "I will not kill myself." He went through this exercise with his mother and his father, with some rejoinders from them, and then looked at me and said, "I have done this before and I still don't feel any differently. I still am afraid that if things got too bad, I would try to kill myself again, and next time I won't just try." I responded, "Will you be that part of you that has not allowed you to kill yourself in the past–the part of you that didn't take quite enough pills, that allowed yourself to be found, that survived after your heart had stopped beating?" His eyes widened and he nodded. "Will you put the rest of you in the other chair and talk to the rest of you?" He said, "I will not let you kill me. I want to be alive and stay alive." He then screamed, "I will not let you kill me!"

"Will you be the other part of you?" I asked. He sat in the other chair and responded, "I hear you; you really want to live, don't you?" Then, crying, he said, from the second chair, "I won't kill you. I won't kill myself." He then sat down in the first chair and said spontaneously, "I am the most powerful part of me and I will not let anything happen to me that ends in my death."

That was two years ago and my friend is still alive, is no longer depressed, and is doing very well. He had made a decision as a child that if things got too tough, he could always kill himself and then he had made things get too tough. The experience of making a *redecision,* not just from his Adult, but also while in his Child ego state, was a most powerful one for him. How different this is from Eric's following statement in *What Do You Say After You Say Hello?*

> The electrode is the decisive challenge for a therapist. He, together with the patient's Adult, must neutralize it, so that the Child can get permission to live freely and react spontaneously, in the face of the parents' programming to the contrary, and their threats if he disobeys. This is difficult enough with milder controls, but if the injunction is a demand made by a witch or giant whose features are distorted with rage, whose voice smashes through all the defenses of the child's mind, and whose hand is ever ready to strike humiliation and terror into his face and head, it requires enormous therapeutic power (1972, p. 116).

Enormous therapeutic power? The power is in the patient. Not in the therapist. It always was.

COUNTER-TRANSFERENCE AND TRANSFERENCE

One last issue remains for this paper—our handling of transference and counter-transference. I discussed this at length in a panel at the 1966 American Group Psychotherapy Association Convention. The contents of this panel, unfortunately, were not published in the *International Journal of Group Psychotherapy*.

Counter-transference

I insist that all our trainees are not only taught and supervised by us, but also treated by us. I know of no other way for the supervisor or training analyst to know really what is going on with his trainee or analyst unless he sees him as a whole person—not as a patient on one couch, while someone else sees him as an analyst at the head of another couch. I want to watch and to listen to my trainees as they switch roles from leader to patient, so I can hear how their counter-transference gets in their way. For instance, I observe how a trainee in a group demonstrates frustration as he plays "Why don't you, yes but," and then gets caught in a bear-trap (cf. Simkin, in Sager and Kaplan, 1972) with one of his patients in his own group and ends up frustrated. Or, how he plays "Kick Me" in the group (Child position) and then plays "Now I've Got You, You Son of a Bitch (NIGYYSOB) as leader (Parent position)—the two *Games* naturally being two parts of the same *Game,* "Kick Me" played by his Child, and NIGYYSOB by his Parent. (Of course, his real parent, now incorporated into his Parent, kicked him as a child.)

I teach the trainee to use his feeling responses to alert him to what group members are doing. For instance, if he becomes aware that his foot is kicking, he may ask himself: "Does this have to do with me or with the patient, or both? If it has to do with me, perhaps that patient's facial expression reminds me of my father, and I am in my own *racket*. If it has to do with him, what is he doing that I am responding to, and how can I use my feelings therapeutically?" The following example is cited to illustrate the point: A counselor from the California Youth Authority walked into the first session of a weekend marathon with a beer in his hand. Three hundred and forty-seven of his co-workers from C.Y.A. have been in our marathons, and all of them knew that we allow *no* drinking during the weekend. Someone must have told this person, also. I assumed, therefore, that he was attempting to set me up–in or out of awareness. I went through a series of questions in my head:

A. Is he playing "Kick Me"? (Answer: Probably.)

B. If he is, what will be his payoff? (Answer: He looks like an angry man.)

C. What decision does his anger fit? (Answer: My guess is, "I'll get you even if it kills me.")

D. What was his *injunction?* (Answer: Probably, "Don't Be.")

There is obvious conjecture here, but I am using my feelings of very mild anger to start off a series of thoughts, and immediately drop my anger as I do so.

E. What shall I do?–Alternatives:

1. Kick him? (Answer: Too early.),

2. Confront him with the game? (Answer: Too early.),

3. Ignore him? (Answer: Beer *is* against the rules, won't do that.),

4. Play it straight (Answer: (A)–(A)).

Having decided (4), I said quietly but very straight to him? "One of the rules here is 'no drinking.'" He responded angrily: "Moralistic bastard!" (I now have answers to A. (Yes); to B. (anger); to C. (I think I'm right; he'll try to get even.); to D. (Yes, his *injunction* is "Don't Be").

During the next 30 hours, he played "Kick Me" at least 87 percent of the time, but refused to enter into any contract; tempted me in all kinds of ways to reject him ("Don't Be"); to throw him out ("Don't Be"); to kill him ("Don't Be"); to fight with him ("I'll Get Even With You if It Kills Me"). I refused all ploys until 4 p.m. Saturday, when I was doing some very delicate and sensitive dream work. I had already asked two psychoanalysts in the group not to get into the dream work, when he came in with a very disruptive interaction, at which point, I said to him very sharply, after five seconds of thought, "Shut Up!" He did. When I was through the work, I turned to him and asked "What did you feel when I told you to shut up?" Our exchange follows:

> Patient: You're a mother-fucking son-of-a-bitch!
> Goulding: That's what you thought; what did you feel?
> Patient: I'll get you, you bastard.
> Goulding: Is that a familiar feeling?
> Patient: Damn right!
> Goulding: What's the feeling?
> Patient: Anger, you stupid prick!
> Goulding: Are you often angry?
> Patient: Always!
> Goulding: Are you interested in knowing how you get there?
> Patient: Nah!
> Goulding: OK, when, or if you are, will you let me know?
> Patient: Fuck you!
> Goulding: It seems to me that you continue to ask me to be angry at you so that at some point I will be angry enough to ask you to leave. Does that fit?
> Patient: Heh, yeah, it does. I've been fired or transferred from more jobs than anyone in Y.A.
> Goulding: Want to know how you do it?
> Patient: I guess so.
> Goulding: Do you say that to get me off your back, or are you interested?
> Patient: (Smile) Go ahead, Doc, maybe I really will learn something!

To summarize this brief interaction, I concluded that the trainee did have a "Don't Be" *injunction*. He did decide, "I'll get even with you even if it kills me." He had been in many street fights, bar room fights, drove a car recklessly, and at high speeds, and the like. He did some fine work, made a redecision to "live and enjoy" and, at last report over a year later, he had sold his sports car, achieved a professional advancement, and had not had a fight. Any feeling, then, of therapist toward patient that *could* be labelled counter-transference can be used by the properly trained and skillful therapist.

Transference

The same patient, described under counter-transference can be used as an example to illustrate the handling of the transference phenomenon. Obviously, carrying the beer was a hostile act toward us, challenging our authority, which later on was shown as a familiar first move in the *Game.* I allowed him to use me as a target until the proper time. I then asked him to use the same words that he had used towards me (saying them over again) to all members of his family, as we placed them (in fantasy) in various chairs. In this way, his negative transference was *immediately* worked through. The same procedure, with variations, is used in all cases of negative transference. We do not use a long term analysis of the neurotic transference, but immediately put it where it belongs. In the same way, in training group transactions with negative feelings, we very rapidly expose and confront the *racket* and the *Game,* and then use the retrogressive method discussed on page 249.

THERAPIST QUALIFICATIONS

The Western Institute for Group and Family Therapy generally trains only people with advanced degrees in medicine, psychology or social work. Ministers, priests, rabbis, and other members of the clergy who have advanced degrees as well as people who do not have advanced degrees but who are being paid to do therapy in probation and parole work or other areas of corrections are also trained. Other T.A. institutes, however, do not require these conditions for training in T.A. As a result, the International Transactional Analysis Association has not established pre-requisites for T.A. training other than for advanced membership as a Teaching Member. To become a Teaching Member the candidate must have either an advanced degree or six years of practical experience do-

Figure 1

INTERNATIONAL TRANSACTIONAL ANALYSIS ASSOCIATION

A NON-PROFIT EDUCATIONAL CORPORATION

3155 COLLEGE AVENUE

BERKELEY, CALIFORNIA 94705

TELEPHONE (415) 653-1420

CLASSIFICATION OF ITAA MEMBERSHIP[1]

Class	*Requirements*	*Fees*	*Privileges*
Subscription to Journal	Open to libraries and institutions	$ 7.50 Libraries and Institutions	Receipt of Journal
Associate Member (AM)	Application	$ 12.00 Annual Dues	Receipt of Journal Special registration fee for Annual Summer Conference
Regular Member (RM)	Successful completion of Official TA 101 course and exam. (101 at Summer Conference is applicable)	$ 25.00 Annual Dues	Receipt of Journal and listed as member Special registration fee for Annual Summer Conference
Special Member (SM)	Successful completion of 101 Course and exam. (101 at Summer Conference is applicable) Approved Special Membership Contract on file with ITAA main office 100 hours training Appearance before and approval of Examining Board (Tape-recorded work samples of at least 3 hours length must be brought to the exam)	$ 25.00 Initiation $ 25.00 Annual Dues	Teach members of specialized field Apply T.A. in specialized field Attend clinical meetings, congresses Voting status Special registration fee for Annual Summer Conference
Clinical Member (CM)	Successful completion of Official TA 101 course and exam. (101 at Summer Conference is applicable) Approved Clinical Membership Conract on File with ITAA main office 87% attendance at 202 for one year and 3 presentations.	$100.00 Initiation $ 25.00 Annual Dues	Practice T.A. (Treatment of patients is dependent upon local regulations) Attend clinical meetings, congresses Voting status Special registration fee for Annual Summer Conference May receive referrals for therapy and

	Two groups for one year with 50 hours supervision or its equivalent. TA Presentations Appearance before and approval of Examining Board. (Tape-recorded work samples of at least 3 hours length and log sheet must be brought to the exam)	Supervise training of clinical trainees
Provisional Teaching Member	Teaching Membership Contract approved by PTM Board on file with main ITAA office	
Teaching Member (TM)	CM held for minimum of two years (Formal postgraduate education or state license or six years practical experience.) Approved Teaching Membership Contract on file with ITAA office Teach two 101s in physical presence of a TM Supervision of two clinical trainees under supervision of a TM Sponsor 10 regular member candidates 1,000 hours of TA treatment of patients. 700 hours of teaching and training Complete oral examination by Examining Board.	$ 75.00 Initiation $ 25.00 Filing Fee $ 25.00 Annual Dues
		Teach 101s and sponsor a 202 Supervise training of teaching and clinical member candidates Attend clinical meetings, congresses Voting status Special registration fee for Annual Summer Conference May receive referrals for training and therapy from ITAA office

Substitute Training: Requirements for SM, CM, or TM may be waived by the Examining Board in cases where the trainee is located in a community without access to the continuous supervision of a TM or an advanced seminar. Precise working of substitute training must be put in the advanced membership contract. This listing supersedes previous membership classification requirements.

Training Standards Committee, January 6, 1973

1. Courtesy of International Transactional Analysis Association, Berkeley, California.

ing therapy. A chart of the Classification of the International Transactional Analysis Membership is reproduced in Figure 1.

RESEARCH RESULTS

We have followed up our own and our trainees' patients and T.A. participants who have made no-suicide decisions over a five-year period. So far, over 800 of these depressed people are reported to be alive, and none have in any way attempted suicide. In addition to these data, we have hundreds of letters in our files that attest to the effectiveness of T.A.

SUMMARY

Our primary interest through T.A. is to create an environment in which the patient can discover that he supports bad feelings by *Games, fantasies,* and *displacement;* that he holds onto his bad feelings to support his *scripts* and *decisions* in order to obey the *injunctions* that at one time he obeyed in order to survive psychologically and/or physically; that *now he obeys because it is familiar,* and because he thinks he doesn't know any other way. He does, however, know other ways of behaving, and he finds other ways. He may be asked to try out other ways in the group, as a Gestalt experience.

We object to long months or years of individual and/or group therapy that fosters dependence, maintains transference, and strokes sickness. We encourage rapid, decisive therapy, aimed at *immediate* autonomy, independence, and a feeling of accomplishment. We build upon strength, stroke strength, and confront people that even in their resistance they are strong and tough. But, we ask: "Is there not a better way to be tough?" We encourage persons to be loving, to be free of archaic demands and archaic injunctions, to live in the here-and-now, rather than the there-and-then, even while planning for a better tomorrow—*not trying to progress, but being creative, spontaneous, autonomous, intuitive, intimate, aware, enthusiastic, and starting right now!*

SUGGESTED READINGS

Berne, E.: *Transactional Analysis in Psychotherapy.* New York, Grove Press, 1961.

Berne, E.: *The Structure and Dynamics of Organizations and Groups,* Philadelphia, J. B. Lippincott, 1963.
Berne, E.: *Games People Play.* New York, Grove Press, 1964.
Berne, E.: *Principles of Group Treatment.* New York, Oxford University Press, 1966.
Berne, E.: *What Do You Say After You Say Hello?* New York, Grove Press, 1972.
Berne, E.: *Sex in Human Loving.* New York, Simon and Schuster, in press.
Campos, L., and McCormick, P.: *Introduce Your Marriage to Transactional Analysis.* Transactional Analysis Institute, Stockton, California, n.d.
Ernst, K.: *Games Students Play (What to Do About Them).* Millbrae, Calif. Celestial Arts (n.d.).
Fagan, J., and Shepherd, I. L. (Eds.): *Gestalt Therapy Now.* New York, Harper/Colophon Books, 1971.
Goulding, R. L.: New directions in transactional analysis: Creating an environment for redecision and change. In C. J. Sager and H. S. Kaplan (Eds.): *Progress in Group and Family Therapy.* New York, Brunner/Mazel, 1972.
James, M., and Jongeward, D.: *Born to Win: Transactional Analysis With Gestalt Experiments.* Reading, Mass., Addison-Wesley (n.d.).
Lieberman, M. A., Yalom, I. D., and Miles, M. B.: *Encounter Groups: First Facts.* New York, Basic Books, 1973.
McCormick, P., and Campos, L.: *Introduce Yourself to Transactional Analysis.* Berkeley, California, Transactional Publications, 1969.
Perls, F.: *Gestalt Therapy Verbatim.* Moab, Utah, Real People Press, 1969.
Perls, F.: *In and Out of the Garbage Pail.* New York, Bantam Books, 1969.
Polster, E., and Polster, M.: *Gestalt Therapy Integrated.* New York, Brunner/Mazel, 1973.
Simkin, J. S.: The use of dreams in Gestalt therapy. In Sager, C. J., and Kaplan, H. S. (Eds.): *Progress in Group and Family Therapy.* New York, Brunner/Mazel, 1972.
Transactional Analysis Bulletin, 1962-69, Trans. Pubs., Inc., Berkeley, Calif.
Transactional Analysis Journal, 1970-73, Trans. Pubs., Inc., Berkeley, Calif.

REFERENCES

Berne, E.: *Games People Play.* New York, Grove Press, 1964.
Berne, E.: *Transactional Analysis in Psychotherapy.* New York, Grove Press, 1961.
Berne, E.: *What Do You Say After You Say Hello?* New York, Grove Press, 1972.
Fagan, J., and Shepherd, I. L. (Eds.): *Gestalt Therapy Now.* New York, Harper/Colophon Books, 1971.
Goulding, R. L.: New directions in transactional analysis: Creating an en-

vironment for redecision and change. In C. J. Sager and H. S. Kaplan (Eds.):*Progress in Group and Family Therapy.* New York, Brunner/ Mazel, 1972.

Lieberman, M. A., Yalom, I. D., and Miles, M. B.: *Encounter Groups: First Facts.* New York, Basic Books, 1973.

McCormick, P., and Campos, L.: *Introduce Yourself to Transactional Analysis: A T.A. Handbook.* Berkeley, California, Transactional Publications, 1969.

CHAPTER XI

GESTALT THERAPY IN GROUPS

James S. Simkin

GESTALT IS A GERMAN WORD meaning whole or configuration. As one psychological dictionary puts it: ". . . an *integration* of members as contrasted with a summation of parts" (Warren, 1934, p. 115). The term also implies a unique kind of patterning. Gestalt therapy is a term applied to a unique kind of psychotherapy as formulated by the late Frederick S. Perls, his co-workers, and his followers.

Dr. Perls began, as did many of his colleagues in those days, as a psychoanalyst, after having been trained as a physician in post-World War I Germany. In 1926 he worked under Professor Kurt Goldstein at the Frankfurt Neurological Institute where he was first exposed to the tenets of gestalt psychology but ". . . was still too preoccupied with the orthodox approach to assimilate more than a fraction of what was offered" (Perls, 1947, p. 5). Later Dr. Perls was exposed to the theories and practice of Wilhelm Reich and incorporated some of the concepts and techniques of Character Analysis into his work.

While serving as a Captain in the South African Medical Corps, Perls wrote his first manuscript in 1941-1942 outlining his emerging theory and application of personality integration which later appeared as a book, *Ego, Hunger and Aggression*. The term "Gestalt Therapy" was first used in 1949 as the title of a book on Perls' methods written by him and two co-authors, Ralph Hefferline of Columbia University and the late Paul Goodman of New York City.

GROUP PSYCHOTHERAPY AND WORKSHOPS

In Gestalt therapy the emphasis is on the present, on-going situation, which, of course, involves the interaction of at least two people–in individual therapy, the patient and the therapist. This interaction becomes expanded to more than two people in the group situation and may involve an interactive process among several people or may involve the interactive process at any given moment between two people with each of the other participants involving themselves as they are ready. In Gestalt therapy it is not necessary to emphasize the group dynamics, although some Gestalt therapists do so. All Gestalt therapists focus at one time or another on the interactive process between the therapist and the group member in the here and now and/or the interactive process between group members as it is ongoing.

Perls preferred the term workshop to group psychotherapy and in a paper written in 1967 indicated the values of workshop versus individual therapy as follows:

> To the whole group it is obvious that the person in distress does not see the obvious, does not see the way out of the impasse, does not see (for instance) that his whole misery is a purely imagined one. In the face of this collective conviction he cannot use his usual phobic way of disowning the therapist when he cannot manipulate him. . . . Behind the impasse . . . is the catastrophic expectation. . . . In the safe emergency of the therapeutic situation, he (the patient) discovers that the world does not fall to pieces if he gets angry, sexy, joyous, or mournful. The group supports his self-esteem; the appreciation of his achievement toward authenticity and greater liveliness also is not to be underestimated. Gestalt therapists also use the group for doing collective experiments—such as talking gibberish together or doing withdrawal experiments in learning to understand the importance of the atmosphere. . . . The observation by the group members of the manipulative games of playing helpless, stupid, wailing, seductive or other roles by which the neurotic helps himself in the infantile state of controlling, facilitates their own recognition (1967, p. 17).

THEORETICAL FOUNDATIONS

Man is considered a total organism functioning as a whole, rather than an entity split into dichotomies such as mind and body. With the philosophical background of humanism, *a la* Otto Rank, the organism is seen as born with the capacity to cope with life. This is opposed to what I call the original sin theory of human development–that the organism must learn to repress or supress its instinctual strivings in order to become "civilized." The emergence of existential philosophy coincides historically with the development of Gestalt therapy. Wilson Van Dusen (1960), in an article "Existential Analytic Psychotherapy," believes that there is only one psychotherapeutic approach which unites the phenomenological approach with existential theory, and that is Gestalt therapy.

The theoretical model of the psychodynamic schools of personality–chiefly the Freudian School–envisions the personality like an onion consisting of layers. Each time a layer is peeled away, there is still another layer until you finally come to the core. (Incidentally, in the process of "analysis" of the onion, you may have very little or nothing left by the time you come to the core!) I envision the personality more like a large rubber ball which has only a thick outer layer and is empty inside. The ball floats or swims in an environment so that at any given moment only a certain portion is exposed while the rest is submerged in the water. Thus, rather than inventing an unconscious or preconscious to account for behavior that we are unaware of, I suggest that the unaware behavior is the result of the organism not being in touch with its external environment because of being mostly submerged in its own background (internal environment) or in contact with (usually preoccupied with) fantasies.

In *A Review of the Practice of Gestalt Therapy,* Yontef (1971) summarized the theory of Gestalt therapy. He reasoned that organismic needs lead to sensory motor behavior. Once a configuration is formed which has the qualities of a good gestalt, the organismic need which has been foreground is met and a balance or state of satiation or no-need is achieved.

> When a need is met, the Gestalt it organized becomes complete and it no longer exerts an influence—the organism is free to form new gestalten. When this gestalt formation and destruction are blocked or rigidified at any stage, when needs are not recognized and expressed, the flexible harmony and flow of the organism/environment field is disturbed. Unmet needs form incomplete gestalten

that clamor for attention and, therefore, interfere with the formation of new gestalten (Yontef, 1971, p. 3).

As Perls, Hefferline, and Goodman (1951) put it, "The most important fact about the figure-background formation is that if a need is genuinely satisfied, the situation changes" (p. xi).

EXAMPLE OF A FIRST SESSION IN A GESTALT WORKSHOP

The following excerpt is an example of how one workshop started. Following a short introduction, a suggested exercise involved each of the participants and very quickly one of the participants asked to work.

> Jim: Good evening. I'd like to start with a few sentences about contract and then suggest an exercise. I believe that there are no "shoulds" in Gestalt therapy. What you do is what you do. What I do is what I do. I have a preference. I prefer that you be straight with me. *Please* remember, this is a preference, not a should. If you feel that you *should* honor my preference, then that's *your* should! When I ask you, "Where are you?" and the like, my preference is that you tell me—or tell me that you're *not* willing to tell me. Then our transaction is straight. Any time that you want to know where I am, please ask me. I will either tell you, or tell you I am unwilling to tell you—so that our transaction will be straight.
>
> Now for the exercise. Please look around the room and select someone you don't know or don't know well—whom you would like to know or know better . . . O.K.? Now here are the rules. You may do anything you like to "know" the other person better, except talk! John?
>
> John: The lady with the brown sweater.
>
> Jim: Marilyn, are you willing to be "known" by John?
>
> Marilyn: Yes.
>
> Jim: Elaine, please select a partner.
>
> Elaine: That man—I believe he said his name was Bert.
>
> Jim: Are you willing, Bert?
>
> Bert: My pleasure!
>
> Jim: Nancy?
>
> Nancy: I would like to know Agnes better.
>
> Agnes: That's fine with me.
>
> Jonathan: Well, that leaves me to Phil.
>
> Jim: Yes, unless you're willing to include me.
>
> Jonathan: No thanks. I'd rather get to know Phil! (group laughter)

The group breaks into dyads and for several minutes the person who has asked to know the other is the aggressor "exploring" the other with his sensory modalities (touch, taste, smell, etc.), lifting, pulling, dancing with, etc. Then the partners in the dyad are asked to switch and the "aggressor" becomes the "aggressee" as the exercise is repeated.

> Jim: O.K., I am interested in knowing more about your experience. If you have made any discovery about *yourself* and are willing to share, please tell the rest of us what you found out.
> Bert: I discovered that I felt very awkward and uncomfortable when Elaine was the aggressor!
> Elaine: I sensed your discomfort and found myself concerned with what you thought of me.
> Bert: I would like to work on my always having to be "masculine"— my avoidance of my passivity.
> Jim: When?
> Bert: Now!
> (At this point Bert leaves his chair in the circle and sits in the empty chair across from the therapist.)
> I feel anxious. My heart is pounding and my hands feel sweaty, and I'm very aware of all of the others in the room.
> Jim: Is there anything you would like to say to the others?

For the next 15-20 minutes Bert worked in the "hot seat." When he finished, the therapist turned his focus (awareness) back to the group.

"IN THE NOW"

The following examples are taken from my training film, *In the Now*. After my introductory comments, Al moved from the group circle to the "hot seat." He was very eager to start. His work with me is presented verbatim from the film. It concludes with the last several minutes of the film which involved primarily an exchange between Al and Colman, another participant.

> Jim: Okay, now I would suggest we start with getting in touch with what we're doing in this situation now. Most people are interested, or at least they say they are interested, in changing their behavior. This is what therapy is all about. In order to change behavior, you have to know what you're doing and how you do what you do. So, let's start with your examining, focusing your awareness and saying what you're in touch with at this moment. Say where you are, what you're experiencing.

(Al gets up and moves to the hot seat across from me.)

Al: I feel as though I got the catastrophe by sitting over there suffering, and I still feel it at intervals. But I really haven't felt so much like a patient in all the time I've been a psychologist. I think it's for this special occasion. Last night at four o'clock in the morning I awoke . . . well, it started at nine . . . I started blushing in the groin, you know. I thought it was a flea bite 'cause we got five new dogs . . . pups. I couldn't find the flea. By four o'clock in the morning, I was blushing here and here, in my head, and I couldn't sleep, I was itching so. And I got an antihistamine. By nine or ten in the morning the itching went away and then coming here and I get this chest . . . my chest hurts.

Jim: How about right now?

Al: I'm sweating. I sweat and I'm warm.

Jim: What happened to your voice?

Al: It got low and warm and I wiggle a little.

Jim: And now?

Al: I feel a tension I carry around a good deal up here—a band that grabs my head like that and pulls me together like I'm puzzled.

Jim: Play the band that's pulling on Al. "I am Al's band and I . . ."

Al: I am Al's band containing him. I'm his crazy megalomania—want to run the world his way.

Jim: Tell Al what your objections are to his running the world his way.

Al: He's a nut . . . to think he can run the world his way—or a child.

Jim: Now give Al a voice and let Al talk to the band.

Al: I know how to run it as well as anybody else. Why shouldn't I?

Jim: You sounded like a fairly reasonable nut or child at that moment. . . . And now?

Al: Back to my gut. I make myself suffer to recognize I can't take what I want.

Jim: Okay, what is it that you want that you're not taking at this moment?

Al: Well, I very reluctantly thought of the milk and the world as one.

Jim: You're reluctantly not taking the milk and the world at this moment.

Al: I'm sure that's not what I said. I reluctantly *thought* of the milk. I didn't want to talk about that. I'd rather be a megalomaniac than an infant asking for warmth (mother's milk).

Jim: Can you imagine anything in between those two . . . the infant and the megalomaniac?

Al: It's a long way, yeah. You know I'm an extremist. Let's see a bite-size. Yeah, how about just writing an article on art therapy, which I've scheduled for the last three years? I haven't done that. I would like it just to flow and to come out without any pain, without giving up anything else.

Jim: So you want to be the breast.

Al: I want to be the breast! To be the giver, to flow. Oh, well, I hadn't thought of it that way.

Jim: Well, think of it that way. Take a couple of hours. Imagine yourself a big tit.

Al: It's a very feminine thing to be, a breast.

Jim: Yeah.

Al: Give a little.

Jim: Yeah.

Al: Give a lot.

Jim: Yeah.

Al: You get . . . you capture your son with that milk. You hold onto him.

Jim: Al?

Al: Yeah.

Jim: Would you be willing to be as tender, soft, feminine as you know how?

Al: It's a threat.

Jim: What's a threat?

Al: To follow your suggestion would be a threat . . . of what? Makes no sense.

Jim: Okay. Do the opposite. Whatever the reverse of being soft, tender, loving, feminine is for you.

Al: Be masculine.

Jim: Show me.

Al: It's something like *"practice"* . . . you know fatherly, uh, *"shut-up!"*

Jim: Yeah, do a little scowling with it. That's it.

Al: *"Shut-up!"* So it's not puzzling, it's uh, it's father. *"You burnt the soup! Leave the table,"* and then a kind of fantasy of mother crying. I sort of regret that my father died before I became friendly with him again.

Jim: Say this to him.

Al: I'm sorry. (Sigh) Well, inside I said I'm sorry you died.

Jim: Outside.

Al: I'm sorry.

Jim: Say this to him outside.

Al: I'm sorry you died too soon (for me).

Jim: Give him a voice.

Al: I haven't the slightest idea what he would say. I thought of his excusing me. He says, "You, you didn't know any better. You were young and angry."

Jim: Your father sounds tender.

Al: He may be the father I wanted. I never, I don't think of him as a tender man but . . .

Jim: It's the voice you gave him.

Al: Yeah. I may have underestimated him.

Jim: Say this to him.

Al: Dad, I guess I did, I underestimated you.

Jim: Say this to Al.

Al: Al, you underestimated me. You could have been closer. . . .

Jim: (Interrupts) No, No. Say this sentence to Al. "Al, I underestimate you."

Al: Al, I underestimate you. You can do a good deal more than you're doing. Then I put myself down and say, "You're crazy to expect so much from yourself," and don't do anything . . . like going from do everything to do nothing. Just sit and don't create it. I feel a little phony to accept your interpretation so easily.

Jim: You see what you just did?

Al: I puzzled myself?

Jim: You said, "I feel a little phony. . . ." There came your band.

Al: And it hurts here (points to stomach). It didn't hurt there for a long time. Now it's back. What happened? I'm supposed to know? So I've got a blind spot. I'm entitled.

Jim: Your blind spot happens to be Al Freeman.

Al: A total blind spot?

Jim: You're not entitled to that blind spot. What are you doing?

Al: Puzzling. You're playing God and telling me I'm not. I'm not God? That was a . . . I didn't expect to say that at all, really.

Jim: What just happened?

Al: I exposed something, I guess. It was quite unintended.

Jim: Yeah.

Al: I was just going to argue with you, and I came out with my manic side. I don't often do that.

Jim: You just did.

Al: It slipped. I'm sorry. . . . I'm not sorry; I'm glad; I'm glad. Whew!

Jim: What do you experience right now?

Al: Warmth. I love having people laugh, especially with me. So I guess everybody wants it. Wants warmth and love.

Jim: God never makes excuses or gives reasons.

Al: No?

Jim: *I* know.

Al: I give you permission to be God. I understand. Yeah, you have warmth. I give you . . . I give you warmth. What else do you want? The world? You can have the world. Just be sure to give it back . . . in ten minutes. God is an imposter, because I'm God. And that other one is a fake. I really could do the whole thing myself.

Jim: Yeah. Now you're catching on.

SAYING GOOD-BYE

Jim: There's quite a bit of . . . unfinished business that sometimes accumulates during a workshop . . . especially in the area of resentments and appreciations. Now you don't have to have any appreciations or resentments, you may have some other unfinished business. If you have any unfinished business, now is the time to bring this out.

Colman: I want to talk to Al.

Al: Go ahead.

Colman: I left last night and you bothered me. And I feel that you're haunted, you're a . . . mezepah (warlock) and you came here looking and you saw what happened to me. And you asked me a question which was really a statement. You've done that animal trainer bit before, is what your question stated. This guy showed you, and you wouldn't believe. And last night when I came to you . . . to relate to you, you almost took it.

Al: I pulled away because you damn near broke my glasses.

Colman: Yeah.

Al: That's why.

Colman: O.K. Go ahead. Still with the mezepah.

Al: With your hug. No, you're perceiving it . . . badly. I bought it; I did not have any notion whatsoever as to whether you had created that idea, the trainer, on the spot.

Colman: I don't want . . . don't give me that. When I came to you last night . . . and I tried to convey to you my feeling, it wasn't your glasses. O.K., your glasses were incidental, but you turned to me and you said: "Oh, yeah, now I see why you do that."

Al: I said I had no idea. . . .

Colman: Better late than never. You couldn't take it that I felt for you . . . you had to put it off on me that I had to do it . . . you can't eat it, you can't taste it.

Al: O.K., I feel its unfinished business. . . .

Colman: And I still like you.

Al: Let's, let's, hear what's behind it, then.

Jim: Oh, shut up!

Colman: And Jim . . . I don't mind crying; it makes it hard to talk.

I . . . I did come . . . entirely as . . . I say, I think, a scoffer. Go
ahead, do me. But I think it's beautiful, and I do appreciate it.
Thank you, and all you beautiful people.
Jim: Could you add one more sentence, Colman? Remember that the
"it" in Gestalt therapy is "I." Your sentence was "it's beautiful."
Colman: I think I'm beautiful.
Jim: I do too.

RESEARCH IN THE AREA OF GESTALT THERAPY

The final chapter in Fagan and Shepherd's *Gestalt Therapy
Now* is the only research article in the book. It is concerned with
the problems of the reluctant witness. Commenting on the difficulties in doing research in the area, Fagan and Shepherd said:

> Most often, hard data are difficult to obtain: the important variables
> resist quantification; the complexity and multiplicity of variables in
> therapist, patient, and the interactional processes are almost impos-
> sible to unravel; and the crudeness and restrictiveness of the mea-
> suring devices available cannot adequately reflect the subtlety of the
> process. However, the fact that the task is difficult does not reduce
> its importance, and the need for many questions to be asked and an-
> swered by the more formal procedures available to researchers (Fa-
> gan and Shepherd, 1970, p. 241).

I have been interested in assessing the effectiveness of Gestalt
therapy in workshops as contrasted with weekly therapy. During
the years 1970 and 1971, I gathered systematic feedback from
people coming to residential workshops, and I compared the feedback of these patients with feedback that I obtained from patients
whom I had been seeing in a more traditional manner the previous
two years. Seventy-five percent of the patients who attended the
residential workshop reported that they received what they came
for or more. This claim was made by 66 percent of those who
were in weekly therapy with me. The percentage of patients who
claimed that they received no help, or got worse, was approximately equal for those coming to residential workshops and those
coming for weekly therapy (14%). The remainder in both the
traditional and the workshop style were people who claimed they
"got something" from the experience. (It is interesting to note that
patients who had either the individual or group work on a
"spaced" basis and the workshop on a "massed" basis favor the

massed basis by a ratio of about 9 to 1.) Systematic feedback data have been obtained from over 200 people who have attended both workshops and traditional therapy.

I have also experimented with training in Gestalt therapy and have data on the results of an experiment massing close to 300 hours of training into a three-month period. What I attempted was to provide an intensive training experience for five therapists in a residential setting. The number of hours available was comparable to (or more than) the number of hours of training in the more formal institute training styles. Using personality inventories, peer group ratings, the A.B. Therapists Scale, my clinical impressions of the trainees and other systematic measurements, I have some preliminary evidence which supports the possibility of successfully massing training in a three-month period. A follow-up study, in which the five therapists returned for a week seven months after their training, indicated that the *directions* of change (shown during the three-month period) continued. In addition, the quality of their work in dealing with patients showed a consistent positive increase as reflected by both patient's and supervisor's rating of their work.

Yontef (1969) discusses some of the possible research areas in Gestalt therapy. He also discusses the attitudes of Perls and his co-workers concerning research.

GOALS

In Gestalt therapy the patient is taught how to use awareness in the service of himself as a total functioning organism. By learning to focus awareness and thus discovering what *is,* rather than what *should be,* or what *could have been,* or the ideal of what *may be,* the patient learns to trust himself. This is called in Gestalt therapy the optimum development of self-support. Through awareness, the splits which have been developed, can be reintegrated. The patient can become more whole as he begins to deal with his avoidances, which have created holes in his personality.

SELECTION AND GROUP COMPOSITION

During the period from 1960 through 1970, this writer has had a wide variety of ongoing groups. These were psychotherapy groups, psychotherapy groups for couples, and training groups in Gestalt therapy. All of the patients in the therapy groups were previously patients in individual Gestalt therapy. The range of time that a person was in individual treatment prior to entering a group was anywhere from a few sessions to two or three years. Each therapy group was balanced with an equal number of male and female patients. Attempts were made to ensure the heterogeneity of the groups by bringing in as wide a range of age, occupation, presenting problems, etc., as was possible from the sources available to this writer. One typical group had an actor, a student, two housewives, a physicist, an x-ray technician, an attorney, a nurse, a drama coach, a psychologist, and a painter. The age range for this group was from the early twenties to the late fifties. There were equal numbers of men and women.

The therapist reserved the right to bring new people into the training groups and the therapy groups. The group participants in the therapy groups, however, could veto, during the initial session, the continued participation of a new member. This veto was not available to the therapists in-training. In the couples group there had to be a unanimous agreement on the part of all couples, including the therapist and his wife, for the introduction of a new couple into the closed group.

In the training groups, all of the therapists in training were licensed or license-eligible psychiatrists, clinical psychologists or social workers with the exception of a couple of school psychologists whose function included group counseling in the school system. In the training groups there was also an attempt to keep a balance of the sexes. However, this was not always possible because there are more males than females in the helping professions. There was also a preponderance of psychologists in the training group. Audio-tape was used in all three groups and occasionally video-tape was available for some of the work.

Psychotherapists who wanted to participate in the training groups were required to have a minimum of one individual session to determine their suitability for training and working within the Gestalt therapy framework. Sometimes, I would recommend personal therapy rather than training. At other times, I would suggest concurrent therapy with the training. Some of the psychotherapists were admitted for training without being required to seek personal therapy.

GROUP SETTING AND SIZE

Most of the psychotherapy groups met in my Beverly Hills office in a room about 15 feet by 15 feet with wood panelled walls. The couples group and the training groups, as well as a Wednesday morning group, met in the living room of my home. The room was about 18 feet by 24 feet in size, with a large number of upholstered chairs, couches, thick rug, pillows, et cetera.

Psychotherapy groups are ordinarily limited to a maximum of 10, and frequently a minimum of 8. Training groups, the Wednesday morning therapy group (which was co-led by one of my associates in training), and the couples group were somewhat larger, usually limited to 12 people.

FREQUENCY, LENGTH, AND DURATION OF GROUPS

Groups would meet once a week for a two-hour session. Occasionally the larger groups, such as the couples group or training group or the Wednesday morning group, would continue beyond two hours. All of the above-mentioned groups were open-ended with the exception of the couples group which was a closed group.

Approximately one-third of the group patients were also seen in individual therapy on a once a week basis or less frequently. None of the couples were in individual therapy concurrently and none of the therapists were in regular individual treatment.

The typical group patient had about 70-80 hours of group treatment over a period of eight months to a year. Some group members were able to terminate treatment within three to six months (25-50 hours of therapy). Others had been in group as long as three years when I discontinued practice in Beverly Hills.

The training groups began with one group in 1968. By 1969, there were two, and these two continued until I left Southern California in July of 1970. Average attendance in these groups was 30 sessions (60 hours). However, many of the therapists in training also participated in 5-day workshops with me at the Esalen Institute.

The couples group began in the fall of 1969 and terminated at the end of June, 1970. Average attendance for this group was 25 sessions (50-60 therapy hours). One couple terminated before the group stopped.

GESTALT THERAPIST QUALIFICATIONS

The typical Gestalt therapist who is currently being trained at one of the existing Gestalt therapy institutes is a licensed or license-eligible psychotherapist usually from one of the three major disciplines which are licensed to practice psychotherapy in the United States. In most states these are psychiatrists, clinical psychologists and clinical social workers. Typically, the Gestalt therapist is trained in an institute or in a closely supervised apprenticeship with a senior Gestalt therapist over a period of several months to two or three years.

I have experimented with intensive training and offered a condensed three-month training program consisting of over 120 group hours and over 60 individual hours plus about 100 or more hours collateral training (reviewing tapes, peer group supervision, didactic sessions, etc.) (see Research Section).

In addition, I am currently experimenting with several one-month intensive training programs to see whether it is possible to train Gestalt therapists via this modality as opposed to the more traditional spaced learning situations offered at the Gestalt therapy institutes throughout the country. In the spaced learning model, the Gestalt therapist trainee typically works two to four hours a week in both group and individual settings. In addition to a didactic or theoretical seminar once a month, he is required to attend a minimum of a weekend or a longer workshop every two to three months. At some of the Gestalt therapy institutes, the advanced trainees co-lead introductory seminars with institute members, as part of their experiential training.

WORKSHOP STYLE—TRAINING/TREATMENT

A good deal of the work done in Gestalt therapy is conducted in the workshops. Workshops are scheduled for a finite period of time, some for as little as one day. Some are weekend workshops ranging from 10 to 20 or more hours, and others are more extended ranging from a week through several months in duration. A typical workshop consists of one Gestalt therapist and 12 to 16 people treated over a weekend period. Given longer periods (ranging from a week on up to a month or longer) as many as 20 people can be seen by one therapist. Usually, however, if the group is larger than 16, there are co-therapists.

During the six-year period that Fritz Perls and I did training workshops at the Esalen Institute (1964-1969), we would work with 24 people. Each group of 24 was divided into two subgroups consisting of 12 people each. One group would meet in the morning with Dr. Perls while the other group met with me. In the afternoon the reverse would take place with Dr. Perls' morning group meeting with me in the afternoon and my morning group meeting with him. In the evening the 26 of us would meet together.

Since workshops have a finite life, there are just so many hours available to the participants. Usually, there is high motivation on the part of most participants to get into the "hot seat," that is, to be the focus of attention and to "work." Sometimes, rules are established so that no one can work a second time till each participant has had an opportunity to work once. At other times, no such rules are set. Thus, depending on a person's willingness, audacity, and drive, some people may get to work several times during a workshop.

As in group psychotherapy, the workshop style stimulates some of the participants who at the moment are not "working." They become aware of some of their own unfinished business as some one in the "hot seat" is working through an unfinished situation of his own. There is an atmosphere created in the therapeutic situation which allows people to get in touch with and be willing to work on significant unfinished business.

USE OF THE "HOT SEAT" AND OTHER TECHNIQUES

In a recent article, Levitsky and this author have described in some detail the use of the "hot seat" and other techniques used in Gestalt therapy. Many therapists follow Perls' lead in the use of the "hot seat" technique and will explain this to the group at the outset. According to this method, an individual expresses to the therapist his interest in dealing with a particular problem. The focus is then on the extended interaction between patient and group leader ("I and Thou").

As therapist and patient work together occasions arise in which the patient is asked to carry out some particular exercise, e.g., "Could you repeat what you just said, but this time with your legs uncrossed?" or "Could you look directly at me as you say this?" The attitude with which these exercises are carried out is an important element. The patient is gradually educated and encouraged to undertake these exercises in the spirit of experiment. One cannot really know the outcome beforehand even though a specific hunch is being tested. The spirit of experiment is taken seriously and the question raised, "What did you discover?" The discovery is the most potent form of learning (Levitsky and Simkin, 1972, p. 140).

ETHICAL CONSIDERATIONS

Gestalt therapists view people as having the capacity to cope with life. Rather than impose on their patients their own values or strictures on how to live, the Gestalt therapists are interested in having their patients/trainees discover for themselves what values fit their own way of looking at life. Thus, patients are asked to experiment, to examine, to pick and choose, and to taste before swallowing.

The basic drive or energy in Gestalt therapy is oral aggression. Perls contended that this was necessary in order to be able to taste, and to discover what is nourishing and what is toxic, then to destructure the ideas, or food, or whatever, and to assimilate, following tasting.

Based then on the assumption that the person can be self-regulatory, the Gestalt therapist encourages experimentation to discover what "fits." Naranjo (1971), in his article titled "Present-Centeredness: Technique, Prescription and Ideal," says, "There are a number of implicit moral injunctions in Gestalt therapy," and he lists nine of these. He believes that these nine include living now, living here, stopping imagining, stopping unnecessary thinking, expressing, giving in to unpleasantness and pain, accepting no shoulds or oughts other than your own, taking full responsibility for one's own actions, feelings and thoughts, and surrendering to being who you are. He further indicates that although such injunctions as part of a moral philosophy are paradoxical to the point of view of Gestalt therapy which is anti-injunctions, the paradox is resolved when these points of view or injunctions are looked at as statements of "truth rather than duty" (p. 50).

I believe the basic ethical attitude of the Gestalt therapist is that if you experiment you have the possibility of discovering what is suitable for you. If you swallow whole, there is no possibility of growth, no matter how potentially nourishing the food, idea, etc., may be. A number of Gestalt therapists believe that the goal in Gestalt therapy is maturation and growth and that maturity, which Perls defines as "the transition from environmental support to self-support" can only be accomplished through the focusing of awareness and discriminating what is useful for oneself.

Of great immediate concern in terms of ethics is the aptness of the Gestalt therapist. Shepherd points out that,

> Since Gestalt techniques facilitate access to and release of intense affect, a therapist using this approach must neither be afraid nor inept in allowing the patient to follow through and finish the experience of grief, rage, fear, or joy. The capacity to live in the present and to offer solid presence standing by are essential. Without such presence and skill the therapist may leave the patient aborted, unfinished, opened, and vulnerable—out of touch with any base of support, either in himself or available from the therapist. The therapist's capacity for I-thou, here-and-now relationships is a basic requirement and is developed through extensive integration of learning and experience. Probably the most effective application of Gestalt techniques (or any other therapeutic techniques) comes with personal therapeutic experiences gained in professional training workshops and work with competent therapists and supervisors (Fagan and Shepherd, 1970, p. 238).

In addition, Shepherd points out the following as one of the possible consequences of Gestalt therapy:

> The consequences of successful Gestalt therapy may be that by teaching the patient to be more genuinely in touch with himself, he will experience more dissatisfaction with conventional goals and relationships, with the hypocrisy and pretense of much social interaction, and may experience the pain of seeing the deficiencies and destructiveness of many social and cultural forces and institutions.

Simply stated, extensive experience with Gestalt therapy will likely make patients more unfit for or unadjusted to contemporary society (Fagan and Shepherd, 1970, p. 238).

LIMITATIONS OF GESTALT THERAPY

I consider Gestalt therapy as the treatment of choice for people who are "up in their head" most of the time. On the other hand, with people who are given to acting out, that is, who do not think through or do not fully experience their behavior, I would hesitate to use Gestalt therapy as a treatment of choice. A good rule of thumb is that for experienced therapists, Gestalt therapy is usually an effective tool if used with populations they feel comfortable with. Gestalt therapy has been used successfully with a wide range of populations including children, adolescents and adults.

For some Gestalt therapists the use of Gestalt therapy in groups is limiting. Shepherd maintains that the therapist may, by becoming too active, foster passivity of others in groups, while working with someone in the "hot seat." Thus, facilitating the growth of one person may at the same time be

. . . defeating his own goal of patient self-support. In this case, the group too responds passively, regarding the therapist as an expert or magician, and themselves as having little to contribute without his special techniques and skill (Fagan and Shepherd, 1970, p. 237).

Shepherd also considers another limitation to be the theoretical emphasis on awareness and self-support. This magnifies the role of the individual as the individual *per se,* and de-emphasizes some of his important ongoing relationships and the impact of the world about him.

This may mean that relationships may too often be viewed as projections and as clearly secondary in importance to the internal happenings, and the marked influence of family and other external pressures and difficulties may be ignored (Fagan and Shepherd, 1970, p. 238).

John Barnwell's work with ghetto adults in a poverty program (Simkin, 1968), and Janet Lederman's (1969) work with six- to ten-year-old behavioral problem children in the heart of an urban poverty area underline the point of view that the therapist's competence with certain populations is much more important than the technique as such.

SUMMARY

In Gestalt therapy the emphasis is on the here and now relationship between the therapist and the patient or among the therapist and patients in the group or workshop setting.

The group is used as the safe emergency in which the person in distress is encouraged to be himself. The primary attitude fostered is one of experimentation–of "trying on for size."

The basic assumption is made that the patient, rather than the therapist, knows what's suitable. He (the patient) is encouraged to chew and taste before swallowing or spitting out. Responsibility for what is nourishing or toxic is always that of the person who is doing the exploring.

Awareness is the primary tool and maturation the goal in Gestalt therapy. The philosophical underpinnings of Gestalt therapy are existentialism and humanism. What is rather than what was, could be or should be, is emphasized.

Most Gestalt therapists are busy practicing their art rather than evaluating it. Thus far there has been very little traditional research in the area of Gestalt therapy.

One of the most common forms of doing Gestalt therapy is through workshops. These may vary from a day to several months in duration and may be lead by one or more therapists. Most Gestalt therapists work with one person at a time in the "hot seat" rather than dealing with the group's dynamics.

A common feature of the work in Gestalt therapy is the emphasis on experiments and exercises. The therapist is frequently active in mobilizing the group members. This may lead to a dependence on the leader to initiate action. There is also the danger of inept therapists using what is a deceptively powerful approach to stir up affect which they do not stay with and facilitate to completion.

Gestalt therapy is the treatment of choice for people who are "up in their head." It is not for people who act out their impulses. It is most effective in the hands of competent well-trained clinicians.

SUGGESTED READINGS

There has been a sharp increase in interest and the practice of Gestalt therapy during the past decade (1963-1973). At the time this chapter is being written (early 1973) there are several Gestalt therapy institutes throughout the United States with at least three offering systematic training (Cleveland, San Francisco and Los Angeles).

Several books have appeared in the last three years ranging from a collection of ten older articles collected by Pursglove (1968) and twelve original articles in *Festschrift for Fritz Perls* (Simkin, 1968) to the excellent collection of 25 articles in the book, *Gestalt Therapy Now,* focusing on theory, technique and the application of Gestalt therapy by Fagan and Shepherd (1970).

Kogan (1970), unhappy with the (then) absence of a systematic bibliography of source material in Gestalt therapy, collected and published a pamphlet which lists books, articles, papers, films, tapes, institutes and the *Gestalt Therapist Directory.* He includes approximately 90 references. Fagan and Shepherd list over 60 references. Yontef (1971) cites 45 references.

During 1972, two chapters dealing with Gestalt therapy appeared in two different books. In the Sager and Kaplan (1972) collection, Simkin's "The Use of Dreams in Gestalt Therapy" appeared under the "New Approaches" section, and in Solomon and Berzon's (1972) collection Levitsky and Simkin have a chapter dealing with the use of Gestalt therapy in small groups.

Perls' autobiographical book, *In and Out of the Garbage Pail* (1969b), and Simkin's interview of him in 1966 (n.d.) give much of the historical background of the development of Gestalt therapy. Also of historical interest are the two excellent papers written by F. Perls' widow, Laura Perls (1953, 1956).

Practically none of the Gestalt therapy literature has been channeled through conventional sources during the three decades of its existence. Major exceptions are Fritz Perls' (1948) article in the *American Journal of Psychotherapy* and Polster's (1966) more recent article in *Psychotherapy.*

Until 1969, the only films depicting Gestalt therapy were all of

F. Perls.[1] His are still the primary sources (over 30 varied films) with one exception: Simkin's (1969) training film. No Gestalt therapy library is considered complete without the two basic books, *Gestalt Therapy* by Perls, Hefferline and Goodman (1951, 1965), and *Gestalt Therapy Verbatim* by F. Perls (1969a).

REFERENCES

Barnwell, J. E.: Gestalt methods and techniques in a poverty program. In Simkin, J. S. (Ed.): *Festschrift for Fritz Perls*. Los Angeles, Author, 1968.

Fagan, J., and Shepherd, I. L.: *Gestalt Therapy Now*. Palo Alto, California, Science and Behavior Books, 1970.

Kogan, J.: *Gestalt Therapy Resources*. San Francisco, Lodestar Press, 1970.

Lederman, J.: *Anger and the Rocking Chair: Gestalt Awareness with Children*. New York, McGraw-Hill, 1969.

Levitsky, A., and Perls, F. S.: The rules and games of Gestalt Therapy. In Fagan, J., and Shepherd, I. L. (Eds.): *Gestalt Therapy Now*. Palo Alto, California, Science and Behavior Books, 1970.

Levitsky, A., and Simkin, J. S.: Gestalt therapy. In Solomon, L. N., and Berzon, B. (Eds.): *New Perspectives on Encounter Groups*. San Francisco, Jossey-Bass, 1972.

Naranjo, C.: Present-Centeredness: Technique, prescription and ideal. In Fagan, J., and Shepherd, I. L. (Eds.): *Gestalt Therapy Now*. New York, Harper Colophon Books, 1971.

Perls, F. S.: *Ego, Hunger and Aggression*. London, Allen and Unwin, 1947. (New York, Random House, 1969.)

Perls, F. S.: Theory and technique of personality integration. *American Journal of Psychotherapy, 2:*565, 1948.

Perls, F. S.: Workshop vs. individual therapy. *Journal of the Long Island Consultation Center, 5*(2):13, 1967.

Perls, F. S.: *Gestalt Therapy Verbatim*. Lafayette, California, Real People Press, 1969(a).

Perls, F. S.: *In and Out of the Garbage Pail*. Lafayette, California, Real People Press, 1969(b).

Perls, F. S., Hefferline, R. F., and Goodman, P.: *Gestalt Therapy*. New York, Julian Press, 1951. (Republished: New York, Dell, 1965).

---

1. A complete list of F. Perls' films may be obtained from Psychological Films, 105 West 20th St., Santa Ana, California 92706; Films, Inc., 1144 Wilmette Avenue, Wilmette, Illinois 60091; and Gestalt Therapy Films, Science and Behavior Books, Inc., 577 College Avenue, Palo Alto, California 94306. Each of these sources distribute some of Perls' films.

Perls, L.: Notes on the psychology of give and take. *Complex, 9:*24, 1953.

Perls, L.: Two instances of Gestalt therapy. *Case Reports in Clinical Psychology,* Kings County Hospital, Brooklyn, New York, 1956.

Polster, E.: A contemporary psychotherapy. *Psychotherapy: Theory, Research and Practice, 3:*1, 1966.

Pursglove, P. D.: *Recognitions in Gestalt Therapy.* New York, Funk and Wagnalls, 1968.

Sager, C. J., and Kaplan, H. S. (Eds.): *Progress in Group and Family Therapy.* New York, Brunner/Mazel, 1972.

Simkin, J. S. (Ed.): *Festschrift for Fritz Perls.* Los Angeles, Author, 1968.

Simkin, J. S.: *In the Now.* A training film. Beverly Hills, California, 1969.

Simkin, J. S.: The use of dreams in Gestalt therapy. In Sager, C. J., and Kaplan, H. S. (Eds.): *Progress in Group and Family Therapy.* New York, Brunner/Mazel, 1972.

Simkin, J. S.: Individual Gestalt Therapy: *Interview with Dr. Frederick Perls.* Audio-tape recording. A. A. P. Tape Library, No. 31. Philadelphia, Pennsylvania, n.d.

Solomon, L. N., and Berzon, B. (Eds.): *New Perspectives on Encounter Groups.* San Francisco, Jossey-Bass, 1972.

Van Dusen, W.: Existential analytic psychotherapy. *American Journal of Psychoanalysis, 20*(1):310, 1960.

Warren, H. D.: *Dictionary of Psychology.* New York, Houghton-Mifflin, 1934.

Yontef, G. M.: *A Review of the Practice of Gestalt Therapy.* Los Angeles, Trident Shop, California State College, 1971.

CHAPTER XII

RATIONAL-EMOTIVE GROUP THERAPY

Albert Ellis

INTRODUCTION

SEVERAL METHODS OF PSYCHOTHERAPY employ group therapy for expediency reasons–because it is more practical and cheaper for the clients and not because it fits in with the theory that ostensibly underlies these methods. Thus, psychoanalysis involves a utilization of and a working through of the transference between the analyst and the analysand; and with the multiple transferences that presumably occur in group analysis and the consequent impossibility of dealing with, let alone resolving, truly analytic group therapy becomes impossible to manage, and is rightly eschewed by classical analysts.

Rational-emotive therapy, however, basically uses an educational rather than a medical or psychodynamic model (Ellis, 1962, 1969a, 1971, 1972a, 1972b, 1973). Consequently, like most teaching, it is almost inevitable that it be done in groups as well as individual sessions. Moreover, although it is usually used in small group sessions–with from 8 to 13 clients on a once-a-week basis–it is done at times with much larger groups, such as a class of 20 or 30 students or a public workshop at which more than a hundred people may be present. Its group aspects are also adaptable to audio-visual presentations, since it can be taught and practiced by tape recordings, films and TV tapes, live radio and TV presentations, bibliotherapy, programmed instruction, and other forms of mass media presentations. As much or more than any other contemporary form of psychotherapy, therefore, it is truly group oriented; and frequently the rational-emotive therapy (RET) practitioner uses group processes as the method of choice rather than because special circumstances practically force him or her to do so.

287

DEFINITION OF GROUP PSYCHOTHERAPY

As indicated in the previous paragraph, there are two basic forms of group psychotherapy: (1) *small-scale group therapy,* where the group usually consists of from 8 to 13 individuals who meet to discuss their emotional (and practical) problems and tend to do so regularly, once or twice a week; (2) *large-scale group therapy,* where the group may consist of 50, 100, or even more individuals, who meet to discuss their emotional (and practical) problems and may do so on a one-shot basis, irregularly from time to time, or on a frequent regular basis. Small-scale group therapy (GT) is much more prevalent today than is large-scale, and most of this article will be about the RET version of this type of group meeting.

In small-scale GT, the participants are interested in getting to the roots of their emotional disturbances, understanding the difficulties of the other members of the group, and helping themselves and their fellow members to (1) rid themselves of their current symptoms and function better in their intrapersonal and interpersonal affairs and to (2) minimize their basic disturbability, so that for the rest of their lives they will tend to feel appropriately rather than inappropriately emotional and to needlessly upset or over-inhibit themselves to a significantly lesser degree than they often tend to do when they first join the group. In RET groups, the therapeutic goal is definitely symptom removal; but, more importantly, it is for each of the members to achieve a profound philosophic change and (more specifically) to accept (though not necessarily like) reality; to give up all kinds of magical thinking; to stop awfulizing, catastrophizing, and demonizing about life's misfortunes and frustrations; to take full responsibility for his or her own emotional difficulties; and to stop all forms of self-rating and fully to accept oneself and others as being fallible and human, never superhuman or subhuman.

ILLUSTRATIVE GROUP PROTOCOL

Here is an excerpt from a fairly typical session of RET group therapy. The main presenter is David, a 28-year-old school social worker, who is not only anxious with his clients but has great trouble presenting his cases in group supervision sessions because he is afraid of being criticized and scorned by his chief supervisor and other members of the supervision group. During the first ten minutes of the present session, he tells the group about his problems and several members and the therapist question him to try to pinpoint what he is most anxious about and under what condition his anxiety is at its worst. The session continues:

1. David: When I hear the criticism of my supervisor and supervision group, I take it to its illogical extremes—which is, I don't listen to it any longer. I withdraw. I turn off emotionally.
2. Therapist: Because I don't know everything I *should* know about what they're asking me? I can't answer them *perfectly* well?
3. David: Yes.
4. Mary (a 33-year-old housewife): But isn't that because your worth as a person is being involved there?
5. David: Maybe.
6. John (a 45-year-old psychiatrist): Let's get back to more specific examples of when you feel hurt and small. In your description, you mentioned feelings of incompetency. Let's assume that you do act incompetently. Let's assume that it's really dyed-in-the-wool incompetence. How does the *feeling* of incompetence come about?
7. David: I suppose that what you're trying to get me to say is that in order to be competent, I must be competent 100 percent of the time.
8. Mary: "I suppose you want me to say." I have a feeling that you think we're all trying to program you.
9. David: I guess . . . I know by the book what the rational answer is, and I can give you the rational answer. But it's obviously not the way I am behaving at the moment I turn off.
10. Therapist: Well, let me ask: "When you give the rational answer, do you believe that it's *true?* Or do you believe you just give it because you read it in one of my books?"
11. David: I believe that that's probably what I know. I think I *do* know what's going on. But I'm not very successful at working at it, at feeling that the criticism of me that the supervision group is making is not really all that important.
12. Joan (a 28-year-old artist): Oh, when you do see what's going on, when you feel put down by criticism, how *do* you work at it? Or *do* you work at it?

13. David: I say to myself, "I am being defensive. I am closing myself off." I'm feeling put down by the situation or by people.

14. Therapist: O.K. So you see you have a *symptom,* a poor way of reacting to the situation or to people. Now—that could be negative. For you say to yourself, "Oh, shit! I'm defensive. What a louse I am for being defensive!" What else do you say? For I got the feeling before, when you talked about the supervision group's criticizing you, that (a) you were putting yourself down for being criticized, and then (b) you were putting yourself down *again* for being defensive after they criticized you. Now, what do you do to stop putting yourself down for both (a) and (b)?

15. David: Well, I typically say, "I am here in order to get feedback on my cases and how I am doing with them." And, "It is not reasonable for me to behave defensively to the feedback that I am getting."

16. Therapist: I still hear you *describing* that "I'm idiotically doing something." But I don't hear you *attacking* what you're telling yourself to *make* yourself defensive about their criticisms of you.

17. John: When you were answering that, you could give the rational answer and that's *probably* what's going on; it seemed to me that it's just not *clear* to you what's really going on. You're in a fog. How could you find out more precisely what really *is* going on?

18. David: I don't know. How *could* I find out? Oh, I could act *as if* that's what's going on and challenge it. How, at the moment I am upset, do I know what's going on? I *don't* know.

19. Joan: Why can't you ask yourself, "Why am I upset?"

20. Therapist: Or, better, "What am I *doing* to upset myself?"

21. Mary: Maybe. . . . It's very difficult if the only thing you want to do is to *stop* the feeling. One suggestion is that you'd better *prolong* the feeling of shame about their criticism, and examine your thinking and your feelings about having the shame, rather than just concentrate on stopping feeling ashamed.

22. Therapist: Or rather than concentrating on "Oh, shit! I'm having this terrible, this idiotic feeling!"

23. Mary: Right!

24. David: Or hating myself for having it.

25. John: Right!

26. David: Well, I'm more likely to hate myself for having the feeling of not being able to take the criticism and for turning off.

27. Therapist: Right. But that isn't the solution. That's psychoanalytic-type insight: "Oh, shit! I'm doing it!" But it's not rational-emotive therapy.

28. Rose (a 37-year-old teacher): To get back to what Mary said, I see you, for example, imagining this "put-down" situation, and lying on your bed with the tape recorder going, and letting it run in a stream of consciousness kind of way. Perhaps just talking out all these kinds of things that come into your head (about what your feelings are like when in that situation, getting more criticism from your supervision group) will help you get much more in touch with the kinds of things that are exaggerating and escalating your feelings of being put down, your feelings about yourself and so on.

29. David: Let me ask you a question, Rose, "Do you feel, from the description I gave, that I *wasn't* in touch with my feelings?"

30. Rose: Yes, I felt so. I felt, as you said before, that you really wanted to cry and squelched the feeling. But if you did feel like crying and cried, what was it going to get for you?

31. David: Well, I suppose that if I did cry and people heard me cry, all those people are going to feel very sorry for having done this to me—criticized me.

32. Therapist: And change their behavior, if they hear me cry and moan!

33. David: Yes—and change their behavior.

34. Joan: David, you say you want feedback from your supervision group. But you also said that you feel that some of what you get is really not feedback, but a putdown. And I'm wondering if what you're calling putdown, is, in fact, feedback that you can't accept—suggesting that you're really not looking for feedback but you're looking for approval for what you're doing. And when you don't get it, you *call* it a putdown.

35. David: Yes, I think you've got a well-taken point there. It occurs to me that negative feedback or constructive criticism, which is what I'm probably getting, is somehow tied in my head with loss of love, or loss of approval.

36. Therapist: And with *horror* at this loss. But suppose Joan is right and that you always are going for positive feedback, for approval, and saying, "It's horrible not to get it!" Then what's the *next* step? Which I don't think you're taking!

37. David: I could ask myself, *"Why* is it horrible?"

38. Therapist: Do you do that? I haven't got any indication, so far today, that you got to that step. You say, "Yes, I'm wrong for feeling it's horrible to be criticized." Or: "Yes, I'm wrong for feeling defensive." I get *that*. But do you ever say, *"Why* is it horrible to not be approved?"

39. David: If I do it, it's very superficial.

40. Joan: And seldom, I guess!

41. John: I think further, though, before you ever ask that question, I think it's important to find out whether you *are* thinking that.
42. Therapist: But he did seem meaningfully to agree with Joan that he *is* thinking that.
43. John: He's thinking that; but what *exactly* is going on inside him? Whether he's thinking that or whether he's thinking in some other terms.
44. David: My strategy is to behave so that people will respond to me in a sort of, uh, positive, loving kind of way.
45. Joan: Instead of really facing the fact that "I *do* think it's terrible if they don't. And shit!—I'd better *give up* that belief!" You immediately jump back to point A, the Activating Event, and say, "How can I change A, so that they'll approve of me?" So you're really skipping over B, your Belief System, which is creating your turned-off, escape from feeling at point C.
46. John: I still think you're very unclear about the nature of that Belief at B. For you to spell out that Belief more specifically would be the thing.
47. David: I don't know *how* to do it. What do you want me to do?
48. John: For example, when you're feeling hurt or feel like crying, have you sat down and tried to figure out what's going on in your head—what kind of feelings are happening?
49. Mary: David, I've got a feeling that you're saying one thing and feeling something else right now. You're just looking exasperated.
50. David: I feel kind of frustrated. I'd—I really made touch with what Joan said.
51. Therapist: But you're not making touch with what John said. John is telling you exactly what he would like you to do and then you say, "I don't know what you want me to do."
52. David: I can't see concretely what to do.
53. Therapist: But he's being concrete. Except, John, you may be lousing David up with the word *feeling*. Forget about that word! Let me repeat what John said. Let's suppose you *feel* very hurt. Now I think it's fairly clear what you frequently do to avoid feeling that way. You said it a couple of minutes ago: "I immediately try to change my behavior and change that behavior so I won't feel hurt."
54. David: Yes, that's what I usually do. I turn right off and feel practically nothing.
55. Therapist: Now, instead of letting yourself just do that, and keep doing that self-defeatingly and never get to the source of your problem or how to solve it, John is telling you (1) "Stay with your feeling," and (2) "Look exactly for what you're do-

ing, what you're saying to yourself, to create the hurt. Take the responsibility for hurting yourself. And look *precisely* for your Beliefs, at B, which lead you to create it. Don't just *infer* what these Beliefs are. Because that's what you're doing; you're inferring it from the book. "Well, I *guess* I must be saying this and this to myself when I feel hurt and withdraw." But John is saying: "Don't *guess*. Look *for* what you are actually believing, actually saying to yourself. There's something precise there; and it may not be the sentence we're using, or those you read in the book."

56. Joe (a 50-year-old accountant): There are two reasons for prolonging the feeling of hurt that you're trying to avoid having: (1) so that you can see more precisely what you're thinking to create it, and (2) so that you can challenge your idea that you can't tolerate this feeling. So it seems that a major suggestion for the first step, is for you to prolong the feeling—so you can use it to examine the feeling itself and to check the idea that you can't stand it.

57. Therapist: Yes, stay *with* it. And then do what John is suggesting—which is, first, "What am I doing to create it?" and then also, "Why can't I tolerate it?" For that is another thing you're probably saying to yourself: "I can't tolerate the feeling of hurt. I *must* get rid of it immediately!" But we'd like to *see* that you're saying that. You're just inferring it. And you don't really *see* what is going on in your head just before you have the feeling and attempt to squelch it. Most people, when they at first infer what they're saying to themselves, later manage to see it as clear as a bell—as I say in one of my books. But you somehow manage to skip seeing it clearly. And you say, "Well, I *guess* I'm saying that." Then you don't get on to the next step: "Well, if I *am* saying that, why the hell do I have to *believe* what I'm saying?" You're not contradicting your belief because you're not *really* admitting what you're saying. Now, is that clear?

58. David: Yes.

59. Therapist: But why wasn't it clear before? John said it pretty well. Why wasn't it clear when he said it?

59a. David: I don't think he said it that clearly. It has to be clearer, for me to get it, than he put it. When you're saying to me, it's very clear, very specific, very concrete. I understand it. It's very direct.

60. Joan: And he also said it more vigorously. Was it the vigor?

61. David: No, I don't think so.

62. John: He was more direct, though. Is that it?

63. David: I think it was the directness. That's what I respond to. (To John): I had a feeling that you wanted me to say something but I wasn't sure what you wanted me to say.
64. Joan: So you started debating with yourself, "What'll I say? What'll I say?" Is that right?
65. David: Yes. I wasn't able to zero in on John's wavelength, because I wasn't sure of where he was going.
66. John: Do you find it difficult to think that I'm simply inquiring, just asking?—rather than having some previously conceived idea that you've got to come up with?
67. Therapist: But you *do* have a preconceived idea. That's horseshit, to pretend that you don't!
68. John: Oh, I do, but . . .
69. Therapist: Yeah! So he says to himself, "He's inquiring, when he knows fucking well what the answer is! So why is he inquiring in that fashion?" So—you're giving him an extra problem!
70. John: To an extent. But specifically—I suspect he's thinking something along the lines we reached with him.
71. David: But, John . . .
72. John: But the exact *nature,* that I don't know.
73. David: I realize that it would be better if you could evoke this from me. But if I can't go with you, perhaps the next best thing is to be more direct and tell me what you think I am doing.
74. Therapist: You'd better take a flyer and say, "Isn't it *x?* Isn't it *y?* Isn't it *z?*"
75. David: Yes.
76. Therapist: You're doing it too nondirectively. "What *is* it?" That sometimes works. But with confused people, it often does more harm than good.
77. David: Yes, I think it does in my case.
78. Mary: We seem to be coming to the end of the session. Why don't we give David some homework?
79. Therapist: Yes. What would you suggest for yourself, David?
80. David: Well, you all suggested, which I think is good, that when I begin to feel hurt, that I prolong that feeling rather than moving to my defensive kind of comfortable avoidance.
81. Mary: Stay with your feeling and . . . ?
82. David: Try really to experience or come in touch with what in fact I am saying to myself to cause these feelings. And to challenge those statements. And also to challenge the statement that I can't *stand* the feeling.
83. Mary: Well spoken!
84. John: Yes, let me emphasize that maybe the first few times exploring it or investigating it can be the prime thing to do before

you get in there and start questioning it too much. I find you really have to do it two or three times before you really discover all the crap that's going on in your head, before you really ferret out all those meanings you believe that accompany your feelings.

85. Joe: On the other hand, he might be able to start on one of them, see clearly what his meaning is, and knock it down before he starts on the other meanings. Even if he doesn't discover all of his horseshit, if he hits on one irrational idea and knocks it down, it may help him later discover the others.

86. Therapist: Right! Let's not be perfectionistic! And also, I want to emphasize what you said before, David. At one time you *were* in touch with your feelings—you cried, whined, et cetera —and you found out that it *didn't* lead you to the thoughts behind these feelings; and this release of feeling *did* lead you to other, pernicious things: like feeling very sorry for yourself, feeling depressed, and being unable to do anything. The trouble with your kind of instruction, John, is that when *some* people emphasize getting in touch with their feelings in the manner that you recommend, they do it much too *well,* and mull around in the juices of their own goddamned negative feelings! So it's an interaction thing, the best way of doing it: of letting yourself feel the feeling—and looking pretty quickly for the self-defeating and irrational ideas *behind* your feelings, and then, as we especially emphasize in RET, disputing, challenging, and *changing* these self-defeating feelings.

87. John: I am only suggesting that Dave *find out* what's going on, since that's the first step to *changing* feelings.

88. Mary: But they interact, they go together. I agree that we should not try to get David to be too perfectionistic—so that he first has to find *all* that's going on, then find *all* his thoughts behind his feelings, and then contradict *all* these defeating things. It's a little utopian!

89. Therapist: Yes, and I don't think that David works this perfectionistic way. I don't think that many people work that way.

90. Joe: And working that way may not be necessary to produce change in David.

91. Mary: Right!

92. John: Maybe, on the other hand, though, he could use. . . . Oh, when your turning off happens, David, you could investigate your thoughts more than once, and not assume that you have found them all the first time you do so.

93. Therapist: Oh, yes. Once you start working on it, as several of the group members are saying, you can later work on another aspect of your thinking, and then another aspect, and then still

another aspect. You do not have to do it all at once, the first
time. Is that clear, David?
94. David: Fine, I'll try that.

DISCUSSION OF PROTOCOL

Many of the main aspects of RET group work are illustrated
in the excerpt from this session. Let me make the following points
in this connection:

Response 4: Mary brings up the possibility that David's real
problem is his worth as an individual; that is, his downing *himself,*
his *total being,* if he fails in a single major aspect of his life, such
as in the eyes of his supervision group. She does this not merely
because David has already shown, in previous sessions or earlier
in this one, that he is overconcerned about his worth as a person
but because, on *theoretical* grounds, RET holds that this is a basic
problem of *most* humans. They not only rate their *performances*
(which is often good and happiness-producing) but rate *themselves* (which is illegitimate and shame-producing). RET constantly fights against this *self*-rating tendency; and as a member
of an RET group, and consequently one of its practitioners, Mary
raises the issue of self-rating and asks David if this is not one of
his fundamental problems.

Response 9: David says, "I know by the book what the rational answer is," because he (and the other group members) read
such recommended books as Ellis and Harper (1972), *A Guide
to Rational Living,* Ellis (1962), *Reason and Emotion in Psychotherapy,* and Ellis (1971), *Growth Through Reason.* Bibliotherapy is a strong part of RET; and it is frequently found that it aids
the therapeutic process appreciably. But one of the main purposes
of individual and group RET sessions is to make sure that the
client actually *thinks through* rather than *passively parrots* some
of the rational ideas he partly gets through the reading.

Response 12: Joan rightly emphasizes that David's "knowing"
that "the criticism of me that the supervision group is making is
not really all that important" and will do him little good unless he
consistently *works* at applying this knowledge whenever he feels
shame in his gut or acts defensively to run away from this shame.
In RET, the client is not only shown, to use a superstition model,

that he irrationally believes that viewing a black cat *can* hurt him, but he is also shown that he'd better work and work to *dis*believe that superstition before he can expect to become unaffected by the thought of seeing a black cat. Unless he *actively proves to himself,* many times, that his seeing a black cat can *not* possibly harm him, he is not likely to think that it will not merely because he "knows" that he is superstitious about black cats.

Response 14: The therapist is not only active in RET group work but is frequently the *most active, meaning the most actively teaching,* member of the group. He encourages other members to use the RET system to help therapize the individuals bringing up concrete problems; but he also supplements what these group members say, particularly if they omit important aspects of an issue. Here, he brings up the point that clients not only *feel* inadequate and worthless because they condemn themselves (rather than their poor performances); but also, once they *recognize* their self-downing feelings, they frequently denigrate themselves again for *having* such negative feelings. He tries to encourage David to see that he is damning himself *twice;* for the original criticism he receives from his supervision group and for his feeling depressed *about* that criticism.

Response 16: The therapist emphasizes the main cognitive aspect of RET: the client's *attacking* his own irrational ideas about others' criticizing him, once he has *seen* and *understood* that he has these ideas. This is one of the main differences between RET and many other "insight" therapies. The latter may clearly reveal to the client what he is thinking to create his "emotional" disturbances, but they rarely try to persuade him, as RET does, to directly and vigorously attack, challenge, or dispute these ideas. RET teaches him a logico-empirical method (that is, the basic method of science) of *disputing* his unrealistic and irrational hypotheses about people and the world. Without this kind of active disputation, at first done by the therapist and then taught to the client to do for himself (for the rest of his life), RET simply wouldn't be RET.

Response 20: The therapist (and other group members) remind David that he is not merely *getting* upset or *being made* upset by some external people or events. He is specifically *doing* something, *himself,* to bring on his feelings of disturbance (or his defenses against these feelings). In RET, each client is urged to take *full responsibility* for his dysfunctional feelings, and never to hold that *others* made him have such feelings. He is taught to say, "I made myself angry," or "I upset myself," rather than "It made me angry," or "You upset me." RET theory and practice says to the Davids of the world: "Since *you* are doing something to upset yourself, and since you can almost invariably change what *you* are doing, let's get you to find out exactly *what* you are doing (including what you are telling yourself), so that you can many times *un*do it. The so-called *why* of your upsetness is rather meaningless unless it concretely includes *what* you are doing to make yourself upset."

Response 27: When the therapist says that David has psycho-analytic-type insight, he means that he has, at most, only the first of three insights that are stressed in RET. Insight No. 1 is the client's realization that he *has* some kind of symptom and that it *is* psychologically caused: that is, connected with some antecedent process (such as his innate and acquired tendencies to condemn himself when he makes some "serious" error). Insight No. 2 is his realization that, no matter how, when, and where his basic irrational ideas arose (how and why he originally started blaming himself for his mistakes), he *now* actively carries on this self-defeating process. This *continuation* or *here-and-nowness* of the irrationality is really the issue, rather than its supposed (and often unrevealable) origin. Insight No. 3 is his realization that since he very vigorously still holds on to his fundamental irrational ideas (and may even have a strong biological tendency to keep believing in them), nothing short of persistent *work and practice* at disbelieving them is likely to change them significantly. The therapist, in this response, is really urging David to acknowledge the importance of Insights No. 2 and 3, now that he seems to have Insight No. 1.

Response 36: A little more explicitly than the other members of the group, the therapist emphasizes the *horror* that David feels whenever he gets negative feedback or criticism. This, again, is the essence of RET: to show the client not merely that he thinks that something, such as criticism of himself by others, is *bad* but that it is *awful, horrible,* or *terrible.* For when a human evaluates something as bad, inconvenient, unfortunate, or disadvantageous, he normally stays within the realm of reality: for these are empirically *provable* assessments. Thus, David may be able to show how it would truly be unpleasant or inconvenient to him if he kept getting negative feedback from his supervision group, and thus was shown to be a fairly inadequate therapist. But he cannot (nor can anyone else) possibly show that such an unpleasantry or inconvenience is truly *awful* or *horrible.* Why? Because *awful* means *more than* unfortunate. And it means that because David's poor therapeutic behavior is disadvantageous, he *shouldn't* or *mustn't* behave in that manner, and is a *rotten person* if he does.

But–of course–nothing in reality can be *more than* unfortunate. *Shouldn'ts* and *mustn'ts* are magical fictions, categorical absolutes, that have no true existence. And David, *as a person,* cannot be entirely rotten, even though some or much of his behavior may be poor and ineffectual. So RET, through the therapist and the group members, tries to keep teaching David to give up these absolutistic, demonological *awfuls, shouldn'ts,* and *rotten person* concepts, and to live thoroughly in reality (which can be disadvantageous enough, without his dreaming up imaginary *horrors* to add to these disadvantages).

Response 45: Joan tries to get David back to the essential A-B-C's of RET. According to rational-emotive theory, David experiences an Activating Event, at point A, his being responded to negatively by members of his supervision group. Immediately, at point C, his emotional Consequence, he reacts with feelings of anxiety or depression, and then with a defense against these feelings, numbness or avoidance of the "traumatizing" situation at A. He tends to believe wrongly, as most disturbed individuals do, that A causes C–that the Activating Events cause him to feel anxious or to retreat defensively. However, B, his Belief System, is the real issue. At B, he first has a set of rational Beliefs (rB's): "How unfortunate for them to be so critical of me! I wish I were a better therapist and they criticized me less! How annoying to be found out like this!" If he stayed rigorously with these Beliefs, and did not magically *add* to them, he would feel appropriately sorry, sad, frustrated, and irritated–and would usually be motivated to get even more feedback from his supervision group, at point A, and to change his therapeutic behavior which is encouraging them to criticize him.

But, being a human (and innately and by training predisposed to think magically and demonologically), David goes on to a very important set of irrational Beliefs (iB's): "Isn't it *horrible* that they are so critical of me! I *have to be* a better therapist and be criticized less! I'm *a thorough ass and rotten* if they keep seeing me in this negative light!" These highly irrational, unvalidateable Beliefs cause him to feel anxious and depressed and to make himself numbly run away from facing his critics.

If he sticks with the RET framework, he will, no matter how hard it is for him to do so, force himself to acknowledge his painful feelings, at C, to see clearly the irrational Beliefs (iB's) with which he is creating them, and to Dispute them, at D. His Disputing follows the logico-empirical method of challenging any hypothesis: *"Why* is it horrible that the members of my supervision group are so critical of me? *Where is the evidence* that I have to be a better therapist and be criticized less? How does their seeing me negatively *prove* that I am truly a thorough ass and a rotten person?"

If David will persist at this kind of rational-emotive attack on his irrational Beliefs, he will almost always tend to end up with a new Effect, at E: that is, with a restatement of a rational, empirically-based conclusion: "Well, it really is too bad that my supervision group sees me as being so ineffectual as a therapist; but that's all it is, too bad! Now, in order to improve this bad position that I'm in, why don't I heed their suggestions, change some of my procedures, become a more effective therapist, and gain more approval from them. In fact, whether *they* approve of me or not, why don't *I* use their criticism to help me as a therapist so that *I* can better enjoy myself and help others in that capacity?" If he comes to this kind of conclusion, David will almost always find that his feelings of anxiety and depression will vanish and that he will not have to drive himself into defensive numbness.

So Joan (and then John) try to help David to see the A-B-C's of his disturbance and to work through them, at D.

Response 53: The therapist, attempting to clarify what John has been saying to David, tries to get David to stay with his feelings of anxiety, instead of immediately retreating from them; and then to look specifically for his ideas–his irrational Beliefs (iB's)–with which he creates such feelings. But instead of vaguely *inferring* what these Beliefs are (which he can do on the basis of RET theory), he endorses John's point that David would better concretely *search for* these Beliefs.

Response 56: Joe, who has been silent up to this point, comes in to reinforce what John, the therapist, and others are saying to David. In RET, again, *all* the group members are encouraged to be therapists toward any one member who raises a problem. The theory says that the more of this kind of thing that occurs, the more likely is the problem-presenting member to be helped. Moreover, by helping talk him out of his difficulties, the other group members (most of whom have similar philosophic problems of downing themselves when *they* make errors and are socially criticized) are likely to talk themselves out of their *own* basic irrational Beliefs.

Response 63: If David is right, and it was directness rather than more democratic or Socratic questioning that he responded to, this is an important point that is often overlooked in therapy. It is conventionally assumed, especially by psychoanalytic or client-centered therapists (Freud, 1964; Rogers, 1951, 1961), that if the client comes to his basic insights into himself largely on his own, or with a minimum of therapist teaching, he will be most benefited. But RET theory says that this is all very well with *some* clients, but that others are so confused and befuddled when they come to therapy that direct teaching is likely to help them more than any kind of nondirective reflection of feeling (Ellis, 1962, 1971, 1973).

Anyway, in this particular instance John's somewhat objective and nondirective questioning of David mainly induced David to say to himself, "I wonder what 'right' answer he wants me to give? What is it he wants? What *is* it he wants?" This only helped to create greater anxiety in himself, and less likelihood of *giving* this "right" answer. When the therapist and other group members, however, much more directly *gave* David the "right" answer and then asked if it was correct in his case, he was much more able to handle this answer, to reflect on it, and to make it his own. Even though the therapist largely restated John's original points, David felt much more comfortable with this restatement and was able to use it. Direct teaching, in his case, paid off much better than more "democratic" indirectness.

Response 76: The more David is asked about why he did not respond to John but did respond to the therapist's restatement of what John said, the more it appears that he is one of those confused people who can use considerable therapeutic direction; and that with him, as with many such people, open-ended questioning can do more harm than good. Perhaps John's line of questioning would have eventually paid off, if the other group members were not present to interfere with it. But perhaps it would have only continued to help drive David into a greater state of confusion. Anyway, the therapist, seeing what was happening, did not hesitate to intervene and try to help David in another way. And his active intervention seems to have paid off, at least in this particular instance. In other instances, it is possible that it would have been more disruptive than helpful. But, in general, it is found that highly directive and didactic presentations of RET material within a group session, especially to confused clients, frequently gets excellent results—and sometimes gets them when other less directive techniques are not helping the client appreciably.

Response 78: In RET, *in vivo* or activity homework assignments are frequently given, since it is held that clients not only talk themselves but act themselves into disordered behavior; hence it is highly valuable for them to act in a less disordered way before they become truly habituated, in thought and feeling as well as in behavior, to that new and healthier way of life. Typically, clients who are nonassertive are given graduated homework assignments of approaching members of the other sex, trying for new jobs, or otherwise acting more assertively. And clients who are hostile and avoidant are given assignments of deliberately jumping into "hostility-creating" situations (such as visiting hated relatives) and training themselves how to think and feel less hostilely while they are doing so.

In David's case, he is given the assignment of staying with his uncomfortable (anxiety-inciting) feelings; to challenge his irrational Beliefs (iB's) that he can't *stand* these feelings, and to find his other basic irrational Beliefs, such as the idea that he is a horrible person if he continues to draw negative criticism from his supervision group, and to actively Dispute these Beliefs until he gives them up. Urged on by the group to these assignments, David largely carried them out during the next few weeks and seemed to benefit considerably in terms of being able, first, to keep in touch with his feelings of anxiety and, secondly, to minimize these feelings. Two months after the session that is reported herewith, he was able to report back to the group that he was one of the most open individuals, now, in his supervision group and that he had no difficulty facing this supervision groups' criticism of his therapy sessions.

Response 86: The therapist points out that although it is advisable for David to get in touch with his feelings of hurt about criticism, being *too much* in touch with such feelings, as he used to be, has its own distinct disadvantages and is not to be recommended. The *reason* for getting in touch with one's feelings, in RET, is not merely to acknowledge them and to feel them but to *change* them when they are self-defeating. Moreover, RET doesn't assume that if a client *merely* reveals and expresses his feelings that he or she automatically will change for the better. It hypothesizes, instead, that a truly therapeutic understanding of one's feelings includes the understanding of the philosophies which one is employing to create them, and a radical changing of these philosophies when they consistently lead to poor results–such as anxiety, depression, and hostility.

Response 88: Just as RET combats human perfectionism in general and shows how it is the root of much evil, it combats perfectionism in therapy itself. The goal of RET is not to have the client *perfectly* understand or change himself, since he is always going to remain a quite fallible human and to have difficulties and problems of one sort or another. Its goal is to have him eliminate much of his *needless* emotional pain and suffering, but not to make him truly unemotional, or even devoid of appropriate negative emotions, such as sorrow, regret, and extreme annoyance when he is faced with truly obnoxious Activating Events. RET mainly teaches human tolerance–including tolerance of imperfect therapeutic results!

RESEARCH RESULTS OF THE PROCESS

Little research has been carried on, to date, in regard to the specific process of rational-emotive group therapy. But a good many research studies have been done which show, first of all, that the basic theories of RET–especially, the theory that human emotions and behaviors are caused by Belief Systems (B) rather than Activating Events (A) in their lives; and that if a therapist or experimenter helps them change these Belief Systems, they will concomitantly experience a significant change in their emotional and behavioral Consequences (C). Thus, evidence favoring the ABC personality constructs of RET has been presented by Beck (1967), Carlson, Travers, and Schwab (1969), Davison and Valins (1969), Kilty (1970), Lazarus (1966), Mowrer (1938), Nisbet and Schachter (1966), Pastore (1950, 1952), Schachter and Singer (1962), Valins and Ray (1967), and many other researchers.

In regard to the specific use of rational-emotive or related therapeutic methods with groups of individuals, in an attempt to change them from a "disturbed" or "maladjusted" or "neurotic" state to one where they were less disturbed, better adjusted, or less neurotic, there have been surprisingly many of these studies, considering that RET was created in the mid 1950's and did not begin to be widely known as a therapeutic method until the late 1960's. And almost all of the therapeutic experiments that have been done with RET or similar cognitive-behavior procedures have helped validate its practices. Thus, in regard to large-scale group therapy, RET has been found to be effective in studies made by Argabrite and Nidorf (1968), Crawford (1971), Gustav (1968), and Hartman (1968).

When used with more conventional small-scale therapy groups, RET and related therapies have been found to change significantly symptomatic behavior and/or disordered emotionality in a good number of studies with a large variety of different kinds of individuals. Most notable in this respect have been the studies of Dr. Donald Meichenbaum and his associates at the University of Waterloo in Ontario, Canada (Meichenbaum, 1971, 1973; Meichenbaum, Gilmore, and Fedoravicius, 1971; Steffy, Meichenbaum, and Best, 1970). Not only have these researchers shown, in a very ingenious set of studies, that cognitive modification works better than desentitization or other forms of behavior therapy which do not stress cognitive approaches, but they have also tended to prove that group therapy along RET lines is often more effective than individual therapy along similar lines. The work of Dr. Maxie Maultsby, Jr. (1969), testing the effectiveness of group and individual RET procedures with individuals suffering from psychosomatic ailments, also produced corresponding conclusions.

Other experiments testing the effectiveness of RET (and RET-related) group therapy have been carried out by many researchers, including Burkhead (1970), DiLoreto (1971), Herman and Tramontana (1971), Karst and Trexler (1970), Miller (1972), O'Connell and Hanson (1970, 1971), Sharma (1970), Trexler and Karst (1972), and Velten (1968). These, and a batch of new controlled experiments on RET which continue to be reported in the scientific literature, tend to show fairly conclusively that RET not only works (as many other studies on its individual effectiveness have shown) but that it also works unusually well when used with small and large groups.

GOALS OF THE TREATMENT

The main goals of RET group therapy are the same as those of RET individual therapy: namely, teaching clients that *they* are responsible for their own emotional upsets or disturbances; that they can change their disordered emotionality and behavior by changing their beliefs, values, and philosophies; and that if they acquire radically new and profoundly held belief systems, they can almost automatically learn to cope with almost *any* unfortunate activating events that may arise in their lives and keep themselves, at worst, deeply sorrowful and regretful but *not* anxious, depressed, self-deprecating, and hostile about these activators. Some of the important group-oriented goals and methods that are used in RET are these:

1. Since the essence of RET is to help teach the individual how to accept *the existence of grim reality* and to try to change it by concerted work instead of by whining, magic-oriented demandingness, *all* group members are encouraged to reveal and discourage the presenting individual's perfectionism and dictatorialness. All members are also taught to parse logically, vigorously undermine, and empirically contradict the disordered, disturbance-creating thinking of each of the other members.

2. The therapist usually is exceptionally active, probing, challenging, confronting, and directive. He persistently models rational thinking and appropriate emoting. He is not only a trained scientist, but teaches the scientific, or logico-empirical, method to the group members, so that they can apply it effectively to their personal and emotional lives.

3. Both the therapist and the group consistently give activity-oriented homework assignments to group members. Some of these assignments (such as speaking up in group itself) may be carried out and monitored during the regular sessions. Other assignments (such as making social contacts) are to be carried on outside the group but regularly reported and discussed during group sessions. It has often been found that such assignments are more effectively given and followed up when given by a group than by an individual therapist.

4. RET includes a number of role-playing and behavior modification methods–such as assertion training, *in vivo* risk-taking, and behavior rehearsal–which can partly be done in individual sessions but which are more effective in group. Thus, if a member is afraid to tell people what he thinks of their behavior, he may be induced to do so with other group members.

5. The group is deliberately arranged as a kind of laboratory where emotional, gestural, and motorial behavior can be directly observed rather than obtained through the client's secondhand reports. Angry or anxious individuals, who might be at home with an individual therapist and be able to hide their feelings from him or her, can often be more easily unmasked in group, where they have to interact with several of their peers.

6. In RET, clients frequently fill out written homework report forms and give them to the therapist to go over. In group sessions, a few homework forms are often read and corrected so that all the members of the group, and not merely the individual handing in the form, may be helped to see specifically what disordered emotional Consequence was experienced (at point C); what Activating Events occurred to spark it (at point A); what rational and irrational Beliefs the individual told himself or herself (at point B) to create the dysfunctional Consequences; and what kind of effective Disputing could be done (at point D) to minimize or erradicate the irrational Beliefs that led to the defeating Consequences. By hearing about other group members' main problems and how they dealt with them on the Homework Report, clients are helped to use these Reports more efficiently themselves.

7. The individual gets valuable feedback from the group as to how he malfunctions and what he is probably foolishly telling himself to create this malfunctioning. He also learns to view others and to give them feedback; and, more importantly, gets practice in talking them out of their irrational Beliefs, and thereby consciously and unconsciously talking himself out of his own self-defeating irrationalities.

8. One main purpose of RET group sessions is to offer members a wider range of possible solutions to their problems than they might normally receive in individual sessions. Out of ten people present at a given session, one may finally zero in on a presenter's central problem (after several others have failed) and another may offer an elegant solution to it (after various ineffectual or lower-level solutions have hitherto been offered). Where a single would-be helper may give up on a difficult issue (or person), some group members may persist and may finally prove to be quite helpful.

9. Revealing intimate problems to a group of people may itself be quite therapeutic for the client. In regular RET small-group therapy he discloses many ordinarily hidden events and feelings to a dozen or so of his peers; and in RET public workshops he may reveal himself to a hundred or more people. Especially if he (or she) is shy and inhibited, this kind of disclosure may be a most useful risk-taking experience–as the therapist will often

emphasize by showing the inhibited person that he has opened himself and actually received little of the criticism and attack he falsely predicted and that, even if he is disapproved or laughed at, he can still accept himself and find this censure *unfortunate* rather than *awful*.

For many reasons such as those just cited group processes are particularly useful in Rational-Emotive Therapy; both small-scale and large-scale groups tend to be extensively used by leading cognitive-behavior therapists, such as Berne (1972), Corsini (1966), Dreikurs (Dreikurs and Grey, 1968), Ellis and Harper (1971, 1972), Lazarus (1971), Low (1952), and Phillips and Wiener (1966).

SELECTION AND GROUP COMPOSITION

There are various procedures in selecting and maintaining a RET group. My own regular small-scale groups usually consist of a maximum of 13 members, with a therapist and an associate therapist. Most of my regular clients are encouraged to join a group; and many of them only have one or two initial individual sessions before they join. Group members are of all ages, usually ranging from about 20 to 60, and including all kinds of diagnostic categories. Groups usually have a fairly equal number of males and females. Once a member joins a group, he or she may have concomitant individual therapy sessions regularly or irregularly. Most group members only choose to have them irregularly and therefore mainly learn the principles and practices of RET in the course of a group process. Clients who are distinctly shy or who have problems relating to others are particularly encouraged to join a group, since working out their difficulties with their peers is better for them than only working with an individual therapist (who may well be a special kind of person to them and therefore *not* representative of the people they associate with in real life).

GROUP SETTING AND LENGTH OF SESSIONS

My RET groups meet once a week in my regular office in New York City which is furnished with three large sofas and extra chairs. I mainly lead the group for an hour and a half each week, followed by a 45 minute aftersession, which is led by my co-leader (one of the Fellows in training at the Institute for Advanced Study in Rational Psychotherapy). After two and a quarter hours per week with me and the associate leader, the group can then continue its discussions for another hour or so on its own, if it chooses to do so. Every six months, as part of the regular group therapy process, each group is given (at no extra cost to the members) a 14 hour marathon, mainly led by its co-leader, with my assistance.

All groups are open-ended. That is to say, once a member joins, he can attend group for a minimum of five weeks and then (after giving two weeks' notice) can drop out at any time. Those who drop out are usually soon replaced by new members. When a member joins, he therefore comes into a group which is filled mostly with old members who have been in attendance for a period of several months to two years, and who help "teach him" (during regular sessions and aftersessions, and in private contacts they may have with him during the week) "some of the ropes" of RET. New members are also "softened up" for the group process by (1) having one or more individual RET sessions; (2) reading various pamphlets and books presenting the RET viewpoint (particularly, Ellis (1969b), *How to Live With a Neurotic;* Ellis and Harper (1972), *A Guide to Rational Living;* and Ellis (1962), *Reason and Emotion in Psychotherapy;* and (3) attending workshops, recordings, lectures and films on RET given regularly at the Institute.

THERAPIST AND COUNSELOR QUALIFICATIONS

As far as can be arranged by the Institute for Advanced Study in Rational Psychotherapy, all RET group processes sponsored by the Institute are led by highly qualified therapists or counselors. The Institute operates a full-time postdoctoral training program for psychologists, psychiatrists, counselors, and psychiatric social workers; and it also gives a certificate to professional therapists and counselors who cannot participate in its full-time program but who are able to attend several of its all-day training workshops and to obtain a number of supervision sessions with qualified RET supervisors. Some of the Institute's branches, such as those in Chicago and Seattle, also maintain their own professional training programs.

When the Institute's ethical policies are strictly followed—

which they normally are by therapists and counselors maintaining affiliations with it, but which of course they may not be by individuals who self-appointedly call themselves "rational-emotive therapists" without its consent or backing–RET groups (including regular small-scale groups, marathons, and workshops) are led only by qualified professionals (or by supervised trainees) in the field of mental health and by those who have supplemented their basic psychological, social, or other work training with postgraduate work in RET. Unlike the encounter movement, which often welcomes group "leaders" who have no training other than a few weeks' work in Esalen-type "growth" centers, the Institute tries to see that all RET individual counselors and group leaders are first professionally trained, are bona fide members of their own professional organizations, and are subject to the ethical rulings of these organizations.

At the same time, the Institute recognizes the place of self-help, RET-oriented groups, such as Associated Rational Thinkers (ART) groups which were originated by Dr. Maxie C. Maultsby, Jr. and which have branches in various parts of the United States. Dr. Abraham Low (1952) pioneered in self-help groups and founded Recovery, Inc., which teaches principles of anticatastrophizing and antiawfulizing to its own lay members. Like Recovery groups, ART groups are normally led by non-professionals who have their own rigorous training program to help themselves and their co-members, mostly in the course of group processes, discuss and learn the principles of rational thinking and rational living. These ART group leaders, however, are *not* rational-emotive therapists and are not qualified to direct regular RET group processes.

LIMITATIONS OF THE TREATMENT

Rational-emotive group therapy and counseling have intrinsic disadvantages and limitations, especially when compared to more individualized RET processes. In small-group procedures, for example, group members can easily, out of over-zealousness and ignorance, mislead other members and at times even present them with harmful directives and views. They can give poor or low-level solutions, e.g., continuing to show a disturbed person, for example, what "practical" methods he can use to make himself more successful in his life, rather than what deeper philosophic changes he can make in his disturbance-creating outlooks.

Group therapy, even when employing an organized and efficient procedure like RET, has its inevitable ineffectualities. The best-intentioned group members can waste time in irrelevancies; lead the problem-presenter up the garden path; sidetrack and defuse some of the therapist's main points; hold back because they inordinately look for the approval of other group members; bring out their own and others' minor instead of major difficulties; and otherwise get off on various nontherapeutic limbs. Group members can also bombard a presenter with so many and so powerful suggestions that he or she is overwhelmed and partly paralyzed. They can give poor homework assignments or keep presenting so many new problems that old assignments are not sufficiently checked upon. They can allow a member, if the therapist does not actively intervene, to get away with minimal participation and hence make minimal change in his or her disordered behavior. They can become overly frustrated and hostile and can irrationally condemn a participant for his symptoms or for his continuing resistance to working at giving up his symptoms.

RET group therapy, consequently, is hardly a panacea for all ills; nor is it suitable for all individuals who know that they are emotionally disturbed and who come for help. Some clients are not ready for it and would better have some amount of individual RET before they enter a group. Others–such as compulsive talkers or hypomanic individuals–may benefit considerably from group work but are too disrptive to the group (and require too much monitoring and training); hence it is best to exclude them and to have them work out their problems in other modes of treatment. My own belief is that the great majority of disturbed clients can benefit as much, and probably more, from group therapy than from individual treatment alone. But *the majority* hardly means *all!*

SUMMARY

Man is exceptionally prone to self-defeating thinking and inappropriate emoting and behaving. Perhaps, unless he radically changes his entire biosocial makeup, he will always be. He can significantly change his cognitions, emotions, and behavior, however, in a number of ways—most of them accidental and some of them designed. Considering the enormous amount of needless emotional suffering that he tends to experience—including many and often prolonged periods of intense anxiety, depression, guilt, feelings of worthlessness, and hostility—he would be wiser if he clearly understood precisely what he was thinking and doing to create his so-called emotional upsets, and if he exerted the choice (which he uniquely has as a human being) to think and to act differently, and thereby undo his needless emotional upsets and arrange for their infrequent subsequent occurrence.

He (and, of course, she) can most elegantly do this if he avoids preoccupying himself with A, the Activating Events of his life and if he fully acknowledges and feels but resists endlessly re-experiencing C, the inappropriate emotional Consequences which frequently follow from, and falsely seem to stem from, A. He has the choice, instead, of keenly discerning, parsing, examining, modifying, and uprooting B (the irrational Beliefs about which he so easily tends to convince himself regarding the Activating Events at A).

A troubled human being can decide to work persistently at changing his or her irrational Beliefs; or can get help in doing so from straighter-thinking, friends, books, lectures, demonstrations, tape recordings, and other sources. He can rationally-emotively help himself in a large-scale group or class; and he can also work with an individual therapist or group leader. If he chooses a small-scale group process, and if he picks a cognitively-oriented group that also helps him attack his stubbornly held irrationalities by selected evocative-emotive and active-behavioristic techniques, he will avail himself of a multifaceted, comprehensive therapeutic procedure. I stoutly hypothesize that this kind of group therapy is most likely to lead him to a quicker, deeper, and more elegant solution—to the ubiquitous human condition of childishly demanding that he and others be perfect—than other forms of contemporary psychotherapy.

SUGGESTED READINGS

Ellis, A.: *Reason and Emotion in Psychotherapy.* New York, Lyle Stuart, 1962.

Ellis, A.: A weekend of rational encounter. In Burton, A. (Ed.): *Encounter.* San Francisco, Jossey-Bass, 1969a.

Ellis, A.: *How to Live With a Neurotic.* New York, Award Books, 1969b.

Ellis, A.: *Growth Through Reason.* Palo Alto, Science and Behavior Books, 1971.

Ellis, A.: *Executive Leadership: A Rational Approach.* New York, Citadel Press, 1972a.

Ellis, A.: Emotional education in the classroom: The Living School. *Journal of Clinical Child Psychology, 1*(3):19, 1972b.

Ellis, A.: *Rational-emotive Group Psychotherapy.* A filmed interview with Dr. John M. Whiteley. Washington, D. C., American Personnel and Guidance Association and New York, Institute for Rational Living, Inc., 1972c.

Ellis, A.: *Humanistic Psychotherapy: A Rational Approach.* New York, Julian Press, 1973.

Ellis, A., and Harper, R. A.: *A Guide to Successful Marriage.* Hollywood, Wilshire Books, 1971.

Ellis, A., and Harper, R. A.: *A Guide to Rational Living.* Hollywood, Wilshire Books, 1972.

Maultsby, M. C., Jr., Stiefel, L., and Brodsky, L.: A theory of rational behavioral group process. *Rational Living, 7*(1):28, 1972.

Meichenbaum, D. H.: *Cognitive Factors in Behavior Modification: Modifying What Clients Say to Themselves.* Waterloo, University of Waterloo, 1971.

Trexler, L. D., and Karst, T. O.: Rational-emotive therapy, placebo, and no-treatment effects on public-speaking anxiety. *Journal of Abnormal Psychology, 79:*60, 1972.

REFERENCES

Argabrite, A. H., and Nidorf, L. J.: Fifteen questions for rating reason. *Rational Living, 3*(1): 9, 1968.

Beck, A. T.: *Depression: Clinical, Experimental and Theoretical Aspects.* New York, Hoeber-Harper, 1967.

Berne, E.: *What Do You Say After You Say Hello?* New York, Grove Press, 1972.

Burkhead, D. E.: The Reduction of Negative Affect in Human Subjects: A Laboratory Test of Rational-Emotive Therapy. Unpublished doctoral dissertation, Western Michigan University, 1970.

Carlson, W. A., Travers, R. M. W., and Schwabe, E. A., Jr.: A laboratory approach to the cognitive control of anxiety. Paper presented at the American Personnel and Guidance Association Convention, Las Vegas, March 31, 1969.

Corsini, R. J., and Cardono, S.: *Role-playing in Psychotherapy: A Manual.* Chicago, Aldine, 1966.

Crawford, W. K.: Altering the behavior of troubled students. Mimeographed, 1971.

Davison, G. C.: Anxiety under total curarization: Implications for the role of muscular relaxation in the desensitization of neurotic fears. *Journal of Nervous and Mental Disease, 143:*443, 1967.

DiLoreto, A.: *Comparative Psychotherapy.* Chicago, Aldine, 1971.

Dreikurs, R., and Grey, L.: *Logical Consequences: A Handbook of Discipline.* New York, Meredith, 1968.

Ellis, A.: *Reason and Emotion in Psychotherapy.* New York, Lyle Stuart, 1962.

Ellis, A.: A weekend of rational encounter. In Burton, A. (Ed.): *Encounter.* San Francisco, Jossey-Bass, 1969a.

Ellis, A.: *How to Live With a Neurotic.* New York, Award Books, 1969b.

Ellis, A.: *Growth Through Reason.* Palo Alto, Science and Behavior Books, 1971.

Ellis, A.: *Executive Leadership: A Rational Approach.* New York, Citadel Press, 1972a.

Ellis, A.: Emotional education in the classroom: The Living School. *Journal of Clinical Child Psychology, 1*(3):19, 1972b.

Ellis, A.: *Rational-emotive Group Psychotherapy.* A filmed interview with Dr. John M. Whiteley. Washington, D. C., American Personnel and Guidance Association and New York, Institute for Rational Living, Inc., 1972c.

Ellis, A.: *Humanistic Psychotherapy: A Rational Approach.* New York, Julian Press, 1973.

Ellis, A., and Harper, R. A.: *A Guide to Successful Marriage.* Hollywood, Wilshire Books, 1971.

Ellis, A., and Harper, R. A.: *A Guide to Rational Living.* Hollywood, Wilshire Books, 1972.

Freud, S.: *Collected Papers.* New York, Collier Books, 1964.

Gustav, A.: "Success is—": Locating composite sanity. *Rational Living, 3* (1):1, 1968.

Hartmann, B. J.: Sixty revealing questions for twenty minutes. *Rational Living, 3*(1):7, 1968.

Herman, S. H., and Tramontana, J.: Instructions and group versus individual reinforcement in modifying disruptive group behavior. *Journal of Applied Behavior Analysis, 4:*4, 1971.

Karst, T. O., and Trexler, L. D.: Initial study using fixed-role and rational-emotive therapy in treating public-speaking anxiety. *Journal of Consulting and Clinical Psychology, 34:*360, 1970.

Kilty, K. M.: Some determinants of the strength of relationship between attitudinal affect and cognition. *Journal of Social Psychology, 84:*1, 1970.

Lazarus, A. A.: *Behavior Therapy and Beyond.* New York, McGraw-Hill, 1971.

Lazarus, R. S.: *Psychological Stress and the Coping Process.* New York, McGraw-Hill, 1966.

Low, A. A.: *Mental Health Through Will-Training.* Boston, Christopher Publishing Co., 1952.

Maultsby, M. C., Jr.: The implications of successful rational-emotive psychotherapy for comprehensive psychosomatic disease management. In manuscript, 1969.

Maultsby, M. C., Jr., Stiefel, L., and Brodsky, L.: A theory of rational behavioral group process. *Rational Living, 7*(1):28, 1972.

Meichenbaum, D. H.: *Cognitive Factors in Behavior Modification: Modifying What Clients Say to Themselves.* Waterloo, University of Waterloo, 1971.

Meichenbaum, D. H.: Cognitive modification of test anxious college students. *Journal of Consulting and Clinical Psychology,* 1973, in press.

Meichenbaum, D. H., Gilmore, J. B., and Fedoravicius, A.: Group insight versus group desensitization in treating speech anxiety. *Journal of Consulting and Clinical Psychology, 36:*410, 1971.

Miller, S. B.: The contribution of therapeutic instructions to systematic desensitization. *Behavior Therapy and Research, 10:*139, 1972.

Mowrer, O. H.: Preparatory set (expectancy)—a determinant in motivation and learning. *Psychological Review, 45:*62, 1938.

Nisbett, R. E., and Schachter, S.: Cognitive manipulation of pain. *Journal of Experimental and Social Psychology, 2:*227, 1966.

O'Connell, W. E., and Hanson, P. G.: Patients' cognitive changes in human relations training. *Journal of Individual Psychology, 26:*57, 1970.

O'Connell, W. B., and Hanson, P. G.: The negative nonsense of the passive patient. *Rational Living, 6*(1):24, 1971.

Pastore, N.: A neglected factor in the frustration-aggression hypothesis. *Journal of Psychology, 29:*271, 1950.

Pastore, N.: The role of arbitrariness in the frustration-aggression hypothesis. *Journal of Abnormal and Social Psychology, 47:*728, 1952.

Phillips, E. L., and Wiener, D. N.: *Short-term Psychotherapy and Structured Behavior Change.* New York, McGraw-Hill, 1966.

Rogers, C. R.: *Client-centered Therapy.* Boston, Houghton-Mifflin, 1951.

Rogers, C. R.: *On Becoming a Person.* Boston, Houghton-Mifflin, 1961.

Schachter, S., and Singer, J. E.: Cognitive, social and physiological determinants of emotional state. *Psychological Review, 69:*379, 1962.

Sharma, K. L.: A Rational Group Therapy Approach to Counseling Anxious Underachievers. Unpublished doctoral dissertation, University of Alberta, 1970.

Steffy, R. A., Meichenbaum, D., and Best, J. A.: Aversive and cognitive factors in the modification of smoking behavior. *Behavior Research and Therapy, 8:*115, 1970.

Trexler, L. D., and Karst, T. O.: Rational-emotive therapy, placebo, and no-treatment effects on public-speaking anxiety. *Journal of Abnormal Psychology, 79:*60, 1972.

Valins, S., and Ray, A. A.: Effects of cognitive desensitization on avoidance behavior. *Journal of Personality and Social Psychology, 7:*345, 1967.

Velten, E.: A laboratory task for induction of mood states. *Behavior Research and Therapy, 6:*473, 1968.

CHAPTER XIII

CONJOINT FAMILY THERAPY

Martha Hays
(Reviewed by Virginia Satir[1])

M Y THERAPY CENTERS around the application of concepts of interaction. The therapy deals directly with the present rules and processes of individuals by exploring their family system. An overlapping network of examination occurs as the therapy uncovers family rules and processes. I see the family as an operating unit with rules for its maintenance, and all the individuals within this unit as functioning with uniqueness (Satir, 1965). This unit is a system with rules related to precedence, too, so that when separate rules conflict with family rules, there is an awareness of what will happen next.

I see behavior as the result of the family interactions (Satir, 1965). Appropriate behavior occurs as individual members fulfill their particular role contract in the context, or the continually changing situation. Appropriate behavior signals further enjoyment and development of self, as well as furthering the common goals of the family. Inappropriate behavior signals dysfunction. I see a symptom as a report. The child in trouble reports that the marital unit functions with some discrepancy. His symptoms distort, but make obvious, his experience of inhibiting communication (Satir, 1964).

Communication is the means by which needs are met (Satir, 1972). A human being cannot get his needs met if he cannot communicate. Within the family system one learns how or how not to

---

1. The editor of this book felt a need to include material which represents the basic ideas and spirit of my work. Since I was unable to find the time to do it myself, Martha Hays, a gifted graduate student, prepared the following chapter using all of my published material. I believe it to be essentially accurate in its representation.

317

communicate. Families that deal with a created or invented reality, that deny what seems to be objectivity, will produce members that report this by their symptoms. Often I find that dysfunctional families infrequently use direct questions. They hint rather than speak to each other, or they prefer to suppress questions. I see anxiety, hostility and finally helplessness as the outcome of a family process that suppresses questions (Satir, 1965). Suppose that now I were speaking rather than writing, and that you had to report what I say. If you miss something, if you do not understand, and you cannot ask questions, you become anxious. If you miss hearing to any significant degree, you become hostile. If you continue missing you will finally become helpless.

Of course, questions are risks. If families fear being exposed by questions, they forbid or dilute this risk. Families in which self-esteem is low frequently do this. I believe that if the two architects, the male and the female who got together sexually to begin the family, have high self-esteem, their building will produce a system in which all members value self. All members in this kind of system can speak of and can raise question about what they individually perceive as reality. All members, as well as the family unit itself, will make and use flexible, appropriate, satisfying and subject-to-change rules (Satir, 1972). This family unit will form a linking to society that is open and hopeful.

One of the main emphases in my therapy is that of strengthening self-esteem (Satir, 1964). I am a positive person, who believes that people try to do the best they can with what they know. I see my work as having two main parts, learning and experience. I teach each person, relating to him through his uniqueness, by allowing and encouraging him to experience. Family members need to experience self and each other. I use talk, clear communication which at times sounds simplistic and repetitious in my search for the thing being explicitly communicated to me. I use exercises and games that I have developed to accelerate and intensify the experience of family communication (Satir, 1972). These exercises and games rely on the human imagination and the human senses. I work to deepen awareness and to intensify appreciation for communication. Looking, listening, paying attention, getting understanding, and making meaning are all part of this. Most of my structured experiences show the importance our bodies have in communication. I do not believe a person who is saying one thing and whose body contradicts him. I think a person is leveling with me when all of him is congruent. His body, its tonus, his movement, his words, his voice tone, his facial muscles–when all come to me on one level, then I can hear what a person says. I am able to experience him clearly, and I can believe him.

The purpose and the methods of my therapy allow persons to know that they can communicate. They can be safe because they can be known by others, and they can know others. In therapy I work to help them realize that the outcome of communication, or what actually happens, depends upon themselves. Whether or not a family is a good place to be and to live, and to enjoy, depends on the knowing and the being known. The appreciation of the knowing and the being known causes family members to be conscious of value. They value themselves and each other, building self-esteem. They respect self and others enough to choose to be clear. They communicate clearly to show self and others who they are, and where they are. They can trust because of the openness. The unit that this kind of family makes is a good place to be (Satir, 1964).

THEORETICAL FOUNDATION OF THERAPY

The main premise underlying the idea that symptoms are a family production is the notion that all families operate as systems. I see symptoms within individuals as embodiments of family dysfunction within the family system (Satir, 1964). Therapy for the total family unit is logical.

Family systems seem to have order and sequence, and they seem to be reliable. Family members, often unconsciously, know what will happen next. Family systems also appear to be disproportionate. Total growth needs–physical, emotional, social, intellectual–in terms of survival, intimacy, productivity, and making sense and order are rarely met, and are not met equally for all the individuals within a family. The system may meet the needs of some members partially, and some may be left out altogether. The system has order and sequence itself; it has decision-making process, and rules for negotiation and power. Rules of the system control communication. Who speaks, who speaks for whom, who speaks attributing blame or credit to another, all are observable factors of a family system.

From this point of view, the behavior of any family member is entirely appropriate and understandable. Member behavior is appropriate in terms of the family's own system. The behavior of an individual may not fit his own growth needs, nor seem to suit the expectations of other family members, but it does suit the system, or the family situation–its context. Understanding the system, then, allows understanding of the symptom-bearer or the identified patient (Jackson and Satir, 1961).

This approach began as it was observed that families with a schizophrenic child reported that things between the marital pair were pretty perfect (Satir, 1971b). Their crazy son or daughter made life a problem for them. Evidences of personal inadequacies, frustrations, disappointments in the marital relationship were covered up. As the sick child got better, the husband-wife relationship got worse. The pathology was in the unit rather than in the individual. Studying communication patterns of these families led to the double-bind theory. Simply stated, the double-bind theory asserts that the schizophrenic child learns behavior and communication within a situation of simultaneous contradiction. The child receives one message verbally, another non-verbally. For example, a mother may say, "Come close to Mother, Johnny, if you love her," while at that moment expressing rigidity through her gestures (Satir, 1971b).

Now we cannot *not* respond, so if we receive double messages from a survival figure, we are bound into a situation in which meaning, responses, the *shoulds* that we depend on, and expectations assault growth. Children in situations of this sort develop symptoms. But the point is not that inadequate parents produce sick children. *The point is that bizarre, seemingly meaningless behavior from symptom-bearers is appropriate behavior until the situation of the family or the universe of the symptom-bearer is changed.* The communication patterns of continual assault must be changed. In my opinion, these communication patterns are outside a family's awareness. Theoretically, the first step in therapy is to bring these patterns of the family into their awareness.

Early work comparing different kinds of families–families with delinquent members, under-achievers, or individuals with ulcerative colitis, for example–indicates that different kinds of dysfunctional systems lead to different sorts of symptoms. What kind of family develops depends upon the male and the female, the architects of the present family, and upon the families of their previous lives. Clinically and impressionistically it appears that the system a family develops begins in the courtship of the male and the female, develops and is modified as the marriage goes along integrating children into the family. The important thing, however, seems to lie not so much in the obvious. When one is trying to find out the meaning of present behavior, one must uncover the network of rules that the family communication utilizes. What are the rules *now?* Who may do what? Under what conditions? Who may comment, and on what may he comment?

I have found that families with symptom-bearers characteristically have rules that do not clearly allow for recognition of the uniqueness and separateness of each person in the family (Satir, 1971b). First names tend not to be used; members do not look at each other when speaking. Decisions seem to occur as a power struggle rather than as a negotiable process recognizing objective reality. Rules tend to suppress difference; difference seems representative of criticism to family members. In these families, the needs that all human beings have in order to survive, grow, get close to others, and produce are fulfilled, and often distorted, within conflict. The symptoms of these members comment upon the discrepancy between their own growth needs, and the rules of the situation they must depend upon.

Growth is a struggle, and I see each child as struggling to find his own power in a situation where there already are powerful persons who may not value nor help his personal efforts for power. Each child struggles for independence, but he lives within a situation of interdependency. He wishes to be a sexual person, but he may find a confusion of secrecy hiding genital differences (Satir,

1972). As a child who produces, he may find that his worth is measured primarily by his production. He sees, hears, feels, and he thinks–but may he share his perceptions without anyone "dropping dead"–that is, without anyone manifesting anger or pain implying death or destruction?

I assume that symptoms signify frustration of growth. These can be looked at three ways. First, who labelled what behavior as a symptom, or what actual behavior is being called a symptom by whom? Second, what does the symptom say about growth frustration for the person bearing the symptom? Finally, how does this growth frustration maintain survival for the family and maintain relationships? In other words, how does the symptom show the presence of pain, trouble, or confusion in the family?

Recognizing the symptom as appropriate behavior to an inappropriate system has therapeutic implications (Satir, 1971b). The family as one whole unit should be seen together–in one time and in one place. Therapy begins by uncovering and understanding the family's currently operating system. The growth needs of *each* member is seen as taking place in a context. Behavior in contrast is not seen as pathology of the individual, or as isolated, or as "afflicted." This shift makes each person's behavior become understandable, and further, it allows treatment emphasis to shift from "disease" to "growth."

After early exploration has centered around understanding the operation of the current system, how each person is reacting to these rules is uncovered. Then comes the job of changing the system, of education, re-education, and experiences of safe, clear communication while in the presence of the therapist (Satir, 1964). I frequently find in dysfunctional families that members do not ask simple fact-finding questions, nor expect clear answers. As the therapist gets each person to manifest himself clearly in a climate of safety, each person acquires the strength, the know-how, and actually the bravery to do this. As each family member learns to communicate and does communicate, he is able to satisfy his needs more directly. As a family begins talking straight, without conflictual qualifications, begins leveling, the family's rules will begin to change. Changing the rules changes the system.

Pathological atmosphere can become healthy atmosphere (Satir, 1972).

Therapists are therefore concerned with process, more than with outcome. How meanings are sent, how they are received–no matter what the content–is the point. The therapist pays attention to the processes that reveal the network of commitment and contract between family members. The therapist wants to ensure that what is meant is what is said and what is heard. The therapist wants to ensure that each person has esteem, for himself and from his family group.

ATTITUDES I WORK FROM

Over the years I have developed a picture of what the human being living humanly is like. He is a person who understands, values, and develops his body, finding it beautiful and useful; a person who is real and honest to and about himself and others; a person who is willing to take risks, to be creative, to manifest competence, to change when the situation calls for it, and to find ways to accommodate to what is new and different, keeping that part of the old that is still useful and discarding what is not. With healthy human beings feeling and communication are the same. As a matter of fact, when I see a person in which feeling and communication are the same I know the treatment is complete.

The healthy person can do without the hidden; he can see himself the way others see him; he can tell another what he hopes, fears, and what he expects. He can disagree, he can make choices, he can learn through practice (Satir, 1964). He accepts responsibility for his own thinking, his own hearing, and his own seeing. He knows himself. He deals with the actual world, not just his "wish."

As we become more healthy we free ourselves from the harm of the past. We achieve a maturity. Seeing maturity as a "good" is a very important concept in my therapy (Satir, 1964). I think a mature person is in charge of himself. He can make choices; he has the judgment to know that his choices are his limits. He makes decisions on the basis of accurate perceptions about himself and others, and the context in which he finds himself. He acknowledges his choices; he owns his choices (Satir, 1970). Because his decisions are his own, he accepts responsibility for their outcome. Each of us, I think, bears the responsibility of being aware of what we give out to ask the other person to deal with. But at the same time, I have control over the choice of whether or not to act and the course of action I take. For this I can be held responsible to myself as well as to others. I cannot be responsible for what is presented to me; only for my response to it.

These interdependences make us conscious of the way we follow models. We are models for each other. We are responsible for being clear, congruent models.

This vital business that goes on in families is what I call "peoplemaking." Healthy families have healthy people. Dysfunctional families make unhealthy people. A family is a bit like a factory . . . the kind of factory determines the product. Good peoplemaking goes on where self-worth is high; communication is direct, clear, specific, and honest; rules are flexible, human, appropriate, and subject to change; and the linking to society is open and hopeful.

It is my attitude that children in a family reflect the marital situation in which they are reared. Differences do exist. Father is a male and mother is a female. That is a big difference. If either father or mother sees difference of any sort as something to fear, or the source of conflict, then there is a war-like atmosphere with a hurtful, inhibiting set of family rules (Satir, 1972). On the other hand, if difference is seen as pleasant, as an opportunity to explore and to gain understanding, then the family blueprint is a peaceful one where growth and fun and the good things of life can occur. I have found that a person's reaction to differences and to differentness is an index of his ability to adapt to growth and change. It also indicates what attitudes he will have toward other members of his family, and whether he will be able to express these attitudes directly or not.

Blueprints are made up of interdependences and the interactional transactions. The rules, who the models are, what the messages about the desirability of growth are—these things create a blueprint for each individual. He learns to evaluate, and to act on new experiences. He learns whether or not to be close to others. The family is the place where a human being finds out about himself. The family is the place where he first decides whether or not he is worthwhile. He first learns what other people are like. He learns how to relate to others and to the world. The family is the keeper of the essential learnings (Satir, 1972).

Now the teaching process includes the following: a clear idea of what is to be taught, an awareness that each parent has of what he is modeling, a knowledge of how to interest the other in following that model, and the communication to make it work. Families teach to a purpose in peoplemaking. Each person somehow, whether ideally or not, gets involved in the peoplemaking. Each person looks to the family for direction, freedom, encouragement, nuturance, and appreciation for uniqueness.

Persons in an ideal family to me are people who clearly show their own uniqueness, who demonstrate their power, who clearly show their sexuality, who demonstrate their ability to share through understanding, kindness, and affection, who use their common sense, who are realistic and responsible. That may sound like an impossibility, but it is my attitude that persons can try to keep moving in that direction while respecting where they are. The key words are *unique, powerful, sexual, sharing, sensible, realistic,* and *responsible.*

The family is really the place where a person can learn and can develop into this ideal person. But the fact that each person at any single moment in a family is a whole person, is a significant notion to grasp. No matter whether this human being is two weeks old, or 15, or 35, or 80 years old, he is a whole person. He has a right to expect peoplemaking from his family. The disappointment that a grown man experiences at losing a desired job is no more painful than that of a four-year-old child who loses his favorite toy. The experience of disappointment is the same at any age. The feeling in a child who is the brunt of a tirade from an angry mother is no different from the woman's feelings if she has been the brunt of the tirade of an angry husband, or vice versa.

Children seem to thrive on the knowledge that their world of hope, fear, mistakes, imperfections, and successes is a world also known and shared by their parents. Parents who choose authority, rather than honestly expressing feeling, seem phony to their children. If a child becomes distrustful of his parents, he extends the feelings into isolation and general feelings of unsureness, and rebellion.

Now to get back to the key words. I think it not necessary to explain what I mean by "sensible," "sharing," and "realistic." I use those words the same way you do. When it comes to "uniqueness," "power," and "sexuality," I want to go into more depth. Understanding these concepts is important in the family blueprint.

I believe uniqueness is the key word to self-worth (Satir, 1972). We get together on the basis of our similarities, and we grow on the basis of our differences. We need both. It is this combination of sameness and differentness in a human being that I call uniqueness. Helping a child to value the difference between his parents becomes an important part of his learning. Appreciating himself is, too. If infants do not have the opportunity to be treated as unique from the beginning of their lives, it will become difficult to react to them as whole people. They will be handicapped.

Now about the key word, power. Body power develops first. The infant's first cry is most welcome. We greet physical coordination with joy. He is expected to grow and manage his body. I have noticed that parents will have endless patience teaching their child body power, showing joy at each successful effort. I think showing joy at each successful effort is a suitable way to teach the other areas of power, too. The other areas of power are intellectual, emotional, social, material, and spiritual. It is my attitude that if we use patience and respond to the expression of the child's newfound power with joy and approval, we are successful. Emotional power seems scariest, perhaps because adults may not trust their own emotional power.

Another area of difficulty is frequently found as the family teaches sex–in its broadest sense–maleness and femaleness. What a child decides about this reflects, not at all what parents say, but how they enjoy differences.

I have said a lot about teaching, but of course it is not possible to teach family members what to do in every situation. However, I have found that the family that has emphasized the self-worth of whole people will discover that these people know what to do because they have developed judgment as they made their own individual choices all along.

SOME OF THE HOW OF THERAPY

Experiencing and sharing what *is* for family members is the main part of my therapy (Satir, 1964). It begins as two persons look at each other. I want people to experience one another. Suppose you are face to face with me; your senses take in what I look like, how I sound, what I smell like, and if you happen to touch me, how I feel to you. Your brain then reports what this means to you, calling upon your past experiences, particularly with your parents and other authority figures, your book learning, and your ability to use this information to explain the message from your senses. Depending upon what your brain reports, you feel comfortable or uncomfortable–your body is loose or tight. And I am going through the same thing. My senses are taking in. I am in contact with my past experiences, my values and expectations. I feel my body reacting. It is doing something because you and I are looking at each other.

But what our brains "know" about the other are guesses and fantasies, until we check out facts. Let's say you and I are a man and a woman who are in one of the normal life crises. Our adult daughter, Linda, is moving to an apartment of her own. This particular crisis has a heavy sadness for most families. A child's leaving is a big loss. Now, as the man, I take you in, I feel pleasure in your presence, I see an unusual look of resignation about your face, your eyes look sad to me . . . and so I guess that you do not approve of Linda's plan. If I am the woman, I take you in. You are the same contented person that I have felt comfortable with for 25 years, yet there is a clear evidence of concern, which looks like worry to me. I have a fantasy of you explaining to Linda how living in a city apartment can be expensive, lonely, possibly dangerous.

All this takes place in a fraction of a second, before either of us has said a word. When we begin to talk openly, freely, trusting-ly, we find our guesses and fantasies changed. As the man, I hear you say that not only do you approve of Linda's independence, you envy her a little. You share your sadness in anticipating the natural loneliness that occurs when a child moves out. As the woman, I hear that you admire Linda's spirit. When I listen to you talk, you discuss judgment and choice, and you let me understand how you hope we have given her enough choice to help her develop judgment.

In consciously checking each other out, you and I have shared; we have become aware of each other. We are in a very real sense more visible to each other; we have become more accessible. We appreciate each other more as we become more aware. By verbally checking out sensory communication we get a fuller and more accurate dimension. And we can feel more secure. Our verbal communication clarifies, and it brings us closer together. I am always surprised at how loneliness in families disappears as family members learn communication.

Communication is learned. We have learned the how and the what of communication from the first moment of our life. By the time we were five years old, we probably have had a billion experiences in sharing communication (Satir, 1972). We developed ideas about ourselves, about the world, about other people; we learned what to expect and how we could communicate to get what was possible.

I see communication as a huge umbrella that covers and affects all that goes on between human beings. Once a human has arrived on this earth, *communication is the largest single factor determining what kinds of relationships he makes with others and what happens to him in the world about him.* I have found that high self-esteem people communicate directly, openly, and fully. They level with other people, dealing with what is, not what they guess or fear (Satir, 1964). They send congruent messages. Their voice and words match their facial expressions and their body position. The leveling response occurs when people have relationships that are easy, free, and honest. The leveling response is real. If a leveler says: "I like you," his voice is warm and he looks at you.

If his words are: "I am mad as hell at you," his voice is harsh, and his face is tight. The message is single and straight. I trust a leveler because his messages are truths of the moment. I feel good because I know where I stand with him.

In therapy I use exercises that allow people to feel how they are responding. I developed these ideas from listening to literally thousands of interactions among people. It seems to me that I can let people experience the leveling response by contrasting it to other ways we have of responding. I find that we usually use four other ways besides the leveling. These occur to protect the speaker, rather than primarily to communicate to the listener. In other words, self-esteem is low when these are used.

A person may *placate,* so the other person is happy, does not get mad, and so on.

A person may *blame,* so the other person regards him as strong.

A person may *compute;* he tries to deal with what is by saying that it is harmless, or he tries to protect his self-worth with big words.

A person may *distract,* so the other person does not get any relevant message. The distracter does not respond to the point; he seems dizzily off in different directions. He is purposeless and lonely, but he tries not to let anybody know.

For a person to experience the *placating* response, I exaggerate and expand facial and voice messages. I get the placater to feel as he talks to the other person in an ingratiating way, trying to please, apologizing, never disagreeing no matter what. He is syrupy, martyrish, bootlicking. So that a person can really feel his body during placating, I suggest a stance. I get him to go down physically on one knee, wobble a bit, put out one hand in a begging fashion. Be sure to have head up so that neck and shoulders experience placating. Very shortly this placater feels nauseous, if he is listening to himself. He feels strained and headachy. He sounds whiny and squeaky, because he cannot get deep breaths. He must get someone to approve of him, and yet this is impossible as long as he says "yes" to everything.

I have the *blamer* stand with one hand on his hip, the other extended with the index finger pointed. Good blamers get bulging neck muscles and flaring nostrils. They also feel their screwed up face and curled lips, as they tell off, call names, and criticize everything under the sun. Blamers disagree, "You never do anything right. What is the matter with you?" Blamers are bosses, but internally they feel unsuccessful, and are confused about their self-esteem.

The *computer* is ultra-reasonable, correct, distant, monotonous and abstract. He says things like, "If one were to observe carefully one might notice the work worn hands of someone present here." (A leveler could say: Look at my hands. You can tell I work hard!) The computer uses big words. He is rigid, because he has no feeling from the cranium down. He seems calm, cool, and collected; but deep inside he feels a lack of self-esteem, he feels vulnerable. The sad part about the computer is that many people are taught to be this way as an ideal goal. "Say the right words; show no feeling; don't react." That is advice for a robot, not a human being.

The *distracter,* on the other hand, is most reactive, but his reactions are not relevant to what anyone else is saying or doing. To play the distracter, feel yourself as a kind of lopsided top, constantly spinning, but never knowing where you are going, and not even realizing it when you get there. Distracters have mouth, arms, legs, all moving at once. A few minutes of playing the distracter lets a person experience a terrible loneliness and a purposelessness, because the distracter can never be fully present.

Experiencing these four ways of communicating lets people get in touch with their body reactions. Internal feelings experienced earlier come into awareness. These are old ways of communicating, learned perhaps early in childhood. If a person vividly experiences himself in one of these non-functional communication patterns, he is better able to reject this. He is acutely conscious of what he needs and wants to reject. He is better able to learn and use the leveling response. As he begins to become more able with the leveling response his self-esteem goes up, and as his self-esteem goes up he is still more able to level. He feels confident. And so he is confident as he expresses himself. I hope I am not oversimplifying here. To become a leveler takes, besides someone to show you how, guts, courage, and some new beliefs, too. I do not think you can fake it.

I have found that as a person's self-esteem goes up, and as his self-expression is more able, he begins to realize himself as a whole human being. He begins to form mutually satisfying relationships that have satisfactory outcomes.

In teaching communication I am striking out at what I see as the real human evils of this world. For me, the feelings of isolation, helplessness, feeling unloved, low self-esteem, or incompetence are the real evils (Satir, 1972). Certain kinds of communication can change these. I try to make it possible for each person to experience through the leveling response, his ability to deal directly, spontaneously, congruently, and lovingly with others.

THE THERAPIST

I suppose being genuine is really the most important qualification for a therapist. I find that an effective therapist is genuine to each person in a family. He sees each child as a distinct person, just as he sees each adult as a distinct person (Satir, 1964). I try to contact each child at eye level to assure that this genuineness or realness can flow between us (Satir, 1972). This means quite a bit of stooping for me, but I think it is important for any child to experience the mutual respect that comes as two people relate closely at eye level. Since first experiences are very important, this eye-to-eye genuineness helps open and develop my relatedness, and so it furthers what I can do as a therapist.

I see myself as a change agent. I roll up my sleeves and get to work actively helping families change. I try to help them discover their patterns that do not work, and to replace these with patterns that do work. I see a therapist as self-confident, and as curious, too. I go into a family with the attitude of research. I am interested in what actually is going on, not what may seem to be going on, and often not what the family thinks at first they want to be seen as going on. Because of this I think it is vital that therapists have nothing of the "blaming" about them. Helping families in trouble emphasizes research and analysis into their particular dynamics for the purpose of help. For example, I may find in a family someone who is hiding behind the "boss" parental cloak (Satir, 1972). Sometimes I find a boss who is a tyrant. He flaunts his power, knows everything, and parades as a paragon of virtue. He may say, "I am the authority; family members do as I say." Sometimes I may find a boss who is a martyr. He absolutely wants nothing for himself except to serve the other family members. He will go to astonishing lengths to appear as nothing to be considered. He may say, "Never mind me. Family members just be happy." Another boss I may find is the Great Stone Face, who lectures incessantly, very impassively, on all the right things. He'll say, *"This is the right way."*

Now the point of my discoveries, finding such interesting specimen, seems antithetical to most researchers. I am not interested in labeling. My discoveries are for the purpose of knowing what can be done, what can be worked with in a family. All the boss specimen that I have found seem to be suffering from low self-esteem. As a therapist, I'm more confident in beginning to work toward change in the family, as I begin to discover each separate individual (Satir, 1971a). Change begins here.

I find that I work best when I have taken time to feel secure about where the separate family members are. Then I sense where I am in relation to this. This helps me to feel comfortable, and I like to feel comfortable in my work. Work goes best when the therapist enjoys what he is doing. In a very real sense he is having fun. He has a feeling of lightness about what he is accomplishing. In point of fact, I do not think anyone is competent unless at the same time he enjoys what he is doing.

I find, too, that as I am genuine and free, expressing my feelings as they occur, family members pick up on this crucial concept: it is safe to express honest feelings. To be even more emphatic about this: I consider 90 percent of a therapist's work is maintaining a counseling climate of safety, the kind of safe atmosphere in which family members feel and act like they feel OK in expressing their feelings (Satir, 1972). Along with this I probably should mention again my belief that a therapist must never punish. Punishment does not teach. In the same manner, "Obey me" techniques don't work. Perhaps I mean therapists teach by deed, not directive. I recognize that here I am feeling uncomfortable, because I sound too didactic. But this is information, rather than therapy, so I will let it go at that. This contradiction reminds me that as therapists we consciously call the shots as we see them. We deal with the reality, the "what is," as we perceive it. We have common sense and we use it. We do not accept the surface, we uncover. We trust our bodies, too. I have been in families where the air was icy with politeness, or where the air felt stiffling to me because of the boredom. These troubled atmospheres give me the reactions of back and shoulder aches, head pains, or even queasy stomach. I find that by being acutely aware, my body will tell me a lot about a family.

Later when I know the family better, and when they are more healthy, I may share some of my reactions and feelings. One of the bellwether signs of health I find is a sense of humor. When I can look back with a family as they experience the relief of choosing not to go back to dead-end communication, then I feel happy that I am in the presence of health. I understand from my experiences where physical ills must begin. Bodies react humanly to very inhuman atmospheres.

I think the last thing I want to mention about the therapist has a two-fold part. Love and democracy seem related to me, like two parts of one quality. I think good therapists like people with a depth of sincere regard that is love. And they bear this "good will" to all family members. They democratically accept all family members. A situation that always drives this home to me every time I face it, occurs with the child abuser. I see the child abuser as a child grown big reacting to their own growing up. After my first waves of nausea pass, I go to work to help these adults as well as the children with their shame, their ignorance and their burden. And just as in all good therapy, punishment makes matters worse; treatment for these people has to be help in becoming a better person.

MY GOALS

Healthy, nurturing families are made up of physically healthy, mentally alert, feeling, loving, playful, authentic, creative, productive human beings. These human beings can stand on their own two feet; they can love deeply; and they can fight fairly and effectively. They are persons on equally good terms with both their tenderness and their toughness, and they know the difference between the two. These persons compose families in which four things are apparent:

Self-worth is high;

Communication is direct, clear, specific and honest;

Rules are flexible, human and appropriate; they are subject to change; and

The linking to society is open and hopeful.

I think that all healthy families have these parts in common. The healthy family is made up of people who value themselves; each esteems himself and the others; and they are conscious of their value as a group. I have found that people of self-esteem know their families are good places to get their needs met. Their homes are nurturing. These people know it is OK to ask for what they need. They can speak openly of their needs, their disappointments, their achievements, their dreams. Because needs change, really from minute to minute, these people choose rules for their families that accommodate them, that are suitable to them (Satir, 1971a). They find themselves as the value, and so do not arbitrarily follow rules. These people are energetic questioners, too. They are constantly asking: Does it fit? Does this rule, or way of relating in our family, further growth? Does our family encourage our getting our needs met both here, and in the world? In other words, is our linking to society open and hopeful, so that we may expect to have a good time in the world?

Family rules are vital, dynamic, influential forces. These rules are the force that either slows you down or gets you on your way. The importance of these rules just cannot be emphasized too much. In fact, I would say that helping individuals and families to discover the rules by which they live is my goal (Satir, 1972). And I think it is surprising to families to discover their rules. Many families are not even aware of their rule system.

Rules have to do with *should*. Rules also abbreviate what is possible. Rather than beginning anew each time the possibility for a decision or a choice or an action comes up, families depend upon their shoulds. Family members do not have to make a new decision each time on what money is to be used for, who does chores, or what to do about infractions.

A good way that I have for discovering the rules of a family is to have all family members present, and to have them sit down and write their rules. Two hours is about enough time. The family may appoint a secretary if they choose. Now is not the time for argument, nor discussion. Have all the family members add *what they think* their rules are. Maybe this family has a 10-year-old boy who thinks the rule is that he only has to wash the dishes when his 11-year-old sister is *justifiably occupied somewhere else.* He figures he is a kind of back-up dishwasher. His sister thinks the rule is that her brother washes the dishes *when his father tells him to.* It is easy to see misunderstanding resulting here. I listen to irate parents tell me: *He knows what the rules are!* But I frequently find that is not the case (Satir, 1972).

Actually seeing their rules written out helps a family to see whether their rules are fair and appropriate. They can see if their rules are up-to-date. A nurturing family keeps up-to-date rules, and they are adaptable. Our legal system provides for appeals; I think good family rule systems do, too.

After acknowledging what their rules are, a family can confront the question of who makes the rules? Is it the person who is the oldest, the nicest, the most handicapped, the most powerful? Are rules from books, from TV shows, the neighbors, from the families where the parents grew up?

A good family rule system allows freedom to comment on what *is,* not on what should be. I deal with four aspects of this freedom of comment. First, I try to get the answer to: What can you say about what you are seeing and hearing? Expressing fear, helplessness, anger, need for comfort, loneliness, tenderness, or aggression form some of the blocks. Then, I want to know: To whom can you say it? I may find some disjunction like the child who hears a parent swearing, and there is a family rule against swearing. The child may not remind the parent, yet the parent must remind the child if it were the other way around. After this, I need to know: How do you go about it if you disagree or disapprove of someone or something? If your 69-year-old grandmother always loses the phone book, can you say so? My fourth question is: How do you question when you do not understand? Of course, many families do not question at all when they do not understand, but families can learn that they can get clarification. They can get understanding, and they can be understood.

All kinds of seeing and hearing goes on in families. My goal is to get family members to use all their seeing and hearing for closeness, for trust, for support, and for joy. Even the secrets having to do with deformity, jail, illegitimacy, and so on, do exist. Talking around a subject, or hiding the secret does not remove it. Only talking of good, right, appropriate subjects leaves out large parts of reality. These shutting-off attitudes breed low self-esteem, because any family member who is asked in any way to deny his perceptions will be hurt.

The area probably most often placed out-of-touch, or denied, is that of sex. Some families deny that sexual beings, males and females, compose their family. One's sexuality has a vast influence on one's separate individuality. This is important, because uniqueness is the key word to self-worth. The family is the place to learn that it is good to be a female, or that it is good to be a male. I have had contact with family rules as stringent as: do not enjoy sex—yours or anyone else's—in any form. Some families see genitals as necessary nasty objects. Because so much pain comes from repression and inhuman attitudes about sex, I try to get attitudes changed to pride, openness, acceptance, enjoyment, and appreciation. I can say that without exception any person I have seen with problems in sexual gratification in marriage, or who was homosexual, promiscuous, or who was arrested for any sexual crime grew up with some of the taboos against sex. I will go further. Anyone whom I have seen with any kind of coping problem or emotional illness also grew up with taboos about sex (Satir, 1972).

So I believe that anything that *is* can be talked about and understood in human terms (Satir, 1965). My goal is to get family members to realize that expressing themselves honestly gets them in deepest touch with themselves, and with each other, and this means they stand a much better chance of creating satisfying relationships with the outside world.

Now I would like to refer briefly to something I mentioned earlier when I spoke of goals. With people of self-worth, full sharing respects dreams, and I see dreams as the force or impetus of life. Dreams give life something to flow toward. And it seems to me that when a person's dreams, wants, his desires become confidence, he is doing and enjoying doing. He confidently acts his dreams. Family sharing can help this come about.

ILLUSTRATIVE PROTOCOL

The protocol below is from a Symposium on Family Counseling and Therapy that I participated in (Satir, 1971a). When we began–we worked on a stage–it seemed we had some uncomfortable family members, so I tried to get each of the family seated in a comfortable way with his feet upon something secure. As we began to talk, I discovered that Elaine was 4, Jimmy was 6, Jane was 10, and Mary was 11. The parents, John and Alice, were 42 and 34. At that time I had been around for 54 years, so I mentioned that we had a conglomerate of experiences to draw from. We talked of expectations, and then something of family home activity. The family had volunteered, from John's point of view, to learn something about their own family dynamics. The positions referred to as the protocol begins are those that occurred when I grouped the family members close to the persons within the family that each was close to. The arrangement of the two oldest on either side of John, and the two youngest on either side of Alice seemed comfortable to the family. I had begun by trying to get at how they, as a family, lived. We had been working about 15 minutes; now we are learning about some behavior rules.

John: Alice is not nearly as strict with them as I am. I think she would agree with that, and yet her control with them is much better than mine.
Jane: He blows his top.
Satir: He blows his top! All right, all right. But I did feel something change. Did you see something change when you changed your positions? Alice, what kind of explanations would you give for that?
Alice: I guess these two (Mary and Jane) feel as if they don't have to stay within certain bounds when they're with me as they do when they're with him. That's the only explanation that I have. I'm not so good at blowing my top, I guess.
Satir: Do you want to get better?

Alice: I guess so, I mean, I don't know if that would be the solution. I would like to be firmer with them, but I don't want to go into the anger and so forth that is involved with it. We're just so different. I mean, he is a very emotional person and he reacts to every little thing. He just flares up and I don't.

Satir: You know, just let me tell you something that I was feeling. It may or may not be right—that sometimes you ask yourself if you ought to be different from what you are when you don't really believe it. I don't think you really believe you'd like to blow your top, would you?

Alice: Not blow my top. I would like to be able to be more positive.

Satir: Could you give me an example of what you mean by that?

Alice: I would like to be able to say, "No, you are not going to do this," and then make it stick—to be convincing with the children.

Satir: John, what are your feelings as you hear Alice talk at this moment?

John: She and I think differently about this. I'm firmly convinced . . . let me use an analogy. I would not teach without a paddle. I only had to use it three times in 16 years, but it was there. I feel that a recourse to this is necessary. I believe that if you are going to tell somebody something you'd better not tell them anything that you don't enforce, because pretty soon they begin to lose the credibility of it. I feel like that many times she tells them to do things and she doesn't mean to enforce it or, at least, she does not enforce it the way I do.

Satir: Alice do you get that picture? At least that is how John sees you.

Alice: Well, so many times its just easier to do it myself.

Satir: Well, how do you feel about his idea?

Alice: I think many times he is too harsh.

Satir: And what kinds of problems does that make for you?

Alice: Ground-out teeth.

Satir: Ground-out teeth. Would you be willing to try something?

Alice: I guess.

Satir: Would you, John?

John: Let me make one comment. One of the things that I notice, and I think its important, is that when they (Jane and Jimmy and Mary and Elaine) do divide its a result of these two (Jane and Mary) competing. When you talk about tension, this is a more tension-free arrangement, because the competition in the other arrangement does cause tension. But, now let's get on to what you were saying.

Satir: Okay, Elaine, what I'm going to ask you to do is just to let your chair move back a little bit and yours too, Jane. I'd like you to be in a theater somewhere, just watching. If you can stay where you are, I'll put you face-to-face. Now we'll just try this out for size, okay? Alice, I wonder if you could say to John, "I think you're too harsh."

Alice: I think you're too harsh.

Satir: Now, John, would you respond to her?

John: I do my best.

Satir: Alice, how did you feel about what he told you?

Alice: Well, he does do his best. I think he needs to relax more, though.

Satir: He didn't answer you regarding your disagreeing with his harshness though, did he? How did you feel about his not answering that?

Alice: It's a typical answer.

Satir: All right. Let's try it again and you say to him again that you feel he is too harsh.

Alice: I think you're too harsh.

John: I think that I need recourse to violence to make them behave, and I do what I think is right.

Satir: All right, now would you try again. When you (Alice) tell him that you think he is too harsh, will you (John) say to her that you believe that she's wrong.

Alice: I think you are too harsh.

John: I think you're wrong.

Satir: Alice, how do you want to respond to that?

Alice: I think I'm right.

John: I see a fight starting!

Satir: Now, John, you're laughing about it, but could you tell me now how that makes you feel when this comes up?

John: This doesn't come up.

Satir: I noticed that. I know why. I think it needs to, though. All right, could you respond, John. Alice said that she thinks she's right.

John: I think you're wrong.

Alice: This could go on indefinitely.

Satir: Yeah, and this is one of the things out of which there would be no escape, once this happened. Right? So the kids can do it instead. All right, would you move a little closer. Alice, would you just look at him and tell him something that you know that you and he absolutely agree on.

Alice: We need to get off and have some time, just to ourselves.

John: Amen.

Satir: Does that mean you agree?

John: Yes, mam.

Satir: All right, you tell her that you agree with her.

John: I just did.

Satir: No, now you sounded like a preacher.

John to Alice: I thoroughly agree, wholeheartedly!

Satir: Now, Alice, what does that make you want to do?

Alice: Well, I wish we could make some plans to get away.

Satir: Would you tell him something that you want to do with him.

Alice: Well, this really is what we had been planning—to take a little vacation.

Satir: Is it set up?

Alice: Yes, tentatively.

Satir: All right, now what could stop it?

Alice: Child-care problems.

Satir: Okay, now would you discuss your child-care problems?

Alice: We live too far away from either set of grandparents, so we'll have to try and make arrangements to have a friend come in and stay at the house with the children or "farm them out" either in small groups or separately among our friends. We'll be gone about three days.

Satir: How soon is this going to be?

Alice: April.

Satir: April. All right, now you named several possibilities—different children going to different places, and so forth. Would you discuss together, at this point in time, given the information that you have, what you think would be a likely plan.

Alice: Well I've thought of several things.

(Alice and John continue to agree, working out plans. Now I have gotten back to one place they need help. We're working on their disagreeing with each other, rather than their disagreeing through the children.)

Satir: I see, so there is something that scares you about the whole business of the disagreement.

John: Very much!

Satir: What about you, Alice? What objections do you have to disagreeing with John?

Alice: Well, its unpleasant, for one thing.

Satir: Could you go further with that, dear?

Alice: Whatever problems we have, I feel that we could find a better solution than the constant disagreeing and bickering.

Satir: Now let's do something, because one of the problems that I see here is that there is something pretty horrible about the whole business of disagreeing in the family. You haven't found yet a growth way to use the disagreement. So let's play around with something. Maybe by the time we leave we'll be able to know something different about this disagreement.

John: Let me make one comment to Alice that this is by no means an uncommon thing. I just want to tell her that this happens in every family.

Satir: I hear you trying to give Alice some reassurance, John, that she's not so different from other people and neither are you.

John: Essentially, yes.

Satir: John, could you find some ways to talk more simply to Alice?

John: It's difficult for me to talk simply.

Satir: Yeah, every once in a while I have a feeling that I want to get out the dictionary. But anyway, you said that you started out by placating during disagreements.

John: Now this was a number of years ago.

Satir: Long ago?

John: Now she is reasonable.

Satir: Well, would you take the placating stance. Alice, do you remember when he was saying, "Yes, dear," to you, a long time ago?

Alice: No.

Satir: Well, John, this is your recall of this. Which one of these in front of you would you be saying "yes" to.

John: Her (Alice).

Satir: Alice. Well, Alice, now you may not have known this but apparently this was true. Now, John, how did you see Alice reacting when you did this? Blaming, all right. Alice, this may not be your picture, but it is his picture of you. John, what does it feel like for you down there in a placating position?

John: Door mat.

Satir: So you raged inside then. Alice, if you never knew that this was going on, then this would be a whole piece of John that you didn't know about. Now, John, breathe a little, because otherwise you'll get a backache. When you see that stance, Alice, what do you find yourself doing? Is it that way or is it "To hell with you brother" kind of thing? Okay, so you do go "To hell with you brother," and you do what I say . . . with the finger pointed this way. Is that something you've seen, John?

John: Not that reasonable stance.

Satir: Well, wait a minute, though; this time you talk about what you feel, so you apparently haven't seen this.

John: No, I haven't.

Satir: You see it is hard because Alice is looking over there. Alice, would you notice where your finger is going?

Alice: I can't see.

Satir: No you can't see, but you can feel it from behind. You really want to say to him, "Get off my back!" Okay, so he did. Now, John, when you said that you finally stopped; it is very understandable why you stopped and assumed the "reasonable guy" stance. What does that make you want to do, Alice?

Alice: I would like to communicate—to tell him—not to be so reasonable.

Satir: Okay, so what do you want?

John: She hasn't decided yet.

Alice: You talk for me!

Satir: What is it for you? All right, you are at this point now. Alice what do you see yourself doing?

Alice: Not placating, but something similar to that—pleading. It is not quite as much as that.

Satir: All right then kind of like this! You look straight at him. You kind of bend your knees a little and appear to be saying, "Please look at me, please!" All right, children I would like to ask you if you ever have seen these positions between your mother and dad —when he stands like a solid rock of Gibraltar?

Jane: Sometimes.

Satir: What do you find yourself doing when that happens? What do you find happening? What do you feel like you're doing? Do you kind of stand stiff, too? What's your picture?

Jane: (Jane pushes her father.)

Satir: Do you really want to wipe it all out? Push him away. All right, just stand kind of like you want to push him away. Now John you're kind of pleading down here. Where do you think you are? All right, you hold that position for a minute. Elaine, where do you think you are, dear? You're up there too. You want to say you are with your father, huh? Okay. And you've already felt that the two of you are together. Is this something in your family that you've noticed? Jane really tries to get you two to stop.

Jane: I don't like you (father) but . . .

Satir: All right, Jane is in-between.

John: Janes tries to control in our situation.

Satir: Alice, have you noticed this?

Alice: Yes.

Satir: All right, have you seen this in relation to Mary?

Alice: Yes, but not that stance.

Satir: Okay, we're exaggerating this stance, but have you seen this, John?

John: Not clearly.

Satir: Not clearly. Is it beginning to come through now?

Mary: I tell dad what to do. I tell him to be nicer to mommy and I tell her to be nicer to him.

Satir: Well, wait a minute now. There are a lot of pieces here. All right, you can put your arm down further. What I heard you say is that you take your dad off and say, "Now, look, you be nicer to mother." Is that it?

Mary: I tell him what to do to her. I tell him what she'd like. . . .

Satir: All right, you do that right now. Will you tell your father out loud so we can all hear.

Mary: Daddy, when you talk to mommy she can't take all that yelling. Next time you feel like yelling just ask yourself, "Would mommy like the way I say it or would she dislike it?" Just try not to yell.

Satir: Alice, is this something you yourself have been experiencing from Mary?

Alice: Not in those words.

Satir: (To Mary) You want to tell your dad, "Please be nicer to mommy." All right now Mary go over to your mother and tell her what you want to tell her.

Mary: You shouldn't yell.

Alice: I don't yell that much.

Satir: Now Mary, you are saying to your mother, "You be nicer to daddy; he can't help it."

Mary: He can't help it that he yells so much.

Satir: Alice, have you noticed this happening?

Alice: Yes, in a very . . .

Satir: This is only one piece of it. What we're getting at is that when this family reaches a rupture, which is when the two of you have problems where you are objecting and disagreeing, then here is one way that this family operates. Mary is trying to give her father some advice about how to treat his wife, and Mary is trying to give her mother some advice about how to understand her husband. That's what I hear.

As we continued the interview their network of rules continued to come out. We worked on clear communication, and fair disagreements that do not contradict the love family members have for each other. We worked on the family problem of rules coming from *supposed to*. Because this interview uncovered so much, follow-up work was done with the family, so they could better resolve their concerns.

RESEARCH

I am now using a structured interview in six major ways (Satir, 1971b).

1. It provides a method of structuring family behavior and of developing ways of classifying family behavior. Hopefully, our raw data on family behavior will lead to the formulation of appropriate concepts in which we can describe families. Clearly, one of the difficulties in analyzing an individual's behavior, using my systems and communications approach, is that we do not have clear and universal terms in which to describe family systems and family rules.

2. The interview can be used to compare different families task-by-task, and so on.

3. Families may be compared with themselves, at beginning and end of treatment.

4. The interview information may be compared with the information and insight that therapy brings out.

5. The interview may be used diagnostically indicating guidelines for therapy.

6. The interview is part of the therapy. Responding clearly to the interview is a therapeutic experience for a family if it breaks some of their dysfunctional rules (their growth inhibiting, distorting or assaulting rules). Observing that catastrophe does not follow direct level responses forms an important experience for some family members.

Dr. Jules Riskin[2] is working on a set of scales to describe and classify interaction. These scales attempt to show such things as clarity versus congruency . . . or does what is said match how it is said? The scales will deal with concepts like commitment versus avoiding commitment, agreeing or disagreeing, and increased or decreased intensity. So far his results suggest meaningful and significant variables of interaction.

Another investigator, Jay Haley,[3] is trying to develop a more mechanical method for differentiating families and measuring in-

---

2. Associate Director, Mental Research Institute, Palo Alto, California.
3. Research Associate, Mental Research Institute, Palo Alto, California.

teraction. He uses a four-minute sequence of a three-person interchange (father, mother, child) and records the speaking order. Who speaks after whom is significantly different, in that the order is more rigid, in disturbed families. His research has the implication that the family does show patterns, an implication that supports my idea that the family is a system.

The general goal of research is learning to describe, identify, and then use the system for the growth of all family members. The results with both normal and pathogenic families suggest that we are beginning to achieve some of these general research goals.

SUMMARY

Family therapy is of course for families; although I have noticed that three or more people related in any way that are joined by a common task will develop into a family system. So this type therapy is theoretically suitable for many small groups. I think when in groups we shape ourselves into families because for so long the family has been the basic social unit. It almost goes without saying that I think the family still is the basic social unit, and that it will remain so. I see the family as the place where a person can sit down and be known. The family is a small enough group for this. Most families do not exceed the recognized full-group number of 15. In the family group each person is appreciated for his unique value. Each person has a unique place. These places all are at different growth levels. These places balance and accommodate each other.

To give a family group an experience of how they accommodate each other and balance each other, I sometimes provide objects–any objects–that are very different from one another (Satir, 1972). The family is to work out a mobile; they create their mobile by balancing the different objects. There should be as many objects as there are people in the family. Some families will settle for the first balance they achieve; I try to encourage at least three solutions, pointing out the interest and variety. One of the points in the exercise is to see that just as moving one part of the mobile to another place affects all other places, family members do not rearrange themselves without affecting the whole group.

Families who become conscious, thoughtful of others, will have members who consider before changing the family pattern.

I think it's very important to realize that so much family change is what I call normal crisis. These are the natural stresses which are predictable for most people. The crises contain temporary anxiety, require an adjustment period, and require a new integration. After a male and a female decide to begin a family, their first child is their first crisis. There is the conception, pregnancy, and birth. Being the first child is part of the crisis, because he is the guinea pig. I do not see how it can be otherwise (Satir, 1972).

A second normal crisis occurs when this child starts to use intelligible speech (Satir, 1972). This second crisis requires a big adjustment. The third crisis occurs when the child goes to school. The fourth crisis is big; this is when the child enters adolescence. The fifth crisis is when the child has grown to adulthood, and he leaves home. There are heavy loss feelings here. The sixth comes when the young adult marries, expanding the family by adding in-laws. The seventh is the advent of menopause in the woman. The eighth is the climacteric for the man. This crisis is unpredictable, and seems to spring more from the male's idea that he is losing his potency than with anything physical. The ninth comes with grandparenting, which is chock full of privileges and traps. Finally, the tenth comes when death comes to one of the spouses and then to the other.

The changes are normal and rapid. More change goes on in families at a quicker rate than in any other social group that I can think of. Three or four crises may cluster at once, and can indeed make life "worriable."

Frequently, this is when families come for help. If a family has not expected change or emerging differences, if they have cultivated a static condition and homogeneity, they run the risk of falling flat on their faces, and they do need help to get back up. People get born, grow big, work, marry, become parents, grow old and die. In my therapy I try to create awareness and increase communication skills to help families adjust and grow with the squeezes and stresses of life.

SUGGESTED READINGS

Ackerman, N. W.: Behavior trends and disturbances of the contemporary family. In Galdston, I. (Ed.): *The Family in Contemporary Society.* New York, International Universities Press, 1958.

Ackerman, N. W.: *The Psychodynamics of Family Life.* New York, Basic Books, 1958.

Ackerman, N. W.: *Treating the Troubled Family.* New York, Basic Books, 1966.

Ackerman, N. W., Beatman, F. L., and Sherman, S. N. (Eds.): *Exploring the Base for Family Therapy.* New York, Family Service Association of America, 1961.

Asch, S. E.: Studies of independence and conformity: A minority of one against a unanimous majority. *Psychological Monographs, 70:*1, 1956.

Bach, G., and Wyden, P.: *The Intimate Enemy: How to Fight Fair in Love and Marriage.* New York, William Morrow and Co., 1969.

Bateson, G.: Minimal requirements for a theory of schizophrenia. *Archives of General Psychiatry, 2:*477, 1960.

Bell, N. W., and Vogel, E. F.: The emotionally disturbed child as the family scapegoat. In Bell, N. W., and Vogel, E. F. (Eds.): *The Family.* Glencoe, Illinois, Free Press, 1960.

Bernhard, Y., and Bach, G.: *Aggression Lab: The Fair Fight Training Manual.* Dubuque, Iowa, Kendel-Hunt, 1971.

Birdwhistell, L.: The idealized model of the American family. *Social Casework, 51:*195, 1970.

Borke, H.: The communication of intent: A revised procedure for analysing family interaction from video tapes. *Journal of Marriage and the Family, 31:*541, 1969.

Bowen, M.: A family concept of schizophrenia. In Jackson, D. D. (Ed.): *The Etiology of Schizophrenia.* New York, Basic Books, 1960.

Brodey, W. M.: Some family operations of schizophrenia: A study of five hospitalized families each with a schizophrenic member. *Archives of General Psychiatry, 1:*379, 1959.

Calhoun, A. W.: *A Social History of the American Family.* Cleveland, Arthur H. Clarke Co., 1917.

Crow, M.: Preventive intervention through parent group education. *Social Casework, 48:*161, 1967.

Ferreira, A. J.: The "double bind" and delinquent behavior. *Archives of General Psychiatry, 3:*359, 1960.

Fleck, S.: Family dynamics and origin of schizophrenia. *Psychosomatic Medicine, 22:*333, 1960.

Foley, V. D.: Conceptual Roots of Conjoint Family Therapy: A Compara-

348 Basic Approaches to Group Psychotherapy

tive Analysis of Major Theorists. Unpublished doctoral dissertation, Boston University, 1971.

Fromm, E.: *The Art of Loving.* New York, Harper & Row, 1956.

Fry, W. F., and Heersema, P.: Conjoint Family Therapy: A new dimension in psychotherapy. *Topical Problems in Psychotherapy, 5:*147, 1963.

Haley, J.: The family of the schizophrenic: A model system. *Journal of Nervous and Mental Disease, 129:*357, 1959.

Haley, J., and Glick, I.: *Psychiatry and the Family: An Annotated Bibliography of Articles Published 1960-1964.* Palo Alto, Mental Research Institute, Family Process, 1965.

Jackson, D.: The question of family homeostatis. *Psychiatric Quarterly* (supplements), *31:*79, 1957.

Jackson, D.: The family and sexuality. In Whitaker, C. (Ed.): *The Psychotherapy of Chronic Schizophrenic Patients.* Boston, Little, Brown, 1958.

Jackson, D., and Weakland, J. H.: Conjoint Family Therapy, some considerations on theory, technique, and results. *Psychiatry, 24:*(No. 2 supplement) 30, 1961.

Leader, A. L.: Divorced fathers. *Social Casework, 54:*13, 1973.

McPherson, S. B., and Samuels, C. R.: Teaching behavioral methods to parents. *Social Casework, 52:*148, 1971.

Noble, T.: Family breakdown and social network. *British Journal of Sociology, 31:*135, 1970.

Olson, D. H.: Marital and family therapy: Integrative review and critique. *Journal of Marriage and the Family, 32:*501, 1970.

Satir, V. M.: Schizophrenia and family therapy. *Social Work Practice.* New York, Columbia University Press, 1963. (Published for National Conference on Social Welfare, Columbus, Ohio.)

Schul, G. L., and Leichter, E.: The prevention of family break-up. *Social Casework, 49:*143, 1968.

Spitzer, R. J., Jackson, D., and Satir, V.: A technique for training in Conjoint Family Therapy. American Psychiatric Association Meeting, Los Angeles, 1964.

Stackowiak, J. C.: Psychological disturbances in children, as related to disturbances in family interaction. *Journal of Marriage and the Family, 30:*123, 1968.

Sullivan, H. S.: Introduction to the study of interpersonal relations. *Psychiatry, 1:*121, 1938.

Tallman, I.: The family as a small problem solving group. *Journal of Marriage and the Family, 32:*94, 1970.

Watzlawick, P.: A structured family interview. *Family Process, 5:*256, 1966.

REFERENCES

Jackson, D. D., and Satir, V.: A method of analysis of a family interview. *Archives of General Psychiatry, 5:*321, 1961.

Satir, V.: *Conjoint Family Therapy.* Palo Alto, California, Science and Behavior Books, 1964.
Satir, V.: The family as a treatment unit. *Confina Psychiatrics, 8:*37, 1965.
Satir, V.: I am me. *Etcetera: A Review of General Semantics, 11:*463, 1970.
Satir, V.: Conjoint family therapy. In Gazda, G. M. (Ed.): *Proceedings of a Symposium on Family Counseling and Therapy.* Athens, Georgia, College of Education, University of Georgia, 1971(a).
Satir, V.: Symptomatology: A family production. In Howells, J. G. (Ed.): *Theory and Practice of Family Psychiatry.* New York, Brunner/Mazel, 1971(b).
Satir, V.: *Peoplemaking.* Palo Alto, California, Science and Behavior Books, 1972.

CHAPTER XIV

GROUP THERAPY WITH CHILDREN

Haim G. Ginott[1]

G ROUP THERAPY HAS ENJOYED increasing popularity both on the national and international scene. Two factors account for this phenomenon: (1) group therapy has evolved a systematic theory with principles and procedures that can be tested experimentally; and (2) community clinics and individual therapists felt compelled to initiate group treatment in order to meet the growing demands for service.

There is danger in this popularity. The assumption that therapy is either helpful *or* unhelpful is only half true. Therapy, like surgery, can be for better or for worse. Research (Truax and Carkhuff, 1964) indicates that a patient is seldom unaffected by treatment; he is either helped or hurt. This finding puts an awesome responsibility on every therapist: *primum non nocere,* first of all, do no damage. This dictum applies particularly to group therapists. The potential for help or harm is greater in a group. When groups are ill-composed they become not only ineffective but psychonoxious.

This is especially true of child group therapy. An adult can quit treatment when the group becomes too threatening. A child has no choice. He is referred to therapy by his parents or teachers, and remains in treatment as long as they see a need for it. In a poorly selected group, a child may be exposed to devastating experiences. A boy defeated by more capable siblings who is placed in a highly competitive group, will only learn again that he is "dumb." A child stigmatized because of racial or cultural background will only reencounter familiar ridicule in a prejudiced group. A runny-nosed, skinny boy, put in a rough group, will be stamped again as "sissy" and "shrimp." A treatment setting must not replicate the

1. Deceased—1973.

noxious elements of everyday life. Therapy must be a haven from persecution that fosters freedom from fear.

Problems of Selection and Grouping

Group play therapy is the treatment of choice for many children aged three to nine. Preadolescents who are too old for play therapy and too young for interview therapy are seen in different therapy settings (Ginott, 1961; Ginott, 1968; Slavson, 1943). Criteria for admission to group play therapy have been discussed at length by Ginott (1961; In press [b]). Only a resumé will be given here.

Anna Freud (1949) stated, "If infants are insecure and lacking in response owing to a basic weakness in their first attachment to mother, they will not gain confidence from being sent to a nursery group. Such deficiencies need attention from a single adult and are aggravated, not relieved, by the strain of group life" (p. 60). This statement holds true also for therapy groups. These children need individual treatment to strengthen their capacity to establish relationships and to form attachments.

Group therapy is based on the assumption that children will modify behavior in exchange for acceptance. The desire for acceptance stems from satisfactory primary relations with a mother (or substitute) who, by fulfilling the infant's needs, imprinted him with a craving for affection and approval. The basic prerequisite for admission to group therapy is a capacity (actual or potential) for social hunger (Slavson, 1943)–a need to be accepted by peers and a desire to attain status and maintain esteem in a group. In return for peer acceptance, the child is willing to modify impulses and change behavior. He begins to play, talk and behave like other group members.

A play-therapy group is never a random assembly. It requires planned design and complex construction. The final composition is a group in which children exert a remedial impact on each other. A therapeutic group should consist of children with dissimilar syndromes so that each child is exposed to persons and behavior different from and complementary to his own. An effeminate boy needs to identify with more masculine playmates. The dependent child needs the example of more self-reliant groupmates.

The withdrawn need more outgoing group members. Children who live in fantasy need more reality-oriented friends. Aggressive youngsters need groupmates who are strong but not belligerent. Infantile children need to be placed in a group of more mature youngsters. A diversity of remedial models and an atmosphere that invites emulation encourage and lead to corrective identifications.

Age and gender are important considerations in composing play therapy groups. Groupmates should not differ in age by more than twelve months. The shorter the span the better. Yet other considerations may take precedence over age. An infantile child may be assigned to a younger group and a belligerent child to an older group. As they grow in maturity and socialization, such children can be transferred to a group of their own age.

Preschool boys and girls can be placed in the same group. This pattern is in keeping with the general practice of our society. At this age there are no compelling reasons for separating the sexes in educational as well as in therapeutic groups. In kindergarten, boys and girls play together, take naps together and share the same toys and activities. They have a chance to learn about the differences between boys and girls. Mixed groups are especially important for sisterless boys and for brotherless girls.

Same-sex groups are indicated for children of school age. Again, this is in keeping with the practice of society. In school and in the scouts, boys and girls are expected to develop different interests and aspirations. Boys must achieve status in masculine activities, and girls in feminine pursuits. In therapy too, sexual identification of boys and girls needs to be encouraged by provision of models, interests and activities that are culturally differentiated as masculine and feminine.

Children of markedly different IQ's can be placed in the same group. Slow learners are not seriously handicapped in play therapy. Low scholastic ability is easily masked by high facility in the use of tools and materials. The extremely retarded, however, are assigned to more intellectually homogeneous groups.

Play-therapy groups are "open"; new children are accepted during the course of treatment. The reason is practical: children terminate or drop out of treatment and have to be replaced. The number of children in a play group should not exceed five. A larger group becomes overactive: too much happens at once. The therapist is unable to observe all the ongoing activities and to react to each child in light of his dynamics.

An effective play-therapy group affords children opportunities both for action and reflection. The tides of tension in a group must ebb and flow. A group composed only of acting-out children is contraindicated. Belligerent children reinforce each others' aggression, creating a continual state of agitation. A group composed only of quiet children is also unhelpful: it fails to create sufficient tension to bring into play each child's central dynamics. A balanced group is made up of several quiet children and not more than two who are aggressive.

Aims and Means

The aim of group therapy, as of all therapy, is to bring about enduring personality changes. The end result of successful therapy is a strengthened ego, a modified superego, and an enhanced self-image. The corrective elements are identical in all therapies; the effectiveness of a particular method depends on how these elements are utilized. In evaluating any treatment method, the following questions must be answered. Does the method

1. help or hinder the therapeutic relationships?
2. accelerate or retard catharsis?
3. aid or obstruct insight?
4. increase or diminish reality testing?
5. encourage or block sublimation?

Relationship

The presence of several children facilitates the establishment of a desired relationship between the therapist and each child. The group proves especially helpful during the initial phase of treatment. The first encounter with the therapist is often frightening to a small child. He is reluctant to separate from his mother, to follow a strange adult to an unfamiliar room. It is less threatening for him to enter the new situation in the company of two or three children of his own age. In individual therapy, it is not unusual for a child at his first sessions to feel ill at ease, withdraw into himself and spend the time without uttering a word or touching a toy. In group play therapy the presence of other children seems to diminish tension and stimulate participation. The group induces spontaneity in the children. They sense the permissiveness of the setting and the tolerance of the therapist more readily than they do in individual treatment.

The focus of treatment in group play therapy is the individual child. No group goals are set, and no group cohesion is sought. Each child may engage in activities unrelated to other members. Subgroups form and disband spontaneously according to changing needs and interests. Yet the impact of groupmates is an important element of treatment. The therapeutic process is enhanced when a child can be a giver and not only a receiver of attention and assistance. When four-year-old Andy lost his ball he started crying. Five-year-old Bruce said, "Don't cry Andy, I'll find it for you." Bruce stopped his own play, and looked for the missing ball. During the search he kept on assuring Andy that "everything will be all right."

Catharsis

Play therapy provides two media for catharsis, play and talk, so that each child can use his preferred symbolic language. In individual therapy, catharsis is mostly free associative. The child moves freely from activity to activity and from play to play. Seemingly unrelated activities, like verbal free associations, lead to themes about the child's core problems. Group play therapy has an advantage over individual treatment. In addition to free-associative catharsis, it provides also vicarious and induced catharsis. Many children participate covertly as spectators in activities that they crave but fear. A child may follow with eager eyes activities in which he would like to indulge. He is fascinated when another boy spanks a baby doll or stamps on a mother doll. Slowly, he will move from observation to participation. When one child comes forth with a daring activity, others in the group find it easier to do the same. Those who are afraid that "the ice is thin" find courage when they observe others gliding with impunity. The children help each other realize that the playroom is a safety zone where they can rest or roam without fear of dangerous drivers and traffic tickets.

"You can make as much noise as you want," said six-year-old Alan to a newcomer. "Honest, you can. This is our playroom."

Insight

The relation between insight and adjustment is complex. Many disturbed children have an uncanny grasp of their dynamics, whereas most normal youngsters have little insight into the motivation of their behavior. In therapy, children acquire a keener awareness of themselves and their relation to parents and peers. This insight is frequently derivative and nonverbal; it is attained without the aid of interpretations and explanations; it is often a result rather than a cause of improvement.

Groups are conducive to the attainment of derivative insight; self-knowledge is developed through experience in many relationships. In group therapy, children are compelled to reevaluate their behavior and personality in light of peer reactions. When a problem arises, the group forces a confrontation. The child must face the problem, reflect upon it and respond in the very situation that provoked the difficulty.

Grace, a talkative ten-year-old, was in therapy with two quiet girls. She dominated the scene with ceaseless jabber. One day Linda asked, "Why do you always talk so fast, Gracie?" Caught by surprise, Grace mumbled for a moment, and then said, "Because nobody listens to me, that's why. The minute I open my mouth, my mother says, 'Here she goes again!' " "Oh," said Linda, "That's too bad. But . . . we'll listen to you." Linda's question helped Grace face her problem and gain insight into its origin.

A group gives the therapist latitude to plan insight-provoking incidents. For example, when only one gun is provided for three children, conflict will most likely occur. The reaction to conflict enables the therapist to confront each child with his habitual, self-defeating behavior.

Individual therapy is conducive to insight gained through interpretations. Theoretically, interpretations and insights are indicated for neurotic children. Psychoneurosis is a result of unconscious conflicts over the handling of sexual and aggressive impulses towards parents. Though repressed, these conflicts are active and anxiety producing. Defenses and symptoms are formed to ward off anxiety, but the conflicts remain unresolved. Interpretations, properly timed and phrased, can bring insight and relief. Guilt and anxiety over libidinal and aggressive strivings are resolved when, in the security of the therapeutic relationship, repressed conflicts are gradually brought to the awareness of the ego and are worked through. This procedure is feasible only when the therapeutic relationship is intimate. Therefore, the treatment of choice for neurotic children is individual therapy (Ginott, In press [b]).

Character-disordered children, however, benefit little from verbal insight. Character is shaped by experience with persons and situations; it is not changed by words.

Unlike neurotic children, character-disordered youngsters do not suffer great inner stress. Their traits are ingrained, and their behavior is egosyntonic. They gain little from exploration of primary process thinking or from insight into their libidinal strivings. The specific therapeutic aim in treating these children is to build their ego and correct their character. This task cannot be accomplished through the use of insight. Character can be modified only by corrective experiences. This task requires contact that compels and presence that demonstrates. It requires not only a therapist that understands, but a peer group that make demands, offers remedial models and encourages corrective identifications. For the large number of young children who need ego repair and character correction, group play therapy is the treatment of choice.

Reality Testing

From the moment he enters treatment, the child tests the reality of the setting. He tests the reaction of the therapist, the response of the groupmates and the nature of the materials. Unlike individual treatment, group therapy provides a tangible social setting. The group constitutes a miniature society were social techniques can be discovered, rehearsed and mastered. Children compel each other to become aware of their responsibilities in interpersonal relations. Infantile feelings of omnipotence and magic are unmasked and modified by the group. Defensive children learn that they can shed defenses and still remain protected. The emotionally inhibited child learns that he can confide in peers and adults without getting hurt. The silent child learns that he can attain objectives by voicing his desires, and the driven child learns that "they are also served who only stand and wait."

The frustrations and satisfactions encountered in mastering new relations and activities have a direct bearing on the child's ego and self-image. Both are enhanced by realistic success and damaged by repeated failures.

The presence of several children in the room serves to anchor the treatment experience to the world of reality. The group engenders a realistic social outlook. Axline (1955, p. 622) asked, "If play therapy is an experience in self-exploration . . . how does the child learn to expand beyond his self-centeredness to a recognition and appreciation of others?" The answer is, for therapy to become an experience in social learning, children must be provided with activities and situations that demand meaningful interactions with others. Group therapy provides for this need.

In group play therapy, children are exposed to the reality of a friendly yet neutral adult, helpful yet demanding peers, attractive yet challenging materials and tools. In this setting, children are compelled to test themselves in relation to social actualities. For example, a setting that intentionally provides one hammer for several boys who work with wood, is likely to create learning situations.[2] The child who is driven to grab is helped by the therapist and peers to learn more socialized techniques of negotiation and persuasion. The therapeutic gains in this setting will be greater than in individual treatment, where such experiences cannot be encountered.

Sublimation

One of the aims of therapy is to help children develop sublimations that are compatible with society's demands and expectations. The capacity to accept some, repress few and sublimate many primitive urges is the mark of maturity.

---

2. Such frustrating situations may occasionally be planned to test progress, aid insight or spur learning.

Society does not give children much choice in relinquishing infantile gratifications. To infants, culture is cold and cruel. Instead of a soft breast, it offers a hard cup. Instead of instant relief and warm diapers, it offers a cold pot and demands for self-restraint. Civilization says "No" to the small child's greatest pleasures: no sucking of the thumb, no touching of the penis, no picking of the nose, no playing with feces. Children are forced to give up interest in body products as early as possible. This task is usually accomplished by punishment, which leads to repression.

Play therapy offers children opportunities to enjoy forbidden pleasures in acceptable ways. In therapy, children can experiment to their heart's content with sand, mud, paint, clay (brown, of course) and water. In their subconscious, every messy substance represents the real stuff. Play with these soft materials brings substitute satisfaction as well as consolation for the loss of the original pleasures.

Group play therapy provides children with a richer repertory of sublimatory activities than does individual therapy. In individual treatment, a young child may engage in the same activity session after session. For example, he may use water colors and never try finger paints, or he may sift sand and never make mud. This self-imposed play restriction may be due to lack of inventiveness or lack of security on the part of the child. Group play therapy reduces the child's propensity for repetitions. In a group, children teach each other to employ different materials and to engage in a variety of activities, thus increasing each child's stock of sublimatory outlets.

Unlike individual treatment, group therapy provides opportunities for competitive games and for venting hostility against symbolic siblings. In the initial phase of treatment, children displace hostility: they attack, meddle, and interfere. As therapy progresses, sublimations appear. Instead of splashing paint, children color pictures; instead of throwing blocks, they build houses; instead of attacking each other, they shoot at targets. The competitive activities in the playroom reduce sibling rivalry at home.

The Physical Setting

The physical setting is of crucial importance in child group therapy. This fact is not always recognized by those who work mainly with adults in verbal treatment. The room and the equipment influence the therapeutic process for better or for worse. A small room compels unwelcome proximity, causing frustration and irritation. Forced propinquity engenders hostility and intensifies defenses. In a cramped playroom, isolated children withdraw further into themselves, and aggressive children attack others. An auditorium-size room is also contraindicated: it invites wild running and rough play from aggressive children, and it permits withdrawn children to avoid contact with the therapist and groupmates.

The group playroom should be neither too small nor too large. A room of about four-hundred square feet is adequate for group play therapy. The playroom should be soundproofed to preserve confidentality and to tone down noise.

In planning a playroom, every effort should be made to minimize the possibility of physical injury to children. The room should have small windows and no glass doors. Lights, windows, and one-way mirrors should be protected with wire mesh. The walls should be sturdy and readily repaintable; the floor should be waterproofed and unwaxed. The furniture must be functional and hard to break. Office desks with stuffed drawers, decorated chairs, telephones and personal books, have no place in a playroom. Their protection calls for the setting of too many limits and conflicts with the therapist's ability to maintain free-floating attention.

THE THERAPEUTIC ENCOUNTER

Into a room full of toys and play materials enter three, four or five young children. They may be aggressive or submissive, talkative or silent, infantile or pseudomature. They may exhibit conduct disorders, neurotic syndromes or psychosomatic reactions. Regardless of symptom, however, they have something in common: to their parents they are problem children who must change.

This very expectation is perceived by the child as rejection. He senses that at least part of himself is considered bad, ugly and undesired. The therapeutic antidote to this partial rejection is total acceptance. Like fresh air, it should permeate the atmosphere. Even before the therapist meets the children, this attitude is conveyed to their parents. The therapist helps them with preparation for separation—he assists in formulating a nonthreatening announcement about the forthcoming treatment.

"We made arrangements for you to come to a playroom to play."

"Why?"

"Because it's good for children. It helps them understand themselves better."

This brief statement is more helpful than the following long explanations which focus on symptoms: "You have been wetting the bed, you bite your nails and you are always in trouble in school. You need help! Maybe a psychologist can straighten you out."

If the child protests, a longer explanation, also unhelpful, usually follows: "When you have a toothache, you go to a dentist. When you have heart trouble, you go to a heart specialist. When you have mental problems, you go to a psychologist."

The parent's concentration on symptoms intensifies the child's defenses and increases his resistance to therapy.

The therapist accepts each child as he is. When the child enters the playroom, he is *not* bombarded with words. He is *not* met with questions or long explanations. He is *not* asked, "Do you know why you are here?" (Implication: "You would not be here if there were not something wrong with you.") He is *not* told, "Your mother said you got problems and I want to help you." (Implication: "He is in cahoots with mother, be careful!") The therapist does not promise easy friendship nor does he plead for quick confessions. ("I'm your friend, I wish you would tell me what bothers you.") The therapist knows that a child does not come for treatment because he feels troubled. Someone else thinks so—parent, teacher or judge. The child is a captive customer forced into treatment against his will. To him the referring adult may seem sick and in need of help, and often he is not altogether wrong.

The Therapeutic Opening

The therapist's gambit is free of negative implications. He does not begin a new relationship by spotlighting problematic conduct, symptoms or character traits. He knows from experience that young children can grow and change without confessing loudly that they have problems. The therapist's opening statements aim to convey to each child the unique nature of the therapeutic relationship. Essentially, the therapist would have liked to say, "In here you may feel free to express yourself fully—in words and play, in your own time and in your own way. You will be accepted and respected regardless of what you may feel, think, say or do." However, a child cannot understand such a complicated speech, and even if he did understand, he would not believe it. The meaning of therapy can be conveyed only by experience, not by explanation. At the start, the therapist can only inadequately convey his basic attitude by saying, "You can play with these toys all you like during this hour." It takes time for children to grasp the full meaning of this statement. Through experience, slowly, they become aware that it signifies a new freedom to be what they are and become what they can.

The therapist knows that disturbed children need to express many repressed feelings towards family members and authority figures. He accepts the hypothesis that emotional problems stem from faulty experiences in child-parent-sibling relations. His aim is to enable children to experience corrective relationships with an adult as a substitute parent and with peers as substitute siblings. However, the children are not easily convinced that the therapist is different from other adults they have known. They respond to his good will with reactions typical of their past. The submissive child, who habitually relates to adults with compliance, will try to ingratiate himself with the therapist. He will offer to clean the playroom, share candy, or draw pictures for the therapist. The dependent child, who has known love only when helpless, will continue to act cute and meek to gain the therapist's attention. The "wise-guy," who has learned to exploit adults, will try to manipulate the therapist.

The therapist's reactions vary according to the child's history and nuclear problems. To the child's obsequious offer of help, the therapist responds with a neutral comment: "If you want to." His aim is to convey to the child that in this relationship there is no need to be ingratiating and self-effacing. The "angelic" child soon learns that the therapist does not respond to cuteness. The child begins to sense that more mature modes of relating are expected. Provocative children, who invite rejection and criticism, are shocked when the therapist consistently responds with calm acceptance. Their past experience has conditioned them to expect from adults punishment, direction and control. The failure to elicit these familiar responses confuses them. The lack of censure is as unreal to them as would be a sudden removal of gravity. They attempt to verify their picture of adults by "egging" the therapist into anger. They commit acts that in the past brought condemnation and punishment. They "accidently" spill mud on the floor, splash paint on the wall, break a bottle and make a deafening noise. The therapist must be able to bear, without excessive strain, the trying behavior. He may draw comfort from the knowledge that the testing of his permissiveness signifies the beginning of the therapeutic process.

Permissiveness and Limits

The permissiveness of the therapist inevitably engenders regressive behavior in the group. At this phase of treatment regression is anticipated and permitted. However, it is neither encouraged nor sanctioned. It is accepted as a necessary stage in the child's process of recovery. The therapist must be lucidly aware what the permissiveness is and what it is not. If he is restrictive, regression will be hampered and so will improvement. If he unwittingly supports regression, he will encourage endless infantile behavior.

Permissiveness does not mean the acceptance without restrictions of *all behavior,* destructive as it may be. Permissiveness means the acceptance without limits of all *symbolic behavior,* be it hostile, sexual, sadistic or masochistic. All feelings, fantasies, thoughts, wishes, passions, dreams and desires–regardless of their content–are accepted, respected and allowed expression through words and play. Direct acting out of destructive behavior is not permitted. When it occurs, the therapist intervenes and directs it into symbolic outlets.

The unfulfillable nature of some urges makes unavoidable the setting of limits on direct acting out. Certain acts (murder, incest, stealing, vandalism) are absolutely forbidden in our society. They may not be performed in therapy either, except in effigy. Symbolic play enables children to channel even destructive and incestuous urges into harmless outlets.

A child with Oedipal problems may undress and explore a mother doll. Obviously he may not act so toward his mother or his therapist. A child who is angry with his therapist may not hit him. He may draw ugly pictures of him and shoot at them, or he may kick, throw, stab or step on any doll that represents him. By setting limits, the therapist helps the child to express hostility safely. By encountering therapeutic limits, the child learns to distinguish between wishes and deeds. He learns that he may feel all his feelings, but may not act always as he pleases. By preventing undesirable acts while accepting hostile feelings, the therapist reduces the child's guilt and increases his mastery of reality. The child learns that his impulses are not dangerous, that they do no harm and therefore need not be so rigidly inhibited. By mastering a variety of symbolic outlets for aggression, the child learns to accept and control impulses without excessive stress or guilt (Ginott, 1965).

Physical Fighting

During the initial phase of child group therapy, physical fights are likely to break out. Should the therapist intervene and stop the fighting? Opinions differ. Despert (1945, p. 223) allows fighting in the playroom. The rationale is that limits on physical attacks may seem to the child "equivalent to censorship–the type of which is often the basis of his own problems." Slavson (1943) allows fighting among older children in activity groups but not among young children in play groups. He believes that young children need external restraint when they are overaggressive. "Unless . . . checked by someone outside themselves, their aggressiveness gains momentum and increases in intensity" (1943, p. 160). Axline (1947), too, believes that "the ruling out of physical attacks should be one of the limitations of group therapy" (p. 137). Some therapists allow aggressive fights but keep them under control by serving as referees. This practice is undesirable; it turns the therapist into a judge, a role which invites resentment and hostility.

There is little therapeutic gain in allowing children to attack each other physically. Besides the obvious danger of injury, such attacks merely serve to displace aggression from original to substitute siblings. It is more therapeutic to channel aggressive impulses into symbolic actions against family dolls and inflated clowns, and into competitive games and rivalrous play. It must be stressed that the limit on physical fighting among children is not so cut and dried as the limit prohibiting attack on the therapist. A light slap or a mild fight are regarded as normal by children, and the therapist's hurried interferences may be resented. He may appear overprotective and partial. Therefore it is wise to delay setting the limit until some fighting has occurred. The therapist may then intervene and say, "I see it's not play, but a fight. The playroom is for playing, not for fighting." He will then point out acceptable ways of venting anger. "It is easy to see that you are angry at each other. You may draw ugly pictures of each other on the board and shoot at them. You may tell me in words what you think of each other, or you may record what you feel, on the tape recorder." If fighting breaks out again, the therapist will repeat the limit adding, tongue in cheek, "There will be no bloodshed in this playroom; quarrels have to be settled in some other way."

The therapist should be alert to pick up the feelings of all the children involved in the fight, the bully as well as the victim. His tone of voice should be free of criticism, and his choice of words should preserve the children's self-respect. The therapeutic process requires that the therapist consistently adhere to his role as a firm though kindly figure in whom the child can find an ally for his struggling ego.

In dealing with a child who has broken a limit, the therapist must maintain a calm authority and must not become argumentative and verbose. He must not be drawn into an intellectual discussion about the fairness of the limit, nor should he give the child a long rationale for it. It is unnecessary to explain to a child why he must not hit the therapist, beyond saying that "people are not for hurting," or why he must not break the window, beyond saying that "windows are not for breaking." A limit not only conveys a restriction; it also asserts a desirable human value.

Defiant youngsters who insist on breaking limits and attacking the therapist or groupmates may be transferred to a group of older children. Instead of continuing their defiance, such children will most likely look for the therapist's friendship as a protection against the actual or anticipated aggression of the other children. The older group members convey directly and without ceremony that limits must be observed.

When should limits be presented? Some therapists believe that limits should be stated at the outset of treatment so that children will not be confronted with them unexpectedly. This writer is of the opinion that limits should not be mentioned before the need for them arises. There is little advantage in starting a relationship by invoking prohibitions on actions that may never occur. The listing of limits may challenge the aggressive children and inhibit the submissive ones.

When Tommy, an eight-year-old Negro boy, first entered the playgroup, he was told by his therapist, "You may play with the toys any way you want to, but you may not hit me or break toys." Tommy became upset and said, "Oh, no sir. I'd never think of hitting you." Tommy hardly touched a toy during the next few sessions.

A group play therapist can expect unpredictable behavior in the playroom. From the start, he must be able to deal effectively with emergencies. Many playroom crises can be forestalled if the therapist knows which limits are necessary and if he has a clear rationale and effective methods for implementing them. For a more comprehensive discussion of this theory as well as the practice of limits, the reader is referred to Ginott (1961).

THE THERAPIST

The capacity to be empathic with youngsters is the outstanding requirement for all child therapists. Group play therapists must be young at heart; they cannot be overly dry and gravely serious.

They must have some of those irrational qualities of youth that enable adults to stand, withstand and understand children. A child therapist must be free of the conventional reactions to dirt, destruction, noise, hostility and profanity.

Therapists with strong needs for order, neatness and decorum encounter difficulties in group play therapy. Despite their efforts to be accepting, they experience anxiety and react with embarrassment. They try to be permissive, but their vicera will not permit it. They can tolerate dirt, destruction and derogatory words for a short while only. When such provocations persist, they experience within themselves anger and disgust. They reach the brink of their endurance. In psychotherapy as in politics, brinkmanship is fraught with danger. The need for constant self-restraint exhausts their energy and leaves them emotionally and physically drained. Not infrequently, they leave the field of child therapy.

Some therapists who come from punitive homes tend to feel resentment toward all parents. It is difficult for them to remain objective when a case history reveals excessive parental cruelty (e.g., a mother punishing a boy with polio by taking away his crutches and rendering him helpless, or a mother of a little girl, who said, "If you want her to obey, take off her glasses. She is blind without them and she'll do anything you say."). Therapy aims to relieve children of their hatred. A therapist who is antagonistic toward parents may unwittingly reinforce a child's hostility towards his family. Parents often sense the therapist's negative attitudes and withdraw their children from treatment.

Some child therapists are imbued with a missionary zeal and a "rush-to-the-rescue" attitude. These "rapport-chasing" adults adore little children but they make poor therapists. In therapy they assume a manner of extreme kindness. They praise the children profusely and show admiration for any trivial act. They even grant direct erotic gratification by indulging in hugging and kissing and other such playful games. Such ardent attempts to become intimate with children fail to inspire confidence and elicit friendship. The excessive show of warmth only serves to increase anxiety in children accustomed to rejection. Direct advances are especially threatening to children with Oedipal conflicts who are overwhelmed when a love object attempts to get too close. Such children need a strong positive relationship with an adult who is willing to remain at a safe distance. A less imposing therapist enables children to form attachments at their own pace.

Some therapists find it difficult to be empathic with bullying, screaming or runny-nosed children, while others overreact to the weak and the meek. A therapist cannot be expected to have the same feelings toward all children. Mild variations in feeling towards patients is a normal phenomenon. Some children are interesting, while others are tiring. These mild likes and dislikes do not hinder treatment if the therapist is objective about his nonobjectivity and makes an effort to resolve his biases.

However, when a child's behavior so gnaws at the therapist that it affects his capacity for empathy, it is best that the child be referred to someone else. The therapist himself may need some help. Therapeutic empathy must be independent of love for a particular child. Mature empathy is an outcome of the therapist's abiding faith in the process of growth and in the catalytic role that he plays in the unfolding of potentialities.

ACTIVITY GROUP THERAPY

For a highly selected number of children (ages 8-12), Slavson (1943; 1947) has originated activity group therapy. It is a form of ego therapy which deals mostly with behavior disorders and character correction, and not with psychosis and intense psychoneurosis.

Briefly, the pattern of an activity group is as follows: Five to eight boys (or girls) meet weekly for a two-hour session in a large and simply furnished room that contains tools and materials for arts and crafts as well as individual and group games. The atmosphere of the setting is distinctly permissive, and the children can use the tools and materials for constructive or destructive activity. They can work or be idle, play or fight, isolate themselves or run in packs, do homework or read comics. A glimpse at an ongoing session might show several children working with tools–sawing wood or making ashtrays–two children playing ping-pong, one child sitting in the corner away from the group, another hammering on the wall, and one running around the room and interfering with the activities of the others.

The therapist in activity groups is neutral and permissive. He does not assign tasks or settle conflicts. Unlike a play therapist, he neither interprets nor sets limits. As a passive participant, he observes and registers the meaning of the behavior of each child and the interactions in the group as a whole. He knows the history of each child, and is attuned to his unique problems. The therapist's attitudes and behavior convey an image of strength. He is calm and collected in face of turbulence. He demonstrates tolerance in face of frustration. He is helpful, friendly and firm. In short, he serves as a desirable identification model and an ego ideal. The role of the therapist is of decisive importance in this form of treatment. Therapy relies primarily on identification and activity, rather than on verbalization.

The materials supplied in these groups include "hammers, saws, wood of various sizes, clay, water colors, copper and pewter dishes, molds for making ashtrays and large sheets of paper [and] . . . equipment for the cooking of simple refreshments" (Slavson, 1955, p. 145). Girls' activity groups are provided with materials for sewing, knitting, weaving, basketry, beadwork, leatherwork and similar crafts.

The physical setting of the activity room is of importance. A room of about six hundred square feet is considered optimal in size. Slavson (1943) suggests "the empirical formula that the activity room should be five times the area of furniture necessary for work" (p. 145). The following furniture is recommended: a long rectangular table (7 x 3 feet) and a small "Isolate" table (3 x 2 feet) for the child who wants to work by himself, a round table where the children can get together for refreshments, a woodwork bench with two vises, a cabinet for supplies and for storing unfinished projects and a pegboard for tools.

The Clientele

The choice and grouping of clientele is of decisive importance in activity group therapy. The optimum number of children in an activity group is six. The number can be increased to eight at later stages of treatment. The age distribution within an activity group is a two-year span. A balanced group is made up of instigators (children who activate the group constructively or destructively), neutralizers (those who check aggression and help establish equilibrium), social neuters (those who exert little effect on the group), and isolates (those who stay by themselves, withdrawn from the group). A balanced group should contain two aggressive and three withdrawn children, and three youngsters who fall between these two extremes.

The basic requirement for admission to activity group therapy is a capacity for social hunger. If a child is truly indifferent to what others think of him, he has little motivation for change. Such a child may enjoy the activity group, but he will not be cured by it. Children with no inner controls are also not suited for this form of treatment. They need more structure, restraint and limits (Ginott, 1959; 1961) and would be traumatized by the permissiveness of the activity group.

Children with strong sexual ties to their parents are not suitable candidates for activity group therapy. Those with intense incestuous wishes are best helped in individual analytic therapy. They need a stronger transference and more verbal exploration than the activity group alone can provide. Also excluded from activity group therapy are children with marked deviation in conduct or symptoms: the overly sadistic and masochistic, the brain-damaged, the physically crippled and the sexually perverted. Activity group therapy is suited primarily for children who are relatively overcontrolled or undercontrolled, but it is not suited for either of these extremes. It is a treatment of choice for children with infantile, effeminate or schizoid character, the mildly neurotic and those with reactive behavior disorders.

Slavson (1943) recommends activity group therapy for clinical settings only, not for residential institutions. In institutions, the proximity between treatment and residence results in a too-great carryover of behavior from one setting to the other. The unconditional permissiveness of activity group therapy engenders relaxation of inner controls and temporary regression which cannot be tolerated in everyday community living.

SUMMARY

Group play therapy is the treatment of choice for many young children aged three to nine. The chapter discusses problems of selection and grouping and offers guidelines for admission. The aim of group play therapy is defined and the identifiable variables common to all therapy are listed. The unique contributions of group play therapy to the establishment of a therapeutic relationship, to the evocation of catharsis, to the derivation of insight, to the testing of reality, and to the development of sublimations are pointed out and evaluated. The physical setting suitable for group play therapy is outlined. The implication of permissiveness and the application of limits are discussed at length. Attention is called to the qualities of an effective group play therapist. The chapter also discusses activity group therapy–a treatment method suited for a strictly selected group of older children.

REFERENCES

Axline, Virginia M.: *Play Therapy*. Boston, Houghton, 1947.

Axline, Virginia M.: Play therapy procedures and results. *American Journal of Orthopsychiatry, 25:*618, 1955.

Despert, J. Louise: Play analysis. In Nolan, N. D. C., and Pacella, B. L. (Eds.): *Modern Trends in Child Psychiatry*. New York, International U. P., 1945.

Freud, Anna: Nursery school education: Its use and dangers. *Child Study, 26:*35, 1949.

Ginott, H. G.: The theory and practice of "therapeutic intervention" in child treatment. *Journal of Consulting Psychology, 23:*160, 1959.

Ginott, H. G.: *Group Psychotherapy with Children*. New York, McGraw, 1961.

Ginott, H. G.: *Between Parent and Child*. New York, Macmillan, 1965.

Ginott, H. G.: Innovations in group psychotherapy with preadolescents. In Gazda, G. M. (Ed.): *Innovations to Group Psychotherapy*. Springfield, Illinois, Charles C Thomas, 1968.

Ginott, H. G.: Interpretations and child therapy. In Hammen, E. F. (Ed.): *Interpretation in Therapy: Its Role, Scope, Depth, Timing and Art*. New York, Grune, in press (b).

Slavson, S. R.: *An Introduction to Group Therapy*. New York, The Commonwealth Fund and Harvard U. P., 1943.

Slavson, S. R. (Ed.): *The Practice of Group Therapy*. New York, International U. P., 1947.

Slavson, S. R.: Group psychotherapies. In McCary, J. L. (Ed.): *Six Approaches to Psychotherapy.* New York, Dryden, 1955.

Truax, C. B., and Carkhuff, R. R.: For better or for worse: The process of psychotherapeutic personality change. In Wigdon, Blossom T. (Ed.): *Recent Advances in Behavior Change.* Montreal, McGill U. P., 1964.

SUGGESTED READING

For a more detailed presentation of group therapy with children, see Ginott, H. G.: *Group Psychotherapy with Children: The Theory and Practice of Play Therapy.* New York, McGraw, 1961.

PART III

GROUP
COUNSELING

CHAPTER XV

GROUP COUNSELING: A DEVELOPMENTAL APPROACH[1]

George M. Gazda

IN FIGURE 1 BELOW the relationship among various group procedures is illustrated. These relationships have also been supported by means of a survey of group experts (Gazda, Duncan, and Sisson, 1971). Group experts who responded to a questionnaire did not make clear differentiations among group counseling, encounter groups, T-groups, and sensitivity groups. That is, they defined them similarly based on such criteria as type of clientele served, degree of disturbance of clientele, setting of the treatment, goals of treatment, size of group, and length and duration of treatment. These groups, however, were viewed as distinctly different from guidance groups and therapy groups. More specifically, they were in the middle of the continuum shown in Figure 1, i.e., they

1. Parts of this chapter are reproduced from Gazda, G. M. *Group Counseling: A Developmental Approach,* 1971. Courtesy of Allyn and Bacon, Inc., Boston, Massachusetts.

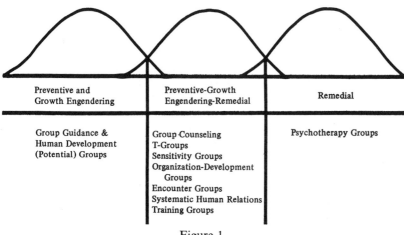

Preventive and Growth Engendering	Preventive-Growth Engendering-Remedial	Remedial
Group Guidance & Human Development (Potential) Groups	Group Counseling T-Groups Sensitivity Groups Organization-Development Groups Encounter Groups Systematic Human Relations Training Groups	Psychotherapy Groups

Figure 1.

375

were viewed as partially remedial, partially growth-engendering and partially preventive. Guidance groups were viewed as preventive and therapy groups as remedial.

Group counseling has been defined as follows:

> Group counseling is a dynamic interpersonal process focusing on conscious thought and behavior and involving the therapy functions of permissiveness, orientation to reality, catharsis, and mutual trust, caring, understanding, acceptance, and support. The therapy functions are created and nurtured in a small group through the sharing of personal concerns with one's peers and the counselor(s). The group counselees are basically normal individuals with various concerns which are not debilitating to the extent requiring extensive personality change. The group counselees may utilize the group interaction to increase understanding and acceptance of values and goals and to learn and/or unlearn certain attitudes and behaviors (Gazda, Duncan, and Meadows, 1967, p. 305).

Group counseling is perhaps best differentiated from group therapy at the same time that both are defined by Brammer and Shostrom's (1960) use of a series of adjectives in which counseling is described as

> educational, supportive, situational, problem-solving, conscious awareness, emphasis on "normals," and short-term. Psychotherapy is characterized by supportive (in a more particular sense), reconstructive, depth analysis, analytical, focus on the unconscious, emphasis on "neurotics" or other severe emotional problems, and long-term (1960, p. 6).

Although these differentiations were applied to individual counseling and psychotherapy, they are equally applicable to group counseling and group psychotherapy.

Eddy and Lubin (1971) have defined sensitivity [group] training, T-group, and encounter groups as follows.[2]

> 1. Sensitivity [group] training: Sensitivity training is one of the first and most generic terms in the field. It originally referred to the small group training conducted by the National Training Labora-

---

2. From Eddy, W. B., and Lubin, B.: Laboratory training and encounter groups. *Personnel and Guidance Journal, 49:*(8), 625, 1971. Courtesy of the *Personnel and Guidance Journal.*

tories. Currently, it is used by some to subsume all small group training approaches. However, most practitioners do not find it a useful term because it is frequently used so broadly (to include group therapy, for example) that it has lost its power to define (p. 627).

Eddy and Lubin recommend the use of the term laboratory training over sensitivity training because

> . . . it is used to refer to an educational method that emphasizes experience-based learning activities. Participants are involved in a variety of experiences, usually including small group interaction, and their behavior provides data for learning. Thus laboratory training involves learning by doing. The subject matter of such programs deals with some aspect of human interaction, and the goal is to be more aware of and responsive to what is going on. A specific laboratory training program may run from a few hours to two or more weeks and may contain a combination of elements designed to provide experiential learning. . . . (p. 627).

2. T-group

> A basic element of most laboratories is the *T-group* (T for training). In the standard NTL-type of T-group, participants find themselves in a relatively unstructured environment in which their responsibility is to build out of their interaction a group that can help them meet their needs for support, feedback, learning, etc. The behaviors exhibited by members as they play out their roles provide the material for analysis and learning. Thus, T-group members have the opportunity of learning ways in which their behavior is seen by others in the group, the kinds of roles, ways of being more sensitive to the feelings and behaviors of other group members, methods for understanding group behavior dynamics, etc. Time is usually provided for trainees to integrate what they have learned and plan to apply their new knowledge after the laboratory ends (p. 627).

3. Encounter groups

> *Encounter groups,* as we define the term, refers to intensive small group experiences in which the emphasis is upon personal growth through expanding awareness, exploration of intrapsychic as well as interpersonal issues, and release of dysfunctional inhibitions. There is relatively little focus on the group as a learning instrument; the trainer takes a more active and directive role;

and physical interaction is utilized. Other modes of expression and sensory exploration such as dance, art, massage, and nudity are currently being tried as a part of the encounter experience (pp. 627-628).

4. Organizational Development groups

Although Organizational Development (OD) groups was a category not included in the survey (Gazda, Duncan, and Sisson, 1971) cited previously, this procedure has its origin in laboratory training group procedures and would likely be placed in the same area of the continuum as the T-group. Golembiewski (1972) has characterized OD as follows:

> OD basically reflects a variety of group-oriented strategies for conscious and deliberate change in social systems. In essence, changes in group level phenomena such as social norms and values are seen as the primary motivators of organizational change, via their influence on the behaviors of individuals (p. 13).

5. Systematic Human Relations Training

According to Carkhuff (1971), systematic human relations training

> . . . derives from the systematic application of training to those ingredients or conditions found to be effective in all helping and human relationships. Basically, the model indicates that all human relationships, including counseling and teaching, may have constructive consequences. The dimensions which can be rated to account for human effectiveness include responsive conditions (responding to another person's experience) such as empathic understanding, respect and specificity of expression, and initiative dimensions (initiating from one's own experience) such as genuineness, confrontation and interpretations of immediacy.
>
> Systematic human relations training, then, involves a systematic step-by-step succession of reinforcing experiences in which the trainee learns to communicate first the responsive dimensions then the initiative dimensions. The trainees also learn systematic problem-solving activities in order to enable them to help their helpees to develop courses of action (p. 231).

A DEVELOPMENTAL APPROACH

Heretofore, no systematic attempt has been made to provide an approach to *group counseling* that was applicable to all age levels.

Previous attempts have "singled out" methods of group counseling with children, with adolescents, or with adults. Slavson (1945), however, long ago recognized the need for differential treatment for different age groups in *group therapy.* "Group therapy," he said, "is practiced on different levels, and in discussing its functions in therapy, it is necessary that these levels be kept in mind" (p. 201).

My experience also has demonstrated the need for a position that allows for and accommodates a different emphasis with different age groups in group counseling. The developmental approach to group counseling, therefore, utilizes the developmental task concept (Havighurst, 1948, 1952, 1953) with subsequent coping behaviors, to serve as broad guidelines for the group counselor. Havighurst defines developmental task as follows:

> A developmental task is a task which arises at or about a certain period in the life of the individual, successful achievement of which leads to his happiness and to success with later tasks, while failure leads to unhappiness in the individual, disapproval by society, and difficulty with later tasks (1952, p. 2).

Havighurst (1952) also cites two reasons the concept of developmental task is useful to educators. His reasons seem equally applicable to counselors and counseling: "First, it helps in discovering and stating the purpose of education [group counseling] efforts" (p. 5). He describes timing to mean *teachable moment* (1952, p. 5). Readiness for group counseling is determined by the dissonance between the developmental task and its subsequent coping behavior.

Zaccaria (1965) gives a more comprehensive interpretation of developmental tasks than does Havighurst. His interpretation includes Havighurst's (1952) "bio-socio-psychological" emphasis, the "vocational developmental" emphasis of Super *et al.* (1957, 1963), and Erikson's (1950, 1959, 1963) "psychosocial crises." Since Zaccaria's description of the developmental tasks concept is more inclusive than Havighurst's I have utilized all three approaches in developing the guidelines for use by the counselor in assessing an individual's progress along his developmental pathways. Difficulty with the mastery of a developmental stage signals to the parent, teacher, counselor, and significant others that assistance or corrective action is necessary. Group counseling through the approach I have outlined in this chapter should help to provide this assistance.

Our society and much of western culture is organized on the basis of an expected progressive development in the biological, sociological, and psychological realms of its citizens and, as such, the concept of developmental task has general applicability. For example, our schools are organized on a preschool and kindergarten, early elementary school, middle school, and high school basis; state laws govern marriageable ages of its citizens; federal laws govern legal retirement age; and so forth (Muuss, 1962).

Although there are wide ranges in the biological, social, and psychological development of individuals, there are classifiable periods between and within age groups. Several individuals (Blocher, 1966; Brammer and Shostrom, 1960; Erikson, 1950; Havighurst, 1952; Super *et al.,* 1957, 1963) have developed various classification schemes for the developmental phases. For group counseling purposes, the phases can be divided into (1) early childhood or preschool and early school, ages 5-9; (2) preadolescent, ages 9-13; (3) adolescent, ages 13-20; and (4) adult. That there is sometimes considerable overlap between age groups, is well documented. There is also a special discrepancy between the sexes at the end of the latency period and beginning of pubescence–beginning between ages 8-13 for girls and 10-15 for boys. The group counselor, therefore, must be alert to individual differences and organize his groups to accommodate them. Since "Little is known as to what the values of a group to a child of 3 or 4 may be" (Slavson, 1945, p. 203), the emphasis of my approach begins with the kindergarten child of age five.

Systematic Human Relations Training, *a la* Carkhuff (1969ab), provides a theoretically and empirically sound method for training those professionals, e.g., teachers, who are not technically included among the "helping" professionals. When combined with the rationale and methodology of Developmental Group Counseling, it makes possible the training of "functional professionals" (Carkhuff, 1970). Now this combined application of Carkhuff's Systematic Human Relations Training with Developmental Group Counseling is of vital importance because it makes possible the extension of Developmental Group Counseling through *functional professionals* (i.e., persons who do not have the paper credentials –certificates, degrees, or licenses–but who are in fact capable of serving as facilitators or helpers) to the culturally different, the educationally deficient and even the mentally retarded.

The typical group counselor today is a middle-class WASP. He will be unable in many instances to transcend the racial, cultural, ethnic, economic, etc., barriers between himself and many who desperately need counseling assistance. Thus he must extend his role of group counselor to group trainer also. In this role he can be prepared to be guided by the basic tenets of Developmental Group Counseling (Gazda, 1971) and Systematic Human Relations Training (Gazda *et al.,* 1973; Gazda, Walters, and Childers, in press). For example, he will very often be alien, if not alienated, to the Black Community as a whole. Nevertheless, there will be those within the Black Community who could serve as functional professionals to reach those beyond the reach of a middle-class WASP. Somewhat analogous to AA and Synanon, volunteers from within a given cultural or problem area (e.g., the Black Community, alienated youth, etc.), must be given training to function as facilitators or helpers.

The expressed effort to go through others who are capable of reaching and assisting the culturally different, etc., is an example of "reaching" them by moving through media (persons, in this case) that are most "natural" to them whether or not their problem or potential problem is the result of inadequate coping behavior for a given developmental task or an alienated feeling towards those of different color, age-group, or economic condition.

In addition to stressing the necessity of reaching others through "functional professionals," the Developmental model described herein focuses on the need to utilize activities and media that are most natural to a given group–especially age-group, but also ethnic, socio-economic, etc., group. Therefore, the potential group leader must be flexible enough and skilled enough to substitute an active sport or game such as basketball for a chess game for ghetto youth if he expects to approach or "reach" them through *activities* that are natural/comfortable for them.

DYNAMICS OF GROUPS

Leadership

Counselor's Ability to Help

Truax (1969) reported that one-third of trained professionals functioning in roles purported to be "helping" such as psychiatrists, counselors, social workers, etc., did in fact help their clients or persons seeking help from them; one-third actually harmed their clients; and one-third had no measurable positive or negative effect. And he concluded that the more helpers we train with our old methods the farther behind we are getting. Further evidence to corroborate Truax's conclusion is presented in Truax and Carkhuff (1967), Carkhuff and Berenson (1967), and Carkhuff (1969ab).

Essentially, the conclusion has been reached that traditional methods of preparing professionals in the field of human relations have not been at all effective and that considerably more care should be shown in certifying professional helpers. Carkhuff (1969a) has outlined the most comprehensive method to date for the selection and training of both lay and professional helpers. His conclusion, based on a vast amount of research (Berenson and Carkhuff, 1967; Carkhuff, 1969a, 1969b; Carkhuff and Berenson, 1967; Truax and Carkhuff, 1967; Rogers, Gendlin, Kiesler and Truax, 1967) suggests that the effective counselor or helper must offer high levels of the facilitative or "core" conditions of *empathy, warmth,* and *respect* as well as the more action- and activity-oriented conditions of *concreteness, genuineness,* appropriate *self-disclosure, confrontation,* and *immediacy* (Carkhuff, 1969a, p. 21).

Truax and Carkhuff (1967, p. 1) described the effective counselor as integrated, nondefensive, and authentic or *genuine* in his therapeutic encounter. They also described him as one who provides a non-threatening, safe, trusting, or secure atmosphere by his acceptance, unconditional positive regard, love or *nonpossessive warmth* for the client. And finally, he is able to "be with," "grasp the meaning of," or *accurately* and *empathically* understand the client on a moment-by-moment basis.

The qualities of the most effective encounter group leaders obtained in a study of 17 encounter groups and their leaders by Lieberman, Yalom, and Miles (1973) included moderate use of stimulation and executive behavior, high in caring, and utilization of meaning attribution (leader's role in giving meaning to group members' experiences). The strongest association with positive outcome was meaning attribution.

Perhaps most important from the several reports of research cited above is the concurrence that the counselor must first demonstrate that he is a healthy human being who has proven that he possesses the qualities described by Truax and Carkhuff (1967) and Carkhuff (1969a) and that his counselees or "helpees," *a la* Carkhuff (1969a), do in fact improve their behavior as a result of the help he provides them. Details for determining one's level as a helper are described in Carkhuff (1969a), in Gazda *et al.* (1973), and in Gazda, Walters, and Childers (in press). It behooves every prospective helper to determine his level of functioning and, if it is not a facilitative level, to raise it or discontinue his role as a "helper."

Goldstein, Heller, and Sechrest (1966, Ch. 8) reviewed the research pertaining to the orientation of group psychotherapists and its effect on clients. They concluded that there was a major need to research the group therapist's orientation from a perspective which also considered the *interacting* influence of stage of therapy, patient and therapist personality and behavioral characteristics, therapist and patient goals, and other related variables.

Leader Orientation

The qualities of a group counselor who is likely to be helpful were outlined above. At this point emphasis will be placed on relating the effects of his interaction to what happens in a counseling group. Once more we need to turn to the group dynamics research for direction. Goldstein *et al.* (1966), following a review of research in both group psychotherapy and group dynamics, concluded that the research

. . . pointedly provides basic evidence for the prediction of more favorable patient response to a leader-centered versus a group-centered therapist orientation in the early stages of group psychotherapy. . . . However, in spite of its less favorable early effects, there is a considerable body of group dynamics research suggesting that the group-centered approach is very likely to result in patient behavior much more highly related to a favorable therapeutic outcome than would be the case if an essentially leader-centered approach persisted beyond the first 10 to 20 therapy sessions (p. 377).

The findings reported by Goldstein *et al.,* are based to a considerable extent on patient expectancies of group leadership. In this regard they found:

In sum, these diverse studies focusing on leadership expectancies in psychotherapy and other settings appear to converge in the general conclusion that the more discrepant the expectancies, the less the attraction to the group, the less the satisfaction of group members, and the more the strain or negative affect between leader and led or therapist on patient (p. 375).

If one can conclude that patients seeking group psychotherapy or, similarly, counselees seeking group counseling will approach the experience expecting direction and assistance from the leader, a rule of thumb to follow would be for the group counselor to be more active in the early group sessions and to move gradually from a leader-centered approach to a group-centered approach as counseling proceeds. This practice should reduce counselee initial hostility, increase receptiveness, and provide the best overall plan for building a therapeutic climate.

This rule-of-thumb procedure is congruent with the model described by Carkhuff (1969a), the model which seems to have the greatest support for application to group counseling. Carkhuff, in describing guidelines for the communications of empathy (a prerequisite for developing a facilitative base), stated that especially at the beginning of helping the helper would find that by increasing his verbal responsiveness, he would not only provide a model for an increasingly active helpee but he would also serve to increase the probability of accuracy in communication.

In the beginning of a counseling group, the counselor is actively trying to build the facilitative base of mutual trust and caring through the utilization of interchangeable responses that incorporate the core conditions of empathy, respect, and warmth. As the counselees develop this base, they will provide cues that indicate they wish to explore their problems beyond the initial depth to a greater depth. The group counselor assists the counselees to move toward a greater depth of exploration which, in turn, leads to greater understanding and eventual positive action through the application of the more action-oriented core conditions of concreteness, genuineness, appropriate self-disclosure, confrontation, and immediacy (Carkhuff, 1969a).

STRUCTURING. Structuring refers to the counselor's orientation of group members. Research results support the use of the following procedures:

1) Be positive in building expectancy states. Group members should be told that (a) they most likely will like and be liked by other members of the group (Schachter, Ellertson, McBride, and Gregory, 1960); and (b) the group was set up to consist of individuals who share similar opinions and values (Festinger, Schachter, and Back, 1950).

2) Stress the hard work that will be involved in the group counseling process. This should increase the effort expended by counselees (Cohen, 1959; Yaryan and Festinger, 1961; Zimbardo, 1960).

3) Stress the careful screening that went into selection of the group members. (This procedure should increase the attractiveness of the group to the counselees—see research reviewed by Goldstein *et al.,* 1966, pp. 344-348.)

4) Define the norm of the group as different from the usual social norm; that is, that it is appropriate and beneficial to discuss one's personal concerns in the counseling group. Reinforcement of this new norm should make the transition to self-disclosure and revelation of one's problems more acceptable to group members (Bonney and Foley, 1963).

GOAL SETTING. Several studies have shown that clarity of group goals and means of achieving them increase the group's attraction for members, generate greater group cohesiveness, and reduce intragroup hostility. Is group cohesiveness, however, desired in group counseling? Truax (1961) studied the effects of cohesiveness in therapy groups and made the following observation:

These results indicate that cohesion, long a central concept in the analysis of small group behavior, is also of importance in the analysis of group psychotherapy; successful group psychotherapy groups are cohesive. . . . These findings . . . point to a variable unique to the group setting and one which is susceptible to external manipulation (p. 16).

A counselee's purpose for seeking help or goal setting should be verbalized in initial interviews before he enters a group; however, he is encouraged to repeat these in the first session of the group. Therefore, to increase the possibility of goal achievement through group counseling, the counselor should encourage the counselees to verbalize their goals as specifically and concretely as they can in the beginning and to increase their specificity as clarity occurs through the counseling experience.

Berne (1966) has referred to goal setting as the therapist-patient contract. He considers the contract to exist between therapist and the institution which employs him and between the therapist and patient. Therefore, the patient should know the therapist's institutional obligations which may impinge on the patient's goals. For example, if the counselor has an obligation to report use of drugs by counselees, the counselee should know this and thus not place himself in jeopardy. Berne (1966) also cautions that the contract between therapist and patient may need to be amended from time to time as determinants underlying symptoms or responses are made more explicit. The same opportunity for goal modification should be applied to group counselees.

Occasions arise wherein subgroups develop within a counseling group and frequently they begin to compete with each other to the point of creating severe friction within the total group. This situation usually calls for reconstituting the group or instituting a superordinate goal such as the counselor's introducing a legitimate threat to the total group that is sufficient to bring together the warring factions in a total group effort to counteract the outside threat. The threat might be impending loss of a meeting place, the revocation of institutional time for group counseling, or some other administrative threat to the group's existence.

NORM SETTING. The concept of norm setting has particular relevance to group counseling in that it is equivalent to what is expected and/or allowable in the group. The norm may be either explicit or implicit, but in either case the group members know what they are permitted to do with its subsequent rewards and what they are forbidden to do with its subsequent punishments.

Included in the setting of group norms, of course, is the group counselor. He is active both in assisting the group develop the norms and is himself being influenced by the group with respect to the role or roles he will be expected to follow within the group. The counselor's actions are especially significant in determining group norms in the first few sessions. His own modeling such as responding empathically and showing warmth and respect to all members, supporting shy members, etc., can go a long way toward setting the climate for the group. That is, when the group is most in need of leadership early in its Exploratory Stage, the counselor has perhaps the greatest opportunity to influence its direction. Bonney (1969) contends that the leader

> should assume an active though not highly directive part in the for-
> mation of the group's norms. Ideally the setting of norms should
> emanate from the group itself. . . . The eventual acceptance of a
> group norm should . . . be left to the consensus of the group and not
> forced by the leader, particularly in the early stages of the group's
> development (p. 167).

Stages of Group Development

A number of group therapists and group counselors (Bach, 1954; Bonney, 1969; Gendlin and Beebe, 1968; Mahler, 1969) have identified stages or phases through which counseling and therapy groups purportedly pass, ranging from three phases (Gendlin and Beebe, 1968) to seven (Bach, 1954). The stages through which counseling groups progress are most clearly visible in closed groups, i.e., groups that retain the same membership throughout the duration of the group's existence. In open groups or groups that add new members as old members terminate and especially when the influx of new members is frequent, the stage development is affected and, as Gendlin and Beebe (1968) have noted, the old members reach a Tired Phase because of the con-stant necessity of the old members assisting the new members through the Breaking Through Phase—the phase during which the member experiences an explosive freeing and growth process. With open groups, then, it is incumbent upon the counselor to know the potential effect of too rapid a turnover in an ongoing group. It is necessary to protect the Sustaining Phase (Gendlin and Beebe, 1968) or work phase of the core members of a group and to prevent them from reaching the Tired Phase.

Hill (1961, 1963, 1965) has developed an Interaction Matrix based on a hypothesis that therapy groups proceed along two dimensions of *content* and *work* and through approximately 16-20 cells or levels of interaction. The Hill model has many of the same elements that were included in the model developed by Carkhuff (1969a). The Carkhuff model adapted to my phases of group development is shown in Figure 2. This model emphasizes the necessity of building a facilitative base through high level expressions of empathy, respect, and warmth in the early phases of developing sound relationships. Building a facilitative base is prerequisite to the implementation of the action-oriented dimensions at later stages in helping relationships. The action-oriented dimensions are geared to changing behavior. The facilitative-action oriented dimensions include genuineness, specificity or concreteness of expression, and appropriate self-disclosure by the leader, whereas the action-oriented dimensions include the leader behavior just cited plus *appropriate* confrontation and immediacy or "telling it like it is" between leader and helpees in the here-and-now.

The amount, the kind, and the timing of counselor intervention in groups, therefore, is related to the stage or phase of a group's development. It cannot be independent of the stage, however, since the group is influenced by counselor behavior and vice versa. It has been my experience that counseling groups go through four rather definite stages. These stages usually occur in the given group session and across sessions. They are (1) Exploratory Stage; (2) Transition Stage; (3) Action Stage; and (4) Termination Stage. These four stages are named similarly by others. For example, Bonney (1969) refers to the Exploratory Stage as the Establishment Stage and Mahler (1969) calls it the Involvement Stage. Both Bonney and Mahler have a second or Transition Stage. The Action Stage can be equated to Mahler's Working

	Phase I (Downward or Inward Phase of Self-Exploration) Initial Stage of Individual Dimensions	Intermediary Stages of Individual Dimensions	Stage 3 Action	Phase II (Upward or Outward Phase of Emergent Directionality and Action) Final Stage of Individual Dimensions
COUNSELOR OFFERED CONDITIONS FOR THERAPEUTIC CHANGE (PART A)[3]				
EMPATHY	Level 3 (interchangeability)	Levels 4 and 5 (additive responses)		Levels 4 and 5 (emphasizing periodic feedback only)
RESPECT	Level 3 (unconditionality)	Level 4 (positive regard)		Levels 4 and 5 (regard and conditionality)
CONCRETENESS	Levels 3 and above (specificity of exploration)	De-emphasized (abstract exploration)		Levels 4 and 5 (specificity of direction)
GENUINENESS	Level 3 (absence of ingenuineness)	Levels 4 and 5 (self-disclosure and spontaneity)		Levels 4 and 5 (spontaneity)
CONFRONTATION		Level 3 (general and open)		Levels 4 and 5 (directionful)
IMMEDIACY		Level 3 (general and open)		Levels 4 and 5 (directionful)
GROUP (COUNSELEE) STAGES IN THERAPEUTIC CHANGE (PART B)[4]	Stage 1 Exploratory	Stage 2 Transition	Stage 3 Action	Stage 4 Termination

3. From Chapter 7 of *Helping and Human Relations: A Primer for Lay and Professional Helpers. Vol. 2. Practice and Research*, by Robert R. Carkhuff. Copyright © 1969 by Holt, Rinehart and Winston, Inc. Reprinted by permission of Holt, Rinehart and Winston, Inc., New York.

4. From Chapter 5 of *Group Counseling: A Developmental Approach*, by George M. Gazda. Copyright © 1971 by Allyn and Bacon, Inc. Reprinted by permission of Allyn and Bacon, Inc., Boston.

Figure 2

Stage. The fourth or Termination Stage is equivalent to Mahler's Ending Stage.

Exploratory Stage

During this stage the group members introduce themselves and describe the goals that each hopes to achieve. They also agree on some basic ground rules. Following the initial session the counselees usually engage in social and superficial discussions about themselves each parrying with the other to present himself in an acceptable fashion. This is the kind of activity in which members assign to each other what Hollander (1964) has called "idiosyncratic credits." Bonney (1969) has referred to this as the "process by which the group consciously and unconsciously, assigns power and influence, in varying degrees to each member of the group" (p. 166). It is also a means of establishing various roles that each person will first assume in the group. Hidden agendas begin to emerge and the group begins to establish norms that will eventually become the unofficial but controlling ground rules.

It is especially important that the group counselor be actively helpful during the Exploratory Stage. He shows his helpfulness by clarifying goals for the group and the group means for achieving them, by telling the group something about himself and, most importantly, by modeling the facilitative dimensions of empathy, respect, warmth, and genuineness. In the Carkhuff (1969a) sense, he gives consistently minimally facilitative or better responses, i.e., he consistently gives responses to each counselee that are *interchangeable* with those of the counselee–interchangeable especially with respect to the affect expressed by the counselee and also to the content or message expressed. It is during this initial or Exploratory Stage that a facilitative base of mutual trust and caring is built. Without this, the group fails to reach the next stage in its development.

Transition Stage

The Transition Stage occurs at a point when one or more counselees begin to self-disclose at a level significantly deeper than the "historical" type of disclosures heretofore given in the group. At this point the group members experience a feeling of threat since the typical social group does not usually function in this manner. The members may attempt to block the self-disclosures with overly supportive responses or by attempts to change the subject–more precisely to revert to the superficial conversation of a historical nature found in the Exploratory Stage.

To move the group as a whole through the Transition Stage to the Action Stage, or work stage, requires high levels of *perception* or sensitivity and accuracy in *timing* of counselor responses. The counselor must be able to encourage volunteers to self-disclose at a level that gives them a feeling of involvement and simultaneously he must be able to hold the anxiety level of the more threatened group members to a level that will not force their defense systems to over-react. Following the Carkhuff model for moving from counselee exploration to understanding to action, the counselor must be able to give responses that are at least minimally action-oriented, i.e., he must begin to add the facilitative action-oriented dimensions of genuineness, concreteness and appropriate self-disclosure to those of empathy, respect, and warmth. The counselor, himself, should be willing to self-disclose, when appropriate, at a depth equal to that of his most advanced counselee, in that way he models for the counselees who are beginning to involve themselves in the action-oriented dimensions of problem resolution, i.e., goal-related work.

Action Stage

The Action Stage is synonymous with the work or productive stage of a counseling group. Also, it involves the implementation of the action-oriented dimensions, *a la* Carkhuff's model, of confrontation and immediacy plus the facilitative-action dimensions of genuineness, concreteness, and appropriate self-disclosures.

The group counselor must orient the counselees toward a belief that their condition will not change until they take definite steps (action) to modify it. Insofar as the counselee's goal can be achieved by modifying his behavior in the group itself, he should be encouraged to do so and rewarded when he does. In this regard talking about how he is planning to change is no longer defensible; he must demonstrate it in the here-and-now of the group experience. The counselor utilizes appropriate confrontations and shares with the counselee his here-and-now feelings about the counselee's in-group behavior. He also encourages other group members to do likewise.

In the final analysis counselee action is goal related and dependent upon behavioral modifications to be employed outside of the group settings. It is encouraged in the form of *homework* to be done and then reported back to the group at the next session. Attempts that fail to achieve the desired goal can be appraised and modified, even role-played in the group, until counselee satisfaction is achieved.

If the group counselor has involved all group members in the action phase of group counseling, he will seldom need to confront group members himself. Rather the group members will confront each other and the group counselor will be more of a gatekeeper of group safety. He will be one of the most expert timing devices in the group—the one who can best predict when a given counselee is ready to be confronted with decision making and/or action. In this view he not only confronts but solicits, through his openness, confrontation by the counselees.

Termination Stage

The Termination Stage begins with a tapering off of counselee self-disclosures, especially in new areas of concern. In a closed group with a preset termination date, the tapering off usually begins naturally two to three sessions before this date and frequently includes half-hearted attempts by the counselees to continue the sessions beyond the preset deadline. Not unusual during the last three or four sessions is the initiation of a "going around" procedure wherein each member solicits frank feedback from every other member. Also common during the Termination Stage is a general and spontaneous need of counselees to tell how much the group members and the group experience have meant to them. They are reluctant to see the group experience terminate and they usually make plans for a group reunion at some specific date in the future.

The group counselor's responsibility at termination is to reinforce the growth made by group members and to make sure that all group counselees have had the opportunity to work out their differences with the counselor and other group members before leave taking. If any member of the group, for whatever reason, continues to require counseling, the counselor must assume this responsibility or assist him in a mutually satisfactory referral.

COUNSELEE SELECTION AND GROUP COMPOSITION

General Guidelines

Frank (1952), Slavson (1953) and Hulse (1954) have pointed to our lack of knowledge in arriving at optimum composition for therapy groups. A similar observation can be made for group counseling. Research has not clearly demonstrated ideal combinations of members for maximum growth through group counseling. Nevertheless, certain guidelines have been utilized and are presented here for consideration, possible application, and research. My experience leads me to concur with Lowrey and Slavson (1943) *that the most essential element in a therapy group is the skill and insight in grouping, and the second most important factor is the personality of the therapist.*

Lieberman, Yalom and Miles (1973) comprehensive study of 17 encounter groups showed that the leader's theoretical rationale was not related to positive changes or growth of group members. Rather, leader characteristics/behaviors were significantly related to group members' changes.

Previous citations in this chapter of the finding of Carkhuff and Truax regarding leader/counselor characteristics point to the important relationship of the counselor's characteristics and counselee outcome. These researchers have established the fact that effective helpers must function at high levels on the core dimensions. What has not yet been adequately established is the relationship between effective leaders and group composition. Can effective leadership alone lead a poorly composed counseling group to growth, or must the group itself possess at least minimal conditions before even effective leaders can produce growth? My convictions lie with the latter part of this question.

Based on a rather thorough review of the literature, Truax and

Carkhuff (1967) concluded that conclusive research on the question of what type of client, patient or counselee would benefit most from counseling or psychotherapy has not been done; however, those counselees who are likely to improve or deteriorate can sometimes be predicted. Even then this may be more a factor of the leader's ability to provide a therapeutic relationship than a true picture of what the counselee is like. Nevertheless, they did find research data to support some *tentative conclusions* related to counselee selection for individual and/or group counseling. Their findings (Truax and Carkhuff, 1967, Ch. 5) are summarized as follows:

1. Matching of counselee and counselor types is critical where the counselor is quite restricted in his ability to show understanding, warmth, or genuineness to all but a narrow range of individuals.
2. Counselee readiness is a moderately good predictor of the degree of positive change. In this regard, counselees who have high expectations and high regard for the counselor tend to show the greatest immediate change while those who differ on the aims and methods of counselor help tend to terminate treatment quickly.
3. The research evidence is unclear regarding the characteristics of counselees likely to benefit most from counseling or therapy. In general, the counselees with the greatest felt disturbance and the least overt disturbance show the greatest improvement at posttreatment.
4. The greater the initial psychological disturbance but the lesser the initial behavioral disturbance, the greater the predicted improvement *during* treatment.
5. Counselor liking or disliking for the counselee will affect outcome. Higher therapeutic conditions are offered to counselees who are liked by the counselor.
6. Social class variables (e.g., occupational and educational level, and intelligence) regarding type and duration of counseling offered, reflect general prejudices of the profession but do not necessarily reflect the counselee response to counseling.
7. Counselee hope or initial expectations of help through counseling is a major factor contributing to the likelihood of its actually occurring.
8. Degree of counselee change is independently influenced *both* by the level of therapeutic conditions offered by the counselor

and the initial degree and type of personal disturbance of the counselee.

9. Accurate empathic understanding seems to be more critical for outcome with nonverbal counselees while nonpossessive warmth and genuineness tend to be equally effective in producing preferred outcome with both verbal and nonverbal counselees.

10. The therapeutic conditions of accurate empathy, nonpossessive warmth, and genuineness are of equal importance in producing personality change in the most disturbed and least disturbed counselees.

11. Level of self-exploration by the counselee is a crude predictor of counselee outcome, i.e., the greater the degree of counselee self-exploration, the more likely the outcome will be positive. (The Truax Depth of Self Explorations Scale in Truax and Carkhuff, 1967, Chapter 5, can be used to obtain a measure of counselee level of self-exploration.)

The guidelines which have been cited above for rule-of-thumb selection of counselees come from both the individual and group counseling research literature and include characteristics of the counselee and counselor. However, the group setting is unique and creates greater problems for predicting possible counselee reaction(s). McGrath and Altman (1966), in their extensive review of small group research concluded: "Actually very few data are available about the role of personality characteristics of members on various group phenomena. Rather, such properties should be studied with respect to the composition of the group" (p. 57). They further concluded ". . . there is very little research on group composition, and what there is gives an unclear picture" (p. 60).

The Lieberman, Yalom, and Miles (1973) study has added some new information of relevance to the problem. In their study they found that the nature of the group as a social system is important. More specifically, they found that

> . . . Groups with norms that favor moderate emotional intensity and confrontation, supportive peer control, and those with looser boundaries of what could be legitimately discussed showed higher learning. Groups that were more cohesive, more involving, and more harmonious during the latter part of their life were better as learning environments.
> . . . group members who liked their groups, who participated ac-

tively, and who were valued by other group members learned more; marginal or deviant members tended to have negative outcomes (p. 76).

With respect to the group counseling research, Anderson (1969) made this observation in his three-year review of the literature:

> Group counseling research reflects little interest in client selection or client preparation as a major independent variable. The available data suggest that people who are affectively oriented, flexible, highly motivated to change, and sufficiently well-adjusted to interact rationally with others function well in counseling groups (p. 212).

Following a comprehensive review of group dynamics and group psychotherapy research, Goldstein *et al.* (1966) developed the following hypothesis concerning group composition: "On a variety of interactive, communicative and compatibility criteria, prediction of subsequent within-group behavior will be more accurate when based on direct behavioral measurement than on interview or psychometric measurement" (p. 329). In order to apply the above principle, they proposed three criteria as guidelines: (1) consistency or typical performance, (2) relation to task success, and (3) objective observation (1966, p. 333). To determine consistency of counselee behavior in a group, two means were suggested: (a) trial groups (see also Bell and French, 1955; Blake, Mouton, and Fruchter, 1954; Borgatta and Bales, 1955; and Gazda, 1968), and (b) simulated groups.

Trial or preliminary grouping is possible where there is a relatively large pool of potential counselees, such as in schools or other institutional settings. Potential counselees are placed in a large temporary group, observed for three or four sessions, and then placed in a permanent group based on their needs and contributions and the needs of the permanent group to which they are added (in the case of open-ended groups) or a new group (closed) when a new group is being organized.

The simulated method for screening consists of a prospective member's listening, via audio tape, to a simulated group experience and responding as if he were a member. This method allows the prospective group counselee to be observed regarding his reaction to type of group leadership and group members. Blake and Brehm (1954) and Bass (1960) describe this method in more detail.

To relate task or group success (therapeutic outcome) to group composition, Goldstein *et al.* (1966) suggested the study and application of findings of characteristic rate of group member interaction, leadership behavior, the effects of group cohesiveness on outcome, and related therapy group dimensions.

Group cohesiveness was found by Truax (1961) to be one of three group conditions significantly related to intrapersonal exploration by counselees in groups. Most of the research in support of group cohesiveness as a powerful agent in affecting behavior is in the field of group dynamics or from non-therapy oriented groups (see Goldstein *et al.,* Chapter 9). Bach, a group therapist, with a group dynamics orientation had this to say about group cohesiveness in therapy groups:

> This principle of cohesiveness is most relevant to the therapy group, for much of the therapeutic process is mediated by all members. The most unique feature of group therapy is the co-therapeutic influence of peers, not of the doctor alone. Traditionally, the doctor is thought of as having the most influence, but in group therapy this is actually not necessarily so, because the relatively low degree of cohesiveness between doctor and patient as compared with the often very deeply involved peer relationships between the patients gives the co-patient a greater power of effective influence (1954, p. 348).

After a careful consideration of the research relevant to group composition for therapy, Yalom (1970) made the following statement:

> On the basis of our present state of knowledge, therefore, I propose that cohesiveness be our primary guideline in the composition of therapy groups. The hoped for dissonance will unfold in the group, provided the therapist functions effectively in the pretherapy orientation of patients and during the early group meetings. . . .
>
> A cohesive frame of reference for group composition is by no means inconsistent with the notion of demographic heterogeneity; however, it does set limits for the degree of heterogeneity. . . . It makes eminently good sense to suppose that the greater the range of interpersonal relationships clarified within the group, the more universal the carryover will be. . . . However, the demographic varia-

tion must be conceived within the general rubric of cohesiveness; too extreme a variation breeds deviancy and undermines cohesiveness (p. 204).

After surveying individual therapy research, group therapy research, and group dynamics research Goldstein *et al.* (1966) generated the following *hypotheses* relative to the means of achieving cohesiveness in therapy groups:

1. Therapy group cohesiveness may be increased by intergroup competition (p. 407).
2. Therapy group cohesiveness may be increased by the temporary inclusion, within the therapy group of a "deviant plant" (p. 411).
3. Therapy group cohesiveness may be increased by dissolving or re-orienting diverging subgroups. The creation of a series of groupwide tasks characterized by superordinate goals with inherent task appeal and demanding interdependent linking across all group members for task completion will result in such subgroup dissolution or re-orientation (p. 417).
4. Therapy group cohesiveness may be increased by differential reinforcement by the therapist or patient group-oriented verbalizations versus individual-oriented verbalizations (p. 421).

Although the Goldstein *et al.* review of the literature which led to the generation of the above hypotheses did not include *group counseling* literature per se, there is little or no reason to doubt that the findings apply equally to group counseling. In order to achieve objective observations of group behavior for predicting outcome a number of interaction process scales were suggested by Goldstein *et al.* (1966), such as those by Bales, Carter, Heyns, Steinzer, Benne and Sheats, and Fouriezos, *et al.* A significant omission in their list is the Hill Interaction Matrix, HIM-A and HIM-B (Hill, 1961, 1963, 1965, 1967). Hill (1967) has stated that "With the HIM-B or HIM-A the pattern of preferences for a group leader or group member can be determined and, by extension, the composition of the group can also be determined and the compatibility of the members with each other and the leader can be measured" (p. 12). There is considerable evidence now building in the related literature to suggest that the Hill instruments, including HIM-G, can also be used to predict outcome of a counseling group as a whole–though perhaps not for each individual participant.

The Multidimensional Evaluation Structure Analysis (Stone, Coles, and Lindem, 1970) represents an addition to the scales for evaluating group interaction that shows great promise for use in selecting members for groups based on the use of paired-comparison ratings. This carefully designed, computer-programmed instrument has great potential for composing groups, giving members feedback, and monitoring group process.

Still another category for predicting an individual's behavior in a group consists of personal interviews and other measures of psychological appraisal. Research data (Goldstein *et al.,* 1966) do not support this means as effective in predicting within-group behavior of members. However, Schultz's (1966) FIRO-B or three-dimensional theory of interpersonal behavior, with his several questionnaires, holds considerable promise as do the indexes of Discrimination and Communication recently developed by Carkhuff (1969ab). The use of biographical data such as used by Dr. Owens of the University of Georgia's Department of Psychology for predicting group interaction has not even been attempted and leaves an entire area open to research. Other techniques which already have been employed with limited success are Bach's (1954) use of MAPS Figure Grouping, the Life Space Drawings and a number of situational and psychodramatic tests described by Goldstein *et al.* (1966, p. 326).

Both Ginott (1961) and Slavson (1964) believe that a person's capacity for "social hunger" is a primary prerequisite for placement in a therapy group. Ginott, in particular, applies this criterion in the selection of children for therapy groups. According to Slavson (1964), "Social hunger has the same relation to group psychotherapy as transference does to individual psychotherapy." Slavson defines social hunger as ". . . the desire to be with people and belong with others" (p. 492).

Social hunger provides the group counselor with a good rule-of-thumb procedure for selecting group counselees; however, it is insufficient in itself, since it is difficult to appraise. Insofar as they are related to counselee readiness or hope, the previous guidelines, based on research cited by Truax and Carkhuff (1967), lend credence and specificity to their application in counselee selection.

Screening Interview

A diagnostic interview is held with each prospective group counselee to give the counselor an opportunity to describe the ground rules for and responsibilities of the group and to enable the counselor to ascertain the counselee's readiness and acceptability for a group counseling experience. The diagnosis is often useful for effective empathic understanding on the counselor's part and it is essential for him also to know the degree of seriousness of the counselee's problem (Truax and Carkhuff, 1967), since prospective counselees, who are experiencing a serious crisis in their lives, should be seen individually. They tend to dominate a group with their immediate needs and prevent others from getting help and this often turns the group against them because they monopolized the time.

Not all counselors can help all counselees; therefore the group counselor must know himself and his limitations in this regard. The diagnostic interview permits the counselor to determine whether or not his prospective group counselee has a problem similar to one that the counselor has been unsuccessful in solving in his own life. The counselee should be referred to someone else if he has a problem which the counselor has proven inadequate in solving. Carkhuff (1969a) makes this point very succinctly:

> If the helper cannot establish himself as a person who is himself living at more effective levels than the distressed person, if the helper cannot establish that given the same circumstances he could bring about a more effective resolution, there is no meaningful basis for helping (p. 45).

The screening interview provides the counselor the opportunity to go over the ground rules of the proposed group with the candidate. The rules are carefully explained in this interview, and are reviewed again at the beginning of the group during the first session and at other times throughout the counseling session as often as is necessary for their communication and clarification. The screening interview also serves as a hurdle to group membership which makes it more appealing upon admission—providing the initiation is not too severe (Goldstein *et al.*, 1966).

To heighten the candidate's appeal for the counseling group, he is told (after the counselor has decided to accept him) that he will very likely find the other group members to be congenial and helpful. A review of research by Goldstein *et al.* (1966), suggests that this type of positive pre-membership structuring leads to increased acceptance of members for each other and resultant group cohesiveness.

Ground Rules[5]

Following the counselor's hopeful and positive introduction in the screening interview, he reviews for the candidate the following ground rules that the candidate will be expected to follow as a member of the group.

1. That he will set a goal or goals for himself before he enters the group, or at the very latest, as early as he can isolate and define his direction of change. And that he will revise these goals as clarification and/or experience dictates.
2. That he will discuss as honestly and concretely as he can the nature of his troubles, including the successful and unsuccessful coping behaviors he has employed.
3. That, when he is not discussing his own difficulties, he will listen *intently* to the other group members and try to help them say what they are trying to say and to communicate his understanding, caring, and empathy for them.
4. That he is to maintain the confidentiality of all that is discussed in the group. (There are no exceptions to this rule other than those things that pertain to him only.)
5. That he will be on time and attend regularly until termination of the group (if a closed group) and until he has met his goals (if the group is open-ended).
6. That he will give to the counselor the privilege of removing him from the group if the counselor deems it necessary for the counselee's health and for the overall benefit of the group.
7. That he will concur that all decisions affecting the group as a whole will be made by consensus only.
8. That he should inform the group counselor in private, before the group is constituted, of individuals who would, for various reasons, constitute a serious impediment to his group participation.

---

5. The following ground rules are written at a level used with adolescent and adult groups. They are modified and abbreviated for children's groups—especially as the ground rules are related to voluntary participation of the counselees.

(I feel that the "cards should be stacked in the counselee's favor" as much as possible; therefore those individuals who could inhibit the counselee should be excluded from his particular group if at all possible.)

9. That he may request individual counseling interviews, but that what is discussed in these interviews should be shared with the group at the appropriate time and at the discretion of the counselor and himself.

VALUES AND UNIQUENESS OF GROUP COUNSELING

There are certain features and values of group counseling and psychotherapy in general that should be recognized. These values and unique features are cited below with full awareness that they are not limited to Developmental Group Counseling and that all have not been experimentally validated. Lacking experimental validation, the value and unique features of group counseling (therapy) are supported by reference to agreement among experts.

Respondents to a national survey (Gazda, Duncan and Meadows, 1967) cited the following advantages–values and uniqueness:

1. Approximates a real life situation, or small community of peers, through which each member can test reality, practice identification, obtain feedback and support, share ideas, feelings, and concerns, leading to personal growth and improved interpersonal relations;
2. Provides for more economical and better use of counselor's time;
3. Facilitates an effective use of peer group pressure;
4. Makes certain individuals (e.g., the defensive, shy, dependent, and school behavior problem) more amenable to individual counseling.
5. Enables counselees to serve as co-counselors;
6. Provides a method for counselor training; and
7. Implements subsequent individual counseling.

Still other statements regarding the values and uniqueness of group counseling and/or group psychotherapy are reported in the literature and summarized as follows:

1. The client discovers that he is not alone or unique with his problems; that others have similar problems, too (Beck, 1958; Bennett, 1963; Broedel, Ohlsen, Proff and Southard, 1960; Cohn, Combs, Gibian, and Sniffen, 1963; Eiserer, 1956; Gawrys and

Brown, 1965; Spielberger, Weitz, and Denny, 1964; Super, 1960).

2. The counselee is encouraged to attack his problems, etc., through the effect of the group acceptance and rewards—support (Andrews, 1964; Beck, 1958; Broedel *et al.*, 1960; Bugental, 1962; Eiserer, 1956; Knowles, 1964; Ohlsen, 1964; Prados, 1953; Strang, 1958; Super, 1960).

3. The group represents a microcosm of social reality (real life) for the members and enables them to test their behavior (interpersonal relations) against social reality (Andrews, 1964; Beck, 1958; Bennett, 1963; Berger, 1962; Bugental, 1962; Cohn *et al.*, 1963; Eiserer, 1956; Gawrys and Brown, 1965; Ginott, 1961; Goldman, 1955; Hinckley and Herman, 1951; Knowles, 1964; Strang, 1958).

4. The group provides the counselees a relatively safe place to try out behaviors and experiment with possible changes (Beck, 1958; Bennett, 1963; Berger, 1962; Cohn *et al.*, 1963; Gawrys and Brown, 1965; Goldman, 1955; Whitaker, Stock and Lieberman, 1964).

5. The counselee learns to give as well as receive help in the role of co-counselor (Bennett, 1963; Eiserer, 1956; Gawrys and Brown, 1965; Knowles, 1964; Ohlsen, 1964; Spotnitz, 1961).

6. The group counselees have the opportunity to learn from each other by observing how others attack and solve problems (Beck, 1958; Eiserer, 1956; Samuels, 1964; Spotnitz, 1961; Strang, 1958).

7. The group counseling experience may lead to the counselee's seeking further counseling on an individual basis (Cohn *et al.*, 1963; Gazda and Ohlsen, 1961; Harris, 1965).

8. The counseling group may represent to some counselees a family group and thus provide the media through which the counselee can work through family problems (Knowles, 1964; Scheidlinger, 1948; Slavson, 1943).

9. Broedel *et al.* (1960), Kraft (1961), and Ohlsen (1964) emphasize the unique value that group counseling holds for the adolescent who has strong needs to identify with and be accepted by his peer group.

10. Group counseling or therapy sometimes provides a greater economy in the use of the counselor's or therapist's time (Beck, 1958; Bennett, 1960; Lodato, Sokoloff, and Schwartz, 1964).

LIMITATIONS AND DISADVANTAGES

The limitations and disadvantages of Developmental Group Counseling are not believed to be any different from those of any other form of group counseling or psychotherapy. For example, when authors were asked to list the limitations and disadvantages of group counseling as a part of a survey questionnaire, their responses in order of frequency included the following:

> . . . inappropriate treatment for certain problem types, e.g., sociopathic or psychopathic children, and the severely disturbed; difficult to control confidentiality, depth of involvement, collusion of unhealthy effects, and anxiety level; requires a more skillful counselor, including a greater sensitivity and expertness in group dynamics; is difficult to select appropriate combinations of group members; permits certain participants, e.g., the shy and withdrawn, to refrain from participation; does not provide for adequate individual attention for some counselees; can be difficult, especially in the school setting, to arrange a convenient time for a group meeting; does not represent an economical use of counselor's time; may lead to acceptance of the group milieu which may become artificial; and it is difficult to train adequate practitioners (Gazda, *et al.* [1967] p. 307).

Several other group counselors and group psychotherapists (who were not respondents to the survey questionnaire) point out possible limitations and disadvantages:

1. The group pressures may cause certain members to lose their individuality in their attempt to conform to group codes (Strang, 1958; Whitaker, Stock, and Lieberman, 1964).
2. Some members may use the group to escape or as a refuge (Eiserer, 1956; Goldman, 1955).
3. The threat of group ostracism to some members may be overwhelming (Beck, 1958; Strang, 1958).
4. Improper grouping can lead to certain group members being harmed (Ginott, 1961; Samuels, 1964; Strang, 1958).

Still other limitations of group counseling and therapy are cited. Beck (1958) calls attention to the unsuitability of group therapy for those lacking communication skills; the lessened control of the group therapist, the unpredictability of group process, intragroup jealousies, and lack of opportunity for depth treatment at critical moments. Prados (1953) cites as a weakness the tendency of members to act out unconscious infantile impulses, and Spotnitz (1961) cites the tendency of some participants, because of group comfort and a decrease in the urgency to tackle their problems, to drop out of therapy prematurely.

Therapists who practice psychoanalytic psychotherapy on an individual basis frequently contend that the use of a group interferes with or makes impossible the development of a transference relationship and hence is not effective therapy. Some psychoanalytically-oriented group therapists feel that the transference relationship between counselees and therapist is sometimes interfered with by the presence of other counselees.

In summary, it seems possible that the same elements that make for a potent therapeutic climate and force are those that also add greater risks to the treatment, e.g., the presence of several counselees in a group decreases the counselor's control and thus subjects the counselees to greater risks of the group's ostracism, pressure, rivalry, breaking of confidence and the like, with the possible resultant harmful effects. Still other limitations or weaknesses of group counseling lie in the difficulty to bring together regularly a number of counselees at the same time and the reduced ability of the counselor to focus on nonverbal behavior.

We shall now turn our attention to the application of Developmental Group Counseling to the various age-groups and illustrate the application with a protocol.

APPLICATION OF A DEVELOPMENTAL APPROACH TO GROUP COUNSELING FOR CHILDREN FIVE TO NINE YEARS OF AGE[6]

One of the developmental tasks for children from five to nine is "achieving an appropriate dependence-independence pattern" (Tryon and Lilienthal, 1950). Using this task with its appropriate coping behaviors as an early warning system for detecting potential trouble for given children, a teacher has referred three children who are having difficulty performing appropriate coping behavior to accomplish successfully this task. The children are two boys and a girl. The girl is an eight-year-old shy, overly dependent child. One boy is aggressive and too independent for his own safety. He is seven years old. The other boy is nine years old, and, prior to the recent birth of a male sibling, appeared to be making

---

6. From Gazda, G. M.: *Group Counseling: A Developmental Approach,* 1971. Courtesy of Allyn and Bacon, Inc., Boston, Massachusetts.

good progress in his dependence-independence functioning. With the arrival of a new baby brother, this nine-year-old boy became very dependent on his teacher (a female) and his parents, and stayed very close to his teacher and his mother. The group counselor is a young woman in her mid-twenties.

A group has been carefully selected to provide potential models for each child and also to contain some built-in controls—namely an older boy whose age and size alone can assist the counselor in controlling the one younger but aggressive boy. The counselor also has obtained extensive case data on each child and has decided in interviews with the teacher and parents that the common problem for each child is a need to develop appropriate behavior to cope with the task of achieving a proper balance between dependence and independence.

The counselor uses a free-play setting for the first three or four sessions. She meets the group for 45 minutes and holds the sessions in a playroom. During this time the children can play with a variety of toys and materials. The counselor shows an interest in each child and makes every effort to establish rapport or build the base of mutual trust and liking for one another. After rapport has been established, the counselor begins to structure the last half of each play session. At first she does this through story reading and telling and through the use of puppets. She introduces vicarious models in this way and verbally rewards appropriate dependence-independence behavior. Moving from puppets to dolls, she structures situations and asks the children to use the dolls to work out solutions. She rewards appropriate solutions verbally and asks for re-plays of inappropriate solutions until they approach appropriate coping behavior for dealing with the dependence-independence task.

As the children show progress with vicarious modeling, the counselor also sets up sociodramas and psychodramas revolving around school and family situations for the group to use in modifying their behavior. Finally, the counselor moves into the realm of the here-and-now relationships between herself and each child and those between each child. She models for the child by encouraging their appropriate independence from her and by rewarding appropriate dependence also.

The media selected for their play and action qualities are used to promote relationship development and problem resolution and are not therefore in themselves a primary focus of the treatment. The counselor is always conscious of the *timing* of her moves and of the purpose of her techniques. She moves from the least threatening situations in the beginning to the more threatening but more relevant procedures as the children show signs of growth. The above procedure or model provides ample opportunity for vicarious and real-life modeling and numerous opportunities for implementing other learning principles of desensitization, shaping, operant conditioning, discriminate and assertive training, and reciprocal inhibition. The deliberate use of these principles represents the science of play group counseling, whereas the when and how of implementing them represent the art of this form of treatment.

The maximum size of a play group for counseling should be five. If a co-counselor is utilized, one might include six or seven children. The size is determined by the degree to which the counselor is able to maintain adequate control over the group. Since young children have few social controls, the counselor must limit the size to retain the control.

GROUP COUNSELING FOR PREADOLESCENTS (AGES 9-13)

Since preadolescents prefer to associate with members of the same sex group, this is the only age group where the preferred method is to segregate by sex for counseling. Because the preadolescent has greater self-control, the group size can range from five to seven or even larger if co-counselors are used. The composition of the group is balanced to provide adequate models for everyone in the group. Sessions should run at least one hour twice a week or perhaps one and one-half to two hours once a week if twice-a-week meetings are not possible.

English and Higgins (1971) used a client-centered group counseling approach with preadolescents from the fourth and fifth grades and, failing to get significant results, concluded: "Logically, it appears that the client-centered approach places unrealistic demands on preadolescents to assume responsibility and initiative, especially for verbalizing" (p. 509).

Alper and Kranzler (1970) and Kranzler (1968) have suggested that all conventional approaches to group counseling are inappropriate with preadolescents. I concur with this position and therefore recommend the activity-interview model because of the natural inclinations of this age group toward games and activities.

ACTIVITY-INTERVIEW GROUP COUNSELING (AGES 9-13)[7]

Activity-interview group counseling is a composite of activity group therapy, *a la* Slavson, and interview group counseling. In essence an activity, such as checkers, is used to involve the group and to lower the inhibitions and defenses of the group members. The activity itself may provide an opportunity for physical catharsis or a nonsystematized desensitization. It serves the same purpose as systematic desensitization practiced by behaviorally-oriented counselors and therapists. In addition to providing a means for tension reduction through physical catharsis, the activity also provides an opportunity for interpersonal interactions which are the concern of the counselor and members in the group "interview" period following the game or activity. Activity-interview group counseling is a combination of prevention and remediation: thus it is intended for preadolescents, in particular, but also for adolescents and some adults, who are not suffering from debilitating emotional problems.

The activities may be many and varied. They should be chosen by the group counselor according to the needs of the group members. Care should be taken to vary the games or activities in order to provide some success experiences for all members of the group. The athletic-type preadolescent should have the opportunity to demonstrate his talents in team sports like basketball, touch football, and volleyball. In like fashion, the less athletic preadolescent should have an opportunity to experience success in table games such as electric bowling, ping-pong, chess, checkers, and the like. Still other activities such as dancing and swimming (especially for girls) and arts and crafts should be used for those who may have talents apart from the physical or intellective.

7. From Gazda, G. M.: *Group Counseling: A Developmental Approach,* 1971. Courtesy of Allyn and Bacon, Inc., Boston, Massachusetts.

Simulation and gaming constitutes a new and promising medium for use in group counseling with the preadolescent in particular. Games such as the Life Career Game (Varenhorst, 1968) can be adapted for small counseling groups and would provide the less physically competitive preadolescent with a substitute means for showing ability or excellence, such as in problem solving. It would also appeal to the group counselor who has less interest and enthusiasm for the more physically active team sports.

Simulating problem-resolution can serve as a means of vicariously conditioning preadolescents by rewarding choices or decisions that lead the hypothetical person to success experiences and not rewarding or vicariously punishing the hypothetical person's inappropriate choices, decisions, et cetera. Thus, this medium could serve much like role-playing, to protect the real counselee, but go beyond it in complexity of problems, external factors affecting decisions, and so forth. The use of action mazes using two or three members as a team could be arranged and when warranted competition between or among teams could be encouraged. To facilitate total group understanding of appropriate and inappropriate moves through the maze, group discussions could follow the completion of the maze.

Since the activity itself in activity-interview group counseling represents only part of the treatment, those activities that involve simultaneously several, if not all the group members, should be most utilized. The discussion phase (interview group counseling session) usually following the game or activity, constitutes the second part of the treatment. During this period the counselor helps the group members focus on the nature of the interactions that occurred during the activity phase of the treatment. The behavior that occurred during the activity is related to the life style of a given group member.

The counselor builds a strong facilitative base with high levels of empathy, respect, and warmth. Only after having established a feeling of mutual trust and caring does he move the group member into the planning and action phase of the treatment through appropriate self-disclosure, genuineness, concreteness, confrontation, and immediacy, *a la* Carkhuff (1969ab).

The interview or discussion phase need not be held in a formal setting such as a conference room, although such a room should be available when movement from an activity setting is required. The conference room can also be set up as a dual-purpose room including equipment and materials for group activities as well as chairs for the interview phase.

Day[8] (1967) studied the use of activity group counseling on culturally disadvantaged, behavioral problem boys referred for counseling by classroom teachers. The subjects were 25 culturally disadvantaged Negro boys, ranging in age from 11 to 14. They were initially selected through the use of behavior ratings by classroom teachers.

The experimental group met in activity counseling three times a week for five weeks. During this time, the control group received no counseling or guidance activities. Immediately after termination of the experimental groups, activity group counseling was provided for the control group. These students served as their own control for the purpose of statistical evaluation.

A criterion instrument used in measuring the change of classroom behavior was the Haggerty-Olson-Wickman Behavior Rating Schedule B (HOW). The criterion instrument used in measuring change in peer acceptance was a sociometric instrument designed by the investigator. Differences in mean gains for classroom social behavior, classroom emotional behavior, and total classroom behavior were calculated for the experimental versus the control group and for the control group during the control phase versus the control group during the counseling phase.

The results indicate that those students receiving activity group counseling showed favorable gains in classroom social behavior and total classroom behavior (p. < .05). Day concluded:

1. Activity group counseling has an effect on classroom behavior of culturally disadvantaged, behavioral problem students. Social behaviors were particularly affected by the experience of activity group counseling. Emotional behavior was also affected by activity group counseling, although nonsignificantly.

---

8. From Blakeman, J. D., and Day, S. R.: Activity Group Counseling. In G. M. Gazda (Ed.), *Theories and Methods of Group Counseling in the Schools,* 1969. Courtesy of Charles C Thomas, Springfield, Illinois.

2. Written evaluation by teachers confirmed that twenty-three of the twenty-five subjects were seen as significantly improved in classroom behavior.

3. Activity group counseling was seen by the participants as a very positive experience. All of the subjects in this study expressed a desire to continue counseling in groups. Each student rated the experience as being both helpful and pleasant.

4. Activity group counseling can be conducted within the confines of the typical school setting using facilities in the school (1967, p. 103).

Blakeman[9] (1967) investigated the effects of activity group counseling on the classroom behavior of seventh- and eighth-grade problem boys of Caucasian origin who ranged in age from 11 to 14. Forty-nine boys were recommended by teachers and then interviewed as possible participants for the study. From this group 40 boys volunteered to participate. This investigation included group activity meetings that were held weekly after school for one hour over a period of six weeks. The activities included touch football, golf, table tennis, swimming, and visits to a nearby confectionary. Criterion instruments for behavioral improvement were the Self Evaluation Picture Tests (SEPT) and the Haggerty-Olson-Wickman Behavioral Ratings Schedule (HOW). An independent examination of the experimental group indicated that activity group treatment had a positive effect upon the self-evaluation and classroom behavior of these behavioral problem boys. Evaluation of the data further indicated that experimental subjects changed in the desired direction, and no regression was noted over a four and one-half month period. Blakeman concluded:

1. It can be stated with reasonable sureness that activity-group treatment effects desirable changes in boys' self-evaluation to significant degrees.

2. Graduate training programs can easily incorporate activity group counseling experiences and practicum courses for trainees. A variety of activities seem appropriate as a setting for activity group

---

9. Blakeman, J. D., and Day, S. R.: Activity Group Counseling. In G. M. Gazda (Ed.), *Theories and Methods of Group Counseling in the Schools.* Courtesy of Charles C Thomas, 1969, Springfield, Illinois.

treatment. All of these are available within the school confines (pp. 69-70).

The following protocol illustrates the dual-purpose setting used with a group of black preadolescent "problem students," ranging in age from 11 to 14 in the Day study previously described. The protocol includes portions taken from the sixth group session. The setting is a dual-purpose room in which six black boys are milling around the room. Some are reading; others are drawing; one is throwing darts. J. (the subject of discussion) is very active. The counselor is a white male.

Protocol

J.: I'm not gonna' tell anything in the meeting today because everything I do, R. tells Mr. A.

R.: I did not tell!

Co.: Let's hear about this.

J.: I am not going to say anything.

R.: He went and shot off his big mouth, and because I told Mr. A. now he is mad at me.

J.: Ah Peanut, that isn't either what happened. That isn't the first time you've done this, Peanut. I've been playing with you all day and you've been doing it all along. Every time you touch him he gets mad. Just touch him a little bit and he gets mad; he's a baby.

Co.: How about that Group? How would you handle that?

W.: J. is to blame; he is always to blame. He's a great big bully.

J.: I didn't touch him. I know what I'm gonna' do about it! I'm just not gonna' associate with anybody in this group anymore.

R.: Don't worry; it will pass over.

J.: No, it won't pass over, R. I'm the only one around this school that even likes you a little bit, and I don't see how I can like you now. You're gonna' be so lonely. I'm the best friend you got and you did me dirty and that's all I'm gonna' have to do with you.

Co.: It sounds like J. is pretty mad this time.

M.: I think they are both at fault. I think they are both babies.

Co.: Let's talk about the basketball game we played yesterday.

J.: I'm not going to talk. Every time I talk, somebody tells on me, I've been in the office more than anybody this year, more than any of you punks.

Co.: J., it sounds like maybe you are blaming R. for some of your problems.

J.: This is part of the office and every time I may do something wrong, R. goes to Mr. A. and tells him all about it.

Co.: Do you consider this part of the office? Is this like the principal's office?

J.: It was before you came. I don't mind if he tells you, but I don't want him telling Mr. A., and I don't want him telling the principal.

R.: J., you think I am the cause of all your problems.

J.: The way I feel about it, if I weren't around you everything would be all right. That's what I'm gonna' do; stay away from you.

Co.: It sounds like R. is responsible for everything you had had to go wrong this year, J.

J.: Most all of 'em, anyway.

Co.: Most all of them?

J.: Yes, all of them. Everything I've been in trouble with is 'cause of him.

Co.: It sounds like J. and R. have had everything to say, so far. What do some of the rest of you think? I wonder if some of the other boys might not be able to help you out.

J.: Every time I see two or three boys beat up on him, fight him, jump on him, I help him. Now, first time things go wrong, he runs in and tells Mr. A. I'm through with him.

Co.: We don't seem to be getting very far with this argument; why don't we try something. Why don't we try J. and R. just being quiet for a minute and let some of the other boys give some of their opinions of how they might handle a situation like this.

J.: No, I'm not through yet. I want to talk some more. I don't like Peanut, and I'm not having any more to do with him.

R.: I think Mr. Counselor has a good idea; let's try that.

T.: I think they both got problems. I think they both need to work on 'em .

M.: I think we ought to put them together and let them fight it out.

Co.: It seems to be a lot of buzzing, but no one wants to say things directly to J. or R. about the situation. I get the idea that all of you would like to, but you're kinda' frightened of what they might say back.

J.: I think the way to settle this whole thing is if I don't associate with R. anymore. When he gets tired of not associating with me, he'll come around and say, "Let's make friends again," and then we'll be friends.

Co.: I'm still puzzled about your saying R. is responsible for all your problems.

J.: Yes, he is. And even though you want me to say something, I'm not gonna' say nothing different. He is responsible for all my problems. Let's do something different; I'm tired of this. I don't want to be talking all day long. I'm mad at this group.

Co.: It seems like J. doesn't feel like the group is satisfying him any more. How do the rest of you feel?

Group: It's great; it's what we want. Let's do it.

W.: Let's get J. out of the group if he doesn't like it.

H.: If he wants out, let's get him out.

L.: Yeah, let's get him out, if he doesn't want to be in the group; let's get him out.

Co.: I guess the boys are saying, J., that the door is open.

J.: Well, one thing about this group is that when we do play basketball or football, we got a sorry bunch of players. None of them really want to play ball. They're just a bunch of goofoffs. We got a sorry bunch of players.

M.: That's what you say. You shoot all the time anyway, how would you know? You never pass it to anyone. Why don't you try to teach some of the boys how to play rather than chewing at them all the time?

R.: Well, I'd like to say something. I tell you this. When J. has the ball, even if you're wide open, he won't pass it to you. He won't pass it to any little boys. All he wants to do is shoot or pass it to one of the big boys. He keeps on dribbling like he don't know or even hear. All he does is shoot.

M.: I think J. and I are the best basketball players in here and I think we play harder than any of the other boys. I think J. doesn't like the other boys. He never passes. I try at least to be good to them.

J.: Yeah, W., L., and T., they're no good. They won't even play. They lose interest in the game, and if you don't keep on them all the time, they won't even play. No sense to pass to them, anyway. They just dribble and lose it. They're no good anyway.

L.: The group wasn't formed just for basketball. There is other reasons, too. Someone else might be good in football. You just want to be the big hog in everything you do, J.

Co.: It seems like some of you boys felt like being good in basketball was the main purpose in the group, while others seem to think that there are other purposes in the group.

T.: Yeah, keep us out of trouble.

J.: I'd like to talk now. Now, you say I don't pass the ball, but who in here does pass the ball? Every time I pass to T. or W., they lose the ball. Every time. So why pass to them? Just lose it if I pass it to them.

W.: What are you talking about boy? You don't even know what you are talking about.

J.: Now you answer that, W. Why would I pass it to you? Now . . . if you see somebody that ain't gonna' do no good with something that is given to them, why give to them? Why do it? Why give it to them?

Co.: It seems like J. sees a different purpose for the group. He wants to be a good basketball player and have a basketball team. Some of the rest of you don't feel that way.

M.: Well, I think anybody that don't know how to play ought to learn, and I think this is a good place to learn to do things. I think J. is wrong. I think we ought to be teaching boys to learn.

J.: The time to learn is not while you're playing the game. The time to learn is on your own in your own yard. Besides that, you can't teach boys that don't want to learn. Some of these boys would rather play dodge, so go let them play dodge, but when they come on a basketball floor, they ought to play basketball and they ought to try to be good. If they don't show a lot of interest, they shouldn't ought to be out there.

W.: I'm no good at basketball, but I think that I'd have a lot of fun playing basketball if J. weren't there.

R.: J. always shoots the ball so when we get back to this meeting, he can just talk about what he did during the game.

Co.: Let's take a look now, boys, at what we are doing. It seems as though everybody is ganging up against J., and it seems like we're trying to tell him that he's not a very good sport when it comes to playing basketball. I think maybe we're being a little hard on him.

J.: Don't worry about me. I don't feel bad.

M.: I think this is good because I think J. needs help. I think he needs help badly not only in basketball but all over.

J.: I don't think I need no help.

M.: Yes, you do need some help. You need lots of help.

J.: You can't help me.

Co.: M., what do you see he needs help in?

M.: He needs to learn how to keep his mouth shut, and he needs to learn how to act.

J.: I don't need no help from none of you, I don't want any help from anybody.

Co.: You don't want any help, from any of us?

R.: That's his main problem. When somebody tries to help him, he won't let them. It is the same thing he was saying. If he won't help himself, how can we help?

J.: Be quiet. Oh, shut up, Peanut. Peanut, will you shut up! I'm leaving this group. I'm through with this group. This group can't help me. I don't like this group, any of you, and I'm not gonna' be in the group. I am through with you, and I don't want anything to do with you or anybody in this group.

Co.: Sorry you feel this way, J. It sounds like we have been a little hard on you today. It seems like the boys had a lot on their minds.

R.: Yes, it is true.

J.: I'm quitting. I don't want anything to do with you. I don't want to come to any more of the group meetings. Count me out.

Co.: We'll leave it up to you, J. Whatever you decide is all right with us. I think, though, that we should leave it open if you would like to come back.

J.: I won't come back, and I won't have anymore to do with it.

M.: I hope you do come back, J. I like you. I just think there are some things you need to work on.

W.: Yeah, we like you, J. I'm sorry that you are so mad.

R.: I like you too, J., even if you are mad at me. And if you don't want to be in the group, I don't think you should have to be.

(Session Ends)

J. says that he is quitting and is very angry. J. comes back to counselor during the week, however, and apologizes for getting angry. He comes back to the group and is a model group member.

The protocol illustrates a very action-oriented approach on the part of the counselor. He assumed that he had a good relationship built with J. and the group. The counselor and the group members showed empathy, warmth, respect, self-disclosure, genuineness, concreteness, immediacy and confrontation—with a rather heavy emphasis on confrontation. If J. had not previously experienced the counselor and group members as helpful individuals, the result of this session would not have been so positive.

GROUP COUNSELING FOR HIGH SCHOOL-AGE PERSONS

Group counseling has been described earlier as being preventive, growth-engendering, and remedial. It is preventive to the extent that a person has access to accurate information that he can use to make wise decisions. It is growth-engendering to the degree that the person's potential may be released through greater self-understanding and self-acceptance. It is remedial to the degree that a person's inappropriate habits and attitudes are modified.

The most natural and efficient medium through which the typical adolescent and adult communicate is the spoken word; therefore interview group counseling is the preferred mode of treatment for adolescents and adults. The preferred size is 8 to 10; the preferred composition is heterogeneous without a wide age range and without extreme differences in intelligence, seriousness of problems, culture, and the like. High school freshmen and sophomores can be combined by age group as can juniors and seniors. Sophomores and juniors can also usually be combined; however, mixing freshmen with juniors and seniors is generally contraindicated. There are a variety of possible meeting schedules including one and one-half to two hours one day a week, one and one-half hours to two hours twice a week, and perhaps a 12 to 24 hour marathon added to either of the above procedures as a part of the overall program. The duration of the treatment should be a minimum of 8 to 10 weeks and preferrably 12 weeks or longer, depending upon the needs of the students. Video feedback can be adapted to a typical interview counseling group. The setting for an interview group should be a room capable of seating comfortably 8 to 10 people in a circular fashion with no table or other obstacle within the circle's center.

The following interview group counseling protocol consists of excerpts taken from the first session of a counseling group composed of high school juniors and seniors. The group consisted of four girls and two boys. Their common concern or interest was planning for college. The protocol begins following the introductions. The writer was serving as the counselor.

Protocol

Cathy: I've been in classes at ――――― High School where we are phased. We have Phase 1, Phase 2, and Phase 3. If you are in Phase 1, you are supposed to have advanced ability and you are supposed to be able to learn easily; therefore lots of times people say, "Well you should be able to do this because you have your ability already." I think that I am often on my own. In some cases this is good, but when you've been in this type of class all your life, you get sort of tired of hearing it and sometimes you *can't* do it by yourself. I'd just like to express that people who *can* do things need encouragement, also. You can't just say, "Here, do it." You've got to give them some attention, too.

Sue: Well, yeah, I agree with that, about the phases and all. You do get tired of it when you are in it all the time. I think a lot of kids that aren't in the top phases are hurt by thinking they are stupid and they don't put out what they could.

Jean: The teacher doesn't realize that when she has a class she's dealing with different types of students that have different interests and backgrounds. Instead of relating to the kids themselves, she's saying, "Okay, this is what we've got to learn," not "This is what will help you." This is where they are at fault. The teachers may take the easy way out and don't go to the trouble of relating to the kids and giving them something meaningful. This applies to all kids, not just to the elite.

Counselor (Co.): I heard Cathy saying that even though she's involved in accelerated classes, she gets to a point at times where she'd like to be encouraged too, noticed by the teacher, and not told, "You're on your own because after all you are an accelerated student."

Cathy: That's it exactly. Of course you have some teachers that are different. Like I say, when you have been in these classes for years, you get it all over and over. You know, that you're in a phasing class and that you can do this or that without any trouble but you would still like to be encouraged and know that the teachers care not only about what you're learning, but they care also about you.

Jean: Another thing is wrong with phasing. I think the slower phase groups could get a lot more, because I think these kids have a lot to offer, but they don't get a chance. Sometimes, too, the top phase kids think they're real smart, and they think the other kids are stupid.

Co.: Jean, you think its bad, then, for some kids to get the idea that there are other kids that are stupid and they got all the brains and they get kind of conceited.

James: I see myself thinking that way sometimes. I think there are people sometimes that don't have the mental power, and being in a lower phase kind of makes them feel inferior. I don't really think they are inferior, but I've had feelings like that sometimes.

Cathy: I've been in classes that were not phased, too. You do learn a lot, but still you feel held back because you have to go along with the class and lots of phase students are interested in just learning. I was in an unphased class and we just didn't move fast enough. You get bored so you just sit back and let things slide because you can easily keep up with them with no trouble at all, but it's still good to be in a class with different types of people.

Bev.: I'm inclined to agree with Cathy because I know this girl who, when she was in the 6th and 7th grades, wasn't in phasing. Although she was really young she was kind of slow. The teachers would give it to her and she's the kind of person that has to have care with it to show her that you want her to learn. And when she didn't, she just failed and failed. She was held back. So when they started the phasing, you know, most of the teachers in the lower phasing care about you a lot more, it seems like, and now she's almost an honor roll student. She's graduating this year and she's making almost straight A's. And I don't think she could have done it if she hadn't had phasing, because now everybody takes time with her and she feels like she can do it rather than they just give it to her. She's doing real well now.

Co.: So you think phasing helped her because she was performing at a low level, but the extra care motivated her to do better and she probably is achieving at her capacity now.

Bev.: Uh-huh.

Bill: When Cathy brought this up I was thinking of what I wanted to bring up in this group session and it was dealing with the teacher. Of course it didn't just affect me personally, it affected the whole class but it did affect me personally, too. She was the type that doesn't give anybody any attention. She goes up and stands in front of the classroom and talks to "it." You've got to have the teacher to encourage you, I think, no matter what phase you are or at what level of learning you are. You probably could do the work on your own but you've just got to feel like you have someone standing by you, willing to help you that you don't get lots of times in the school classroom. I feel like they are inefficient.

Co.: Do any of you have anything you'd like to say to Bill about that?

Sue: I agree with him. In three of my classes—I have the same teacher for two of them—and in the one class my teacher will come in there and just give it to you, over and over and over. I'm not the kind of person that you have to say—well, I get along with my teachers, real good. But I don't like to be talked to like I'm just a machine sitting there—to feed me. One teacher did act like that, and I didn't do well at all. I didn't care if I had my homework done. It was a good thing I liked that subject or I wouldn't have done anything. I think I brought my book home twice. But in one class it was real hard for me and I knew this teacher cared about me, because she would stay after school to help me. I didn't do as well but I studied, where in my other class I didn't even try. I'd pay attention in class because you have to and that's how I got good grades in there, but in the other I didn't do as well but I tried a lot harder.

Co.: So whether your teacher cares or not is pretty important to you as to how you perform.

Cathy: That's my thing in school. If the teacher doesn't care about me, I just don't care about the subject.

Co.: Cathy, it sounds like you're saying the same thing as Sue. If the teachers care they turn you on, and if they don't, they turn you off.

Cathy: Yeah.

Bill: It sounds like we're saying that the teacher should be there all the time. But what I mean is that you should be able to feel like she is your friend, and you can go to her when you need her. You should be able to work individually, too, and not let your work depend on her 'cause it's not always going to be that way. I realize like when you get in college, everybody says, "Oh you've got to learn to do it on your own because you know its really personal." But I do believe that a teacher should let you know that she cares about you as a person not just as a student.

Marsha: This may not be related but taking it out of the teacher-student context, you know you always perform better in just everyday life situations if someone cares.

Bill: I play some basketball and I think this is a very similar situation with the coach. You don't perform as well in the sport if you're not interested and the coach isn't interested in you and he doesn't care for you, encourage you to play and all. I think it affects your game.

Co.: So it is very much like the teacher situation.

Bill: Uh-huh.

Sue: I have two older brothers who had some trouble with high school teachers, but they got along fine in college. It seems funny, all of a sudden you have all of this self-realization, you know, and you're going out into the world. Is it the fear of college?

Bill: It might be the atmosphere in the classroom and all, 'cause I don't know, the teachers there just don't tolerate it.

Sue: Well they don't have the problem. They don't have the problem to tolerate. There's never a question.

Bill: I think you're privileged to be able to go to college. If you get thrown out of college, that's it.

(The group moves into a discussion of college requirements, academic, and interpersonal, and the first session ends on this note.)

GROUP COUNSELING FOR ADULTS[10]

The following protocol was taken from a group session with adults very early in the life of a group. The protocol illustrates the application of the core conditions of Carkhuff (1969ab) to a problem introduced by a group member in *interview group counseling*. Since there was no facilitative base built with the counselee, the group counselor and members were careful to begin with interchangeable responses, especially of empathy. The interaction covered only ten minutes of group time and yet led to a decision that the counselee felt was necessary and appropriate.

The counselee was in her mid-twenties. The group was composed of male and female members from their early twenties to their late fifties.

Protocol

> Counselee: Every time the phone rings my heart jumps. I stay worried all the time.
>
> Counselor: You're really pretty sure then that you're going to get some bad news every time the phone rings.
>
> Counselee: Yes, it seems like that I just wait to hear some upsetting news from home.
>
> Group Member A (female): Something then is going on at home that makes you think that something bad is going to happen?
>
> Counselee: Yes, my sister is ill and they're trying to find out what's wrong with her but they tell me that they don't know exactly what it is yet. I feel like maybe I should be there instead of 84 miles away, living my own life.
>
> Counselor: You feel kind of guilty that in this time of crisis in your family that you're not there to help out.
>
> Counselee: Yes, it seems like that every time they've needed me, that I was either away at school or not available. This really has me upset!
>
> Group Member B (male): It is not the first time that they couldn't depend on you to be around? You've been away quite a bit sometimes.
>
> Counselee: Yes. Maybe it wouldn't affect me so badly if this were the first crisis, but it seems like it's just been one a minute in the

---

10. From Gazda, G. M.: *Group Counseling: A Developmental Approach,* 1971. Courtesy of Allyn and Bacon, Inc., Boston, Massachusetts.

last five years, and I'm really feeling guilty. I'm married now, but I still feel like I have commitments to Mom and Dad.

Counselor: You feel that during these five years away from home you weren't doing enough to help your Mom and Dad. Now you are married and you're in less position to help them than you were before.

Counselee: Yes. This is it, and then this is the point that confuses me. They wanted me to go away to school and get an education and get a good job. But then being away from home and getting a good education caused me not to be there when they needed me. Now, I've got a good education and am working and I feel like I should be there with them.

Counselor: After they sacrificed for you, you stayed away and now you feel like you owe them something in return, but you haven't been able to pay them back in some way or other.

Counselee: I guess that's getting to the point. Just marrying and getting your own life, job, house—just how much can you partici-pate in family situations when you are out of school, out of the house, without really feeling like you are giving them less than you really should?

Group Member C (male): You just wish you knew what was a fair return to them (interrupted here by counselee response).

Counselee: Yes.

Group Member C (male): . . . after you're married, and what mar-ried people owe their parents.

Counselee: Yes, especially after they've made sacrifices for me.

Counselor: I get the feeling that you feel that you do need to do more than you have done.

Counselee: Yes, but then on the other hand, I'm wondering if I really should.

Counselor: Sometimes you think you should, and other times you don't know what a fair return is.

Counselee: Yes, so if I could just work out this problem of not being so-so I wouldn't be so concerned with what's going on at home. If it just wouldn't occupy my mind so much. It really is upsetting me! It seems if I could adjust to the fact that Mom and Dad and my sister have a life, Jack (husband of counselee) and I have a life, and we can just do so much and then function normally.

Group Member D (female): Somehow if you can just get settled in your own mind that there has to be this separation and that you can feel comfortable about whether you've been fair to your par-ents.

Counselee: Do you think that it's normal to worry about a sister that is sick and ill, and is it normal to the point that you think about it 80 percent of the time and you really spend your time moping and wondering if something is deadly wrong with her? I just don't know what will become of me, nor would I know how to help Mom and Dad.

Group Member C (male): You really don't think it's normal to spend that much time worrying about her. You're also feeling quite a bit of guilt about her illness and the fact that you can't do more for her and your parents.

Counselee: That's why I'm coming and asking for help, because I don't know whether or not it's normal or not. I kind of feel it is normal, since I do have close ties, and I really do love them—love her and my family. But then I don't have guilt feelings about her illness, 'cause this is something that I did not have anything to do with. I do have a guilt feeling about whether or not I really did help them (parents) enough, or if I'm committing myself to home (when I say home, I mean to Mom and Dad and family) as much as I should. That is the essence of my problem. And then it seems like that because I do have these guilt feelings, and it stays on my mind . . . like I'm always wondering about if something is going to happen. If it is, I say well I should be there. Then if I were there, I wonder how much I really could do.

Counselor: What could you do? You're kind of torn between the feeling that you need to be there on the one hand, and realistically if you were there, you couldn't do anything anyway to change your sister's health, but you might in some way be a comfort to your parents.

Counselee: Yes. Now what are your views on this?

Counselor: I guess all I can tell you Marilyn is what I hear you telling me—that you're pretty miserable right now the way things are, and it is not getting any better, and that you need to take some kind of action to feel better about his relationship between you and your parents, that you need to do something more than you have done. I don't know what's possible, but that is what I heard you telling me—that you feel like you owe more than you've been giving them back.

Counselee: I do feel that I have to do more. I guess now my next move must be to talk to my husband about my feelings and make plans to do something more for my parents but which will be acceptable to him.

SUMMARY

This chapter begins by defining group counseling through placing it in perspective with other group procedures. It is defined as lying on a continuum from prevention to remediation and including aspects of both plus growth-engendering dimensions.

The essence of this chapter is the explication of Developmental

Group Counseling–an eclectic position that includes relationship and learning principles. This position rests on the hypothesis that group counseling must take into consideration the counselee's age and developmental levels–physical, psychological, and vocational –if it is to be relevant to varying age groups. The age groupings for which special forms of group counseling have been described are 5 to 9, 9 to 13, 13 to 20, and adulthood. For each age grouping the preferred type of leadership, group size, setting and media, group composition, and length and duration of treatment, are described. Protocols are used to illustrate group counseling with each age group.

The dynamics operative in counseling groups such as leadership, including essential conditions of a helping relationship, structuring, goal setting, norm setting and stages of group development are related to effective group functioning. Related topics include criteria for group selection and composition, ground rules for group operation, values and uniqueness of counseling groups, and limitations of counseling groups.

A list of carefully selected readings is given at the end of the chapter. These readings have been selected to provide specific references for each of the four age groupings dealt with in Developmental Group Counseling.

SUGGESTED READINGS

Amster, F.: Differential uses of play in treatment of young children. *American Journal of Orthopsychiatry, 13:*62, 1943.

Blocher, D. H.: *Developmental Counseling.* New York, Ronald Press, 1966.

Bandura, A.: Behavioral modification through modeling procedures. In Krasner, L., and Ullman, L. P. (Eds.): *Research in Behavior Modification.* New York, Holt, Rinehart & Winston, 1965.

Blakeman, J. D., and Day, S. R.: Activity group counseling. In Gazda, G. M. (Ed.): *Theories and Methods of Group Counseling in the Schools.* Springfield, Ill., Charles C Thomas, 1969.

Boocock, S. S., and Schild, E. O. (Eds.): *Simulation Games in Learning.* Beverly Hills, Calif., Sage Publications, 1969.

Brammer, L. M.: Eclecticism revisited. *Personnel and Guidance Journal, 48:*192, 1969.

Carkhuff, R. R.: *Helping and Human Relations.* Vol. 1. *Selection and Training.* New York, Holt, Rinehart & Winston, 1969(a).

Carkhuff, R. R.: *Helping and Human Relations.* Vol. 2. *Practice and Research.* New York, Holt, Rinehart & Winston, 1969(b).

Carkhuff, R. R.: *The Development of Human Resources: Education, Psychology, and Social Action.* New York, Holt, Rinehart & Winston, 1971.

Carkhuff, R. R., and Berenson, B. G.: *Beyond Counseling and Therapy.* New York, Holt, Rinehart & Winston, 1967.

Corsini, R. J.: *Roleplaying in Psychotherapy.* Chicago, Aldine, 1966.

Crosby, M. (Ed.): *Reading Ladders for Human Relations.* (4th ed.) Washington, D. C., American Council on Education, 1963.

Erikson, E. H.: *Childhood and Society.* (2nd ed.) New York, Norton, 1963.

Gazda, G. M.: *Group Counseling: A Developmental Approach.* Boston, Allyn and Bacon, 1971.

Ginott, H. G.: *Group Psychotherapy with Children.* New York, McGraw-Hill, 1961.

Glasser, W.: *Schools Without Failure.* New York, Harper & Row, 1969.

Goldstein, A. P., Heller, K., and Sechrest, L. B.: *Psychotherapy and the Psychology of Behavior Change.* New York, Wiley, 1966.

Groups in Guidance: Special Issue: *Personnel and Guidance Journal,* April, 1971.

Haas, R. B. (Ed.): *Psychodrama and Sociodrama in American Education.* New York, Beacon House, 1949.

Hansen, J. C., Niland, T. M., and Zani, L. P.: Model reinforcement in group counseling with elementary school children. *Personnel and Guidance Journal, 47:*741, 1969.

Harms, E.: Play diagnosis: Preliminary considerations for a sound approach. *Nervous Child, 7:*233, 1948.

Havighurst, R. J.: *Developmental Tasks and Education.* (2nd ed.) New York, Longmans, Green, 1952.

Havighurst, R. J.: *Human Development and Education.* New York, David McKay, 1953.

Hinds, W. C., and Roehlke, H. J.: A learning theory approach to group counseling with elementary school children. *Journal of Counseling Psychology, 17:*49, 1970.

Lilienthal, J. W., and Tryon, C.: Developmental tasks: II. Discussion of specific tasks and implications. In *Fostering Mental Health in Our Schools: 1950 Yearbook, ASCD,* Washington, D. C., Association for Supervision and Curriculum Development, 1950.

MacLennan, B. W., and Felsenfeld, N.: *Group Counseling and Psychotherapy with Adolescents.* New York, Columbia University Press, 1968.

McGrath, E., and Altman, I.: *Small Group Research: A Synthesis and Critique of the Field.* New York, Holt, Rinehart & Winston, 1966.

Middleman, R. R.: *The Non-verbal Method in Working with Groups.* New York, Association Press, 1968.

Moreno, J. L., and Kipper, D. A.: Group psychodrama and community-centered counseling. In Gazda, G. M. (Ed.): *Basic Approaches to Group Psychotherapy and Group Counseling.* Springfield, Ill., Charles C Thomas, 1968.

Murphy, G.: Play as a counselor's tool. *School Counselor, 8:*53, 1960.

Nesbitt, W. A.: *Simulation Games for the Social Studies Classroom.* Vol. 1, *New Dimensions.* New York, Foreign Policy Assoc., 1968.

Raser, J. R.: *Simulation and Society: An Exploration of Scientific Gaming.* Boston, Allyn & Bacon, 1969.

Scheidlinger, S.: Three approaches with socially deprived latency age children. *International Journal of Group Psychotherapy, 15:*434, 1965.

Simulation Games. New York: Western Publishing Co., Inc., School and Library Department. (brochure n.d.)

Slavson, S. R.: Differential methods of group therapy in relation to age levels. *Nervous Child, 4:*196, 1945.

Sturm, I. E.: The behavioristic aspect of psychodrama. *Group Psychotherapy, 18:*50, 1965.

Super, D. E., Crites, J., Hummel, R., Moser, H., Overstreet, C. B., and Warnath, C.: *Vocational Development: A Framework for Research.* New York, Bureau of Publications, Teachers College, Columbia University, 1957. Monograph No. 1.

Super, D. E., Starishevesky, R., Matlin, N., and Jordaan, J. P.: *Career Development: Self-concept Theory.* New York, College Entrance Examination Board, 1963. Research Monograph No. 4.

Truax, C. B., and Carkhuff, R. R.: *Toward Effective Counseling and Therapy.* Chicago, Aldine, 1967.

Tryon, C., and Lilienthal, L. W.: Developmental tasks: I. The concept and its importance: In *Fostering Mental Health in Our Schools: 1950 Yearbook, ASCD.* Washington, D. C., Association for Supervision and Curriculum Development, 1950.

Varenhorst, B. B.: Innovative tool for group counseling: The Life Career Game. *School Counselor, 15:*357, 1968.

Zaccaria, J. S.: Developmental tasks: Implications for the goals of guidance. *Personnel and Guidance Journal, 24:*372, 1965.

Zaccaria, J. S.: Some aspects of developmental guidance within an existential context. *Personnel and Guidance Journal, 47:*440, 1969.

REFERENCES

Alper, T. G., and Kranzler, G. D.: A comparison of the effectiveness of behavioral and client-centered approaches for the behavior problems of elementary school children. *Elementary School Guidance and Counseling, 5:*35, 1970.

Anderson, A. R.: Group counseling. In Glass, G. V., and Thoresen, C. E. (Eds.): *Review of Educational Research: Guidance and Counseling, 39:*(2), 209, 1969.

Andrews, E. E.: Identity maintenance operations and group therapy process. *International Journal of Group Psychotherapy, 14:*491, 1964.

Bach, G. R.: *Intensive Group Psychotherapy.* New York, Ronald Press, 1954.

Bass, B. M.: *Leadership, Psychology and Organizational Behavior.* New York, Harper, 1960.

Beck, D. F.: The dynamics of group psychotherapy as seen by a sociologist, Part I: The basic process. *Sociometry, 21:*98, 1958.

Bell, G. B., and French, R. L.: Consistency of individual leadership position in small groups of varying membership. In Hare, A. P., Borgatta, E. F., and Bales, R. F. (Eds.): *Small Groups.* New York, Alfred A. Knopf, 1955.

Bennett, M. E.: *Guidance and Counseling in Groups.* (2nd ed.) New York, McGraw-Hill, 1963.

Berenson, B. G., and Carkhuff, R. R. (Eds.): *Sources of Gain in Counseling and Psychotherapy: Readings and Commentary.* New York, Holt, Rinehart and Winston, 1967.

Berger, M. M.: An overview of group psychotherapy: Its past, present and future development. *International Journal of Group Psychotherapy, 12:*287, 1962.

Berne, E.: *Principles of Group Treatment.* New York, Oxford University Press, 1966.

Blake, R. R., Mouton, J. S., and Fruchter, B.: The consistency of interpersonal behavior judgments made on the basis of short-term interactions in three man groups. *Journal of Abnormal and Social Psychology, 49:* 573 1954.

Blake, R. R., and Brehm, J. W.: The use of tape recording to simulate a group atmosphere. *Journal of Abnormal and Social Psychology, 49:*311, 1954.

Blakeman, J. D.: The effects of activity group counseling on the self-evaluation and classroom behavior of adolescent behavior problem boys. Unpublished doctoral dissertation, University of Georgia, 1967.

Blocher, D. H.: *Developmental Counseling.* New York, Ronald Press, 1966.

Bonney, W. C.: Group counseling and developmental processes. In Gazda, G. M. (Ed.): *Theories and Methods of Group Counseling in the Schools.* Springfield, Ill., Charles C Thomas, 1969.

Bonney, W. C., and Foley, W. J.: The transition stage in group counseling in terms of congruity theory. *Journal of Counseling Psychology, 10:*136, 1963.

Borgatta, E. F., and Bales, R. F.: Interaction of individuals in reconstituted groups. In Hare, A. P., Borgatta, E. F., and Bales, R. F. (Eds.): *Small Groups*. New York, Alfred A. Knopf, 1955.

Brammer, L. M., and Shostrom, E. L.: *Therapeutic Psychology*. Englewood Cliffs, New Jersey, Prentice-Hall, 1960.

Broedel, J., Ohlsen, M., Proff, F., and Southard, C.: The effects of group counseling on gifted underachieving adolescents. *Journal of Counseling Psychology, 7:*163, 1960.

Bugental, J. F. T.: Five paradigms for group psychotherapy. *Psychological Reports, 10:*607, 1962.

Carkhuff, R. R.: *Helping and Human Relations,* Vol. 1. *Selection and Training.* New York, Holt, Rinehart and Winston, 1969(a).

Carkhuff, R. R.: *Helping and Human Relations.* Vol. 2. *Practice and Research.* New York, Holt, Rinehart and Winston, 1969(b).

Carkhuff, R. R.: Systematic human relations training. In Gazda, G. M., and Porter, T. L. (Eds.): *Proceedings and a Symposium on Training Groups.* Athens, Ga., College of Education, University of Georgia, 1970.

Carkhuff, R. R.: *The Development of Human Resources: Education, Psychology, and Social Change.* New York, Holt, Rinehart and Winston, 1971.

Carkhuff, R. R., and Berenson, B. G.: *Beyond Counseling and Therapy.* New York, Holt, Rinehart and Winston, 1967.

Cohen, A. R.: Communication discrepancy and attitude change: A dissonance theory approach. *Journal of Personality, 27:*386 1959.

Cohn, B. Combs, C. F., Gibian E. J., and Sniffen A. M.: Group counseling, an orientation. *Personnel and Guidance Journal, 17:*355, 1963.

Day, S. R.: The effects of activity group counseling on selected behavior characteristics of culturally disadvantaged Negro boys. Unpublished doctoral dissertation University of Georgia, 1967.

Eddy, W. B., and Lubin, B.: Laboratory training and encounter groups. *Personnel and Guidance Journal, 49:*(8), 625, 1971.

Eiserer, P. E.: Group psychotherapy. *National Association of Women Deans and Counselors Journal, 19:*113, 1956.

English, R. W., and Higgins, T. E.: Client-centered group counseling with pre-adolescents. *Journal of School Health,* Nov., 507, 1971.

Erikson, E. H.: *Childhood and Society.* New York, Norton, 1950.

Erikson, E. H.: Growth and crises of the healthy personality. *Psychological Issues, 1:*50, 1959.

Erikson, E. H.: *Childhood and Society.* (2nd ed.) New York, Norton, 1963.

Festinger, L., Schachter, S., and Back, K.: *Social Pressures in Informal Groups.* New York, Harper, 1950.

Frank, J. D.: Group methods in psychotherapy. *Journal of Social Issues, 8:* 35, 1952.

Gawrys, J. J., and Brown, O. B.: Group counseling: More than a catalyst. *School Counselor, 12:*206, 1965.

Gazda, G. M.: A functional approach to group counseling. In Gazda, G. M. (Ed.): *Basic Approaches to Group Psychotherapy and Group Counseling*. Springfield, Illinois, Charles C Thomas, 1968.

Gazda G. M.: *Group Counseling: A Developmental Approach*. Boston, Allyn and Bacon, 1971.

Gazda, G. M., and Ohlsen M. M.: The effects of short-term group counseling on prospective counselors. *Personnel and Guidance Journal, 39:* 634, 1961.

Gazda, G. M., Duncan J. A., and Meadows, M. E.: Group counseling and group procedures—Report of a survey. *Counselor Education and Supervision 9:*305, 1967.

Gazda, G. M., Duncan, J. A., and Sisson, P. J.: Professional issues in group work. *Personnel and Guidance Journal, 49:*(8), 637, 1971.

Gazda, G. M., Asbury, F. R., Balzer, F. J., Childers, W. C., Desselle, R. E., and Walters, R. P.: *Human Relations Development: A Manual for Educators*. Boston: Allyn and Bacon, 1973.

Gazda, G. M., Walters, R. P., and Childers, W. C.: *Human Relations Development: A Manual for Health Science*. Boston, Allyn and Bacon (in press).

Gendlin, E. T., and Beebe, J.: Experiential groups: Instructions for groups. In Gazda, G. M. (Ed.): *Innovations to Group Psychotherapy*. Springfield, Illinois, Charles C Thomas, 1968.

Ginott, H. G.: *Group Psychotherapy with Children: The Theory and Practice of Play Therapy*. New York, McGraw-Hill, 1961.

Goldman, G. D.: Group psychotherapy and the lonely person in our changing times. *Group Psychotherapy, 8:*247, 1955.

Goldstein, P., Heller, K., and Sechrest, L. B.: *Psychotherapy and the Psychology of Behavior Change*. New York, Wiley, 1966.

Golembiewski, R. T.: *Renewing Organizations: The Laboratory Approach for Change*. Itasca, Illinois, F. E. Peacock, 1972.

Harris, W. K.: A beginning counselor's experience with group counseling. *School Counselor, 13:*47, 1965.

Havighurst, R. J.: *Developmental Tasks and Education*. Chicago, University of Chicago Press, 1948.

Havighurst, R. J.: *Developmental Tasks and Education*. (2nd ed.) New York, Longmans, Green, 1952.

Havighurst, R. J.: *Human Development and Education*. New York, David McKay, 1953.

Hill, W. F.: *Hill Interaction Matrix Scoring Manual*. Pocatello, Idaho, Author, 1961.

Hill, W. F.: *Hill Interaction Matrix (HIM) Scoring Manual*. Salt Lake City, Utah, Dye, Smith and Co., 1963.

Hill, W. F.: *Hill Interaction Matrix (HIM)* (Rev. ed.) Los Angeles, University of Southern California Youth Studies Center, 1965.

Hill, W. F.: Group therapy for social impact: Innovation in leadership training. *American Behavioral Scientist, 11:*(1), 1, 1967.

Hinckley, R. G., and Herman, L.: *Group Treatment in Psychotherapy.* Minneapolis, University of Minnesota Press, 1951.

Hollander, E. P.: *Leaders, Groups and Influence.* New York, Oxford University Press, 1964.

Hulse, W. C.: Dynamics and techniques of group psychotherapy in private practice. *International Journal of Group Psychotherapy, 4:*65, 1954.

Knowles, J. W.: *Group Counseling.* Englewood Cliffs, New Jersey, Prentice-Hall, 1964.

Kraft, I. A.: Some special considerations in adolescent group psychotherapy. *International Journal of Group Psychotherapy, 11:*192, 1961.

Kranzler, G. D.: Elementary school counseling: An evaluation. *Elementary School Guidance and Counseling, 2:*286, 1968.

Lieberman, M. A., Yalom, I. D., and Miles, M. B.: Encounter: The leader makes the difference. *Psychology Today, 6:*(10), 69, 1973.

Lodato, F. J., Sokoloff, M. A., and Schwartz, L. J.: Group counseling as a method of modifying attitudes in slow learners. *School Counselor, 12:* 27, 1964.

Mahler, C. A.: *Group Counseling in the Schools.* Boston, Houghton Mifflin, 1969.

McGrath, J. E., and Altman, I.: *Small Group Research: A Synthesis and Critique of the Field.* New York, Holt, Rinehart and Winston, 1966.

Muuss, R. E.: *Theories of Adolescence.* New York, Random House, 1962.

Ohlsen, M. M.: *Guidance Services in the Modern School.* New York, Harcourt, Brace and World, 1964.

Prados, M.: Some technical aspects of group psychotherapy. *International Journal of Group Psychotherapy 3:*131, 1953.

Rogers, C. R., Gendlin, E. T., Kiesler, D. J., and Truax, C. B. (Eds.): *The Therapeutic Relationship and Its Impact: A Study of Psychotherapy with Schizophrenics.* Madison, Wisc., University of Wisconsin Press, 1967.

Samules, A. S.: Use of group balance as a therapeutic technique. *Archives of General Psychiatry, 11:*411 1964.

Schachter, S. Ellertson, N., McBride, D., and Gregory, D.: An experimental study of cohesiveness and productivity. In Cartwright, D., and Zander, A. (Eds.): *Group Dynamics.* Evanston, Ill., Row, Peterson, 1960.

Scheidlinger, S.: Group therapy—Its place in psychotherapy. *Journal of Social Casework, 29:*299, 1948.

Schutz, W. C.: *FIRO: A Three-Dimensional Theory of Interpersonal Behavior.* New York, Holt, Rinehart and Winston, 1960. (Republished:

The Interpersonal Underworld. Palo Alto, Calif., Science and Behavior Books, 1966.)

Slavson, S. R.: *An Introduction to Group Therapy.* New York, The Commonwealth Fund, 1943.

Slavson, S. R.: Differential methods of group therapy in relation to age levels. *Nervous Child, 4:*196, 1945.

Slavson, S. R.: Common sources of error and confusion in group psychotherapy. *International Journal of Group Psychotherapy, 3:*3, 1953.

Slavson, S. R.: *A Textbook in Analytic Group Psychotherapy.* New York, International Universities Press, 1964.

Spielberger, C. D., Weitz, H., and Denny, J. P.: Improving the academic performance of anxious college freshmen. *Psychological Monographs, 78:*(13), 1964 (Whole No. 590).

Spotnitz, H.: *The Couch and the Circle.* New York, Alfred A. Knopf, 1961.

Stone, L. A., Coles, G. J., and Lindem, A. C.: *Multidimensional Evaluation Structure Analysis (MESA): A Complete Multidimensional Scaling System for a Multiplicity of Purposes.* Grand Forks, North Dakota, Judgmetrics, 1970.

Strang, R.: *Group Work in Education.* New York, Harper, 1958.

Super, D. C.: Group techniques in the guidance program. In Farwell, G. F., and Peters, H. J. (Eds.): *Guidance Readings for Counselors.* Chicago, Rand McNally, 1960.

Super, D. E., Crites, J., Hummel, R., Moser, H., Overstreet, C. B., and Warnath, C.: *Vocational Development: A Framework for Research.* New York, Bureau of Publications, Teachers College, Columbia University, 1957. Monograph No. 1.

Super, D. E., Starishevesky, R., Matlin, N., and Jordaan, J. P.: *Career Development: Self-concept Theory.* New York, College Entrance Examination Board, 1963. Research Monograph No. 4.

Truax, C. B.: The process of group psychotherapy. *Psychological Monograph, 75,* 1961 (Whole No. 511).

Truax, C. B.: A new approach to counselor education. Paper presented at the Canadian Guidance and Counseling Association Convention, Edmonton, Alberta, Canada, June, 1969.

Truax, C. B., and Carkhuff, R. R.: *Towards Effective Counseling and Psychotherapy: Training and Practice.* Chicago, Aldine, 1967.

Tryon, C., and Lilienthal, J. W.: Developmental tasks: I. The concept and its importance. In *Fostering Mental Health in Our Schools. 1950 Yearbook of ASCD.* Washington, D. C., Association for Supervision and Curriculum Development, 1950.

Varenhorst, B. B.: Innovative tool for group counseling: The Life Career Game. *School Counselor, 15:*357, 1968.

Whitaker, D., Stock, D., and Lieberman, M. A.: *Psychotherapy Through the Group Process.* New York, Atherton Press, 1964.

Yalom, I. D.: *The Theory and Practice of Group Psychotherapy.* New York, Basic Books, 1970.

Yaryan, R., and Festinger, L.: Preparatory action and belief in the probable occurrence of future events. *Journal of Abnormal and Social Psychology, 63:*603, 1961.

Zaccaria, J. S.: Developmental tasks: Implications for the goals of guidance. *Personnel and Guidance Journal, 24:*372, 1965.

Zimbardo, P. G.: Involvement and communication discrepancy as determinants of opinion change. *Journal of Abnormal and Social Psychology, 60:*86, 1960.

CHAPTER XVI

BEHAVIORAL GROUP COUNSELING

Carl E. Thoresen and Beverly Potter

THE BASIC OBJECTIVE of all counseling and psychotherapy is changing people's behavior—how they think, how they feel, what they say to themselves and how they act with others. In this chapter an approach to group counseling and therapy is presented that holds promise as an effective and efficient way of helping persons change.

BASIC RATIONALE

Counseling in groups has long been recognized as an effective way of helping persons clarify their concerns and learn ways of doing things more effectively. This understanding and doing is, of course, facilitated by the presence of several persons sharing common concerns. Unlike the one-to-one counselor-client setting, a group environment is a rich milieu where a great variety of behaviors can be learned. The group setting can provide a good approximation of many "real life" experiences, helping persons transfer actions carried out in the group into their everyday life. In this way the group serves as a laboratory for learning, a time and place to consider, observe, try out and receive information on certain actions.

In this chapter we offer a working model of behavioral group counseling. In developing this model we have drawn upon the writings and experiences of many other writers (e.g., Lazarus, 1967; Varenhorst, 1969; Rose, 1972). We acknowledge that theoretical rationales and group techniques actually used often have little in common. Many group approaches labeled, for example, as Gestalt, client-centered, or bioenergetics employ "behavioral" techniques without necessarily acknowledging them theoretically. We share the views of recent critics of counseling and psychotherapeutic research (e.g., Strupp and Bergin, 1969) that the best remedy for the theoretical sickness of therapeutic strategies is to be openly empirical. What works? With whom? Let the questions of "why" follow from answers to the questions of what helps people change.

A Working Definition

Some writers, most notably Lazarus (1971), have advocated a "technically eclectic" stance. "Technical eclecticism does not imply a random melange of techniques taken haphazardly out of the air. It is an approach which urges therapists to experiment with empirically useful methods . . ." (p. 33). Others have defined behavior therapy as only employing techniques derived and validated by modern learning theory (e.g., Eysenck, 1971). We believe that social learning theory as presented by Bandura (1969) offers a valuable theoretical rationale. However, at present, the practitioner, i.e., the group counselor, must be eclectic in an empirical fashion.

Some Assumptions

Many assumptions and biases are involved in any approach to group work. Some of the important ones we make are as follows:

1. What people do—human action—is largely influenced by current environmental experiences. The current environment, however, can also be changed by the person's actions. Thus, the person's environment influences and is influenced by what the person does.
2. All behavior (internal as well as external) is observable and measurable in some way and is also susceptible to change by similar methods.
3. Human behavior is composed of internal actions (thoughts, self-instructions, images, physiological responses) and external actions (spoken words, gestures, physical-motoric movement, and other non-verbal responses) and client goals concern changes in both kinds of actions.
4. Counseling in groups is best viewed as an educational process where teaching and learning takes place.
5. Data should be gathered continuously and systematically by each group member during all phases of group treatment, including the time period after the group terminates.
6. Each group member should have at least one "client goal" stated

in performance terms, i.e., stating what actions, under what circumstances, and to what extent the client is going to do by the end of the group.

7. Each member should have individualized behavioral objectives (sub-goals) to accomplish during and/or between group sessions.

8. The person's environment, especially the actions of the other persons, is often the "client," i.e., the problem resides in the environment that must be modified.

9. The group counselor works within a "clients as their own counselors" framework, i.e., teaching clients the skills of behavioral problem-solving and self-management.

10. Direct verbal and non-verbal interaction in the group is not necessarily the best or sole means of helping clients change. Use of media within the group (e.g., videotapes) and individual tasks between sessions is often effective.

These assumptions, in a sense, represent the ideology from which we function–a network of concepts, beliefs and ideas that guide our actions as group counselors. We act as if these premises and assumptions are true, but hold them tentatively, subject to change based on the data of experience. Many group approaches, of course, share some of these assumptions. Hence, they are not unique to the behavioral approach described here.

THE MAJOR STEPS

Identifying Problems

Behavioral groups are organized to achieve a particular purpose, such as remedying a particular problem experienced by several persons or preventing certain problems from developing. Hence a group can serve several high school students who, for example, lack friends or can offer help to a group of teachers in learning how to manage stress and tension. To illustrate the major steps used in behavioral groups, we will present information from two recent groups, referred to hereafter as the friendship group and the teachers' group. Figures 1A and 1B provide selected information on two members in each of these groups. Figure 2 graphically portrays the major steps in behavioral group counseling.

The initial step is to identify a problematic situation. Although

FRIENDSHIP GROUP

Pre-Group Interview

	NORA	MARK
Operationalize the Problem:	Nora is afraid to approach other people and she lacks the skills to initiate and maintain a conversation. She has no friends.	All his friends are in the motorcycle club. Little motivation to attend school and do homework. He has the skills to approach people, carry on a conversation and establish a friendship.
Formulate Goal(s):	To learn to approach and talk to people. To establish one friendship.	To meet at least one other person with whom I have common interests and with whom I want to establish a friendship.

First Group Session

Discuss alternative strategies to achieve each member's goal.

	NORA	MARK
Generate Alternatives:	1. Modeling (in and out of group) 2. Behavioral rehearsal 3. Read: "How to Win Friends and Influence People" 4. Shaping (progressive steps carried out in environment) 5. Join clubs	1. Join appropriate clubs 2. Expand interest areas 3. Relax criteria for selecting possible friend 4. Advertise in Berkeley Barb

Group members evaluate the various alternatives.

	NORA	MARK
Evaluate Alternatives:	1. Read book: provides helpful points but does not teach behavior 2. Join clubs: Nora does not have skills to interact, resulting in possible failure and rejection	1. Advertise: probably elicit inappropriate people; possible self-devaluation; parents would disapprove; peers would ridicule.

Group members select strategy which seems to have the most potential for helping member reach goal.

	NORA	MARK
Select Strategy:	Use shaping, modeling, behavioral rehearsal.	Join a club, expand interest, relax criteria for a friend.
Gather baseline data:	Behavioral Objective #1: For the next week, Nora will count the number of times she approaches and talks to another person and the number of times she is approached and talked to (parents excluded).	Behavioral Objective #1: Mark will record the amount of time he spends with the motorcycle club each day this week.

Approximations to Goal(s):

Second Group Session

Group discusses the baseline data: What did they learn?

Group helps Nora analyze the steps she needs to make to reach her goal.

Behavioral Objective #2: Nora will select one popular person in the cafeteria and observe behavior at least once every day this week. Record observations.

Group helps Mark analyze the steps he needs to make to reach his goal.

Behavioral objective #2: Mark will make a list of the activities he enjoys and his other interests.

Behavioral Objective #3: Mark will make a list of the qualities he desires in a friend.

Third Group Session

Group evaluates how successfully the behavioral objectives were carried out.

Discuss observations Nora made in cafeteria. What is the first step in approaching a person?

Model and rehearse: Approaching a person and asking a simple question.

Behavioral Objective #3: Once each school day Nora will approach at least one person and ask a question, i.e., "What time is it?" "Is there an assembly this week?"

Discuss Mark's interests and what he expects in a friend.

Behavioral Objective #4: Mark will make a list of the clubs and activities offered by the school, the community center and the Free University.

Fifth Group Session

Group evaluates how successfully the behavioral objectives were carried out.

Discuss experiences in approaching a person, asking a question and making a statement about the basketball game.

Behavioral Objective #4: Once each day, Nora will observe a person, make a statement about his behavior, and ask a question.

Behavioral Objective #5: Gather data on baseline behavior. (Repeat B.O. #1.)

Discuss experiences at meeting of the Radio Ham Club. Identify one person Mark would like to know better. Rehearse: How to invite Franklin to his house.

Behavioral Objective #5: Mark will invite Franklin to his house this weekend to see his shortwave radio.

Behavioral Objective #6: Gather data on baseline behavior. Mark will record the amount of time he spends with the motorcycle club each day this week. (Repeat B.O. #1.)

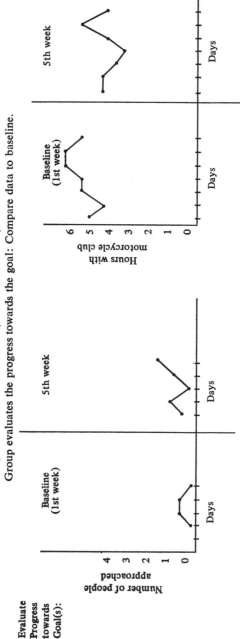

Sixth Group Session

Group evaluates how successfully the behavioral objectives were carried out.
Group evaluates the progress towards the goal: Compare data to baseline.

Evaluate Progress towards Goal(s):

Discuss experiences with observing, making a statement to the person and asking a question. Models and rehearses: Listen to a statement made by someone, follow it with an appropriate statement and ask a question.

Behavioral Objective #6: Each day Nora will observe one person, make a statement about his behavior, ask a question, listen to their response, and make an appropriate statement followed by a question.

Behavioral Objective #7: Collect data on baseline behavior.

Discuss Franklin's visit to Mark's house.

Behavioral Objective #7: Twice during the following week, Mark will call Franklin to "rap" about radios.

Behavioral Objective #8: Collect data on baseline behavior.

**Terminate
Group:**

12th Group Session

Group evaluates how successfully behavioral objectives were carried out.

Group evaluates the progress made towards the goal: Compare data to baseline.

Maintenance: Nora will volunteer to be a science tutor at the Drop-In Center. Nora will join the "dating problems group" to learn how to talk to boys.

Maintenance: Mark will continue to attend the Radio Ham Club and will work with Franklin on the club project.

Follow-up: The group will meet again in four weeks to discuss the progress and any problems.

Figure 1A. **Metagoal:** To learn skills necessary to develop and maintain a satisfying friendship.

TEACHERS' GROUP

Pre-Group Interview

	ANGIE	DALLAS
Operationalize the Problem:	Angie experiences anxiety at home and at school. The anxiety increases when she is confronted with discipline problems and when she is talking to colleagues. Angie has many fears about failing.	Dallas frequently worries about teaching when going to sleep which results in insomnia.
Formulate Goal(s):	To reduce anxiety when confronted with discipline problems and when talking to colleagues. To increase her self-esteem.	To reduce the frequency of insomnia.

First Group Session

	ANGIE	DALLAS
Generate Alternatives:	Leader elicits suggestions from members and offers suggested approaches to problems.	
	1. Systematic desensitization 2. In vivo relaxation 3. Use tranquilizers 4. Increase positive thoughts	1. Systematic desensitization 2. In vivo relaxation 3. Read a boring book in bed 4. Thought-stopping
	Members and leader evaluate each alternative. Which is most likely to help member achieve his goal?	
Evaluate Alternatives:	Tranquilizers: The use of drugs will not teach Angie how to control anxiety herself.	Reading: Dallas has tried this method and has had only occasional success.
Select Strategy:	Group discussion reveals that members experience anxiety in many common situations. Thus group desensitization and in vivo relaxation supplemented with members doing self-desensitization is selected as the major strategy.	
Gather Baseline Data:	Behavioral Objective #1: Each day this week each member will subjectively rate (from 1 to 10) and record anxiety level once every waking hour.	
Approximations to Goal(s):	Behavioral Objective #2: Each member will make a list of all school-related anxiety-provoking situations and bring them to the next meeting.	
Gather Baseline Data:	Behavioral Objective #3: Angie will count and record the number of positive and negative self-thoughts every day this week using wrist counter.	Behavioral Objective #3: Dallas will record the time he goes to bed and the approximate time he falls asleep each night this week.

Second Group Session

Group evaluates how successfully the behavioral objectives were carried out.

Group discusses and compares each member's baseline data on level of anxiety and the anxiety-provoking situations.

A group hierarchy is developed in the group.

Teach physical relaxation exercises and simple meditation techniques to all group members.

Behavioral Objective #4: Each member will practice relaxation exercises at least once each day this week for 20 minutes.

Behavioral Objective #5: Each member will continue to gather data on the baseline behaviors. (Repeat B.O. #1 and #3.)

Behavioral Objective #6: Angie will compile a list of her "positive qualities."

Third Group Session

Group evaluates how successfully the behavioral objectives were carried out.

Begin group desensitization: Relax group and present first three items on group hierarchy.

Behavioral Objective #7: Behavioral Objective #6:

Each group member will practice relaxation-meditation exercises at least once each day this week for 20 minutes.

Behavioral Objective #8: Behavioral Objective #7:

Each member will continue to collect data on baseline behaviors.

Behavioral Objective #9: Each time Angie looks at Behavioral Objective #8: Dallas will practice re-

her watch, she will subvocalize a self-thought. laxation and meditation exercises for 30 minutes each

night before going to bed.

Fourth Group Session

Group evaluates how successfully behavioral objectives were carried out.
Group evaluates the progress towards the goal: Compare data to baseline.

Evaluate
Progress
towards
Goal(s):

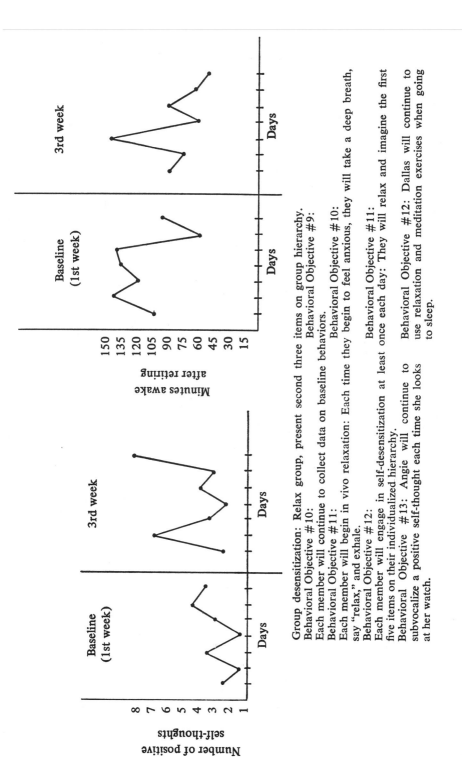

Number of positive
self-thoughts

8 7 6 5 4 3 2 1

Baseline
(1st week)

Days

3rd week

Days

Minutes awake
after retiring

150 135 120 105 90 75 60 45 30 15

Baseline
(1st week)

Days

3rd week

Days

Group desensitization: Relax group, present second three items on group hierarchy.

Behavioral Objective #10:   Behavioral Objective #9:
Each member will continue to collect data on baseline behaviors.

Behavioral Objective #11:   Behavioral Objective #10:
Each member will begin in vivo relaxation: Each time they begin to feel anxious, they will take a deep breath, say "relax," and exhale.

Behavioral Objective #12:   Behavioral Objective #11:
Each member will engage in self-desensitization at least once each day: They will relax and imagine the first five items on their individualized hierarchy.

Behavioral Objective #13: Angie will continue to subvocalize a positive self-thought each time she looks at her watch.   Behavioral Objective #12: Dallas will continue to use relaxation and meditation exercises when going to sleep.

Eighth Group Session

Group evaluates how successfully the behavioral objectives were carried out.

Group evaluates the progress towards the goal: Compare data to baseline.

Group desensitization: Relax group and present last three items from hierarchy.

Maintenance: Angie will continue in vivo relaxation and cueing herself to think positive thoughts. She will join Raymond Health Spa where she can take saunas.

Maintenance: Dallas will continue in vivo relaxation when retiring. He will enroll in the self-hypnosis course offered by the Free University.

Follow-up: The group will meet again in six weeks at Angie's house for a pot-luck supper to share progress and problems.

Terminate
Group:

Figure 1B. Metagoal: To learn self-management of stress and anxiety.

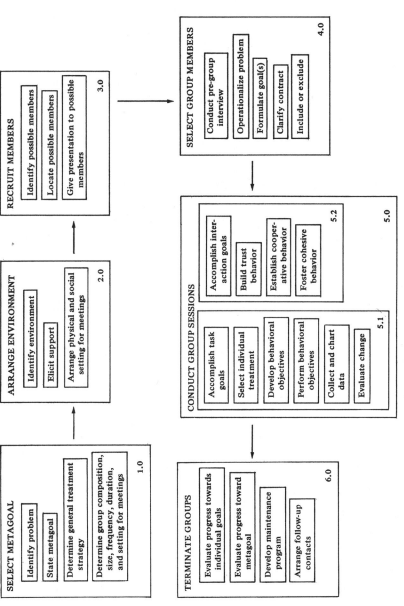

Figure 2. Major steps in behavioral group counseling.

problems sometimes come to the counselor from persons request-
ing help for themselves, it is important to identify potential problem areas which might be prevented. For example, a high school
counselor observed that several students consistently sat alone in
the cafeteria and walked by themselves. Conferences with teachers, parents and other students provided further evidence that
many students felt isolated and lacked friends. "Teaching" students how to meet new people and how to develop satisfying
friendships was identified as an important kind of preventive counseling. However, counselors in educational institutions should not
restrict their clientele to students. Frequently, working directly
with the teachers, parents, or administrators is effective. For example, on several occasions a counselor heard teachers complaining about their inability to deal with their feelings of stress and
frustration. With an eye on preventing future problems, the counselor decided to offer help by working with teachers in a group on
the management of stress and tension.

After a problem area has been identified in behavioral terms,
the question of individual or group counseling is considered. Although the efficiency factor in group counseling is an important
incentive, it should not be the determining factor. The intervention
strategy used is determined by the goals of treatment. If group
counseling would better facilitate the behavior in question, it
should then be selected as the model of treatment. Generally, a
group approach is optimal for goals concerning interpersonal or
social behaviors because the group itself is a social environment
where one can learn and practice new behaviors. Group counseling is not limited, however, to interpersonal change. Behavioral
group counseling can be used to alter a broad range of behavior—
from acrophobia and aggressive behavior to weight problems and
vocational concerns (cf. Thoresen and Hosford, 1973).

The Metagoal

After the counselor decides to utilize a group counseling intervention in a specific problem area, the next task is to specify the
desired outcome or metagoal for the group. The group's metagoal
identifies the focus of the group—the performance area in which

each member seeks change. The specific and explicit statement of the metagoal is crucial because confusion and ambiguity about the general goals of a group often cause frustration and failure. Studies have demonstrated (e.g., Raven and Rietsema, 1957) that persons with a clear picture of the group goal and the path to accomplishing it typically like their own task and the group task more, experience less hostile feelings, are better able to perceive different social roles in the group, and are more responsive to group influence than persons in groups in which goals and means are unclear.

Metagoals are broader than the members' goals, but are narrower than traditional goals such as "to enhance mental health" or "to foster self-actualization." The metagoal should be stated explicitly enough that it (1) points to a general treatment strategy, and (2) makes it possible to assess the extent to which the group achieves the metagoal. Behavioral counselors do not, of course, use the same techniques with every group. Instead, they try to select an overall procedure or combination of procedures most likely to help each member accomplish individual goals and, simultaneously, move the group as a whole towards the metagoal. In the friendship group, the metagoal was to learn the skills needed to develop and maintain satisfying relationships. In accord with this objective, the counselor relied primarily on the techniques of modeling and behavioral rehearsal, combined with social reinforcement for participation. The counselor who worked with the teachers' group had a different metagoal: the self-management of stress and tension. The major techniques involved variations of group desensitization.

Arranging the Environment

A counseling group does not exist in a vacuum; it is conducted within the context of several physical and social environments. The environments include the organization offering the service, such as a school, a recreation agency, or church, and the people who are affiliated with the organization as well as families of group members and members' peers. To be successful, the group counselor must gain some support of the environment. This is especially true when the concept of group counseling is first being introduced. Misunderstanding and confusion about the purposes of counseling groups can lead to many problems. Many parents, teachers and administrators equate all counseling groups with sensitivity, encounter, or awareness experiences and will take action to terminate what they believe is a harmful and unethical experience for students. In other situations, some persons believe their authority is being ignored or challenged when they learn *indirectly* about the group. Teachers, for example, sometimes feel that students are being excused from classes to attend a group session simply to avoid schoolwork or to talk very critically about them. Such problems can be reduced if the necessary efforts are made to arrange the environment.

The counselor first analyzes who constitutes the environment. When working with students in a school situation, this almost always includes those with administrative responsibility for the counseling program as well as the school. The counselor should meet with the relevant administrators to discuss the student problem situation and why group counseling is the appropriate intervention. The metagoal, techniques, nature of student participation and length and duration of sessions should be explained. Administrators in this way have an opportunity to make suggestions, voice concerns and provide support. In the same way, the counselor meets with teachers and with interested parents. Often, this gives other concerned persons an opportunity to feel involved in the program and to provide support.

Sometimes a verbal descripton does not suffice. Misgivings and misconceptions may still exist due to the negative "propaganda" about groups often portrayed in the mass media. Because a picture can be worth a thousand words, we have found it helpful to provide brief demonstrations of how groups function. A recent film entitled Behavioral Group Counseling (Counseling Films, 1973) has also been used to clarify what happens in a group.

Recruiting Members

The behavioral group counselor *actively* recruits members. For example, many students can be reached by visiting their classes and briefly discussing the group to be started. In a college setting, visits to dormitories and announcements in the campus paper have been effective. The following ad in the campus paper produced over fifty calls in three days: "Lonely? Trouble making friends? Group starting soon. Call X2108." Obviously, the traditional method of "wait and see," i.e., sitting in the office and waiting to talk to people who come is inadequate. The group counselor must reach out into the environment of prospective clients. If they are underachievers, he goes to the remedial reading class; if they are alienated students, he goes to the communal living group, the coffee shop; if they are troubled teachers, he goes to a teachers' meeting, the lunchroom, or for a beer on Friday.

An effective way to introduce group counseling is to describe it to potential members and answer their questions. The counselor begins by introducing himself and describing briefly his role in the organization and his concern about the problem area the group will deal with. The metagoal, what activities will happen in the sessions, confidentiality, commitment, and how one can join, are described. The counselor suggests that anyone interested in the group can talk with him privately without an obligation to join. We have found that showing the film on behavioral group counseling cited earlier in conjunction with an introductory talk is very successful in conveying information and stimulating client interest. Some "behavioral" group leaders have brought with them a member from a previous group to talk about the purpose of the group and how it was beneficial.

Pre-Group Interview

The pre-group interview with each prospective member is crucial in establishing an effective group. The first portion of the interview is devoted to explaining the metagoals and exploring the person's concerns. Attention is given to what the person can do well (e.g., leadership experience) as well as areas of difficulty. Possible techniques to be used in the group are discussed. The counselor expresses warmth, acceptance and a genuine concern for the person as a way of establishing some degree of trust and rapport. A major task of the counselor at this time is to evaluate the compatability of the person's major concerns with the group metagoal.

A basic characteristic of behavioral counseling is that client concerns are stated in terms of observable client actions. Further, these actions as goals are idiosyncratic, tailored to the individual situation. Usually, persons conceptualize their problems in global terms–"I'm lonely and depressed. . . . I have a withdrawn personality . . ." and are not clear about what changes they seek. One of the purposes of the pre-group interview is to help the client pinpoint the problem in more specific performance terms and start to decide on a terminal goal. To achieve this objective, the counselor cues and probes to find out what the person is currently doing that he finds disatisfying: When does he do it, how often, under what circumstances? The counselor starts to help the person specify what he would prefer to be *doing,* under what conditions and to what extent. This, of course, is a demanding task and one that is not always clarified in the pre-group interview. Sometimes the first few group sessions are used to help certain members clarify their problem and develop a clear goal.[1] A group counseling goal should meet four criteria: (1) it must be a goal desired by the client; (2) it must be compatible with the group's metagoal; (3) the counselor must agree to help the client achieve this goal; and (4) the goal must be stated so that behavioral assessment is possible.

A second objective of the pre-group interview concerns commitment. The prospective group member should make a verbal and/ or written commitment to group process and goals. The contract approach accomplishes both these objectives. The contract specifies the metagoals of the group and the techniques employed for their accomplishment, the member's goals and appropriate behavior, as well as the leader's goals and behavior. In Figure 3 these behaviors are categorized as task and interaction behaviors.[2]

---

1. One of the most difficult skills to learn as a group leader is assisting persons to clarify their concerns and to pinpoint what they want to do, i.e., in specifying client goals.

2. The distinction between task and interaction is not discrete. It is presented here more as a conceptual point for the reader than as a point to be discussed with the client in the interview.

The task behaviors are those actions which aid in the accomplishment of the group's metagoal, such as helping other members accomplish their goals, collecting information (data), carrying out outside tasks and participating in group exercises such as modeling and behavioral rehearsals. The interaction behaviors are those actions which facilitate openness and trust within the group, including self-disclosure, responding positively to suggestions from others, and listening carefully.

What the member can expect from the leader is specified in the leader contract. The leader's task goals are to help each member achieve his own goal; interaction goals are to facilitate openness, trust, and cohesiveness in order to develop a safe atmosphere for the accomplishment of the group's metagoal. A contract is a flexible tool that can be used to structure a wide variety of groups. It should be noted that contracts have also been used to facilitate task and interaction behaviors in "sensitivity training" groups (cf. Egan, 1970).

By carefully selecting group members, the counselor can increase the probability of facilitating behavior change. Thus, entry into the group is contingent upon the member's endorsement of the contract. In essence, the client must convince the counselor that he or she is indeed ready for participation in the group by having an appropriate goal, expressing a genuine commitment to accomplish this goal and agreeing to help others reach their goals.

Use of pre-group checklist (see Fig. 3) has been helpful for both beginning and experienced group counselors. It ensures that each point will be covered and aids in organizing the interview. Although the contract is often agreed upon verbally, the pre-group checklist, by modifying the wording appropriately for the client, can serve the function of a written contract.

Group Sessions

The group leader has two major goals to accomplish: task goals and interaction goals. Although the two goals are pursued simultaneously, we will discuss them separately.

TASK GOALS. The first two steps which the counselor follows in helping each member, i.e., operationalizing the problem and formulating the goal, are implemented primarily during the pre-

Name ___ Frank Gilette ___

Date ___ October 15, 1972 ___

1. ✓ Metagoal of group:

To learn how to meet persons and develop interpersonal skills needed for satisfying relationships.

2. ✓ Person's concern:

Afraid of new people. Feels always being judged by others. Very nervous in talking in group. No close friends.

3. ✓ Person's strengths, weaknesses:

Good athlete (track, basketball), good appearance, above average grades, some friends, poor voice control, no eye contact, limited conversation skills.

4. ✓ Possible technqiues:

Encouragement, modeling, behavioral rehearsal, contracting, outside tasks between group sessions.

5. ✓ Leader goals:

Task: To help members achieve their goals and maintain change after group terminates.

Interaction: To develop a safe and supportive atmosphere; to help members help each other; to encourage relevant member-to-member actions.

6. ✓ Leader behaviors:

Task: To use individualized techniques; to give relevant reinforcement; to provide necessary information; to assess individual progress.

Interaction: To structure interactions; to use technqiues to facilitate a safe atmosphere; to model appropriate behavior; to give support and encouragement for progress (no matter how modest); to listen carefully.

7. ✓ Member behaviors:

Task: To make commitment to accomplish goals and to help others; to collect information between and during sessions on one's actions; to carry out outside tasks; to participate in group exercises; to offer suggestions to others (including leader); to consider suggestions from others.

Interaction: To honor confidentiality; to encourage and praise others for progress; to give and accept suggestions and information; to cooperate; to listen carefully; to share reactions openly (self-disclose).

8. ✓ Tentative member goals:

To learn how to talk with 2 or 3 others about school and feel relaxed.
To talk on a variety of topics (small talk).
To start to develop one close friendship.

9. ✓ Client requests entry

10. ✓ Leader accepts client for group

11. ✓ Time of first meeting:

October 27, 1:15 to 2:45 p.m.

12. ✓ Location of first meeting:

Group Room (24-A)

13. ✓ Agenda of first meeting:

To get acquainted, share concerns, make goals more specific.

14. ✓ Additional information:

Figure 3. Example of the Pre-Group Interview Checklist for Friendship Group.

group interview. Each member arrives at the first group session with his problem and goal somewhat defined. The leader's major objectives during the first few sessions are to help members further clarify their problems and goals and to consider appropriate treatment strategies.

One member of the friendship group, for example, suggested that Mark advertise for a friend in the Berkeley Barb, a local "underground" newspaper. This suggestion was not rejected simply because it was unorthodox. Geisinger (1971), in fact, has reported success using this method with adults. Any suggestion from members should be carefully evaluated. Consideration is given to (1) estimated probability that the procedure will work, i.e., help member accomplish his overall goal, (2) relationship of member's values to the method proposed, and (3) consideration of possible consequences of procedure.

Even though advertising in the Berkeley Barb may be an exciting adventure for Mark, it might not lead to meeting the appropriate people. Such a step may conflict with Mark's value system because he sees it as a "desperate move." Further, his parents might strongly disapprove. On the other hand, the suggestion of joining a club could put Mark into contact with boys of similar interest, and club membership is generally looked upon favorably by parents and peers. After each alternative strategy has been evaluated, one or more are selected by weighing each one in relation to the others. If none of the alternatives are acceptable, the group then returns to generating more alternatives.

BEHAVIORAL OBJECTIVES. The leader's next objective is to help each member determine the specific steps or means to be undertaken to implement their treatment strategy. Behavioral objectives are plans for specific action which members undertake within and between group sessions in order to move progressively closer to their goal. These action plans constitute the heart of treatment. The group meeting provides the social and physical environment for members to learn and practice behaviors that can be tried outside the group.

Krumboltz and Thoresen (1969) have delineated three criteria of an adequate objective. First, a behavioral objective specifies the behavior to be performed to an extent that it may be reliably recorded by an observer (the person himself is often the observer). This criterion covers covert or internal behaviors such as thoughts (self-verbalizations) and images. Self-recording of covert behavior was performed in the teachers' group. Each teacher rated and recorded his own anxiety level, at specified intervals, on a ten-point scale. Angie also counted the number of times she engaged in a positive self-thought, e.g., "I did well in talking to Mr. Clark." Second, a behavioral objective indicates how much (i.e., how many times, how long, etc.) of the behavior is required to meet the objective. Nora, a member of the friendship group, had an objective that illustrates this criterion: "She will approach at least *one person once on each school day. . . .*" Third, a behavioral objective specifies under what conditions or circumstances the behavior will occur. Dallas' eighth objective stated that he was to practice his relaxation-meditation exercises each night before he went to bed. (This identified the circumstance of the behavior.)

If objectives convey the "whats, whens, and wheres" of actions, then the member can succeed more readily. A vague objective such as "I will be more friendly" is difficult to carry out. It may leave the person confused as to what constitutes "being friendly." Further, it is unclear with whom he should be friendly as well as how much is "more friendly"? Such confusion can result in failure, which in turn can provide data to confirm a person's self-fulfilling hypothesis, e.g., "I'm not worthy of friends." Maximizing the chances of having successful experiences is important. Behavioral objectives represent a series of successive approximations to the goal. Each step should be large enough that some progress is being made, yet small enough that the person can carry out the behavior with a good chance of being successful.

There is no standardized or best method for determining what the series of behavioral objectives should be for a particular person. When persons are enthusiastic about changing, they often attempt to do too much in one step. In forming objectives in the beginning, one rule of thumb is to divide whatever a person wants to attempt into two or three objectives. With some success, the objectives can later cover larger tasks. Nora was so motivated to learn approach behaviors that after the first group session she wanted to approach ten people and ask them a question. The leader suggested that she first observe the approach behaviors of others and then approach at least one person a day and ask a brief question. From observing Nora in the group, the counselor was confident that she would succeed in these objectives. Objectives are individualized based in part on skills the person has already demonstrated. Even when two members have the same goals, the series of behavioral objectives for each will usually be different from session to session.

A major task of the counselor is to go beyond the member's immediate problems and focus on how to *prevent* the necessity of future counseling. The person who repeatedly fails to deal with a problem effectively creates more problems, setting a failure cycle in action. D'Zurilla and Goldfried (1971) have hypothesized that "some individuals behave ineffectively not only because of a lack of successful learning experiences with certain specific situations, but in addition, because of a deficit or some kind of disruption in one or more aspects of problem-solving performance" (p. 110). Although the group counselor cannot prevent future problems from occurring, he can teach members a strategy for handling problems effectively. Helping members attain their goals within a problem-solving context facilitates this learning. In short, the group serves as a laboratory where the members learn a process of problem solving.

INTERACTION GOALS. Helping each person accomplish goals is the major focus of behavioral group counseling. But more is involved than a series of consecutive individual sessions taking place in a group. The leader must conceptualize and relate to the group on two levels: as a collection of discrete persons and as an entity itself. The leader's task goals are aimed at the person within the group; interaction goals are focused on the group as a whole. A wealth of data from the group dynamics social-psychological literature attests to the powerful impact of a group environment on its members. For example, cohesiveness or the likelihood of mutual attraction is one important factor. Studies (e.g., Back, 1951; Berkowitz, 1954) have demonstrated a relationship between level of group cohesiveness and its influence on member behavior. Members in highly cohesive groups typically can be more influenced by each other.

Developing cooperative behavior (a "norm") is another factor. Studies (e.g., Deutsch, 1949) have found that groups ranked high in cooperative actions demonstrate more solutions to problems, acted in more positive ways with each other, and reported fewer communication problems than members in less cooperative groups.

The group leader endeavors systematically to influence the group in order to harness its power in service of the metagoal. This process is set into motion during the pre-group interview when the group is presented in an attractive way and expectations are developed that others in the group will be sharing much in common with each other. The leader sets a norm for cooperativeness during the discussion of the contract, i.e., members are expected to help each other attain their goals. In this way, the leader starts to lay the foundations of cohesiveness, trust, and openness that are built upon during group sessions.

The systematic use of reinforcement, cueing-shaping, modeling, and extinction can be used to develop the group as a whole. Krumboltz and Potter (1973) developed a behavioral model to facilitate trust, cohesiveness and metagoal accomplishment in groups. The concepts of trust and cohesiveness as well as goal accomplishment are defined in terms of *observable member behaviors*. For example, the definition of cohesiveness includes a high frequency of "we" statements (referring to the group as a whole) and member-to-member talk, and a low frequency of negative statements about the group as a whole, positive remarks about a subgroup or clique, and talk directed exclusively at the leader. By listening to a tape-recorded segment of a group session, the leader can count the frequency of "we" statements and member-to-member talk. From this analysis he can develop a specific interaction goal. The leader, for example, might choose to use a group exercise such as having members work briefly in dyads to discuss their similarities with each other. The leader can then re-inforce members when they make statements to other members and when they make references to their similarities with each other. The leader can again count the frequency of "we" statements and member-to-member talk in later sessions to assess the impact of the intervention. Schutz (1969) and Liberman (1972) have also described a number of interaction tasks for developing cohesive, cooperative and trusting behavior. Although the functional rela-tionship of what we have called task- and interactive-goal change in member behavior remains unclear, group leaders should, we be-lieve, work to promote both in their groups.

TECHNIQUES. No standard techniques are employed in a routine fashion. Behavioral group counseling is experimental, drawing in large part on social learning theory as a basis for techniques (Bandura, 1969). Techniques, however, are not restricted to only those for which considerable data exists, e.g., positive reinforce-ment. Sometimes the leader may try out a procedure that is not related directly with research in social learning. The leader, for example, may use a non-verbal exercise described in the Gestalt therapy literature to accomplish a particular objective. Data are gathered to see if the leader's hypothesis is supported, i.e., does the technique bring about observable desired change in member behavior?

Many techniques which have strong empirical support in indi-vidual counseling have not yet been studied systematically in groups. However, adaptations of individual counseling methods in groups can be studied experimentally because each member's progress is being monitored continuously. If a technique holds promise as a way to alter behavior, and if it is possible to assess consequences empirically, then the technique is appropriate for group counseling. The same procedure can, of course, be labeled many different ways. Identification of a technique with a certain theoretical viewpoint is no justification for not using a technique, as long as it is used empirically. In essence, if a technique can be shown to work, then use it.

A combination of techniques holds excellent promise as ways to deal with five areas of action of common concern to group leaders: (1) learning new behaviors; (2) reducing fears, stresses and anxieties; (3) encouraging behavior to be performed that has already been learned; (4) reducing negative, undesirable behaviors; and (5) learning self-control skills to maintain desired changes. This combination can be characterized as "instruct-model-practice-reinforce." For example, Nora did not know how to initiate and maintain a conversation. Modeling combined with shaping or reinforcing successive approximations was used. The desired behaviors of approaching a person, initiating and carrying on a conversation are analyzed and divided into small steps. Nora's first step was to be in the presence of other people and approach them visually and observe. She did this by going to the cafeteria each day and observing the behavior of a popular person. This has the added benefit of teaching her how to select and learn from models in her own environment. Next, Nora learned how to approach a person and ask a simple question in the group. She was instructed in the specific behaviors involved by recalling her experience of observing models in the cafeteria and from suggestions from the other members and the leader. Next, a group member skilled in approaching and asking questions demonstrated or modeled this behavior. The modeling was discussed and Nora rehearsed it in the group. Nora then established an objective to carry out between sessions. When Nora returned to the next group session, she discussed her performance and was socially reinforced for her success. This combination treatment was repeated until Nora learned the complex behaviors required by her goal.

A variety of sources about techniques are available. Krumboltz and Thoresen (1969) present examples of many techniques such as reinforcement, modeling, contingency management, systematic desensitization and combination procedures. Lazarus (1971), Wolpe (1969), and Yates (1970) also present a wealth of information. Kanfer (1973) offers a comprehensive list of references to theory, research and techniques, while Thoresen and Mahoney (1974) review recent research and clinical uses of behavioral self-control techniques. (Also see Mahoney and Thoresen, 1974.)

EVALUATION

Throughout this chapter an emphasis has been placed upon the necessity to specify the problem, the goal, and behavioral objectives in terms of observable behaviors that can be counted and monitored reliably. Collecting data on a systematic basis, typically by means of client monitoring and recording, is the major characteristic of a behavioral approach to counseling. It provides both the client and counselor with information about the client's progress *during* counseling and indicates if counseling is succeeding. If no means of monitoring a behavior can be devised, the behavior has not been adequately defined. If data are not gathered systematically on each group member, then the strategy employed is not a behavioral one.

To foster empirical evaluation, some kind of "design" is helpful. Usually an intensive or "N = 1" design is appropriate (cf. Sidman, 1960; Chassan, 1967; Glass, Willson and Gottman, 1972; and Thoresen, in press). In this method, success is determined by comparing data on a specific behavior collected before treatment (baseline) with data collected on the same behavior during treatment as well as after treatment. In this way, the person serves as his "own control" in that the comparison is with how much the person has changed from the before (baseline) phase. For discussion purposes, we will present how this works with one group member, followed by a brief discussion of how evaluation fits into the flow of the group sessions, how the group as an entity is evaluated, and how the leader evaluates his own performance.

The first step is to specify the problematic behavior. For example, Angie, a member of the teachers' group, frequently had devaluating thoughts about herself and her teaching. An observer, in this case Angie herself, pinpointed the antecedents of behavior, i.e., the context and those events that take place immediately prior to her negative self-thoughts and the consequences, i.e., those events that happen immediately after the negative thoughts. Angie stated that when she was at home, any reference to her job or teaching in general was followed by negative self-thoughts. At work, talking to a colleague or disciplining a student is also followed by negative thoughts. In addition, negative thoughts always seem to result in anxiety, i.e., increased heart rate, "knots" in her stomach, and perspiring. Angie's goal was to increase positive thoughts about herself and about her teaching performance and to reduce self-critical thoughts. Before Angie attempted to make any changes, she first used a wrist counter to record positive and negative self-thoughts. She also charted their frequency each day for a week. This "before treatment" phase provided a baseline, i.e., a quantitative description of the behavior used as a reference point for evaluating change.

The treatment program included cueing and shaping positive self-thoughts. Angie also decided, with the group's assistance, to make going to the hairdresser—something she currently did once a week and really enjoyed—contingent on having an average of at least five positive self-thoughts a day. After Angie compiled a list of her positive qualities, she "cued" herself to subvocalize positive self-statements by attaching a small "happy face" decal to her wristwatch lens. Seeing a decal reminded her to engage in a positive thought. Angie's increase in positive thoughts were socially reinforced during group sessions; she brought her data charts to the sessions and reported what changes had occurred.

Angie continued to count and chart the frequency of positive self-thoughts during cueing and reinforcement. It was now possible to evaluate the effectiveness of the intervention by comparing the data from the treatment phase with the baseline. If the frequency of positive self-thoughts notably increased, the intervention could be considered effective and could be continued. If, on the other hand, the data revealed no substantial change in the frequency of positive thoughts, then the intervention could be judged ineffective. Such a finding would lead to reconsideration of the problem, goals, and method.[3]

Evaluation does not end with the termination of group sessions.

---

3. What constitutes a notable or substantial change is, of course, relative. Visual inspection of the charts can be deceptive. We have used White's "split middle" analysis technique to assess the statistical significance of change in the "slope" and "level" of data between phases (cf. White, 1971). The technique is easily learned and used by members.

To be successful, Angie must demonstrate that the change in positive thoughts has been maintained after treatment. To help maintain change, Angie decided that she would continue the cueing of positive thoughts. Angie placed happy-face decals as cues in several places, such as in her car and in the kitchen. Once a week she would change the location of cues to retain their effectiveness. Angie again monitored her positive and negative self-thoughts during the fifth week after the group ended. She brought these data with her to the follow-up group meeting where these data were compared to the baseline and treatment data. Her data showed an average of nine positive self-thoughts per day during the followup week. She also reported negative self-thoughts at less than five for the entire week.

Generally, it is easiest to have members monitor their own behaviors, although this should be supplemented with information from other observers. Outside observation is, of course, not possible when the target behavior is internal. Sometimes external actions can be observed that relate to the internal actions. In Angie's case, another group member volunteered to record the number of positive self-statements Angie made during each group session. Angie also had her husband rate her once a week on her "attitude" toward herself in terms of her teaching and school in general, i.e., how often did she complain about school, her inadequacy about teaching, and her feelings of despair?

When members have prior experience with self-monitoring, baseline observations can begin immediately after the pre-group interview. In this way members can arrive at the initial sessions with some baseline data. Typically, however, a large portion of the initial session is devoted to discussing self-monitoring, i.e., why it is important and how is it done. Gathering baseline becomes the first behavioral objective. Each member keeps a chart of the behavior as the group continues and typically brings data to each group session.

Part of each session is set aside to evaluate progress and alter behavioral objectives if progress is lacking. Of course, being able to "see" the change is often reinforcing in itself for group members, and can provide excellent motivation. Prior to the follow-up session, each member again monitors the behavior for a specific period of time and brings these data to the meeting. Follow-up data are compared to the baseline and to the data collected during counseling to evaluate the effectiveness of the maintenance program. If the data indicate that the behavior is sliding back to the baseline, the maintenance program is analyzed and changed. The leader arranges to meet with this member again in the future to evaluate the new maintenance program.

What happens in group sessions can be evaluated from session to session. Certain behaviors, such as how often members engage in talk irrelevant to the group's metagoal and how often members direct comments to the leader versus other members, can be identified by the group. Baseline data can be collected by having two members (one for each behavior) count the behaviors each time they occur. The group can formulate a goal and decide on appropriate interventions. The behaviors are then monitored during each session and progress is evaluated. Using this approach during the group sessions has several benefits, such as (1) members' participation in the process increases their commitment to the group, and (2) members are given an opportunity to learn problem solving. Rose (1972) presents a good discussion of various methods of counting and charting behavior during group sessions.

It is equally important for the leader to self-observe and evaluate his own behavior, such as how often he verbally reinforces a member or asks for suggestions. It is difficult, however, for the beginning leader to conduct a group and simultaneously monitor his own behavior. Sometimes the leader can ask a member to observe him using a wrist counter, tally chart, or tape-recording. Sharing the data with the group and asking for suggestions about changing a particular behavior can be very effective. Not only does self-observing and sharing provide information about his own performance, but it models these actions for the group.

A Comment on Qualifications

The leader should be able to act in ways usually described as warm, genuine and empathic. These behaviors are crucial, especially during the pre-group interview, if the leader is to understand each person's major concerns. In addition, these actions greatly enhance the leader's effectiveness to influence members in the group. The leader must also possess a thorough understanding of social learning theory and techniques, coupled with skills of data gathering and analysis.

In many ways, the leader functions as a "teacher" who is responsible for encouraging learning in a variety of ways. Teaching skills are needed, for example, in arranging the group environment so that each member learns how to collect data on his own actions, i.e., self-observation skills. The notion of teaching skills is conceived of here as much broader than the usual "teaching as telling." Indeed, one of the major tasks is for the behavioral group counselor to arrange the environment, including his own behavior, to facilitate self-teaching and self-learning.

How much professional training is needed remains an open question. Clearly, lay persons can readily learn to implement many behavioral group techniques. However, additional training is needed to synthesize theoretical rationales with empirical findings in using and evaluating counseling techniques. The authors have participated in a one-year behavioral systems training program for counselors in which behavioral group counseling skills have been developed (Hendricks, Ferguson, and Thoresen, 1973). However, the training program has not been systematically compared with other variations so that the optimal amount of time and experiences in training still remains unknown.

We believe that the leader should participate at some time during training as a member of a behavioral counseling group. This opportunity gives the prospective leader a firsthand experience of how it feels to be a member who participates in a pre-group interview, makes a commitment to specific goals, works between sessions on behavioral objectives, gathers data on his own actions, and helps others with their goals. Unfortunately, no data exist on this question other than opinions of former students who have reported its value. Hopefully, some controlled experiments will clarify this question as well as those involved with amount and type of training.

Some Limitations

Behavioral group counseling offers a systematic yet flexible approach to a broad spectrum of client problems. As such, it is not limited to a particular problem or a particular technique. A behavioral group will not always be effective under all conditions. Success is limited by the training and commitment of the leader as well as by the environmental conditions (e.g., setting) in which the group takes place. The most critical limitation is "what we don't know about counseling in groups." Controlled empirical studies of group counseling are needed where specific techniques are examined in the light of observed changes in client behavior. Many questions need empirical answers. The structure we have presented should be examined. Questions, such as the relative effect of the pre-group interview, specific versus vague client goals, the use of self-monitoring and charting and how to best maintain behavior change after the group has terminated, need investigation.

A behavioral framework does provide a relevant strategy for research and evaluation, one that makes it possible for group leaders to be far more accountable for their efforts. The limitations of behavioral group counseling are empirical ones which can be reduced with controlled research.

SUMMARY COMMENT

Behavioral group counseling as presented here provides a structure by which many persons can be helped in making changes they desire. A variety of techniques based in part on social learning theory can be used to alter and maintain behavior. The group setting can provide a powerful social and physical environment to bring about change, coupled with behaviorally-stated tasks carried out between group sessions. Group counseling involves far more than insightful discussions.

Behavioral group counseling shares the following features:

1. Each member is helped to develop one or more "client goals,"

i.e., statements of what the person will do, to what extent and under what circumstances, by the end of the group.

2. A variety of techniques based in part on a social learning rationale are tried on an experimental basis.

3. Information or "data" are gathered continuously—usually by each group member (self-monitoring).

4. Each member's own baseline or "before treatment" data serve as the basis of comparison, i.e., the person serves as his own "control" for purposes of evaluating change.

5. Each member works on behavioral objectives as the group proceeds, i.e., engages in certain actions between as well as during group sessions as steps toward their goals.

6. Empirical data are used to measure success; group success is measured by the proportion of members who accomplish and maintain their goals, i.e., their changed behavior.

REFERENCES

Back, K. W.: Influence through social communication. *Journal of Abnormal and Social Psychology, 46:*9, 1951.

Bandura, A.: *Principles of Behavior Modification.* New York, Holt, Rinehart and Winston, 1969.

Berkowitz, L.: Group standards, cohesiveness, and productivity. *Human Relations, 7:*509, 1954.

Chassen, J. B.: *Research Design in Clinical Psychology and Psychiatry.* New York, Appleton-Century-Crofts, 1967.

Counseling Films, Inc.: *Behavioral Group Counseling.* Madison, Wisconsin, Counseling Films, Inc., 1973.

Deutsch, M.: An experimental study of the effects of cooperation and competition upon group process. *Human Relations, 2:*199, 1949.

D'Zurilla, T., and Goldfried, M.: Problem solving and behavior modification. *Journal of Abnormal Psychology, 87:*(1), 107, 1971.

Egan, G.: *Encounter: Group Processes for Interpersonal Growth.* Belmont, California, Brooks-Cole, 1970.

Eysenck, H. J.: Behavior therapy as a scientific discipline. *Journal of Consulting and Clinical Psychology, 36:*314, 1971.

Geisinger, D.: Personal Communication (Behavior Therapist in private practice). San Francisco, 1971.

Glass, G. V., Wilson, V. L., and Gottman, J. M.: *Design and Analysis of Time-Series Experiments.* Boulder, Colorado, Laboratory of Educational Research, 1972.

Hendricks, C. G., Fergusen, J., and Thoresen, C. E.: Toward counseling competence: The Stanford program. *Personnel and Guidance Journal,* *51*:(6), 418, 1973.

Kanfer, F. H.: Behavior modification: An overview. In Thoresen, C. E. (Ed.): *Behavior Modification in Education.* Seventy-Second Yearbook of the National Society for the Study of Education, Part I. Chicago, University of Chicago Press, 1973.

Krumboltz, J. D., and Potter, B.: Behavioral techniques for developing trust, cohesiveness, and goal accomplishment. *Educational Technology,* *13*:26 1973.

Krumboltz, J. D., and Thoresen, C. E.: *Behavioral Counseling: Cases and Techniques.* San Francisco, Holt, Rinehart and Winston, 1969.

Lazarus, A. A.: *Behavior Therapy and Beyond.* New York, McGraw-Hill, 1971.

Liberman, R. P.: Learning interpersonal skills in groups: Harnessing the behavioristic horse to the humanistic wagon. In Houts, P., and Serber, M. (Eds.): *After the Turn On, What?* Champaign, Illinois, Research Press, 1972.

Mahoney, M. J., and Thoresen, C. E.: *Self-Control: Power to the Person.* Monterey, California, Brooks-Cole, 1974.

Raven, B. H., and Reitsema, J.: The effects of varied clarity of group goal and group path upon the individual and his relation to his group. *Human Relations, 10*:29, 1957.

Rose, S. D.: *Treating Children in Groups: A Behavioral Approach.* San Francisco, Jossey-Boss 1972.

Schutz, W. C.: *Joy: Expanding Human Awareness.* New York, Grove Press, 1967.

Sidman, M.: *The Tactics of Scientific Research.* New York, Free Press, 1960.

Strupp, H. H., and Bergin, A. E.: Some empirical and conceptual bases for coordinated research in psychotherapy: A critical review of issues, trends and evidence. *International Journal of Psychiatry, 72*:1, 1969.

Thoresen, C. E.: The intensive approach: Counseling research. *The Counseling Psychologist,* in press.

Thoresen, C. E., and Hosford, R.: Behavioral approaches to counseling. In Thoresen, C. E. (Ed.): *Behavior Modification in Education.* Seventy-Second Yearbook of the National Society for the Study of Education, Part I. Chicago, University of Chicago Press, 1973.

Thoresen, C. E., and Mahoney, M. J.: *Behavioral Self-Control.* New York, Holt, Rinehart and Winston, 1974.

Varenhorst, B.: Behavioral group counseling. In Gazda, G. M. (Ed.): *Theories and Methods of Group Counseling in the Schools.* Springfield, Illinois, Charles C Thomas, 1969.

White, O. R.: The prediction of human performance in the single case: An examination of four techniques. Working Paper No. 15, Regional Resource Center for Handicapped Children. Eugene Oregon College of Education, University of Oregon, 1972.

Wolpe, J.: *The Practice of Behavior Therapy*. New York, Pergamon Press, 1969.

Yates, A. J.: *Behavior Therapy*. New York, Wiley, 1970.

CHAPTER XVII

THE TELEOANALYTIC GROUP COUNSELING APPROACH

Manford Sonstegard and Rudolf Dreikurs[1]

INTRODUCTION

T HE GROUP APPROACH pursued by the writers has in turn been called Adlerian psychology, Individual Psychology, and the Teleoanalytic approach. Alfred Adler was one of the first, if not the first, to use group approaches and, as far as can be determined, the first to use group methods in a school setting, counseling parents and children before groups of teachers in the schools of Vienna. The psychological formulation, which Adler called Individual Psychology to denote the holistic concept of the human organism, resides in the philosophic belief that understanding human behavior necessitates understanding the entire field in which the individual operates.

Individual Psychology, therefore, indicates a socioteleological approach to the understanding of human motivation. In this context man is perceived as a social being and his behavior as goal-directed and purposeful (Dreikurs, 1957).

Group counseling in the strictest sense is a comparatively recent development. Gazda (1968) traces its growth to a period encompassing the last thirty to forty years.

However, group methods were not unknown in remote ages. A unique group approach, the dialogue, was employed by Socrates. Aristotle was aware of the therapeutic effect of the theatre as a catharsis or purgation of the audiences' emotions through psychological involvement in the performance. The Marquis de Sade wrote and directed plays, which were performed by his fellow inmates of the Chorenton Mental Asylum with therapeutic results

---

1. Deceased—1973.

(Corsini, 1957). There is some evidence that group approaches were used by priests in Ethiopia.

Contemporary group counseling methods are essentially a product of the twentieth century. Group counseling is almost exclusively a democratic procedure reflecting the political and social climate of a nation. It is both the child and the midwife of democracy requiring a society based on freedom and equality in order to flourish while at the same time perpetuating those ideals.

Since group counseling thrives only in a free social and political environment, it is not unusual that group techniques have developed and have been rapidly disseminated in the United States. The writers and other group counselors with a teleoanalytic orientation have liberally borrowed from Adlerian group psychotherapy for adaptation to group counseling in the educational setting.

DEFINITION

With the teleoanalytic psychological formulation, the general procedures of group psychotherapy and group counseling are much alike, particularly if adolescents and adults are counseled. Psychotherapy is more complete and directed toward changing the faulty life style. Group counseling does not endeavor to bring about changes in the personality; rather, the focus is on the immediate situation, emphasizing the individual's mistaken goals and a reinterpretation of the individual's concepts of himself and his motives. The approach is not to effect a pervasive psychological change but to help the individual discover and redirect his mistaken intentions. In other words, the therapeutic procedure is to effect motivation modification.

THEORETICAL FORMULATIONS

Before proceeding to a discussion of group counseling, it seems appropriate first to describe the teleoanalytic approach to counseling in general. The technique of counseling or psychotherapy practiced by teleoanalytic psychologists can be described as an uncovering and interpreting form of therapy with a characteristic method of exploration, interpretation, and guidance. Like any specific approach to counseling, it has its own theoretical framework.

Man, in this theoretical framework, is perceived as a social being whose every action has a purpose. The holistic view of man is reflected in the name Individual Psychology. It was meant to indicate the indivisibility of man, who is more than the sum total of all his physical, mental, and emotional processes and functions. In contrast to prevalent mechanistic, deterministic theories, Adler recognized man's creative ability, which permits him to set his own goals and determine his own movements, expressing his total personality, his past experiences, his present attitudes and his ideas about his future. The teleological concept implies self-determination. It does not matter whether the individual is aware of his decisions or not. Consciousness is not required for most functions, be they physical or psychological. Man operates on an economy principle; he is consciously aware only of what he needs or what he wants to know. He uses all his abilities and faculties in line with his intentions. His mind and body, his ability to think and to feel are at his disposal, without the requirement of consciousness, which often would impede rather than assist him.

Man as a social being is primarily motivated by a strong desire to belong. Only within the group can he fulfill the potentialities which he possesses. All human qualities are then conceived as expressions of social interaction; they indicate movement toward others. Social interest, a feeling of belonging, permits and stimulates full social interaction; it is restricted by feelings of inferiority. If the individual feels inadequate or inferior to others, then he doubts his place in the group. Then, instead of moving toward participation, he defends himself against social demands. Maladjustments and dysfunction result from partial or total discouragement. Manifest symptoms of maladjustment are safeguards. They ensure against loss of prestige and against open admission of antisocial or asocial intentions.

Self-deception about one's intentions is part of normal human experience. No one knows himself; no one can be sure of his motivations and intentions. We need subjectivity to participate in social living. We need a biased apperception to move forcefully in a self-chosen direction. Our whole personality is based on a subjective interpretation of life, developed during our formative years.

Personality is the result of training which is less stimulated by heredity and environment than by the child's own interpretation, conclusions and decisions. The basic concept of himself and life, the guiding lines which he has set for himself for orientation toward social participation form a fixed pattern: the life style. Fundamental notions, convictions, and logical assumptions underline the life style and form the "private logic" on which the individual operates.

PHASES OF COUNSELING

Teleoanalytic group counseling can distinguish four phases in every uncovering and interpretative form of counseling: (1) relationship: the establishment and maintenance of a proper counseling relationship; (2) analysis: investigation of dynamics leading to an understanding of the client, his personality and his problems; (3) interpretation: since each school has its own concepts of psychodynamics, of personality development and psychopathology, methods of investigation and interpretation show characteristic differences; and (4) reorientation and reeducation: specific means of promoting changes and improvement characterize the teleoanalytic general orientation. Even though the four phases overlap, each deserves special consideration.

MECHANISMS INHERENT IN THE TELEOANALYTIC APPROACH TO GROUP COUNSELING

A number of mechanisms, germane to group counseling, explain its effectiveness. The educational feature of group counseling is one of these mechanisms. Group counseling is learning. If learning is to take place there must be action, and group participation is the action that is necessary. Without participation by members no therapy can result. The participation can be of a nonverbal as well as a verbal nature. Even though a member of the group merely listens without comment, he may go away with some clarification of his problem. Witnessing disclosures made in a group and hearing the group analysis or "feedback" guided and stimulated by the counselor, can supply the listener with new insights. Testimony for this procedure is sometimes expressed by, "What you say is nothing new, but I have never thought of it that way before." Insight, and thereby an understanding of our own problems through listening to someone else discuss his, is a unique phenomenon of group counseling. A group member identifies with others as he comes to understand their feelings and to accept their ideas. This encourages participation. Universalization is the cementing element in achieving group cohesiveness.

Insight, however, is not the only mechanism for change. The nature of deficiencies and failures makes encouragement appear to be an essential factor in all corrective endeavors. Feeling inferior means having no place in society. This is the most devastating role for any individual. Our competitive culture increases the danger of not measuring up to established standards. A profoundly discouraged individual requires reassurance in every counseling session. This may be done deliberately or it may be a by-product of the session. The success of the counselor in group counseling depends to a large extent upon his ability to provide encouragement. Conversely, failure is generally due to the counselor's inability to encourage. Reorientation and redirection of mistaken goals requires restoration of the counselee's faith in himself, a realization of his strength and ability, and a belief in his own dignity and worth. Without encouragement, insight will not promote change. Imparting to the counselee a sense of worth and value contradicts the many negative social influences to which he is exposed every day.

Peer encouragement often plays a larger role in group counseling than counselor encouragement. Children and parents are often more influenced and encouraged by their own peers than by a teacher or counselor. Group counseling not only helps an individual parent or child to help himself, but members begin to help each other; for participating in a group almost automatically evokes mutual help. Most classrooms are competitive, with each student interested, for the most part, in his own elevation. Under these conditions there is little chance to assume responsibility for one another or to counteract the social isolation in which each student exists. It is generally assumed that children in the same classroom know each other. On the contrary, many are as socially isolated as a hermit. Group counseling helps to dissolve the social wall within which many children live. A kindergartner one day, as the group was about to close its weekly session said, "Can I bring Betsy to the group?" The counselor asked, "Why would you want Betsy to join the group?" "Because she doesn't talk. That's what worries me. Maybe if I could bring her with me we could help her."

Recognizing that the problems of all children are essentially social gives group counseling its special significance in regard to both the diagnosis of the child's problems and their solutions. The group provides a social situation with real meaning. Some youngsters have never had an opportunity to test themselves in a real social situation. They may never have adequately found their place in a family group or been assured a place in the school group. In group counseling each member feels that he has a place despite the various ideas and attitudes which he encounters from his peers. Under the guidance of a counselor he learns how to contend with these as he develops coping devices which are to his advantage when he returns to the family and to the classroom. The problems of each youngster reveal themselves in the group in which he attempts to interact. Therefore, they must be solved in a group. It is in group counseling that a youngster finds that he is equal to others. In counseling groups, deficiencies lose their stigma. Paradoxically, deficiencies may be the necessary qualification for membership in counseling groups, as is the case in group counseling for underachievers. Thus, in a group, deficiencies do not lessen social status, but rather serve as a basis for equality for all group members.

In a democratic society, as contrasted with an autocratic society, an atmosphere of equality is developed. As has been pointed out above, the potentiality for establishing socially positive attitudes is not found in the community or in the school, but it is possible in well-directed counseling groups. The group thus becomes a value-forming agent. Individual counseling does not lend itself to bringing about necessary value changes. The normal family and classroom experiences of a youngster are not usually conducive to correcting his already established faulty value system. They may fortify wrong values. Since all human values are of a social nature, group counseling cannot avoid dealing with values. Social participation in one way or another affects the value system of the students. The impact of social experiences in group counseling is bound to have a beneficial effect on the value system of each participant. It is of extreme importance that teachers and counselors and even neighbors take a more dynamic role in value formation. Adults have largely abdicated their rightful position in serving as norm setting and value forming agents. Because of this, value formation and norm setting have become a prerogative for subgroups in which the youngster attempts to find his place.

SAMPLE PROTOCOL

One sample protocol will not encompass all the mechanisms and features essential to a good group counseling session; however, the following session does illustrate a representative teleoanalytic group approach. This particular incident involved thirdgrade children and was conducted in a school setting.

> Dan: Do you know my Mom? She usually goes every Wednesday night.
> Counselor: What does she think about these meetings?
> Dan: She thinks it is okay and she thinks it helps us.
> Counselor: Do you think it helps to have parents get together and talk about situations?
> Milton: Yes, it keeps the parents going—things are different at home now.
> Dan: It helps both children and parents.
> Counselor: Do you think parents learn something new?
> Dan: We talk about it at home. Mother tells me about the meeting and I tell her about the group meeting.
> Counselor: What have you learned? Have you learned anything from our discussions?
> Dan: I don't think Bill has learned very much. He keeps looking around at things.
> Counselor: You don't think that he has learned very much?
> Dan: He still picks the . . . he still unthreads his socks.
> Counselor: No, but you see. . . . How do you feel about this, Buzz? Dan's attack on Bill? How do you feel about this? Do you think he is. . . . What do you think about what he did?
> Buzz: I don't think he just likes him.
> Dan: He doesn't think that I like him very much. He doesn't really think that I like Bill.

Counselor: Don't you like Bill? Is this true?

Dan: No, I like Bill, but, well, he does things to kind of aggravate people.

Counselor: Does he aggravate you?

Dan: Well, sometimes.

Counselor: But you don't dislike him even if he does. Now, was Bill doing anything that hurt our group this morning?

Dan: Well, he was attracting attention for one thing.

Counselor: I beg your pardon.

Dan: I said he was attracting attention.

Counselor: I was wondering since Dan doesn't have any particular dislike for Bill, why did he point out what Bill was doing wrong?

Dan: Well, he wasn't listening and getting much from the group.

Counselor: Yeah, but . . .

Dan: He should be listening.

Counselor: Umhum, you think he should be listening all the time. Well maybe he was listening. Bill were you listening this morning?

Bill: Oh, I sorta on and sorta off.

Counselor: How do you feel about Dan? Do you feel that he is your friend?

Bill: Oh, ah, it all depends on what times.

Counselor: What do you mean, depends on what times?

Bill: Well, well, once in a while when I am trying to help him out in some way, then he's my friend. But then sometimes I am out at the swing—ah, this is just an example of what goes on and ah, then ah, then, he asked me for it and I say no, it's going. It gets sorta aggravating.

Counselor: Sort of aggravating? Do you have any idea, Fred, why Dan would point out Bill and say that he doesn't think that Bill has learned very much?

Fred: Because he thinks he is perfect.

Counselor: What do you mean by that Fred?

Fred: Well, like that one day he was telling us first his brother was bad and then . . . I mean first he was bad and they changed off.

Dan: Oh, I still get in trouble.

Bill: Well, everybody does. Nobody is perfect.

Dan: I just don't get in trouble as much as I used to.

Counselor: What do you think about Fred's statement that you want to be perfect?

Dan: Well, nobody can be perfect.

Counselor: Maybe so, but do you try to be perfect?

Dan: Well, if nobody can be perfect, I don't see how you can try.

Counselor: But you are trying?

Dan: Maybe so.

Counselor: Would you like to be perfect?

Dan: I don't know.

Counselor: Is it like Fred says?

Dan: If you were perfect you wouldn't have to go to school.

Counselor: Yeah, that's right. But Fred says—I think he said you tried to be or wanted to be perfect.

Milton: I think he likes to be perfect like some people's teeth that are pulled together very good.

Bill: Well then, look at mine, look at mine.

Milton: I agree with Fred that Dan doesn't like swings, he just has to get organized with other games like Army, or Vikings, or War, or Snap Dragons, and things like that.

Counselor: How does this game go, Dan? These games that Milton talks about?

Dan: Well, I am usually, just one of the . . . one . . . one of the sides.

Counselor: But you get them organized?

Dan: Well, I help organize it. To get them into formation; like if we are having a fight with somebody like maybe a dozen on each side, or more than a dozen on each side. Well, they are mostly . . . I pick the side that doesn't have very many. Well, the fewer side and, well. . . .

Counselor: Do you want to finish? How come you stopped?

Dan: I forgot what I was going to say. They don't obey me like they are supposed to obey their commander, and if they don't obey, then I just don't want to be a leader.

Counselor: And you have a tough time getting them to obey?

Dan: Most of the time. They just stay back.

Milton: I think I can explain it in simpler words.

Counselor: Okay.

Milton: Dan has an army, and the army turns traitor and. . . .

Dan: They don't exactly turn, they are already traitors and. . . .

Milton: . . . they create mutiny. But Dan gets out in the nick of time.

Counselor: Against Dan?

Dan: No, they don't go against me, they just don't want to do what I say. So, I just don't want to be a leader.

Counselor: Now, that seems to be . . . Fred, that seems to be the opposite to what you have just said. You said that he wants to be perfect.

Dan: When there are so many, like a dozen or more, then they just don't want to do what I say.

Counselor: Why do you suppose he can't get them to do what he says? Bill, do you have any idea?

Bill: Well, because probably they are trying to make him, like I said a long time ago that he thinks he is it always, and they are trying to show him he isn't it.

Counselor: Oh, he tries too hard to be it?

Bill: Well, ah, you say he tries to be it, and gets it, and then they say, "Oh, ah, pooey to him." Well, he just thinks he is just the wonder of the world or something like that. And, ah, they give up. You know, like that.

Counselor: You think he wants to be the leader because this is going to build him up?

Bill: Ah, hum, umhum!

Milton: I don't.

Counselor: You don't think so? What do you think, Milton?

Dan: I don't want to be leader.

Milton: Well, it's half and half to me.

Counselor: Half and half?

Milton: Well, Dan likes to be a leader, but when they don't obey him he hates to be a leader, and then it's just like that. It comes and goes away, and comes and goes.

Counselor: Do you think that maybe the kids feel that he isn't really interested in them so much as he is interested in himself?

Fred: Yes.

Milton: Dan needs more protection. He needs blind obedience. He has to get them to fear him.

Dan: No, I'm not usually the leader to start out with.

Bill: The school should have new playground equipment. Dan can't get a swing. Never can get anything he wants. . . . Well, that is just life.

Counselor: How do you feel, Dan, when the whole thing collapses? Do you feel that it is your fault? Disappointed?

Dan: Yes.

Counselor: Perhaps he feels that everything should turn out perfectly. If it doesn't he feels it must mean that "I'm not any good; it's my fault." How about in school? What about school work?

Bill: He doesn't pay attention to his school work. He is admired so much for his drawing. His desk gets dirty . . . gets junky. He draws a lot. Can't find anything in his desk. . . . Mike's, Fred's and Buzz's are more bare looking than Dan's.

Counselor: Do you think Dan draws well? Best of anyone in the room?

Bill: Yes, so am I. I am good at making organ books which I am making right now.

Counselor: (asks Buzz about Dan's art ability)

Buzz: (smiles shyly) Yes, Dan says he can't draw very well. Especially his army stuff.

Counselor: Do you think Dan could get A's?

Dan: I do. Mostly in arithmetic, reading and spelling I get A's but not in writing because I am sloppy. Sometimes my drawing . . . well it doesn't get to be what I want. It's hard, you know.

Counselor: (to Dan) It's hard to get it perfect?

Milton: I would like to compliment Buzz's imaginations and Dan's drawing.

Counselor: In what things does Dan really dig in and try to do well?

All Members: Drawing.

Counselor: What determines what schoolwork Dan is going to do well?

Bill: He is good in drawing. If he has a choice he will start working in art.

Counselor:Why?

Bill: The teacher told him to put it away.

Counselor: Why does he draw so much?

Bill: Dan got an F in reading.

Dan: I always get an A in reading. I didn't get an F in reading, you dope!

Counselor: Do you suppose Dan does only the type of schoolwork that he thinks he can do perfectly? What do you think about my idea? Dan works well and really pitches in on subjects that he is good in. Just doesn't work quite as hard on these other things.

(At this point, Dan very skillfully changed the subject; Milton interrupts Dan's talking.)

Counselor: I am wondering if any of you noticed what happened in the group these last few minutes.

Mike: It seems that Bill knows how to aggravate Dan by bringing up things he doesn't like.

Dan: He can't help it. He saw the F on my paper and he just wanted to bring it up.

Counselor: Something else happened. Did anyone notice it?

Fred: Dan changed the conversation.

Counselor: Perhaps he didn't like what we were discussing. What do you think, Dan?

Dan: No, I just thought we had been on one subject an awful long time.

Fred: Maybe Dan is finding out about himself and he doesn't like it.

Counselor: What do you think about what Fred said?

Dan: He could be right.

Counselor: I have another idea. Would you like to hear what I think?

Chorus: Yes.

Counselor: Could it be possible that Dan wants to be something special? So he works hard on that in which he can be something special, like drawing. He doesn't work on other school subjects because other children do well in these and he feels he can't come up to them. What do you think?

Dan: I think it is true.

Counselor: The discussion period is about over but before we leave I should like to ask a question. Did you learn anything from our discussion today?

Dan: I learned that if I try to think of everyone more and not myself so much they might want to be with me.

Milton: I found out that people get bad grades because they say, "That's so hard to do," and they start to draw a stupid picture or something.

Counselor: So, until next week when we meet for another discussion, goodbye.

RESEARCH

More research is needed in the area of group counseling in general and in the teleoanalytic approach in particular. The conclusion that can be drawn from research in the latter area, or with group counseling in general, is that it is inconclusive, a fact, Gazda (1971) points out. Some selected research will serve as an illustration. Palmo (1971) applying the teleoanalytic approach studied the effects of: (1) group counseling with parent and teacher consultations; (2) group counseling without parent and teacher consultation; and (3) parent and teacher consultation without group counseling on the improvement of elementary school children with adjustment problems. A control group was used for comparison. The results indicate that the parent-teacher consultation was the most effective procedure in reducing the adjustment problems of elementary school children as perceived by the classroom teacher and observer. The results also indicate that the group counseling, parent-teacher consultation procedure was not significantly different from the group counseling procedure but both were significantly different from the control.

The purpose of a study by Steed (1971) was to determine the efficacy of the Adlerian counseling technique in modification of the family's interactional process. No significant support was found for more positive interpersonal adjustment.

Sonstegard (1962) found that applying the Adlerian approach to group counseling of fifth-grade underachievers and their parents resulted in improvement in reading achievement, positive changes in conduct and work habits. In a study that is indirectly pertinent, McKelvie (1971) set out to explore techniques providing support personnel for school counselors and for involving students in the educative process by training high school juniors to lead Adlerian-oriented groups of junior high school students. The findings suggest that there are personality correlates which facilitate leadership and that Adlerian techniques can be effectively utilized by high school students in counseling situations.

GOALS OF GROUP COUNSELING

Making group counseling an effective therapeutic agent depends to a certain extent upon the theoretical formulation of the counselor. From the teleoanalytic point of view, an improvement of the group members depends upon reorientation, and a better understanding of the principles of social living and cooperation. Of primary importance is the modification of one's mistaken motivation, the mistaken notion one has of himself. The reorientation means a change in the group member's attitude toward his present life situation and problems.

An incident which had its setting in a social rather than a constituted counseling group might be a pertinent illustration. Fran commented during an informal social conversation that she felt she could be more effective and get more out of life. As the conversation turned to why she felt this way, she related recurring dreams. A counselor who was present casually asked if she remembered anything that happened when she was a little girl. She gave a number of early recollections. The counselor interpreted what they meant to him, namely that she was restricted in her activity to only those things she knew would please others and would be certain to reflect favorably on her. Others present questioned the interpretation. Fran, they said, was much too independent, too poised and sure of herself for this to be true. She was much too dynamic in her pursuit of activities. Since this was a social rather than a dully constituted therapy group the counselor was not sure that he was justified in offering a professional opinion. Further, in such a setting, with the limited psychological data and particularly the negative feedback from the group, he was not certain his interpretation was valid. The discussion ended with the counselor confessing that he could be wrong. Some weeks later he received a telephone call from Fran. She said, "You don't know how much your interpretation has meant to me. It is true, I discovered, I am inclined to do only those things that please, always concerned about the image I project. I am less concerned about that now. Now I do what I think is the right thing to do. You will never know how much this means to me. Isn't it stupid I didn't see this before?"

The effects of successful outcomes of group counseling, regardless of the method and the theoretical basis on which the counselor operates, must become evident in the encouragement and increased self-confidence of the group member, permitting him to participate in the life tasks and society more forcefully and candidly. Reorientation denotes the ability to establish and maintain proper human relationships based on self-confidence and respect for others.

The group has a readily observable impact on each participating member. Perhaps there is a need, as Carl Rogers suggests (Hall, 1967), to eschew "rigid scientific research in the behavioral sciences and return to a much more naturalistic observation of people and their behavior."

Group techniques are more imperative in a democratic society where the authority of the individual has been replaced by the authority of the group. Society puts a premium upon prestige, while the group minimizes its significance. The group attempts to eliminate vanity and anxiety about status; it helps to free the group member from the vertical movement of personal glory by which he constantly measures himself against others. In this way, group counseling attempts to replace detrimental social values. This again characterizes group counseling as primarily an educational process, promoting new values.

In the action and interaction between the members of the group, each expresses his goals, his intentions, his social orientation.

Looking for deep and unconscious psychological processes in the child and his parents is not necessary and is often detrimental, because such introspection usually loses sight of the real problem that exists in the social field in which the child operates.

Many youngsters are not only socially isolated but also develop negative concepts of themselves that no amount of effort on the part of teachers and counselors can eliminate. The group as an educational medium increases one's receptiveness to different ideas, to new facts or concepts. It goes beyond this, however. It helps each member to integrate and really accept new ideas previously completely foreign to his own thinking. For example, Bruce, a bright boy, made little progress in school despite the efforts of both his teachers and parents. He was invited to join a counseling group. One day, after attending a number of sessions, he remarked, "Before I joined this group, I thought I was dumb." Another youngster told his mother, "You know, I'm not so stupid." "What makes you say that?" she asked. "The kids who meet with Mr. Counselor to talk about things think I'm smart." "We've told you this before," she answered. "Yeah, but these guys mean it!" was the confident reply.

Understanding one's own problems through listening to someone else discuss his difficulties is a fundamental benefit of group counseling, be it for children or adults. This is exemplified in the case of one mother who came for individual counseling (Sonstegard, 1964). It became clear after a number of interviews that the necessary reorientation was going to be slow. Therefore, the mother was advised to attend the parent group counseling sessions. During the second group session she interrupted the counselor's discussion with another parent by asserting, "Now I know what I'm doing wrong!" A remark by the other mother had struck a chord that the counselor, in individual sessions, had been unable to do. Thus the counselor is always counseling several mothers simultaneously as the other parents in the group speak up. Each sees himself in others and comes to understand his own feelings, accepts new ideas and, in turn, encourages others to participate.

Interactions then may be of a nonverbal nature. In fact an extremely withdrawn youngster could withdraw still further, and perhaps leave the group if prodded to interact verbally. Withdrawn youngsters are still participating even if they only listen and observe. A sly smile, a movement of the lips or perhaps a twinkle of the eye will be evident as he reacts to the interaction of the other group members. Eventually he overcomes his inhibition and begins to participate verbally as he begins to understand himself through the disclosures of other students' mistaken goals.

THE GROUP SELECTION, COMPOSITION, SIZE, SETTING, AND FREQUENCY OF SESSIONS

As in other areas of group counseling, research is almost nonexistent or has not clearly demonstrated sound criteria for the selection, composition, size, setting, length and frequency of sessions to obtain maximum motivational modification through group counseling. To the writer's knowledge the most thorough treatment of this area of group counseling can be found in Gazda's (1971) comprehensive contribution.

Most of the criterion, lacking adequate research, has been drawn from the practitioner's personal experience with groups. The writers are taking the same liberty but confining the discussion to the school setting.

In the writers' experience groups may be formed in many ways. Children whom the teachers feel may profit from group counseling may be selected by the teachers. Groups are frequently formed with children whom the principal suggests. Parents often ask to have their children included in a group. If the child is receptive to the idea, he or she may invite children to form a group. In any case, the first question the children usually ask at the first meeting is "Why the group?" If the school counseling program is built on sound principles, the counselor can truthfully answer: "We have found that when people have a chance to talk things over in groups it usually helps." The next question that usually follows is, "Why were we selected?" The answer is: "We would like for everyone in the school to have the experience of talking things over, but there are not enough counselors so we invited those who can profit most from group meetings."

Children are not compelled to join a group. Once they become members, they may leave when they no longer benefit from the counseling. Children already in the group frequently ask if they may invite a classmate who is having trouble, because "we may be able to help him." Sometimes children form their own groups and ask for a counselor to lead them. The counselor can suggest to children with whom he works individually that they might profit from group counseling.

Whatever the manner of group formation, no one who wishes to join is turned away, for refusing a youngster the opportunity to become a member of a group is contrary to democratic premises (Sonstegard and Dreikurs, 1973). Several considerations should be kept in mind, however. It is advisable to have an even number of boys and girls in the group. Too divergent an age range should be avoided. Extremely withdrawn children can be mixed in the same group with aggressive acting-out and attention-getting youngsters, to some advantage for all.

Ten to 12 has generally been accepted as a maximum group size. Some counselors prefer groups numbering six to eight. The size of the group depends to a great extent upon the skill and experience of the counselor. Some teleoanalytic-oriented counselors hold group discussions with a whole class numbering 30 pupils.

In a school setting the existence of a group counseling program is generally known to all the children. Most of them are eager to become group members and often they feel slighted if they are rejected. The authors have not formulated any rigid criteria about the composition of the group. In a school setting as well as in private practice, any child who wishes to become a member of a group is given the opportunity to do so. He has only to express a desire to participate and to accept a few ground rules formulated by the group. A typical set of rules follows: (1) one may talk freely about anything one wishes, but one must also respect others' rights to talk freely. (2) All discussions are confidential. (3) Discussions outside the group about group concerns would be doing mischief and might hurt someone. (4) One must attend the group sessions regularly.

The atmosphere of the meeting room is important but not a

crucial factor. The authors, faced with crowded school conditions, have held counseling sessions with youngsters in boiler rooms, auditorium stages, storage rooms, and isolated corridors without excessive handicaps. The group sits in a circle with the counselor. The furniture size is appropriate to the age of the group. Sitting around a table is avoided.

An ideal meeting room should have a carpeted floor. It should be of sufficient size to allow four to five feet of space between the circle and the walls of the room. It should also be devoid of distractions such as noise from music, shop classes, and the corridors.

The counseling sessions should be scheduled to meet consistently at the same time and day of the week as agreed upon in a discussion with the members of the group and the teacher. In the author's experience, 30 minutes seems appropriate for the elementary school children and 50 minutes for junior high and high school students. It is vital that the time schedule be adhered to rather carefully. In the first place, the group members develop a serious and businesslike attitude toward the sessions and, secondly, the teachers are in a position to plan classroom procedures without undue disruption. This is vital where the support and participation of the faculty is indispensable to the success of the group counseling program.

MEDIA

There is nothing inherent in the teleoanalytic psychological formulation which is inimical to the employment of various media, especially in individual counseling. However, the teleoanalytic counselor confines his group counseling primarily to verbal interaction which permits a candid examination of the group member's subjective account of the problem bothering him. Next, the objective elements are examined; namely, his relationship to parents and siblings, the family constellations, how he views his position in the family, and his early recollections. The interpretations of his life style are presented either by group members or the counselor. Frequently the counselor may employ psychodrama with the group dramatizing the situation. Role playing is employed by the teleoanalytic counselor more frequently than play therapy.

It is practical and simple to move into "playing out" an incident rather than talking it out: "show us what happened." Especially if it is a situation which requires a solution such as a conflict situation, the counselor may ask, "Does anyone have a better idea of what could be done?" (Grunwald, 1969). If several different situations are depicted, the counselor discusses with the group solutions they consider to be the best.

Play therapy would likely be used more often and with effectiveness if facilities were provided. The writers have used play therapy as a medium in application of the teleoanalytic psychological formulation in a school setting. However, the availability of necessary space and equipment for play therapy in a school setting often presents difficulties. The school administration is likely to consider this an unproven frill. In only the most affluent schools will the approach be accepted without the adequate data to substantiate its efficacy.

Those counselors who have musical skills often apply another media, music therapy. Music therapy as a therapeutic medium may appeal not only to the counselors but the group members in intensifying the corrective effectiveness of the group counseling process (Dreikurs, 1954).

STRUCTURING OF GROUP COUNSELING

Group counseling must have structure. This is easily discernible in individual counseling, but less so in the group. It is there, nevertheless. As mentioned earlier, certain dynamics of individual counseling apply also to the group counseling process: (1) establishment and maintenance of proper relationships; (2) examination of the purpose of the group members' actions or behavior; (3) revealing to the individual the goals he is pursuing, called psychological disclosure; and (4) reorientation and redirection. However, in contrast to individual counseling, certain specific dynamics are necessary in group counseling.

Relationship

The counselor establishes himself as the group leader, even though a democratic atmosphere must prevail. The effective group counseling relationship is based on mutual respect. It does not mean that each member may do anything he pleases. Firmness and kindness are necessary in all group counseling.

As perceived by the authors, relationship requires more than mere establishment of contact and rapport. Winning the client's cooperation for the common task is a prerequisite for counseling, be it individually or in groups. The group facilitates cooperation. Maintaining it requires constant vigilance.

Analysis

Examining or discovering the child's goals can be done in individual counseling as well as in a group situation. However, the child's goals and movements become more obvious in interaction with the others in the group, in contrast to the limited interaction he experiences with the counselor in individual sessions. The counselor no longer depends exclusively on the student's verbal reports of his interactions with others. He sees him in action during the session. Often the child acts differently in a group than when alone with the counselor. Much of the veneer which the child uses to coverup may be stripped away in the group, as his true personality is openly revealed.

An appropriate illustration follows.

Gale was a bright, charming, fourth-grade girl. Most of the teachers were impressed with her; she was aggressive, but caused no trouble. In Gale's group, and from the same classroom, was Jim, who was also a bright boy but a disturbing element in the class. At the beginning of one group session, with Gale and Jim present, the school principal came into the room. Gale immediately invited him to participate. He accepted, but had to leave to answer a phone call. Gale informed a late-arriving boy that the empty chair beside her was reserved for the principal, and advised him to locate another chair.

Upon the principal's return, the group discussion shifted immediately, Gale took the initiative and subtly began to belittle Jim, while she put herself in a favorable light. This disturbed Jim, and he began to act up. The other boys followed suit. Gale achieved her goal and sat back with a feeling of "See how badly they behave and see how good I am." The expression on her face vividly revealed her triumph. The principal indicated his disapproval of the boys by his non-verbal reaction. Gale had given the principal the most adroit "snow job" imaginable.

The group was well on the way to getting out of hand when the counselor began to change the course of the session with, "I wonder how many of you know what happened to get the boys to act up?" The technique which Gale had used to degrade the boys and upgrade herself had created disunity. This technique would not have been discovered through individual counseling with Jim and Gale. It could only be revealed as it was in the group situation.

Insight

Groups are more effective than individual counseling in helping children gain insight and redirect their mistaken goals. The group facilitates the process of insight. Many would not be able to learn about themselves but for the interaction taking place in the group, the child comes to see himself in others. Thus the psychological disclosures and the interpretations during the group sessions are not only valuable for the child to whom they are directed, but to other members of the group who learn from these disclosures. A sixth-grade girl recognized herself through the counseling of one of her peers. "I used to be like that, always helping the teacher, being good and doing the right things, not because I wanted to, but because I would get in good."

Mistaken goals and erroneous motives among members of the group are similar enough for each member to see himself in others. It appears that this factor should be considered in selection of group members. In other words, the more similar the group, the stronger the mirror effect. Thus there is some advantage in forming groups with common problems, for example, groups of underachievers, of parents, of teenagers, of dropouts and the like.

The statements and opinions of group members often carry more weight than anything the counselor may say. This is equally true for group counseling of parents. In one parent group a father was relating how neither he nor the mother could make their son, Butch, a sixth grader, come home after school to change from school to play clothes. Butch had been spanked, had privileges removed, and had been subjected to numerous punitive actions. He still persisted in going with the boys to play, rather than coming home first to change clothes. The father said, "I told him tonight that the next time he goes to play with the boys without first coming home to change, I am going to take his model airplanes from the ceiling in his room and trample them to bits."

Another father fairly shouted. "You can't do that! That's just being revengeful!" Another member pointed out that there was good reason for Butch's behavior. "How would you like being left out just because you had to go to change clothes?" The counselor inquired, "What do you think of that?" The father admitted that he had not thought of it that way before, but it made sense because Butch had been having trouble making friends. The parents suggested that the father should stop punishing, discuss the problem with his son, and come to a mutual agreement. The counselor asked the father what he thought of the recommendations. "Well, if they (the parents in the group) say it will work, then it must work."

The reactions of the group members were much more significant than what the counselor said. Group members accept each other more in their redirective efforts because they feel the equality which exists among them. In the above case the counselor was able to develop more insight and exert more corrective influence because he had won the active support of the group.

The insight which a counselor helps to develop in the group sessions is not limited to the individual. Very few persons, if any, understand their own behavior. Even though Socrates admonished people to "know thyself" centuries ago, man still does not know himself, and in reality, may never be able to understand himself. But he can and will learn about human behavior in general. So it is that children and parents in groups learn something about themselves and even more about people in general. With this understanding of human nature, they begin to understand themselves. Group counseling is (in reality) a learning process. Experience shows that the group enhances learning and that group counseling as a learning process is enhanced by the group.

Disclosure or insight often becomes an end product in individual counseling as well as in group counseling. However, insight is not an end in itself; it is merely a means to an end. It may not be the basis for behavioral change, but it always is a step in that direction.

Reorientation

The end product is reorientation. The children are helped to re-direct their mistaken goals. Parents learn to give up erroneous concepts about dealing with children, and find out what is effective in influencing children. The change in approaches and relationships becomes evident in the child's improved relationship with his peers, with his teachers, with his siblings and parents and in his more realistic concept of self. The group becomes an agent in bringing about these changes because of the improved interpersonal relationships in the group. There is a greater possibility for each group member to see himself as he is and to recognize his faulty concept of himself and the goals he is pursuing.

COUNSELOR QUALIFICATION

A discussion of group counseling would be incomplete without some attention given to the counselor and his training. What kind of a person does it take to be a group counselor? What are the characteristics? Must he possess a certain personality?

The writers do not maintain that a group counselor must be in possession of unique characteristics. However, it would be difficult to visualize a shy, reticent person achieving any measure of success. Group counseling, especially as applied to children, requires a certain degree of outgoingness. The counselor must have a genuine liking for people, feel comfortable in company with them and enjoy mutual give-and-take (interaction), whether it be congenial or controversial.

The group counselor must have confidence in himself and feel that other people can be justified in having confidence in him. He trusts himself and the children. Consequently, he has no fear of them—no fear that he will not know what to do and that the children will get the best of him or defeat him.

The group counselor must have the courage of his convictions. Here a certain amount of caution is indicated, for a counselor with conviction and courage may often be inclined to play God. However, without conviction he will not command respect. Unless a counselor has respect for himself, he cannot expect the same from members of the group. A conviction of the soundness of his approach leaves him free to listen, relaxed and calm, while he observes the dynamics of the group interaction and the members' verbal and nonverbal participation. He can be firm and kind at once in his interpersonal relationships. He can be friendly without the destructiveness of familiarity.

Basic to the theoretical formulation set forth early in the chapter, the group counselor must assume the responsibility of serving as an interpreter and a guiding agent in the psychological process of change. It is his function to direct, when necessary, the group's interaction into meaningful channels through an understanding of what is taking place. If the counselor fails to assume his proper role, an entire session may be spent in innocuous shop talk. Here the counselor must put into play every skill he has mastered. He must be a true "leader," not an imposing autocrat. He must know when to permit group members to proceed undirected in their exploration. At the same time he must know the precise moment when direction is required. Not only must he be attuned to the appropriate moment, he must also make the right statement or ask the correct question. There are statements and questions that turn off group interaction. The counselor must be sensitive to the kinds of questions and statements that will open significant discussions.

Sensitivity to children, their actions and reactions can be learned. Once it is acquired as a working tool, the professionally growing counselor improves and perfects the skill through continuous practice. Actually, group members can help a less-experienced group counselor to grow as a leader and to acquire effective techniques.

ETHICAL SAFEGUARDS

Group procedures can be used for evil purposes as well as for good. The same would apply to the workings of any profession. Consequently, there is nothing unique about unethical practices in the application of group processes. Most counselors have heard of at least one case where "a group leader permitted participants to be inflicted with abuse which created a situation resulting in psychotic decompensation for a participant" (Gazda, 1971). This would seem to indicate a need for policing such as legislation, certification, accrediting, et cetera.

Paradoxically, the popular group approaches most in vogue are those which inherently possess the greatest potential for unethical practice. In group procedures focused on group members' inner feelings, emotions, and fears, a type of revelation frenzy and soul picking can occur which can result in the psychological paralysis of a participant. Thus the eagerness of the counselor or members to force openness can simply result in the utter retreat of a group member. There is little likelihood of such an occurrence among groups dedicated to the development of self-actualization through outer-directedness and social concern.

There appears to be sentiment against legislation to govern group practitioners, but for professional associations to police their own membership with more adequate training programs, central certification and a published list of certified group practitioners (Gazda, 1971) is commendable. Many other professions have either resorted to or have been forced to resort to legislation. Whether our helping profession will choose to establish workable standards and codes, thus avoiding a situation of forced legislation, remains to be seen.

The teleoanalytic approach has certain safeguards against unethical practices. The counselor does not deal with feelings and emotions. Neither does he dispense advice except recommendations provided parents in study groups and at the Family Education Centers. In group sessions, dwelling upon what the individual group member does is avoided as vigilantly as being engrossed with feelings and emotions. The counselor and group members are concerned with the purposes of behavior: with intentions. The psychological disclosures made by the counselor or group members are in the form of suppositions and are prefaced with: "Do you think perhaps . . . , Could it be . . . , or I get the impression that. . . ." The atmosphere of equality and mutual respect are other elements providing ethical safeguards. Thus, personal attacks, extreme pressures, and ego destruction are minimized. The group members may accept or reject the interpretation. A group member may later, as in the case of Fran, related earlier in this chapter, find disclosure meaningful after she has had time to think about it.

One might be concerned as to the damage the group members might inflict on the counselor. This is especially true if the counselor is lacking in adequate training, skills, and experience. The number of group counselors who have lost their confidence and ended up feeling inadequate makes one realize that ethical responsibility rests with all the members of the group.

PRACTICAL APPLICATIONS

Teleoanalytical psychology is a psychology of use rather than possession. Its application in the group process in clinical and educational settings is common. Since this chapter is written with an educational perspective, it might be interesting as well as instructive to describe in some detail the group process as it applies to family counseling and the role played in the procedure by teachers and administrators.

Family Group Counseling

The application of Adlerian principles of counseling to groups began with counseling families in what has become to be known as Community Child Guidance Centers (Dreikurs, 1951b; Sonstegard, 1954). Group counseling in these Centers is a unique combination of group dynamics, with the group approach taking place at various levels: (1) the family group, where the family as a unit is dealt with rather than with the mother or the child alone; (2) the children's group in the play room, where sometimes play is supplemented with psychodrama or music therapy; (3) the parent group, composed of parents enrolled for counseling; (4) the community group, comprised of visiting parents, teachers, students and others interested in problems of child guidance; and (5) children-adult group where children are interviewed in the presence of adults, but with their parents absent.

Each group situation, related to family group counseling, presents its own dynamics. To present a model of the interrelationship of the various groups, the family group will be considered.

The writers recognize that the problems of the child result from interpersonal relationships in the family group; therefore they deal with all family members at the same time. Wherever possible, all adults in a household are drawn into the counseling session. Frequently, however, the mother is the only one willing to come, though fathers are now taking part more and more. Even though they are reluctant to come at the start, the fathers become more willing to attend as their children show signs of improvement. This holds true as well for grandparents and other relatives who initially resist coming, but are eventually drawn into the counseling relationship. The authors always insist on the participation of all children in the family.

Discussion and counseling deal with the dynamics that operate within the family. Since the problems of the child express his interpersonal conflicts, the counselor deals with all members of the family who unwittingly take part in the conflict. This approach leads to quicker results and a better understanding of the factors responsible for the disturbance.

The child's behavior, regardless of how much disturbance it causes or how abnormal it may appear, must be considered a logical answer to the situation in which he finds himself. First of all, his behavior is a response to the mother's attitudes and her methods of dealing with him, just as it is interrelated with the behavior of his siblings. Sometimes, the "problem" child is not the real problem at all. His purportedly "good" and well-adjusted brother or sister may be a source of the disturbance, pushing the child down and discouraging him.

Examination of the family setting may reveal peculiar conditions which explain the child's reactions and behavior. The basis of the problem may be a conflict between the parents, the child being used as a pawn. Or it may be a conflict between the mother and the grandmother. A mother may be involved in a fight with two men of the family, such as a son and the father, or she may be squeezed out by an alliance of a grandmother with the child. In one particular case, a child's rebellion and unruliness arose from the fact that the mother allied herself with two older daughters against a younger child. However, in each case the child plays an active role, evoking from parents and siblings a reaction to his own intentions and goals.

In each family the interpersonal dynamics are exposed and explained to all the participants and new relationships are stimulated. Counseling consists of interpretations and suggestions of methods for dealing with each problem. The prime objective of all suggestions is to change existing relationships and mistaken concepts of the child.

As a rule the parents are interviewed before the group of parents assembled in the counseling room. Meanwhile, the children are in the playroom with a play therapist, psychodramatist or music therapist. The parents leave as the interview is completed and the children enter the counseling room.

In many instances the parents are called back before the children leave, so that part of the discussion is conducted with all members of the family together. In this way, everybody is given a chance to express his feelings openly and frankly. In the home setting, this kind of open discussion of attitudes and feelings is rarely possible because every statement may lead to quarreling. The counselor helps maintain a calm atmosphere of objectivity and interprets the position of each individual to opposing members of the family. This discussion of mutual problems in a democratic spirit of respect leads to better understanding for all. This begins a "family council," a technique instituted in most cases to carry on the corrective approach as part of daily family life.

The playroom was established as an adjunct to the counseling center as a place in which each child is observed in his relationship to siblings and other children. In the permissive atmosphere of this setting, the child openly expresses his attitudes and approaches, and the playroom director has an opportunity to report his observations of the child to the counselor.

To facilitate reorientation of the child, psychodrama as developed by Moreno (1946) is utilized. The psychodramatist employs the children's characteristic domestic and social problems to lead them to recognize and reevaluate their particular attitudes and approaches. The dramatization experience supplements verbalization in counseling.

The playroom director and psychodramatist or music therapist integrate their approaches to the child and maintain close contact with the counselor, with whom they exchange observations in the counseling room in the presence of all parents and participants. The counselor directs them in their activities by supplying them with information about the basic psychodynamics of each child.

Entirely different group dynamics come into play in the group discussion when the parents are enrolled in the program. They do not only attend sessions when their own cases are scheduled for interview–arranged, in accordance with the severity or urgency of the case, every two or four weeks–but they are invited to attend all sessions. Regular participation is important both for their own reorientation and for the help they give to other parents whose cases are being discussed.

This form of group counseling provides parents with an opportunity to understand their own problems better and more easily, as similar problems are discussed with other parents. Although it is difficult to see ourselves objectively, we have little blocking in clearly understanding a problem with which someone else is faced.

The group helps parents both directly and indirectly. At any point at which a parent has difficulty in seeing what he is doing to the child or what he could do differently, other parents may volunteer to report a similar experience. This is frequently supplemented by a description of the methods used and the solutions found. More important than the direct contribution is the emotional and spontaneous reaction of the group to statements and attitudes expressed by parents during the consultation.

Counseling need no longer be a private affair between parents and counselor, with the possibility that parents may feel misunderstood by the counselor, or question the validity of his opinions. In place of the counselor-client relationship, from which autocratic– and therefore detrimental–elements are not always eliminated, the client is exposed to group persuasion, which he can accept more easily.

Another indirect influence of great importance is the realization by each parent that he shares his problems with many others. Feelings of shame, humiliation, guilt or personal inadequacy are removed, as parents realize that their problem is a universal one. The group situation provides a convincing portrayal of the fact that almost all parents have similar problems with their children, that one's own child is no worse than many others and that it is normal for the children of today to misbehave and to create problems. With this recognition, parents usually lose embarrassment over their own "failure."

The authors consider it necessary to reach and to affect the entire community in its attitude toward and methods of dealing with children. Society is faced with the cultural dilemma that parents in general do not know what to do with their children. Participation in the discussion by visiting parents, teachers, social workers and others interested in children (i.e., those who represent the community), provides principles of education for the whole community, which is effective in the democratic setting of our times.

Frank discussions of the parent's problems in the presence of his neighbors, friends, the child's teacher, his clergyman and his physician can change prevailing concepts in the community. The authors' experience revealed that parents of all economic, racial or religious groups behave in the same way and have similar problems.

Usually a parent is not interviewed until he has attended several sessions. Embarrassment is rare, and if it occurs, it disappears within a few minutes. Within a short time, the entire community becomes aware of the amount of help needed by almost every parent.

The counselor must be sensitive to the group atmosphere to be sure that all who attend feel a part of the group. Usually no one acts merely as a spectator, since all are involved in the problems of their children. The counselor must be on the alert for those who indicate, if only by facial expression, that they would like to make a comment or ask a question. To facilitate constant awareness of the group, the counselor must make provision for a seating arrangement in which all participants sit close together. This can best be accomplished by arranging the chairs in a semicircle of not more than three or four rows deep. The counselor and parents being counseled are seated at the open end of the semicircle. In the experience of the writers, a group of about one hundred or even more can be integrated with proper seating arrangements. Thus while counseling one parent the counselor is simultaneously involving the entire group.

The group comments and the questions raised are usually sincere and express the desire to learn. Occasionally differences of opinion may lead to attempts to involve the counselor in an argument, or the counselor may fall into error of trying to convince the participant by logic. Engaging in pure logic or responding in kind to antagonism is only detrimental, since all emotional expressions are magnified in a group setting. Often group members, if the counselor is alert, can help the counselor to avoid emotional involvement. For example, a member of the group said to a parent who became argumentative, "You must remember your method has not worked. This method works." Thus the group is highly supportive, both to the counselor and to the person who is counseled.

Counseling children before the group of parents is an important aspect of the authors' guidance centers. Any question of the psychological soundness of this approach was long ago dispelled. The technique has been practiced for over a quarter of a century in many parts of the world without any case of adverse effect upon the child being brought to attention. On the contrary, the few minutes spent with the child seem to produce deeper and more constructive impressions in the group than in private sessions. Here the child is reached more easily, and results are quicker.

When the child and his siblings enter the counseling room, they are confronted with a group of adults, sometimes quite numerous. And, if this is the first interview, with the counselor, whom they have not met, this situation is certainly "strange" to them. Interestingly enough, the effect of the strangeness is both profound and extremely helpful. Contrary to the assumption that the child is not "himself" in a perplexing atmosphere, it has been found repeatedly that he expresses himself here more accurately than in the familiar surroundings of home or school, where he may hide behind well-established facades. In many cases the behavior of the children entering the room points to problems diametrically opposed to those cited by parents and teachers. The "problem" child may show a completely adequate performance and adjustment, while the hitherto well-adjusted sibling suddenly reveals his difficulties.

Although the diagnostic and therapeutic efficiency of the situation is obvious, some doubts about the effects of this exposure of the child are often heard. One has to attend several sessions to realize the amazing fact that children are completely at ease, with the exception of a restless or shy child whose behavior would be the same in a private interview. Particularly astonishing is the frankness with which children immediately begin to talk to the counselor.

Their positive response to the adult group may best be explained by the desire of many children to get special attention. They want to be the center of attention and seldom have the chance to get as much as they do in this situation. Many who are show-offs immediately sense their opportunity. The impressive setting enhances their willingness to listen to the counselor, in contrast to their behavior in a private office, where they are often on guard against any adult from whom they expect scolding and criticism or at least preaching.

Because of their sensitivity, children immediately respond to a group atmosphere characterized by interest, sympathy and a desire to help. They are treated as equals from the outset. This is for them a new experience which helps to overcome any barrier they may have set up for themselves before coming into the counseling room.

In our experience, nowhere is every move of the child so characteristic of his deeper attitudes and approaches as in the dramatic, impressive moment when he enters the room. The way in which he moves—particularly the physical contact with or distance from his siblings—the manner in which the children in the family seat themselves, all openly reveal relationships of one to the others.

A short discussion with the counselor centers around a few leading questions regarding the child's relationship to others, followed immediately by a discussion of his goals. They may or may not agree with reports by his parents, since a parent is often the last person to see any change.

There is a strong interaction between the children and the adults present. Both contribute greatly to their mutual benefit. What does the child contribute to the group? Most impressive is the realization by all that parents have greater difficulty than the child in understanding the nature of the child's problems. The children's ability to understand and their response to psychological interpretation contrast impressively with the obvious lack of similar qualities in their parents.

A child's exhibition of the "recognition reflex" when the goal of his behavior is disclosed to him (Dreikurs, 1948) is often both dramatic and convincing to those in doubt about the counselor's previous attempt to explain the child's behavior to his parents. Discussion with children is generally most enlightening to adults, as more pertinent and fundamental issues are discussed with children. In contrast, a great deal of time is spent on insignificant issues with the parents, who fasten their concern on symptoms rather than fundamental issues.

What does the group offer to the child? As previously mentioned, the group provides a setting for a psychologically significant experience for the child. Throughout the interview, he responds to the group as he talks with the counselor. Many of the child's remarks are for the benefit of listeners, often with perfect timing. There is constant interaction between child and group.

As the entire group participates, apparently only listening, adults are often compulsively carried away by their own attitudes toward children. If a child plays stupid, and the counselor understands and ignores, some mother may feel compelled to come to the child's aid. The discussion that follows is equally important for the child as for the others. Some adults have difficulty in sensing a child's goals and provocations, and they do not know when to fall for them and when to ignore them.

With the leadership of the counselor, the group "learns" to behave. As a result, the child is impressed with the new experience. It is important, for example, to know when to laugh and when not to laugh at what the child says or does. By and large, those who attend sessions for any length of time know when to laugh as the child plays to the gallery, and when laughing would be out of place. Only newcomers infrequently violate this psychological need. Generally, the group treats the child as an equal and behaves "properly," an experience seldom offered a child growing up today. One child, on the way home from his first counseling session, remarked to his mother, "You know this is the first time

I have felt that there were people who understood my problem." The concept of group counseling of families spread from Chicago to Iowa, Oregon, and West Virginia. When graduate students taught by Dreikurs at Northwestern University and the University of Oregon began to be appointed to university faculties, his innovations began to spread. The instructors counseled parents and children in front of their graduate classes. This was an actual demonstration of methods, rather than a mere lecture on them. At other universities the classroom became the meeting place for the parents enrolled in the Child Guidance Center.[2] The graduate students who were enrolled for course credit met with the parents. The children, under adult supervision, were in another classroom which served as a temporary playroom. Thus the students learned first-hand not only the methods of counseling, but also the procedure for the organization and administration of a Guidance Center.

Many formulations emanated from Adler's work with parents, teachers and children in a school setting. It is not surprising, therefore, that teachers and counselors find the psychological principles particularly adaptable to the school situation.

Coordinating Group Counseling in the School Setting[3]

The counseling of families before groups of educators became commonplace. Often they were teachers and principals who attended graduate classes in various universities. This opened the way for the most recent development of organizing group counseling in the school; in many school systems it became an integral part of the school's guidance and counseling program. There are four facets to the group approach in a school setting; the group of parents, teachers, administrators and children.

Counseling Parent Groups

Counseling of parents in a school setting follows the same general pattern as that in a Child Guidance Center. In the school set-

---

2. University of Oregon, Southern Illinois University, and West Virginia University.

3. A video tape ampex #1200, or a 16 mm film entitled *Group Counseling of Gifted Underachievers* may be obtained by writing Demonstration Project, Board of Education Office, 1200 Maine Street, Quincy, Illinois.

ting, the principal usually initiates the formation of a group of parents. They usually meet one evening per week for 1½ hours. The evening meetings permit fathers to attend. The children are counseled during the school day.

Counseling Teachers

The teachers meet for a session once each week after school is dismissed (Sonstegard and Graeber, 1960; Stromer, 1966). They also are invited to participate in the groups of parents, and sometimes also in the groups of children. Thus they learn to understand parents and children. The teachers participate in the psychological investigation of each case; they discuss the significance of the behavior which they have observed in their classes, what this means in terms of the child's goals, and what steps need to be taken to redirect his mistaken goals.

Although it is important that the teachers participate and contribute to the psychological investigation and the diagnosis, the most important assignment is redirection and reeducation. Through guided interaction they arrive at the best methods for bringing about changes in behavior.

The discussions are not devoted exclusively to specific cases. Teachers often bring up situations that occurred in their classrooms. The purpose is to discover better methods of dealing with these situations. The freedom of expression is conducive to a free discussion not only of classroom but also of personal problems. As teachers have an opportunity to learn from each other they begin to help each other.

The discussions are also devoted to problems of theory and of the underlying philosophy. The counselor plays the role of an instructor, keeping in mind the need to encourage open discussion.

Inviting teachers and even principals to participate in the children's counseling groups has often had an unexpected effect. One would assume that children might be reluctant to talk freely. Quite to the contrary, they soon discover that what they say is kept confidential and has no ill effect on the classroom situation. They can be frank and at times even critical without fear of retribution. They feel better understood by the educators, who listen to what they have to say.

The teachers and principals learn that accepting the child does not necessarily mean giving approval to what he does. They also learn that it is possible to be firm and kind at one and the same time, and effective limits can be set without getting into a fight. The manner in which the teachers' discussions are conducted encourages teachers also to participate in parent groups. Some have expressed their opinion that they learned as much from attending the parent group sessions as they did from their own group discussions. At any rate, the teacher can contribute tremendously to the understanding of the child whose parents are being counseled. Teachers usually ask that they be informed when families with children in their classrooms are scheduled for counseling, so they can plan to be present–not so much for what they can contribute, but to gain a better understanding of the child.

The participation of teachers in the parent group session helps develop good teacher-parent relationships. The parents are impressed by the teacher being interested enough to take several evenings of her own time to attend. The parents stop being critical of the teacher and they stop blaming her for their child's difficulties. The teacher discovers that blaming parents for the child's behavior or deficiency is not only unwarranted, but useless, even detrimental. Teachers and parents begin to appreciate more what each is trying to do. More important, being together in a counseling situation, they can now coordinate their efforts in redirecting the child (Stormer, 1966).

Counseling Administrators

It is too often assumed that educating teachers to better understand children and improve their instruction will bring about the millennium. It is true that the teacher is the key figure. However, a teacher might be reluctant to put into practice new methods if she feels the principal's indifference or antagonism. The principal's attitude may stem from his lack of understanding of the broader aspects of counseling children and parents. This is the reason for the administrator's counseling groups held once each week. The discussions are informal, usually devoted to questions the principals raise. Even though they center around the principals' main interests, the counselor has an opportunity to discuss the theoretical formulations of the entire group counseling program. He can help them be prepared to answer the many questions which will be asked in regard to the counseling program. He can help them become leaders among the teachers, rather than mere executives.

When principals learn to understand the dynamics of the child's behavior they begin to take the children in as partners in the function of the school. They begin also to give teachers more opportunity to participate as members of the teacher-administrator team.

The application of Adlerian methods of group counseling in schools, as developed in Europe and later in America, requires the coordination of all concerned: the parents, the teachers, the children and the administrators. The teacher plays a pivotal role, for it is her attitude toward the group counseling of the children from her class which will determine to a large extent its effectiveness. The participation of the parents and their attitudes will be influenced by the teacher's attitude toward group counseling. However, it is unlikely that group counseling as described will become an integral part of the school's program without the principal's active participation.

LIMITATIONS

It is difficult categorically to list the limitations of teleoanalytic group counseling without detailed consideration of a number of variables. Given a sound group counseling program and a well trained counselor, the limitations would be confined to the intricacies of the process. To the unsophisticated observer the process is deceivingly simple, "a counselor talking to a bunch of kids," as one observer put it. Actually the process is complicated which may be its chief limitation. To illustrate with one variable:

A group of four fifth-grade girls were discussing Jean's reluctance to make friends. She had a friendly relationship only with Cindy. Debbie liked Jean, but they were not close friends. Without going into the detail of the dialogue, Debbie volunteered that the "kids didn't like Jean." Jean was essentially an "only" child because she was several years younger than her brother. The counselor tried to explore what might be done to help Jean make friends and what others might do to encourage Jean to be more outgoing. This had continued for a number of sessions. Another counselor took over the group sessions and from the previous counselor's notes and the information he had gained from sitting in on sessions surmised that Jean was behaving in a manner which turned her peers away from her. Could it be that Jean by her subtle ways of proving her superiority threatened the other girls? The counselor structured the group session to check out his hypothesis. Many examples of how Jean tried to prove how good she was began to emerge. For example, Jean received a higher grade than Cindy on one of her papers. Jean knew this but she asked Cindy what her grade was anyway. When Cindy gave her the information, Jean sniffed, "I got better than that."

The counselor's guess proved to be correct. He disclosed to the group his idea and got the recognition reflex from Jean. The other members of the group recognized the dynamics of the behavior after it was revealed to them.

The teleoanalytic counselor can be easily misled by surface manifestations and tend to deal with symptoms rather than the dynamics of the behavior. This will, in all probability, do no harm but it will serve no purpose in the redirection of the group members' mistaken goals. It could, in fact, lead to a demise of the group. A reaccounting of a portion of a group session will illustrate the point. A counselor-in-training was having difficulty with the disruptive behavior of members of this group. Kelly was especially disruptive. His disruptions would not start until they were about half way into the 40-minute session. Kelly would get off his chair and crawl about the floor as well as manifest other bizarre behavior. The counselor had tried to deal with the disruption by attacking the symptomatic behavior, talking to Kelly, encouraging him to return to his seat and often admonishing him about his behavior to no avail. The lack of success was understandable because the counselor was concentrating on the surface manifestations rather than dealing with Kelly's mistaken goals or intentions. The practicum supervisor noted that Jim who had been mildly disruptive sat back with a rather satisfied attitude. Kelly's behavior had become exceedingly disruptive causing the counselor much discomfort. The other members of the group also quieted down as if following Jim's lead.

The supervisor interceded at this point, much to the relief of the student counselor, and asked the group if they had noticed what had been going on in the group the last 15 minutes. The comments concentrated mostly on Kelly's behavior: "He acts the same way in the classroom." "The teacher is always 'after him.'" "He acts stupid and makes others laugh." One group member was more perceptive, "Jim thinks Kelly is dumb."

"Did the group members think Kelly was a stupid boy?" asked the supervisor. "He could be smart if he didn't act so dumb," volunteered one member. "Then, if he is smart why does he act dumb?" the supervisor wanted to know. "Jim gets on Kelly an awful lot," the perceptive member observed. Kelly by this time had discontinued his disruptive behavior and was following the discussion intently. Jim suddenly remembered he had permission to leave school early that day. (A little chat with the principal verified this but Jim had set his approved departure up a few minutes.) The session continued without disruptive behavior from Kelly. The other members appeared to be more free and exhibited an accepting attitude toward Kelly.

The supervisor had an interview with the teacher. She was concerned over Kelly's disturbing behavior and expressed the opinion that he was bright and often did excellent work but not often enough. "He was," she said, "a little wild." The supervisor ventured a guess that Jim might be responsible for triggering Kelly's behavior. The teacher laughed about this and commented that Jim was a good student and had little to do with Kelly. The counselor training supervisor suggested to the teacher that she might observe and let him know what she found.

Due to a holiday and other circumstances the group did not meet for two weeks. The members began talking about behavior on the playground and what the teacher was doing about it. No names were mentioned until Jim pointed out a transgression which wasn't serious but was obviously Kelly's. Kelly noticeably stiffened and bounced his head almost imperceptively a couple of times against the back of the chair.

"Did anyone know who had committed that particular transgression?" the counselor wanted to know. Obviously everyone knew. As the group continued to point out further transgressions Kelly began his bizarre behavior. The counselor interrupted the discussoin and one of the members drew attention to Kelly by snickering and saying, "He's acting crazy again." "I wonder what started it," questioned the counselor. "Beats me," chirped one of the members.

"I get the impression that it began when Jim started to point out bad things about Kelly," ventured the counselor. "Do you think that what Kelly does is really that bad?" the counselor quizzed. "Not really, but Jim's mother wants him to be a good boy," the perceptive member pointed out. "Could that have anything to do with Jim's 'bad mouthing' Kelly," the counselor wanted to know. The members did not respond relevantly so the counselor said, "I have some ideas about it. Would you like to hear what I think?"

Everyone except Jim appeared eager to listen. The counselor said, "Could it be . . . ?" He went on to interpret how Jim wanted to be good to please his mother, but he didn't want to risk being a mama's boy. He could escape this by being dare-devil-like and getting others to be bad. His peers did not realize how they nonverbally admired Jim and thus he could have it both ways, being good to gain approval of his mother and tricky enough to have a place among the boys and avoid the "mother's boy" label.

Jim looked about the group with apprehension in his eyes and momentarily crossed his arms on his chest when he saw that the members indicated an acceptance of the counselor's interpretation. "Jim, what do you think of my idea?" the counselor questioned.

This incident relates how dealing with the inner motivations for one's mistaken goals can result in the realization of the unproductiveness of these goals, making a modification of intentions through goal awareness possible.

SUMMARY

Adlerian psychology is characterized by a holistic socioteleological approach; that is, man is a social being whose every action has a social purpose. He is a free agent, able to use his creative ability in setting his own goals and deciding upon his own movements. As a social being, man constantly strives to belong, to find his place among his fellowmen. His ultimate destiny can be achieved only within the group.

Uncovering and interpreting goals are primary characteristics of the Adlerian technique of counseling. There are four distinguishable phases: (1) the establishment and maintenance of a desirable counseling relationship; (2) investigation of the dynamics of behavior; (3) revealing or disclosing of purposes or goals; (4) reorientation. The difference between Adlerian and other approaches to counseling is most evident in areas 2 and 3.

Many of the psychological formulations upon which the present-day Adlerian psychologist structures group counseling evolve from Adler's work with parents and children—first in the schools, then in community centers. Thus the group counseling of families in child guidance centers in America, and later the application of these same principles to teacher and administrator groups and the counseling of children and parents in groups in a school setting, was a natural extension.

Group counseling is significant in a number of respects. It provides for participation in a group of one's peers, which in itself is therapeutic. But more than that, the group is a means of gaining insight and understanding of one's problems through listening to someone else discussing his. The interaction involving himself, previously unacceptable to his own thinking, becomes understood and accepted. The group not only helps the individual parent or child to change, but evokes a desire to help others. The group provides a social situation with real meaning, and under well-directed counseling, it can become an agent for the forming of positive social values and norms.

SUGGESTED READINGS

Dreikurs, R.: The unique social climate experienced in group psychotherapy. *Group Psychotherapy, 3:*292, 1951a.

Dreikurs, R.: Family group therapy in the Chicago community child-guidance centers. *Mental Hygiene, 35:*291, 1951b.

Dreikurs, R.: The dynamics of music therapy. In Bing, Mariana (Ed.): *Music Therapy.* Lawrence, The Allen Press, 1954.

Dreikurs, R.: Adlerian psychotherapy. In Reichman, F., and Moreno, J. L. (Eds.): *Progress in Psychotherapy.* New York, Grune, 1956.

Dreikurs, R.: Group psychotherapy from the point of view of Adlerian Psychology. *The International Journal of Group Psychotherapy, 7*:363, 1957a.

Dreikurs, R.: *Psychology in the Classroom.* New York, Harper, 1957b.

Dreikurs, R.: Group dynamics in the classroom. *Proceedings of the Thirteenth Congress of the International Association of Applied Psychology.* Rome. 1958.

Dreikurs, R.: Early experiments with group psychotherapy. *American Journal of Psychotherapy, 13*:882, 1959.

Dreikurs, R.: *Group Psychotherapy and Group Approaches.* Chicago, The Alfred Adler Institute, 1960.

Dreikurs, R.: *Adult-Child Relations, A Workshop on Group Discussion with Adolescents.* Eugene, Oregon, The University of Oregon Press, 1961.

Dreikurs, R., Corsini, R., Lowe, R., and Sonstegard, M.: *Adlerian Family Counseling.* Eugene, Oregon, University of Oregon, 1959.

Moreno, J. L.: *Psychodrama.* New York, Beacon, 1946.

Seidler, R.: School guidance clinics in Vienna. *International Journal of Individual Psychology, 2*:72, 1936.

Sonstegard, M.: A counseling center in a small community. *American Journal of Individual Psychology, 11*:81, 1954.

Sonstegard, M.: A rationale for interviewing parents. *School Counselor, 12*:72, 1964.

Sonstegard, M., and Graeber, H.: In-service teacher education in counseling. *Midland Schools, 75*:10, 1960.

Stormer, E.: A demonstration of group counseling procedures. *Progress Report #4.* Quincy, Illinois, Board of Education Office, 1966.

REFERENCES

Corsini, R.: *Methods of Group Psychotherapy.* New York, McGraw-Hill, 1957.

Dinkmeyer, D., and Dreikurs, R.: *Encouraging Children to Learn.* Englewood Cliffs, Prentice-Hall, 1963.

Dreikurs, R.: *The Challenge of Parenthood.* New York, Duell, Sloan and Pearce, 1948.

Dreikurs, R.: Group psychotherapy from the point of view of Adlerian psychology. *The International Journal of Group Psychotherapy, 7*:363, 1957.

Gazda, G. M.: A comprehensive appraisal of group and multiple counseling research. *Journal of Research and Development in Education, 7*:57, 1968.

Gazda, G. M.: *Group Counseling: A Developmental Approach.* Boston, Allyn and Bacon, 1971.

Grunwald, B.: Role playing as a classroom group procedure. *The Individual Psychologist, 6:*34, 1969.

Hall, M. H.: A conversation with the father of Rogerian therapy. *Psychology Today, 7:*19ff, 1967.

McKelvie, W. H.: An Evaluation of a Model to Train High School Students or Leaders of Adlerian Guidance Groups. Unpublished doctoral dissertation, West Virginia University, 1971.

Palmo, A.: The Effects of Group Counseling and Parent-Teacher Consultations on the Classroom Behavior of Elementary School Children. Unpublished doctoral dissertation, West Virginia University, 1971.

Sonstegard, M.: The Effects of Group Counseling of Underachievers and Their Parents. Unpublished study, University of Northern Iowa, 1962.

Sonstegard, M., and Dreikurs, R.: The Adlerian approach to group counseling of children. In Ohlsen, M. (Ed.): *Counseling Children in Groups: A Forum.* New York, Holt, Rinehart, and Winston, 1973.

Steed, S.: The influence of Adlerian Counseling on Familial Adjustment. Unpublished doctoral dissertation, University of Arizona, 1971.

AUTHOR INDEX

511

SUBJECT INDEX

A

A. B. Therapists Scale, 275
Abreaction, 74, 75
Abnormal Psychology: An Experimental Clinical Approach, 172
Acting out, 75, 111, 112, 116, 117, 239
  criminal, 124
Action groups, 75
Action phase of psychodrama, 85
Activating event, 299, 304, 307
Activity, 110-112, 116, 117
"Activity group therapy," 12
Activity group therapy with children, 367-369
Activity homework assignments, 302-303
Activity-interview in developmental approach, 408-416
Activity-oriented homework assignments, 306
Adjustment and insight in group therapy with children, 355, 356
Adlerian "open door" treatment, 26
Adlerian-oriented counselors, 26
Adlerian principles, xiv, 13
Adlerian psychology, 468-508
Adlerians, 10
Adult ego state, 234, 237, 244, 254-259
Affect, 150-155, 160-165, 169, 171, 172
Aims and means of group therapy with children, 353
Alcoholics Anonymous, 62, 381, 382
Alienated youth, 381, 382
"All in all," 142
Alternate meeting in psychoanalysis, 108-110
"Alternate session," 13
Alternating roles in psychoanalysis, 106, 107
American College Personnel Association Task Force on Group Procedures, 63
American Group Psychotherapy Association, 12, 13, 33, 63, 238, 256
American Journal of Psychoanalysis, 120
American Journal of Psychotherapy, 284
American Medical Association's Council on Mental Health, 59, 63, 65
American Personnel and Guidance Association, 22-24, 32, 34, 63
American Personnel and Guidance Association Interest Group on Group Procedures, 22-23
American Psychiatric Association, 64
American Psychological Association, 23, 64
American Society of Group Psychotherapy and Psychodrama, 10, 33
Analysis of group counseling research
  controls, 38, 40, 46
  criteria and outcomes, 38, 43-51
  experimental designs, 38, 41-43, 48, 50
  instruments, 38, 40, 47, 48
  nature of the study, 38, 39, 44
  recommendations, 52, 53
  statistics, 49
  test statistics, 41
  treatment, 38, 40, 46, 47
  type of group, 38, 39, 44
Analytic approach, xii
Analytic Group Psychotherapy, 115
Analytic intervention, 114, 116, 117
Annual Review of Behavior Therapy, 172
Antiawfulizing, principles of, 310
Anticatastrophizing, principles of, 310

519